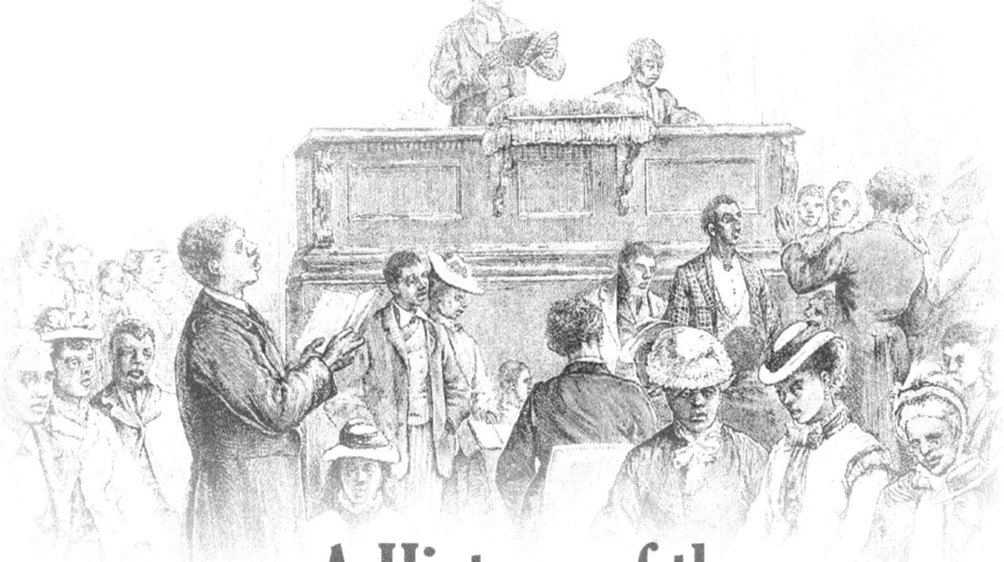

A History of the African American CHURCH

Leroy Fitts

TownsendPress
Nashville, Tennessee

Copyright© 2016. 2019. Leroy Fitts
All rights reserved.
ISBN: 1511751266
ISBN: 13-9781511751261
Library of Congress Control Number: 2015906053
CreateSpace Independent Publishing Platform
North Charleston, South Carolina

ISBN: 978-1-949052-03-9

To My Beloved Son:

Dietrich Emmanuel Fitts
December 21, 1967–May 6, 2014

Contents

Preface ix

Introduction xi

Chapter 1: Formative Influences on African American Religion 1
    The African Background
    African Traditional Religions
    Euro-African Faith Traditions
    Early African Christianity
    The Ethiopian Orthodox Church
    The Coptic Church
    Christianity in the Sudan
    The Atlantic Slave Trade
    Euro-American Religion and African Slavery
    The Established Church in Virginia
    The Quakers and Slavery
    The Moravians and Slavery
    The Baptist Churches and Slavery
    The Methodist Episcopal Church and Slavery
    Evangelization of African Slaves in the New World
    Evangelistic Work of the Methodist Episcopal Church
    The Roman Catholic Church
    Protestants and Catholics in Maryland

Chapter 2: Plantation Missions and the Evolution of Segregated Worship
    Experiences 41
    Secret Worship Experiences among Slaves
    Slave Preachers and Relevant Religious Worship
    Biracial Churches and Racial Discrimination

Chapter 3: The Rise of Separate African American Churches 55
    The African Methodist Episcopal Church
    The African Methodist Episcopal Zion Church
    Separate African American Churches in the Methodist Episcopal Church
    Separate African American Churches in the Methodist Protestant Church
    Separate African American Churches in the Protestant Episcopal Church
    Separate African American Presbyterian Churches

The African Union Church
African American Baptists
Roman Catholic Separate Church Movement
The Westward Expansion: American Frontier
Baptist Separate Movement in the West
The A.M.E. Zion Church Expansion in the West
The A.M.E. Church Expansion in the West
The Westward Spread of the Roman Catholic Church

Chapter 4: The Institutionalization of African American Churches 110
The African Methodist Episcopal Church
The African Methodist Episcopal Zion Church
The Colored Methodist Episcopal Church
Unification Movements in African Methodism
Leadership Crises in African Methodism
African American Baptist Denominations
The Afro-Christian Convention: Congregational Christian Churches
Holiness and Pentecostal Denominations

Chapter 5: Emancipation, Church Growth, and New African American Religious Movements 163
Church Growth among African American Baptists
Church Growth among African American Methodists
The Growth Phenomenon of Pentecostal and Apostolic Churches
The Coming of Cults in the African American Religious Experience

Chapter 6: The Christian Missions of African American Denominations 191
The Lure of Africa
African American Baptist Foreign Missions
Early Missionary Strides of African American Methodists
The Globalization of African American Missions

Chapter 7: The Rise of African American Denominational Schools 235
Antebellum Education of African Americans
White Denominational Schools for African Americans
African American Baptist Schools
African Methodist Episcopal Church Schools
African Methodist Episcopal Zion Church Schools

Chapter 8: The Socio-political Tradition of African American Churches 273
    African American Churches and the Abolitionist Movement
    Slave Revolts and African American Churches
    The Civil War and Reconstruction
    Reconstruction and African American Christians
    African American Churches and Moral Reform Movements
    Segregation and Discrimination Politics in the South
    The Anti-lynching Movement
    The Movement for the Enforcement of Voting Rights
    The Impact of Migration on Churches

Chapter 9: The New Socio-political Tradition of African American Churches 338
    The Impact of a New Cosmopolitan Outlook
    The Civil Rights Revolution
    Interdenominational Organizational Civil Rights Strides
    African American Social Revolution: 1956–1970
    The Black Power Movement and a New Social Agenda

Chapter 10: Emerging Trends in African American Church Life 373
    The Ecumenical Movement and African American Churches
    The Affirmative Action Debate
    The Reparations Movement
    Upward Mobility in Denominational Life
    Women in Ministry
    The Rise of Megachurches
    Exploding Moral Crisis Debates

Bibliography 420

Index 435

Preface

This book emerges from my deep conviction that the African American church has contributed to the historic development of the Christian church in America and throughout the world. It has contributed its insights, values, and practical ministries to the common treasury of the American ethos which has been largely transplanted internationally. The African American church has engaged itself in redeeming ways in dialogue with other traditions and movements, both religious and secular, in the advancement of Western civilization. To be sure, insufficient credence has been allotted to her dynamic and creative presence in the march of Christian civilization. Any history of Western civilization is incomplete without proper consideration of the African American church.

This study is designed to promote inner dialogue within the total denominational experience of African Americans with relevance to pastors, lay church leaders, teachers, and other academics of Christian culture. Through its telescopic view of the total program development of the African-American church experience, the study provides serious minded individuals who are aware of the importance of history with the understanding of the dynamics of progress and change in contemporary life. It is for individuals seeking truth about themselves, their culture, and the hope for an abundant future.

I owe a deep debt to many individuals for providing their input and specialized resources for the completion of this study. Special thanks to the late Dr. Frank P. Lewis of Lynchburg, Virginia, for providing many out-of-print books, old newspapers, and many periodicals relative to the African American church; the library staff of Morgan State University, Coppin State University, Howard University, and Lincoln University for providing me with thousands of African American newspapers from which I have photocopied church history materials for the composition of newspaper-sized scrapbooks. I have created fifty-one volumes of church history materials from many different African American newspapers, arranged in chronological order, consisting of approximately fifteen thousand pages of materials covering approximately a hundred years. The Schomburg Center for Research in Black Culture of the New York Public Library, under the former leadership of Victor N. Smythe, has microfilmed the first twenty-two volumes of my scrapbooks entitled "The Black Church in the News." Also, Mrs. Luke Reynolds provided me the opportunity of purchasing the library of the Clayton-Williams University of Baltimore when it closed several decades ago. The library contained many rare books on African American history and culture. And special thanks to my daughter, Angelique L. Fitts Taylor, who helped in editing the manuscript for publication. To all these special people, I am so grateful.

Leroy Fitts
Baltimore, Maryland

Introduction

The usage of comprehensive terminology to designate church life among African Americans, such as the "Negro church," the "Black church," and currently the "African American church" has been well established in sociological and historical studies. In 1921, Carter G. Woodson published the primary scientific historical study of the African American churches, entitled *The History of the Negro Church*. He was followed by other writers referring to the Black church, such as the 1964 publication of E. Franklin Frazier's *The Negro Church in America*; the 1970 publication by C. Eric Lincoln entitled, *The Black Church since Frazier*; the 1971 publication edited by Hart M. Nelsen, Raytha L. Yokley, and Anne K. Nelsen entitled *The Black Church in America*; the 1988 publication by Edward D. Smith entitled *Climbing Jacob's Ladder: The Rise of Black Churches in Eastern American Cities, 1740–1877*; *The Black Church in the African American Experience* by C. Eric Lincoln and Lawrence H. Mamiya, published in 1990; and *The Black Church in America: African American Christian Spirituality* by Michael Battle, published in 2006. These scholars and many more have utilized comprehensive terminology to designate African American Christian churches. To be sure, the current accepted terminology is the "African American church."

The thesis of this book is that in order to understand the evolution of the African American church one has to search for earlier formative social and theological thoughts and elucidate how they impacted the churches. African American churches did not develop in a vacuum but from earlier ideas and church movements. Religious movements from Africa and Europe impacted the evolution of the African American church.

Initially, Christianity entered North Africa from the Apostolic Period impacted by the existing religions of the Roman Empire. During the genesis of Christianity in Africa, it appeared as a Jewish sectarian movement encountering the religious, social, and political challenges of the Roman Empire. Nevertheless, the novel religious movement survived in an often hostile environment and experienced expansion from Africa through Europe to the New World. It was often challenged by the existence of African traditional religions as they evolved their new cultural forms and increased in vitality. African spirituality with its concept of God as the Supreme Being served as a uniting force across North

African regions. To be sure, transplanted Africans did not come to the New World void of all consciousness of a Supreme Being due to their multiple forms of religious beliefs. Some had been influenced by the monotheistic concepts of Judaism, Christianity, and Islam.

Accordingly, the African American church has its roots in the religious heritage of both the continents of Africa and Europe. However, the main tenets of faith came by way of Europe. European denominational experiences fostered the early development of Christianity among the slaves and free African Americans in the New World. In many profound ways, both African spirituality and what became dominant European Christianity left indelible marks upon the African American church. Many of these marks remained constant throughout the formative stages of Christianity among the transplanted Africans.

The majority of English Protestants and a few Roman Catholics were in the forefront of the evolution of slavery in Colonial America. Their theological and sociological motifs guided public opinion in its acceptance of the institution of slavery. However, it took some time before anything approaching a consensus developed among English Protestants, the majority Christian movement, sufficient for the establishment of the "peculiar institution." For a considerable time, lively debates took place among various Protestant groups, especially Quakers and Methodists, over a Christian justification for the enslavement of Africans. These debates became increasingly intense during the advent of the abolitionists lasting throughout the Civil War era. Forceful sermons by northern abolitionist clergymen and pro-slavery southern clergy were delivered to activate and intensify the debates over slavery. Political addresses, printed materials, books, and other media were utilized in the lively and disruptive controversy over slavery. Divided opinions became the characteristic element of public discourse among Christians and non-Christians, some even suggesting a "divine origin" of slavery.

Generally, negative anthropological concepts were interpreted from the book of Genesis to justify Christian acceptance of slavery, especially in the South where cotton had become "king." Most of the whites from the slaveholding colonies did not believe in the full humanity of Africans. They believed that Africans had not fully evolved into humanity equal to that of Europeans. Hence, the fundamental Christian belief in the "fatherhood of God and the brotherhood of man" was not operative in the situation of the slaves. Many white Christians throughout American history have held tenaciously to negative anthropological concepts based on the Bible for the justification of slavery, and later for the basis of segregation and discrimination. Initially, these socio-religious concepts became the basic presuppositions of the evangelistic mission of white Christian churches among slaves and later emancipated African Americans.

Nevertheless, the vestigial elements of African spirituality, which informed the psychological aspects of Christian conversion, proved sufficient for the early development of secret worship experiences among the slaves which became the future basis for the emergence of the African American church. African American slave preachers and those from the free community were the originators of the separated African American church. However, for a considerable period of time these churches remained partially aligned with their respective white denominational churches. For the most part, these churches had developed from the early trend of inclusion of slaves and free African Americans in biracial white churches based on the emerging styles of denominational evangelism. To be sure, the decision to branch out and start the independent African American church did not emerge abruptly. There were considerable debates even among African American Christians regarding the advisability of starting independent churches. Many opted to remain in the bi-racial denominations.

The potential dynamism of the African American church gained additional importance with the issuance of President Abraham Lincoln's Emancipation Proclamation and the fall of the Confederate States of America, which radically altered the economic and social milieu of former African American slaves. Christian slaves, constituting the majority of the African American population, emerged on the African American church scene and provided tremendous church growth throughout the nation. Most of the traditional denominations experienced a rapid increase in membership, expansion of organizational structures, and the construction of large church buildings to accommodate the needs of the expanding memberships. Specifically, the construction of these new church facilities provided new educational experiences in economic cooperation among African Americans.

Social, economic, and political changes within the African American community also provided for the emergence of Holiness and Pentecostal churches. The twentieth century witnessed an avalanche of small sectarian denominations which challenged the denominational culture and theological tenets of the traditional churches. The new denominations sought to resist the assimilation trend to accept white Christian culture within traditional denominations and instead sought to return to the New Testament understanding of church life. They emphasized the fundamental necessity of holiness and sanctification. To a certain extent, the appearance of African American cults was also a protest movement against the traditional churches, centering on specific charismatic leaders on the fringe of African American Christianity. Cult groups like Father Divine's Peace Movement and Sweet Daddy Grace's United House of Prayer for All People emerged on the religious scene, drawing large followings from poverty-stricken urban areas where illiteracy still remained a factor to be eliminated by the developing schools among the race.

A remarkable missionary spirit among African American Christians emerged, even prior to emancipation, against seemingly unprecedented odds. Given the racist nature of slavery in Colonial America, it seems almost inconceivable that an enslaved people could have dreams of returning to their native land in Africa to evangelize the peoples of the second-largest continent in the world. However, the lure of Africa was sufficient enough for African American churches to develop missionary work on the continent. During the early period of emancipation, African American church denominations developed a global stance toward missionary work. This trend became even more dynamic with the global exposure of church leaders to worldwide cultural, social, and political movements following World War I and World War II. African Americans became increasingly global in their vision for Christian evangelism, political justice, and human rights.

Not only in foreign missions, but the African American church sought to address the educational needs of the race through the emergence of schools. During the antebellum period, African American churches sought to develop survival skills among the race in small settings such as in basements or Sunday school areas. As they became more organizational in structure, some denominations moved forward to organized primary and secondary schools, ministers' institutes, and denominational colleges and seminaries. These schools sought to meet the practical needs of the race by providing curriculum emphasizing trades, professions, and liberal arts. The education of the race was a tremendous task for the churches, with their limited economic and trained human resources. For the most part, the schools had to draw on the skills of white teachers and administrators to provide adequate educational opportunities. Gradually, the trend toward independence in higher education emerged with the employment of more African American teachers and administrators. Nevertheless, the challenge to provide relevant education for the race remained a constant struggle. Following the 1954 Supreme Court decision ending segregation in public education, denominational schools faced a new challenge of having to compete with economically superior institutions for students and highly qualified faculty and administrators. This remained a constant challenge to the survival of African American church schools.

Significantly, African American independent churches evolved as veritable schools of political science in the context of social and religious changes in American culture. Pastors as well as lay members were given unique experiences in democratic procedures during congregational meetings and deliberations in denominational assemblies and conventions. Hence, the African American church became politically oriented in aspects of life and social thought. It became a voice of protest against segregation and discrimination practices so persistent in white churches and American culture. African American preachers from many mainline churches voiced their opinions regarding issues of American democracy as well as international movements for human rights and freedom.

The late twentieth century and early twenty-first century ushered in some social, moral, and denominational innovations in the life of African American churches. Many of the challenges existed earlier, but they encountered the new leadership in ways forcing them to reexamine and reconsider many of the belief systems and practices of modern church life. Advancing secularism, the post-Civil Rights Revolution, the new morality, ecumenism, family planning, gender consciousness, and the new phenomenon of megachurches growing at the expense of traditional churches impacted new church leaders with the challenge of radical change. The new leadership was forced to respond in new ways to the changes in public opinion regarding the nature and purpose of the Christian church in contemporary society in constant transition. Currently, transition is the order of the day almost everywhere in church life.

Chapter 1

FORMATIVE INFLUENCES ON AFRICAN AMERICAN RELIGION

To understand the development of a historic movement, one has to search for earlier formative ideas and elucidate how these ideas impacted the evolution of that movement. It may be rightly said that all history has a history. Therefore, the African American church did not develop in a vacuum but from earlier ideas and movements. A continuity of social, political, and theological ideas with roots in Europe and Africa have impacted the development of a variety of Christian movements incorporated in what is called the African American church.

The African Background

Religion is as old as humanity itself. Early humans found it necessary to reverence higher powers found in the ordinary encounters with their natural environment. Although some primitive religions contained strong naturalistic tendencies, early humans believed that a spiritual dimension underlay the physical manifestations of their reality. This was more or less the universal religious content of early humans' cultural evolution. Africa is believed to have been the home of the earliest people, and the continent witnessed the evolution of religion from its most primitive forms. Hence, a brief survey of the significance of African traditional religions in the evolution of their more cultured forms is necessary for an understanding of Christianity's contact with the continent. The genesis of Christianity in Africa was in North Africa as a Jewish sectarian movement. The young religion faced social, religious, and political challenges as it sought expansion throughout the northern regions of the continent. Politically, it was severely persecuted by the Roman government; socially challenged by Greek cultural traditions; and religiously challenged by the multiplicity of existing competing religions in North Africa. All of these factors must be understood to gain knowledge of how Christianity survived in a hostile environment to experience expansion from Africa through Europe to the New World.

African Traditional Religions

Long before North Africa was conquered by foreign powers, African religions had been definitive of the development of African culture. In fact, the culture of Africa was largely permeated by the sense of sacredness, of religious mystery, and of spiritual powers characteristic of most African religions. However, the emergence of multiple tribes throughout the continent defined their spiritual dimensions differently. Each of the many tribes defined their religious culture ranging from what some European anthropologists defined as animism, fetishism, polytheism, and primitive monotheism. The first descriptive concepts of animism, fetishism, and polytheism were European observations as outsiders from the inner contents of the religious devotees. The inadequacy of this description has been pointed out by Osadolor Imasogie, professor at Nigerian Baptist Theological Seminary, Ogbomosho, Nigeria. Interestingly enough, he summarized critically the European derivative concept of animism:

> Since E.B. Tylor used the word "animism" in 1866 to describe the religion of primitive man, Westerners writing on African religion have invariably equated African religion with animism. According to an evolutionary theory of the origin of religion, animism gave rise to polytheism while the word polytheism was the precursor of monotheism. The implication in using the word animism to describe African religion is that since Africa is still primitive, by Western standards, its religion must of necessity be at the bottom of the supposed line of religious evolution, while Judaism, Christianity, and Islam are at the top since they are monotheistic. The inadequacy of this term as a blanket designation for African religion will be pointed out in connection with the rejection of fetishism as the two concepts belong to the doctrine of sacramentalism.[1]

Imasogie basically rejected the whole idea of defining African religion in terms of primitive animism. This was aimed at adverse concepts of Africans in general resulting from faulty anthropological theories of colonialism.

Accordingly, Imasogie advanced his critique further:

> The term fetishism, which in its Portuguese and Latin derivation implies a work of art, was redefined by E.B. Tylor to signify the embodiment of spirits in material objects. Fetishism, according to Geoffrey Parrinder, later came to be "confused with the so-called pagan worship of gods and veneration of ancestors." Stabbed awake, however, by the fact that the etymology of fetishism forbids its use as an accurate description of any religion; later, a committee of anthropologists was convened to reconsider the matter. Unfortunately, the committee came to the conclusion that while fetishism is inadequate it "might be retained for a limited

class of magical objects in West Africa, that is, the charms, amulets, and talisman which form the subordinate part of the religious complex." Of course, in spite of that decree by anthropologists most people still refer to African religion as "fetishism."[2]

After surveying other Western characterizations of African religion, Imasogie offered the new concept of "bureaucratic monotheism" as a more accurate description of African religions. He pointed out the advantages of this description: "It not only points to the prominence given to the divinities and the socio-political pattern of the African society thereby reflected in the religious expression, it also preserves the intrinsic monotheism which undergirds the African religious experience."[3] Much of Imasogie's new characterization of African religions stems from the seminal work of Mbiti's *African Religions and Philosophy*.

The verity of African traditional religions tends to maintain a substantial belief in a supreme being which nurtures the inner spiritual consciousness of the various devotees to their particular faith traditions. Imasogie pointed out, "Mbiti came to the unmistakable conclusion that 'without a single exception the people have a notion of God as the Supreme Being.'"[4] Mbiti derived his views from detailed studies of religious expressions from more than three hundred tribal groups in various parts of Africa. He observed, "As the Supreme Being, He is self-sufficient, self-supporting, self-containing just as He is self-originating."[5] This widespread concept among African tribes of the Supreme Being or High God may have constituted fertile grounds for Christianity's advancement in Africa, the second-largest continent in the world.

Euro-African Faith Traditions

The African American church has roots in two different continents—Africa and Europe. European denominational experiences fostered the early development of Christianity among the population of slaves in the American colonies. In many profound ways, the impact of European Christianity left an indelible mark upon the African American Christian experience. So pervasive is that mark that many refer to Christianity itself as the "white man's religion." However, even European theology was not devoid of a significant African orientation. Several of the church fathers were from North Africa; the theological school of Alexandria, Egypt, influenced early Christian thought; and the Old Testament was translated into Greek in Egypt. The Egyptian church played a notable role in the evolution of Western Christian thought. In fact, African church fathers like

Tertullian, who created Christian Latin literature; Cyprian, who polished the Latin language; and Augustine, who wrote extensive Christian theological works, became the "fathers" of the Western churches. Bishops from the church of Egypt were in attendance at the formative church councils. Europeans assimilated North African theological thought, refined it, and transported it to the Americas. Hence, European thought and practice derived from African Christianity defined the nature and development of theology, ethics, and denominationalism among African American Christians. The only one area that was left unaffected was the nature of African American spirituality. This area was left to the nurture of African spiritual roots. Initially, slaves were converted as dehumanized Africans in the New World, but not without an inner retention of African religious influences. Although African slaves were separated from their fellow slaves from the same tribe, they were still able at a personal level to retain much of their belief systems. To be sure, their response to the Holy Spirit was fundamentally African. No external force could eradicate the deep inner remains of the flow of African spirituality.

With a similar emphasis, Albert J. Raboteau affirmed the following:

In the New World slave control was based on the eradication of all forms of African culture because of their power to unify the slaves and thus enable them to resist or rebel. Nevertheless, African beliefs and customs persisted and were transmitted by slaves to their descendants. Shaped and modified by a new environment, elements of African folklore, music, language, and religion were transplanted in the New World by the African diaspora.[6]

In a highly significant sociological study of the African American church, E. Franklin Frazier advanced the argument that slaveholders' radical dehumanization strategies to transform free Africans into American slaves was so severe that African slaves were forced to break with their social heritage. Frazier went on to suggest the following:

It is evident, then, that the manner in which Negroes were captured and enslaved and inducted into the plantation régime tended to loosen all social bonds among them and to destroy the tradition basis of social cohesion. In addition, the organization of labor and the system of social control and discipline on the plantation both tended to prevent the development of social cohesion either on the basis of whatever remnants of

African culture might have survived or on the basis of the Negroes' role in the plantation economy.[7]

Frazier's theory was designed to challenge the conclusion of W. E. B. Du Bois's study of the African American church in his 1903 definitive work entitled *The Negro Church*. In this study, Du Bois argued that the church was a remnant of African culture. He said, "From such beginnings arose and spread with marvelous rapidity the Negro Church. . . . It was not at first by any means a Christian Church, but a mere adaptation of those heathen rites which were roughly designated by the term Obe Worship, or Voodooism."[8] This view retained some of the European language suggesting primitive stages of African cultural development. However, Melville Herskovits's *Myth of the Negro Past*, Frazier, and Raboteau reached similar conclusions that African slave culture was characterized by the survival of Africanism.

Early African Christianity

Long before Africans were brought to the American colonies in 1619, Christianity had penetrated the African continent beginning in Romanized North Africa. Evidence of this early penetration may be seen in the Acts of the Apostles. Soon after the death of Jesus Christ, the new faith was brought to North Africa by African Jewish converts to Christianity. Judaism had penetrated North Africa from a very early date. In fact, the inhabitants of Egypt were divided into three classes—Greeks, Jews, and Egyptians. The Jewish population was so great that the celebrated temple of Onias at Leontopolis was built during the reign of Ptolemy VI Philometor. The temple was built by Onias son of the high priest when Onias became a refugee in Egypt. During the Greek Age, the Jews had adopted much of the Greek culture as evidenced by Philo and Josephus. Many of these Greek-speaking Jews had come to Jerusalem to participate in the great Jewish festivals of Passover and Pentecost. Some met Jesus in person, while others were influenced by what they had heard about Him from His disciples. One classic example was the conversion of the Ethiopian eunuch by Philip recorded in the book of Acts. Subsequently, this eunuch with royal connections to the court of Candace (this was the official title of the queen-mother in a kingdom between Aswan and Khartoum) returned to Africa and contributed to the conversion of the ruling class of Ethiopian society. Queen Candace became the first Christian ruler of Africa. She communicated the new faith to the royalty of Ethiopia who thereafter assisted in the infiltration of the faith to the general population of the kingdom.

The Ethiopian Orthodox Church

Interestingly enough, the Ethiopian Orthodox Church traces the historic roots of their faith back to biblical history with the spread of Judaism to Ethiopia when King Solomon reigned in Jerusalem. Prior to the Jewish religion's introduction into Ethiopia in 1000 BC, Queen Makeda, referred to as the Queen of the South, visited King Solomon; a relationship was established that resulted in the birth of King Menelik I of Ethiopia, traditionally believed to be the son of King Solomon. Hence, a direct link between Ethiopian religion and the spiritual roots of Christianity was established by the emergence of the new faith in Ethiopia. Clifton F. Brown, in his article in the *Negro History Bulletin* entitled "The Ethiopian Orthodox Church" said this:

> The date of the effective establishment of the Ethiopian Orthodox Church is generally accepted as 330 A.D. In that year, two Syrian Christians, Frumentius and Aedesius, presented themselves at the Axumite court of Emperor Ezana (c. 325-350). After converting Ezana and other members of the imperial family, Frementius went to Egypt where he was made the first bishop of Ethiopia by the Patriarch of Alexandria, Athanasius. On his return to Axum Frumentius, called by the Axumites, Abuna Salama (Our Father of Peace), worked closely with Ezana in spreading Christianity throughout the kingdom.[9]

Archbishop Yesehaq noted in an article on the Ethiopian church entitled "The Ethiopian Church and Its Living Heritage," delivered at The First Pan-African Christian Church Conference July 17-23, 1988, in Atlanta Georgia, cited the historic consciousness of the Ethiopian masses: "Ethiopians trace their genealogical origin to Adam and Eve; from Adam to Noah, from Noah to Ham, and from Ham to Ethiopia. The name 'Ethiopia' is historically accepted to be not only for today's Ethiopia, but as the universal name for Africa in earlier times."[10] A network of enduring trade developed between Ethiopia and ancient Israel which lasted well into the Roman Period, making possible the spread of Christianity throughout North Africa.

The Ethiopian Orthodox Church has also affirmed this: "Christianity was officially announced as the state religion in the fourth century by King Edna (Ezana, A.D. 320–356), and during the episcopacy of Frumentius, who was consecrated by Patriarch Athanasius of Alexandria. This occurred after Constantine issued his decree of toleration, declaring Christianity to be a legalized religion of the Roman Empire."[11] The Ethiopian church maintained close ties with the Coptic Church of Egypt, which remained unbroken even through one of the greatest Christological controversies to divide the Early Byzantine world: the question of whether Christ of one nature (monophysis) or two perfect natures, one divine and one human. Both the Egyptian (Coptic) Orthodox Church and the Ethiopian Orthodox Church rejected the doctrine of the two natures of Christ promulgated at the Council of Chalcedon in AD 451, remaining resolutely Monophysite. After a short period, the "Nine Fathers of Syria" arrived in the Ethiopian kingdom. These Monophysite holy men established the monastic movement in Ethiopia which would provide centers of literary and artistic activity throughout the following centuries.

The Coptic Church

The emerging church of Egypt encountered an ancient culture rich in a variety of religious traditions. The ancient Egyptians had been through a series of spiritual developments before the advent of Christianity. Emperor worship was just one form of the worship experiences of Egyptians. Animal worship played a vital part in the religious experience of the Copts. Many Copts and Greeks worshipped the god of Hades, known as Serapis. Among other gods were the bull Apis, Sobek the crocodile, a particular fish of the Nile, the wolf, and the goddess Isis. However, many of the priests and upper class still worshipped the "one god" of whom all the other gods were but so many manifestations. The Egyptians had a very strong belief in immortality and spiritualism. The former gave impetus to the great building programs of pyramids by the kings. Christianity had to make adjustments to the existing religious culture of the Copts.

According to early Christian tradition, Christianity was first preached in North Africa during its first period of expansion. The Egyptian church itself attributes its founding to Mark, the interpreter of Peter. Similarly, Eusebius, the first historian of the church (260–339), records this tradition relative to Mark's missionary work in Egypt. He was the first missionary bishop in Africa. Others soon followed and developed the African church as one of the most important centers of the faith. F. P. Noble, in his 1899 work entitled *The Redemption of Africa: A Story of Civilization*, states the following regarding the apostolic missionary activity in Africa:

> (1) Matthew went as a missionary to Ethiopia first and suffered martyrdom either in Abyssinia or India: (2) Simon Zelote's missionary travels included parts of Asia, Egypt, Libya (including Cyrene), and Mauritania;

(3) Jude extended his missionary labors to Libya; (4) Thomas, so Jerome understood, preached the gospel in Ethiopia; and, (5) James the Less labored in Egypt, and was crucified.[12]

While disagreeing with the position held by Noble regarding the ministry of Mark in Egypt, William H. Worrell does state that by AD 200 Christianity had spread among the native Egyptians, and the delta was full of converts. He attributes this to the fact that Christianity came as a simple religion with a firm belief in immortality with the ability to acclimate existing religious thought among the Egyptians. Specifically, he sees the possibility of a synthesis of Christianity and the Osirian cult.[13] Similarly, F. B. Welbourn suggests that:

> Christianity came to East Africa as the "religious" dimension of western civilization. It was concerned not so much with inviting Africans to join what the North African theologian Tertullian called "a third race of men." Rather, it offered to save their souls without challenging at any fundamental level their primary loyalties to their tribes. This form of Christianity would readily be attractive to distant African tribes in the north and western parts of the continent.[14]

The Roman province of North Africa covered modern Tripoli, Algeria, and Morocco.

Gradually, the roots of a synthesized form of Christianity spread downward to areas of East Africa as well as West Africa. Again, Welbourn affirm,

> By the end of the second century there had appeared the "Gospel according to the Egyptians." The "catechetical school" of Alexandria—which was mainly an attempt to reach the intellectual Greeks of the city—was headed by the great figures of Clement and Origen. A century later, Bible and liturgy had been translated into the vernacular languages of Egypt. Paganism was still active (a figure of a priest has been discovered, belonging to this time and bearing the symbols both of the Holy Communion and of the Egyptian goddess Isis). But a genuinely national Coptic Church was growing; the Copts were the indigenous people of Egypt.[15]

Similarly, the Ethiopian church, with its specific form of Christianity following southward trade routes, was partially instrumental in the spread of Christian ideas into lower East Africa. Trade routes between North Africa and native tribes below the Sahara Desert made possible the flow of Christian ideas to the western parts of Africa. These trade routes had been established by merchants of Timbuktu who exported slaves to the Moorish kingdoms north of the Sahara. Apparently, African Christian spirituality as well as Islam, with indigenous tendencies, spread into much of the African continent, especially the Maghrib, very early in the general expansion of Christianity.

Christianity in the Sudan

At an early age, Christianity spread into the Sudan from Egypt before the reign of Emperor Constantine, the first Christian emperor. Some Christians escaped south into Nubia in order to avoid the persecutions instigated by earlier Roman emperors. The faith reached this new area also as a result of merchants who traded in Egypt and the Sudan. After Constantine, the propagation of the faith in Nubia continued through traders and travelers from Egypt. However, the most successful spread of Christianity into the Sudan was the work of Christian missionaries sent to the Sudan by the great emperor of Constantinople Justinian, and his wife Theodora, in the sixth century AD. The emperor's wife Theodora was an Arian, a different Christian body from her husband. She was a very devoted Arian and devoted herself to the encouragement of missionaries and Christian missions. Julian, a priest, approached Theodora requesting her to send missionaries to Nubia to try to convert it to the Christian faith. She conveyed the request of Julian to the emperor, who ordered the Christian mission to be sent to Nubia as quickly as possible. Theodora took the lead in sending Julian to the Sudan to evangelize the people in the Arian faith. In 540, Julian reached Nubia before the mission from the emperor arrived. His work in northern Nubia resulted later in the whole of the area being converted to Arian Christianity. With the later arrival of the mission from the emperor, two rival forms of Christianity were introduced into the Sudan.

Mandour El Mahdi gives the following account of the spread of Christianity into the region by a bishop named Longinus:

> Longinus was also responsible for the conversion of the kingdom of Alwa to Christianity. On his return to Nubia in A.D. 580, the kings of Alwa, who were anxious to follow the example of Nubia, invited him to visit their country and propagate Christianity. He went and Alwa became Christian. While Longinus was in Nubia and Alwa, many of the pagan temples were converted into churches, and many new churches and monasteries were built. The missionaries sent by Justinian went to the kingdom of Makuria, which converted to Christianity in the same period as northern Nubia.[16]

Hence, the influence of these two Christian political leaders resulted in the conversion of many Africans in Nubia, later called the Sudan. This factor is significant for the possible penetration of some degree of the faith into lower East Africa prior to the later colonization period.

The Atlantic Slave Trade

The Age of Exploration ushered in Christian European contact with West Africa. Roman Catholic explorers were pioneers in the early contact with Africans in the western parts of Africa. They were seeking a more profitable trade route to India and other parts of the Orient without having to deal with Moslems in North Africa. During the seventh and eighth centuries, zealous Moslems had infiltrated militarily and religiously into North Africa, posing a major challenge to the North African church. The Arabs advanced into various parts of North Africa with little or no resistance from the existing military establishment as well as the Christian church. The successful spread of Islam was partly the results of strife and doctrinal divisions within the church. Many of the North African Christians converted (some by force) to Islam. After the final stage of the Moslem invasion in AD 665, Christianity was almost wiped out in North Africa, surviving in the small kingdom of Ethiopia. The strong hold of Islam in North Africa was resented by European Christians. Before the Age of Exploration, Europeans traded reluctantly with these Arabs. The Arab middlemen limited the profitability of the trade between Europe and the Orient. Europeans had to trade with these tradesmen for goods from the Orient and human cargo from Africa. However, the European interest in slaves or servants from Africa was limited because the perceived need for these Africans was not economically advantageous. Those who were brought to Western Europe were Christianized and assigned servant positions. Later, adventurous explorers from Europe would change this economic arrangement and radically alter the plight of Africans.

In the early fifteenth century, the Portuguese developed a new kind of ship capable of launching long-distance travel which facilitated the Great Age of Exploration. Of all the countries in Europe, Portugal was in the best position to launch this defining age of Euro-African contact in what was to be called "The Dark Continent." Traditionally, Portugal had always been a gateway to Africa, the first destination of these new ventures. Lisbon and Porto, both excellent natural harbors, were thriving centers of commerce. Socially and politically, it was more stable than other European nations. France and England had been ushered into a state of instability caused by the Hundred Years' War. Prince Henry "The Navigator" was the pioneer in Portugal's drive to penetrate West Africa. In 1419 at Sagres, near Cape St. Vincent, he established a home and sort of maritime college for the double purpose of finding places where there was "a sure and certain hope of profit" and converting the infidel inhabitants thereof to the true faith of Catholics.[17] In 1415 and again in 1418, Prince Henry was engaged in campaigns against the hated Moors and learned of the caravan routes extending from Tripoli, Ceuta, and other Mediterranean towns in North Africa. He encountered some Moorish prisoners who informed him of the abundance of gold, wines, textiles, and slaves southward across the Sahara and the Sudan. These resources were transported from the Senegal and Gambia regions, and from the Gold Coasts on the Gulf of Guinea. News of the rich trade "inspired Prince Henry to seek those lands by way of the seas."[18] He sent forth mariners to explore and trade with African kings along the west coast of Africa, and to search for a river passage to Prester John's alleged Christian kingdom in east Africa. Subsequently, his work was carried on by others interested in gold and slave trade. Once that trade had been firmly established, Portugal sent Cao and Dias farther south on voyages of discovery until finally, Dias reached southern Africa. Initially, these Catholic explorers tried to establish small outposts for trade in slaves and minerals, and the conversion of natives from their pagan religions to the "superior" white man's religion. However, the lure of riches from the slave trade soon overshadowed any missionary considerations.

In 1497, Vasco da Gama sailed with specific instructions to reach India and negotiate with Christians there for a share in the spice trade. The success of these voyages was sufficient for the Portuguese to successfully challenge the monopoly of the hated Arabs in the oriental market, resulting in the partial revitalization of economic life in Europe. Not only was spice from the Orient a lucrative market, but the slave trade was also seen to be profitable. Largely under the encouragement of Prince Henry, the sailors and merchants of Portugal early saw the economic advantages which the African slave trade afforded. The growth in the wealth of Portugal, with the construction of the great castle of Elmina and the two papal bulls which gave them exclusive rights in Africa and sanctioned the enslavement and baptism of captive natives, was not long ignored by other European nations. Soon, other nations followed the enterprising spirit of Prince Henry. Specifically, Spain was captivated by this spirit of exploration. Desiring a share in the Far Eastern trade, they sent Columbus to find a westward route to the Indies. On April 17, 1492, the Catholic monarchs of Castile, Ferdinand and

Isabella, signed the Capitulations of Santa Fe, the agreement by which Columbus would undertake the voyage of discovery to the western Atlantic. However, Portugal had already expanded its slave enterprise. By the time of the death of Prince Henry in 1460, seven or eight hundred slaves were being carried to Portugal annually.[19] Not only were slaves brought from West Africa, but Spain and Portugal also purchased slaves who had been taken from various parts of Africa from Arab traders. These slaves were taken to Spain and Portugal for economic considerations and to be Christianized.

Even after Columbus's "discovery" of the New World in 1492, England, unlike Spain and Portugal, was rather slow to get involved in the Atlantic slave trade. Both Spain and Portugal, with the authorization of the pope, had developed an extensive Atlantic slave trade. Millions of slaves were transported to the New World by these Catholic settlers. The Spanish and Portuguese Catholics had little or no concern for the tremendous horrors African slaves experienced on the ships to the New World. They were simply thought of as regular cargo by the ship captains. For example, on Captain Thomas Phillips's slave ship *Hannibal*, some slaves developed diseases and some committed suicide rather than being transported through the Atlantic slave trade. Many African lives were lost on the voyages while various captains saw this fact only in economic terms. With the evolving triangular slave trade, African slaves were merely thought of as human cargo. With unaffected Christian conscience, the Spanish took the lead in extending the slave trade by promoting a system known as the sale of the *assiento*, which were monopolies or contracts sold to nations or individual corporations for the importation of slaves. These Roman Catholics built New World empires based on slavery.

But the English settlers in the thirteen original colonies were initially more concerned with their security, government with religious freedom, and economic development based on capitalism rather than extensive involvement in the Atlantic slave trade. To be sure, these Protestant settlers realized the need for cheap labor, but such labor could be supplied by indentured servants, Native Americans, and a minimal number of Africans. In 1619, only a few Africans accompanied the English settlers at Jamestown, Virginia. The twenty Africans arrived on a Dutch ship for sale as indentured servants. Historians debate whether these Africans were really slaves or just servants of the colonists. However, this settlement signaled the first African contact with the English colonial development in the New World. It was not until 1672 that the first successful African trading company in England became involved in the lucrative trade. Later,

African slaves would play a major role in the economic development of the colonies.

Gradually, the English settlers, unlike the Roman Catholics of South and Central America, came to realize their need for a greater slave population to sustain their labor force. Winthrop D. Jordan, in his article entitled "Unthinking Decision: The Enslavement of Negroes in America to 1700," remarks,

> When the first fragmentary evidence appears about 1640 it becomes clear that some Negroes in both Virginia and Maryland were serving for life and some Negro children inheriting the same obligation. Not all Negroes, certainly, for Nathaniel Littleton had released a Negro named Anthony Longoe from all service whatsoever in 1635, and after the mid-1640's the court records show that other Negroes were incontestably free and were accumulating property of their own. At least one Negro freeman, Anthony Johnson, himself owned a Negro.[20]

Nevertheless, colonial laws were soon codified establishing the basis for chattel slavery. The earliest example of the legal establishment of slavery took place in 1640 when the Court of Virginia made a distinction between black and white servants. Subsequently, statutory slavery by the colonies occurred rapidly: 1641, Massachusetts; 1663, Maryland; 1664, New York and New Jersey; 1682, South Carolina; 1700, Pennsylvania and Rhode Island; 1715, North Carolina; and 1755, Georgia. These new developments ushered in an expanding involvement in the Atlantic slave trade (millions of Africans became unwilling African Americans) by Protestant Englishmen and other ethnic settlers in the colonies. The slave population in the southern regions far outnumbered that of the North. Forceful economic and social factors caused a radical adjustment in the American settlers' attitudes toward African slaves. Gradually, slaves became viewed in terms of their economic worth and not as fellow human beings.

Euro-American Religion and African Slavery

The majority of English Protestants were in the forefront of the evolution of African slavery in colonial America. However, it took some time before anything approaching a consensus developed among English Protestants sufficient for the establishment of the "peculiar institution." For a considerable time, lively debates took place among various Protestant groups over the slavery issue. Forceful sermons, addresses, printed materials, and other media were utilized in the lively debates over African slavery in the colonies. To be sure, divided opinions were characteristic in most religious bodies and lasted even far into the National Period before the Civil War.

The New England Puritans, who arrived on the Mayflower on December 21, 1620, in Plymouth—where they established the second permanent English settlement—were among the earlier groups to tackle the issue of African slavery. In 1691, the Mayflower settlers merged with the Massachusetts Bay colony to form Massachusetts. In establishing the colonial government, they desired the formation of a theocracy in relations to the Mayflower Compact. Their political temperament was driven by experiences with the religious controversies in England and greater Europe. The Church of England had been established as the result of the controversy of King Henry VIII's (the first Tudor king who ascended the throne in 1485) political decision to challenge the authority of the Roman Catholic pope in English civil and religious matters. While married to his wife Catherine of Argon, the king fell in love with Anne Boleyn and decided to marry her, but the pope would not allow such a situation. In 1529, King Henry called Parliament into a historic session that lasted seven years. Before it was dissolved, the Church of England had severed all connections with the Roman Catholic Church. This act was also partly in response to the advancing Protestant movement in Europe. Also, this effectively resulted in the real birth of the established Church of England under the control of the monarch. New England Puritans, as a Calvinistic-oriented reform movement of post-Reformation England, inherited from England the separatist spirit of defiance against the pope. But they also desired a separation from the worldly concerns of the Church of England. The Puritan movement was not limited to New England but was also found among settlers in other areas like Virginia and other pioneer regions. Moreover, they were not limited to any one denomination. They desired a "pure religion" based directly on the teachings of early Christianity. They desired to make the church perfect as an instrument for promoting true religion and therefore urged the utter rejection of everything that contained Roman error and superstition. But the Puritans had no objections to the connection of the church with the state, or to the church's being controlled by civil authorities. This factor set the stage for the latter controversy of slavery.

The high moral views of New England Puritans did not preclude their acceptance of and involvement in the slave business. According to T. Scott Miyakawa, none of the large denominations—not even New England Congregationalists—

were free of slave-holding members. He affirmed: "The good Puritan felt that God had given him the heathen as his heritage, and in enslaving the Indians and the Negroes he was merely claiming his inheritance."[21] There was a tremendous inconsistency between the theory and practice of these Puritans. In 1641, theoretically the first colonial statute on slavery in Massachusetts read for a dozen words like a charter of universal rights: "There shall never be an bond slaverie, villinage or captive amongst us…unless it be lawfull captive taken in warres, and such stranger as willingly selle themselves or are sold to us." Servitude as a penalty for crime was also provided for in this law.[22] The English clergyman Richard Baxter was one of the first to address the inconsistency involved in their acquiescence to the institution of slavery. In 1673, he addressed a section of his *A Christian Directory* to those masters in foreign plantations who had Africans and other slaves, which was widely read in New England as well as in the mother country. He recognized three legitimate occasions for enslavement: crime, captivity in war, and self-sale. He condemned as incarnate devils those who "go as Pirates and catch up poor Negro's or people of another Land, that never forfeited Life or Liberty, and to make them slaves."[23] This was a direct assault on the African slave trade.

In 1726, Samuel Willard extended the theme expressed by Baxter. In his work entitled *Complete Body of Divinity*, he wrote the last comprehensive statement of covenant theology stating that slavery could be brought about not only by crime, captivity, and self-sale but also by "natural generation," which created new inconsistencies in the debate. He believed that the biblical texts of Genesis 14:14 and 17:12 authenticated his belief that slavery, beginning at birth, fits the reality of African slavery in the New World. However, this did not apply to white indentured servants who could not "inherit or pass his or her bondage."[24] Clearly, racial considerations were involved in his theological position.

William Warren Sweet summarized this pervasive theology in New England and elsewhere:

"As long as this type of theology prevailed in New England, churches could not be expected to raise any protest against the institution. And it is a significant fact that it was not until their Calvinism was radically modified that New England's opposition to slavery began. Many of the most influential Congregational ministers were slave owners, as were John Davenport of New Haven; Ezra Styles, president of Yale; and even

Jonathan Edwards. It is also true that Congregational ministers were interested in the conversion of slaves early on (as was Cotton Mather), and several of the New England churches had Negro members and gave instruction to them, but there was no settled policy developed nor organized work among them."[25]

African slaves were found, although not as many as in other English colonies, in every New England colony. The relatively small number of slaves in New England centered on the limited needs of the type of economic development in that society. Its economy was not like the plantation system of the southern colonies, which required large numbers of slaves.

By 1769, conflicting voices were heard among New England Congregational ministers over the issue of slavery. Dr. Samuel Hopkins, who became the first minister of the First Congregational Church in Newport, Rhode Island, was one of the most forceful voices against the institution of slavery. Initially, he had been involved in holding slaves delivered by the slave trade, but later changed his mind relative to the lack of Christian principle involved in the institution. Upon observing the severe plight of slaves in Newport, Dr. Hopkins soon became "a bitter foe of the institution and began preaching against the evils of the slave trade."[26] Throughout his neighborhood, he saw many of his best friends actively engaged in the slave trade; but it became a matter of Christian conscience for him to speak out loudly against the whole slave business. In 1770, Dr. Hopkins preached a strong sermon "against kidnaping, purchasing and retaining slaves."[27] Some of his wealthiest church members exercised strong opposition to the sermon and left the church. This experience did not deter him from his strong position but made him more adamant, resulting in his house-to-house visitation in the neighborhood urging Christian slaveholders to free their slaves. Near the close of the Colonial Period, his influence was widespread throughout New England. In 1776, he published his most influential work entitled *Dialogue Concerning the Slavery of the African*, which influenced other Congregational ministers to voice opposition to the institution of slavery.[28]

The Established Church in Virginia

The social and religious development of the Virginia colony predates and became more expansive regarding slavery than developments in New England. The establishment of the church in this colony was definitive of the spread of slavery in all southern colonies. Virginia was first in laying the groundwork for the legal precedence of the institution. In 1670, the Virginia Assembly passed a slave law which disallowed lifelong servitude for those Africans who became Christians before their arrival in the colony. Church members, being the only authorized voters, were prominent in this development toward establishing the legal foundation for the institution of slavery. As previously mentioned, Africans were brought to Jamestown, Virginia, in 1619 as indentured servants. This was the defining moment for a later tragedy in the experience of Africans in the British colonies. Initially, these settlers had not developed strong racist sentiments based on negative ontological considerations regarding the Africans. This factor would gradually develop as the trend toward the evolution of chattel slavery.

Religiously, the Church of England established a stronghold in the Virginia colony, for it was the oldest British colony in North America. During the reign of James I (1603–1625), several commercial companies were chartered to plant English colonies in North America, which emphasized.

> …the importance of propagating the Christian religion, and of bringing the "infidels and savages" to human civility and settled government. Religious beliefs and practices of the Church of England were to be maintained. As later in Plymouth, the company was in the control of men of Puritan sympathies. They were neither part of Separatists from the Established Church nor did they reject episcopal polity, but were strongly evangelical in piety and liturgical practices.[29]

The charter granted to the Virginia Company of London in 1606 specified "the true word of, and the service of God and the Christian faith be preached, planted and used" within the several colonies and plantations, not only for the benefit of the colonists but also "amongst the salvage people which doe or shall adjoine unto them."[30] In 1604, political difficulties developed within the London Company which resulted in the colony's becoming a royal colony. Robert Handy states that "the Puritan element was now replaced by a more Anglican one, and the colonial legislature required ministers explicitly conform to the practices of the Church of England."[31]

A growing concern in England for evangelistic work in English colonies led to specific actions on the part of the Church of England. As early as 1679, the Bishop of London took active interest in the religious state of the American colonies. In 1689, Reverend James Blair was appointed commissary for Virginia and urged the House of Burgesses to become committed to a law which would provide for the Christian education of the Native Americans and slaves. Even earlier, in 1665, the Anglican clergyman Morgan Godwin arrived in Virginia to advance missionary work in the colonies. After observing the poor state of religion generally in the colony, he returned to England and sent a strong letter to Governor William Berkeley regarding the religious matter. Subsequently, he spent some time in Barbados where a Quaker pamphlet awakened his distress over the general neglect of slaves' spiritual welfare. When he returned to England, he undertook a campaign of preaching and writing to promote the instruction and baptism of slaves. In his work entitled *The Negro's and Indians Advocate*, Reverend Godwin described and refuted the two basic issues against evangelistic efforts among Native Americans and African slaves which claimed that Africans in particular were not really human and that their Christianization was subversive of the planters' interest and security.[32] Also, the planters suggested that "the African's strange complexion, together with their stupidity and barbarousness, identified them as more akin to the beasts than human, as one woman claimed that you might as well baptize a puppy as a Negro boy."[33] Dehumanization and color prejudice were both expressed in these points of view. These two elements were destined to play a pivotal role in the relationship between African slaves and their masters. Historically, no other form of slavery had made such deep and cruel ontological evaluation of human beings.

In order to counter the strong arguments against the evangelization of African slaves, Reverend Thomas Bray, an English clergyman who spent some time in the colonies observing the poor condition of religion, decided to organize a missionary movement that would paint a more positive picture of African slaves as well as Native Americans. Upon returning to England, he led the way in 1701 for the organization of the Society for the Propagation of the Gospel in Foreign Parts. It was the earliest organized attempt for missionary work in the colonies. The program of the S.P.G. was divided into three branches: "the care and instruction of our people settled in the colonies with emphasis on the spiritual needs of English Christians; the conversion of the Indian savages; and the conversion of Negroes."[34] This represented a slightly modified picture of non-whites in the colonies. The new missionary society had the full support of the Archbishop of Canterbury with the understanding that it would "provide for the administration of God's Word and the sacraments" in those areas where there were no settled Anglican clergy.[35]

Reverend Samuel Thomas was the first missionary sent out by the society to work with Yamassee Native Americans in South Carolina, but the colonial governor Sir Nathaniel Johnson decided to send him to minister to the English settlers on the branches of the Cooper River. However, Reverend Thomas was still able to find some time to work with slaves in the area, teaching them to read the Bible with the objective of their conversion. He was successful in the instruction and conversion of twenty African slaves in the area.[36] When Reverend Thomas died in 1706, Reverend Francis Le Jau came to continue the missionary work of the society. He discovered that some of the planters were open to ministry with their children and African slaves. In conjunction with his work with the children of English settlers, Reverend Le Jau was able to instruct and baptize many Native American and African slaves. After this apparent success, he began to encounter some opposition from other planters over the issue of baptizing slaves. Seemingly, English law suggested that slaves would be liberated upon their baptism into the Christian religion. In an attempt to modify the effects of this law, several colonial legislatures, beginning in Maryland in 1664 and extending through the first quarter of the eighteenth century, declared that baptism did not change the slave's status.[37] In order to clarify the legal situation in England, "Bishop George Berkeley requested the formal opinions of His Majesty's Attorney-General" who replied in 1729 that "baptism made no alteration in the civil status of a slave within the British Kingdoms."[38] Both civil and religious clearance were given for a more aggressive missionary work among the slaves.

The Quakers and Slavery

Voices from a smaller Protestant group were heard in Pennsylvania (a colony founded by William Penn) as early as 1671, beginning with such well-known Quaker leaders as George Fox. Prior to Fox's work, some Quakers held slaves with only moderate opposition, but George Fox, who visited the colony in 1671–1672, became the most influential spokesman against Quaker involvement in the institution. In a Friends quarterly meeting, he admonished slaveholding Quakers to "deal mildly and gently with their negroes, and not use cruelty toward them . . . . and that after certain years of servitude they would make them free."[39] Apparently, he had in mind the system of white indentured servants in the colonies. George Fox realized that although slavery was recognized in the charter of Pennsylvania, there were provisions for freeing slaves under certain conditions after fourteen years of service. In 1711, at the Friends quarterly meeting held in Chester, Pennsylvania, a resolution was passed discouraging the enslavement of any more slaves. In summary, William Warren Sweet remarks, "Year by year after this time on the Chester Quarterly Meeting and the Philadelphia Yearly Meeting discussed the question, particularly of buying and selling slaves"[40] By 1773, the Quakers' annual meeting urged the manumission of all female slaves as soon as they reached the age of eighteen; likewise, all male slaves were to be manumitted at age twenty-one.

Moreover, the Quakers even dared to do journalistic work in the South. They were aware of the powerful effects of good journalism in ending the enslavement of Africans. They were also aware of the fact that there were some few Christians in the South who were sensitive to the slavery issue. In 1820, Elihu Embree, a Quaker in Tennessee, published in the town of Jonesboro the first anti-slavery paper in the South known as *The Emancipator*. This paper challenged Quakers who were guilty of slaveholding as well as other whites in Tennessee. The Quaker challenge to slavery lasted well into the advent of the Civil War. They remained unrelenting in their opposition.

The Moravians and Slavery

The Moravian movement in the United States has roots in Bohemia (1457) and was refounded in Saxony under the impulse of Pietism (1722). The Moravians were once known as the Bohemian Brethren, but the name "Moravians" later became the usage in the English-speaking world. In Europe, they were characterized by their tendency to establish a separated Pietist society within the State Church, thus becoming a denomination and a society under Count Zinzendorf. Part of the society migrated to America and established headquarters in Bethlehem, Pennsylvania, and Winston-Salem, North Carolina. The reasons that caused them to migrate to America were missions to the Native Americans and slaves, Count Zinzendorf's attempts at church union in Pennsylvania, and the threat of suppression in Germany. During the colonial period, residence in their unique communities was restricted to members only. In 1740–1741, they established settlements in Nazareth and Bethlehem, Pennsylvania. In 1753, they established a similar community in North Carolina.

The missionary work of the Moravians was not very successful among African American slaves. However, they were able to evangelize a small group in Winston-Salem, North Carolina. In 1822, this group of slaves and perhaps free African Americans organized the St. Philips Moravian Church, initially called The Negro Congregation. It was first established in Old Salem in a log cabin.[41] However, the Moravian church did not receive the approval of most African American Christians. The movement remained very slow and ineffective.

The Baptist Churches and Slavery

Other Protestant groups like Baptists and Methodists became involved in the institution of slavery during the colonial period as well as the national period until the Emancipation Proclamation issued by President Abraham Lincoln. But again, there were considerable differences of opinions among leaders within these church denominations. Such divisions tended to take on sectional significance, particularly between the North and South. This was due to the demographics of slavery in America. Northern Christians had fewer reasons economically to be dependent on slavery. Farms were relatively small in rural areas, and movements toward a more urban and industrial society emerged in the North. On the other hand, the South's economy assumed a more rural and large plantation development, necessitating the need for a large, cheap labor force. By far, the largest population of slaves was found in the South where large plantations developed. This was especially true with the invention of the cotton gin. Subsequently, slave labor became crucial to economic development in that region. Hence, the contrast between economic needs played a central role in the theological controversy between Christians of all major denominations, including Roman Catholics, in the North and South over the issue of slavery. To be sure, Baptists and Methodists emerged as the largest Protestant groups and participants in slavery.

The story of Baptist beginnings in the English colonies resulted from the plight of Roger Williams, an English Puritan who left his native country seeking religious freedom. He wanted to be free to worship and practice his Puritan beliefs in the New World. Cotton Mather asserted the fact that "many of the first settlers in Massachusetts were Baptists, and as holy and watchful and fruitful and heavenly a people as perhaps any in the world."[42] Early Baptists in America trace their primary roots to the work of Roger Williams, the first who pleaded for liberty of conscience in the colonies, and who became the pioneer of religious liberty in the New World. But upon his arrival in the colony, he soon encountered difficulties from other Puritans regarding civil matters. Governor Hopkins once remarked, "Roger Williams justly claims the honor of having been the first legislator in the world, in its latter ages that fully and effectively provided for and established a full, free, and absolute liberty of conscience."[43] His socio-political concepts of church and state relations led to tremendous encounters with the principal leaders of the Massachusetts colony. He was exiled by the court because of his opposition to church membership rights of suffrage, all laws compelling attendance at church, and all taxed for the support of worship. His position deviated too far from the tradition inherited from the Church of England.

While exiled from Massachusetts, Roger Williams was able to lead a movement for the founding of the Rhode Island colony. He was able to secure a charter from the King of England and became the ruler of the colony based on biblical principles. In 1639, Ezekiel Holliman baptized Roger Williams, the first to be baptized by immersion on a profession of faith, who then administered the same rite to Holliman and ten others. This small group organized themselves into the first Baptist church in North America. Subsequently, emigrants who were Baptists established themselves in other parts of New England and Virginia, and in most principal towns in the colonies. Ironically, many of these same Christians capitulated to the drive for slave ownership. The high principles of the founders of the faith gave way to the economic considerations of participating in the slave-trade business.

One of the earliest evidences of Baptist participation in slavery was the case of the Mill's Creek Church which sent up to the Kentucky Baptist Association this query in 1798: "Has a black slave the right to a seat in the Association?" The prompt answer was sent back, "Yes, provided he be sent as a messenger from a church."[44] At this time, the few converted slaves were worshipping in biracial churches. However, this emerging agitation over the spiritual rights of converted slaves soon became a strongly dividing issue in Baptist churches throughout the colonies, for the decision favorable to slave participation in the Baptist denomination was not readily received by other Baptist churches. In 1795, the Lick Creek Church split over the issue of slavery. Similarly, "a disaffection existing in the Rolling Fork Church, on the account of slavery, the whole church except three withdrew from the association."[45]

The initial decades following the American Revolution were times of spiritual stresses and unremitting social tension relative to the slavery question. In many cases, those African American slave Baptists who had been admitted into the biracial churches were very limited in their privileges and responsibilities. An obvious allusion to this tendency was reflected in an 1802 report of the Dover Baptist Association. Here, it was said that some churches admitted to their church meetings all male members, slave or free. Nevertheless, the report reflected a movement against this tendency:

> By experience this plan was found vastly inconvenient. The degraded state of the minds of the slaves rendered them totally incompetent to the

task of judging correctly respecting the business of the church, and in many churches there were a majority of slaves; in consequence of which great confusion often arose. This circular letter argued and advised that although all members were entitled to the privilege, yet that none but free male members should exercise any authority in the church. The Association, after some debate, sanctioned the plan by a large majority.[46]

Clearly, the association's action made it very clear that the slavery question was sufficient to cause many white Baptists to set aside basic principles of the denomination to accommodate slavery.

Again, the Baptist controversy assumed regional bias resulting in sharp differences between northern anti-slavery Baptists and southern pro-slavery Baptists. Northern Baptists gained inspiration from the evolving abolitionist movement and their social ethics. The Baptist Association of Hancock, Maine, adopted a report in 1836 declaring that in their opinion "of all the systems of iniquity that ever cursed the world, the slave system is the most abominable," and that the only remedy was immediate emancipation. The next year, the same association resolved "that, we as the professed followers of Jesus Christ, have no fellowship or communion with those under the character of Christians continue to hold their fellow-men in bondage."[47] Generally, the anti-slavery Christians, though not all abolitionists, followed a similar trend in speaking against the institution of slavery. On the other hand, the Savannah River Baptist Association considered the conduct of the abolitionists "considerable and meddlesome," and requested their state convention to instruct their delegates to the Triennial Convention of 1841 to demand of the Northern brethren whether "they can acknowledge these fanatics as their co-workers, and to inform them of the impossibility of further cooperation by the Georgia Baptists unless the Abolitionists are dismissed."[48]

Often, key persons in a region can influence the mode of thought and actions of many others regarding socio-political and religious beliefs. Representative of the southern Christian idea regarding slavery was James Furman. He admonished, "We who own slaves, honor God's law in the exercise of our authority." In an interpretation of Furman's position, Donald G. Mathews said,

> These words were not a defiant response to abolitionist rhetoric or a statement about the divine origins of black slavery. They were words of admonition in a letter from a South Carolina Baptist clergyman to a fellow slaveholder suspected of perverseness in his treatment of a male

servant. Furman's message was that we masters may not treat slaves according to our own will because our authority, as all authority, is really delegated by God, and in exercising it, we have a solemn responsibility to convey that fact to servants and thus elevate our relationship with them to a "high moral plane." In writing the letter, Furman naturally assumed that he would not be condemned as an abolitionist meddler, for his statement was not the command of an outsider so much as a confessional prayer acknowledging our common responsibility as masters. His was a brief exposition of the Evangelical slave holding ethic."[49]

In these observations, Mathews rightly summarized the escapist type of Christian ethics assumed by many southern evangelicals regarding the institution of slavery. They sought to justify the system, arguing that Christian social ethics was being operative in the master and slave relationships in the South. They argued that African slaves were better off on American plantations than their previous conditions on the "Dark Continent." In fact, many Christians of most southern denominations held views similar to those in a book published in 1852, written by Reverend Josiah priest and entitled *Bible Defence of Slavery; and Origin Fortunes, and History of the Negro Race*. Reverend Priest made several representative ideas regarding the justification of slavery: "It will not be forgotten, that we have said above, that Ham, one of the sons of Noah, was born black, with all the peculiarities of the true woolly headed negro man, by the direction of Divine power, and contrary to the common dictation of nature.... The circumstance we now allude to, is the name which was given to the youngest son of Noah, the father of the negro race, at his birth, and that name was Ham."[50] To answer any objections, Priest stated, "We answer, that the word Ham, in the language of Noah, which was the pure and most ancient Hebrew, signified anything that had become black; it was the word for black, whatever the cause of the color might have been, the same as the word black, means black in the English tongue."[51] He further argued that God placed the races of men in the proper location on the planet for adaptation: "Among men reckoned in classes, as belonging to distinct families or nations, the earth has also been divided by the operation of the Divine hand, and suited to their several natures. To the white race, the descendants of Japheth, the northern regions of the earth were given. To Shem and his descendants, the red or copper colored race, the middle regions or temperate clime, north of the equator, was allotted. But Ham and his race were given the burning south."[52] In order to be hermeneutically correct in suggesting that God ordained that the sons of Ham would ever be slaves in the Genesis account, Priest stated,

> But lest the reader should become perplexed, respecting the application of this anathema, on account of the text above referred to being in the English, "cursed Canaan," instead of "cursed Ham," as it should have been translated; we state that the Arabic copy of the book of Genesis, which is a language of equal authority with the Hebrew, and originally the very same, reads "cursed Ham," the father of Canaan, a servant of servants shall he be unto his brethren.[53]

Moreover, he went even further to suggest that Africans were fundamentally depraved and inferior to the white race:

> It is utterly impossible to reduce the whites by any process whatsoever to so low a condition, as is found to be the universal state of the negro race, on account of the possession of superior mental faculties, moral feelings, reason, reflections, sympathies, and all the train of qualifications, constituting the image of God, as alluded to, Gen. 1:27. But these qualifications, and this image, are possessed by the negro race in a less degree, which corresponds exactly with the difference there is between the color, forms, and attitudes of the two races.[54]

In order to counter some of the harsh attitudes of the southern brethren, Reverend Francis Wayland, a moderate white Baptist, urged a more conciliatory position less threatening to the preservation of the Union. By the early 1800s, radical positions held by Baptists of the South were severely agitating the political strength of the Union. The abolitionist movement was intensifying its pressure on the pro-slavery elements in American society. While not in substantial agreement with the abolitionists, Reverend Wayland addressed a letter to William Lloyd Garrison in 1831, explaining he did not desire to have *The Liberator*, an Abolitionist publication for propaganda, because although he believed slavery to be wicked and destructive of the best interests of both master and slave, immediate emancipation was neither wise nor just. In 1845, his views had become progressively more radical. In a letter to Reverend Richard Fuller, the noted pro-slavery Baptist who was styled as a devoted master, Wayland argued,

> Jesus Christ has taught us that the hungry, the thirsty, the naked, the sick, the prisoner, the stranger, are his representatives on Earth, and that our love to him is to be measured by the universal sympathy which we

extend to every form of human distress, and he adds, "Inasmuch as ye did in not to one of the least of these my brethren, ye did it not to me." The special representatives of Christ in this country seem to me to be the oppressed, and I fear I must add the frequently lacerated, Christian slave. How shall we stand before the Savior, if we make no effort to comfort and deliver this slave—much less if we count ourselves among the number of his oppressors?[55]

Reverend Francis Wayland further dismissed any socio-political arguments held by proslavery Baptists, asserting, "But it will be said, the abolition of slavery will ruin the Southern States. Should it be so, as you have well remarked, if it be wrong, it ought to be abandoned."[56] Northern Baptists maintained the position that religious and political grounds favored the cessation of slavery. The divided opinions reflected in such men as Reverend Francis Wayland, Reverend Richard Fuller, and Reverend Josiah Priest tended to heighten the stress among Baptists over the issue of slavery.

Generally, this anthropological conceptualization from the book of Genesis reflected the interpretation of southern Christians as well as early Northern Christian slaveholders across denominational lines, which became prevalent in the general population of slaveholders. Most white Christians did not believe in the full humanity of African slaves, nor even that of free African Americans. Christian and non-Christian whites held tenaciously to negative anthropological concepts regarding African Americans.

The Methodist Episcopal Church and Slavery

Lastly, the attitude of Methodist slaveholders maintained positions similar to Baptists and other denominations. In 1784, when the Methodist Episcopal church was formed at the Christmas Conference, a rule was adopted that every slaving-holding member must within a year execute a legal instrument agreeing to free his slaves, while the preachers were required to keep a record of all such transactions in their circuits. All members were required to comply with this ruling within a year or withdraw from the church. This was the most extreme anti-slavery legislation enacted by the Methodist Episcopal church until the outbreak of the Civil War. It was soon found, however, to be extreme, for in less than six months it was necessary to suspend the rule.[57] In 1785, Bishop Coke, because of his strong anti-slavery stand, almost experienced physical violence in Virginia; and Bishop Asbury came to the sorrowful conclusion that "any mention in the South of anti-slavery views might lead to evil consequences for the church."[58] Again in 1796, the anti-slavery constituency of the Methodist Episcopal church sought to adopt a new rule and there was "an attempt made to restrict slavery in the Church," providing that official members must agree to emancipate their slaves, while sellers were to be expelled."[59] The spirituality of the Methodist Episcopal church probably influenced the rather positive attitude of the leadership of the American denomination. Leaders were familiar with the religious sentiments of the founding fathers of the Methodist Movement in England—John Wesley; indirectly, his brother Charles Wesley; George Whitfield; and other members of "the holy club." John Wesley entered Christ Church in Oxford, England, in 1720, where he began reading from the spiritual works of Thomas à Kempis which led him to a deeper spirituality and later influenced him to take the holy orders resulting in being ordained a deacon in 1725 and a priest in 1728. In 1729, John Wesley returned to Oxford and became leader of a "holy club," a group of serious students who had united with Charles Wesley to seek the inner resources of Christian spirituality and the development of their strict methodical approach to daily spiritual living. They were labeled with the taunting name "methodists" from other Oxford students.

Another prominent member of "the holy club" was George Whitfield (1714–1770), who became one of the greatest pulpit orators of the eighteenth century. In 1732, he entered Pembroke College, Oxford, where he later met Charles Wesley in 1734, who invited him to "the holy club," and began a life of extreme asceticism. Later, he was ordained a deacon at Gloucester, June 20, 1736, and became a popular preacher around London. When John Wesley relocated to the colony of Georgia, he invited George Whitfield to come to Georgia and preach, where he conducted a successful ministry. Like others who had been influenced by "the holy club," Whitfield held some high view of Christian manhood resulting in humanitarian socio-political views. He traveled extensively through the Southern colonies and observed the plight of slaves. Hence, he addressed a letter to the planters affirming that his sympathies had been strongly excited by the "miseries of the poor negroes" calling attention to the practice of slave masters, indicating that such behavior encouraged "the savage tribes in Africa to continue their warfare on each other to supply the demand for slaves thus created."[60] He further suggested that the "generality of" them were using their slaves "as bad as though they were brutes; nay worse," worse than their horses, which were "fed and properly cared for" after the labors of the day, while the slaves must grind their corn and prepare their own food; worse even than their dogs, who are "caressed and fondled," while the slaves "are scarce permitted to pick up the crumbs which fall from their master's table."[61]

Perhaps it was this similar spirituality and social ethics that influenced both Bishop Cook and Bishop Asbury to assume a more humanitarian approach to Africans in the New World. Both sought to influence other church leaders with the same spirit. However, their success was partly limited to the denominational level. Nevertheless, this official position of the Methodist Episcopal church appealed to African Americans and led to a significant increase in the number of their membership in the denomination.

Evangelization of African Slaves in the New World

As previously indicated, the strides toward the evangelization of slaves in the colonies were characterized by divided opinions. Protestant settlers had many social and political issues to deal with that precluded any substantial concern for African slaves. First and foremost in their minds was the economic issue of how best to utilize these slaves for the fullest benefit to the masters. The profitability motif figured high on their plane of concerns. Money was in short supply, and the investment in slaves was a significant expenditure for most of the slaveholders. Hence, the evangelization of slaves required outside motivations from evangelistic-minded English churchmen.

As previously mentioned, the Society for the Propagation of the Gospel in Foreign Parts was an early English missionary organization to advance the evangelization of African slaves in colonial America. The society was organized in England in 1701 by Thomas Bray. He had previously organized the Society for Promoting Christian Knowledge. His interest in forming this society was for the establishment of theological and classical libraries for the training of clergy. Members from this society assisted Bray in the organization of the S.P.G. In 1703, the society sent George Keith, a former Quaker, on an exploratory mission to English plantations in colonial America. He was joined by Captain John Talbot on the ship on which he sailed to New Jersey. From this base, he visited other plantations throughout most of the colonies and provided an extensive report back to the society in England. He was not even impressed with the performance of the white clergy among the white settlers. In 1685, he had preached at Woodbridge, New Jersey, at an independent meeting-house, but was still aware of the need of a more substantial clergy presence in the New World.[62] When George

Keith reported back to the society in England, his ministry was exclusively to white settlers, not to the slaves. But he probably mentioned his observations of slaves he encountered to other members of the society.

The real missionary work among the slaves commenced with the ministry of Reverend Samuel Thomas. He extended his ministry beyond the whites in South Carolina to include the religious instruction of slaves. He successfully instructed twenty slaves to read the Bible. These became the earliest members of the biracial church in the colonies. In 1706, this type of ministry was continued by Dr. Le Jau, who instructed and baptized many slaves and Native Americans. In 1714, his missions group included seventy English and eight slaves. All in all, the work among slaves was minimal since their response to Christianity at this early period was very slow. But their word among the English persons settlers was rather widespread. Hudson surveyed the work, reporting that "from the time of its inception until 1783 when it officially ceased operations in the newly independent colonies, eighty-four of its missionaries labored in New England, fifty-eight in New York, fifty-four in South Carolina, forty-seven in Pennsylvania, forty-four in New Jersey, thirty-three in North Carolina, thirteen in Georgia, five in Maryland, and only two in Virginia."[63]

One problem was that many of the planters maintained that converted slaves were more difficult to control. William Wilson Manross refuted this claim by stating, "This opinion was probably based on prejudice, for at a later time it was discovered that Christian negroes made better slaves, and piety became a virtue to be stressed upon the auction block. That development took place, however, after the negroes had become more used to servitude when it was easier to persuade them that submission was a Christian duty."[64] In New York and Philadelphia the society for the Propagation of the Gospel in Foreign Parts maintained catechists to instruct slaves, and their ministry seemed successful. It may be assumed that some of these missionaries were able to convert a few slaves in these colonies. In New York, the catechist was Elias Neau, a French Huguenot refugee who, before migrating to America, had suffered imprisonment for his faith. Although he was a layman, he became very interested in the welfare of slaves which led him to an appointment as the society's catechist in 1704.[65] Elias Neau was a diligent worker for the society in New York. When he arrived in the city, it had a population of 1,500 Native Americans and African Americans. He successfully instructed and baptized a significant number of the African Americans. In 1712, the work of the school was hindered because of a conspiracy on the part of some

African Americans to kill English residents of the city. When the revolt was put down, several African Americans were executed and the catechizing school was burned for the uprising. It was not until 1722 that the school was cleared from the charge and allowed to reopen. Subsequently, the society experienced a limited amount of work in other parts of New York. In 1723, Thomas Barclay reported from Albany that he "had instructed twenty negroes in the catechism."[66] Reverend Samuel Cooke, minister at Shrewsbury, Monmouth County, reported a little success by "baptizing two negroes in 1752."[67] In 1726, the clergy of Virginia reported some success in their ministry to catechize and instruct the slaves whenever the masters were agreeable. However, it was very difficult to persuade masters to permit the society to work on their plantations, resulting in a rather small number of conversions. Masters held strong beliefs that the evangelization of slaves was counterproductive to their economic interests.

In 1743, the society purchased two African Americans to train them as teachers for the work of a school in Charleston, South Carolina. By this time the society had established missions in all the colonies along the Atlantic seaboard. In 1758, the society was able to open schools in Philadelphia; and in 1760, similar schools were opened in Newport, Rhode Island, and Williamsburg, Virginia. In Maryland, the society had a good success story because "most of the clergy were accustomed to instructing the negroes with some regularity" which resulted in the baptism and instruction of a few of them on the eastern shore.[68] In North Carolina, James Moir reported that he had "baptized three hundred whites and sixty negroes."[69] The small number of converts among the slaves reflects the minimal success of the society in colonial America. But the biracial church saw its beginnings in these small groups of slaves who were allowed to worship in white churches. However, they were segregated in these churches either in designated pews, balconies, or chapels, thus reducing the challenges of social contact between the races.

Evangelistic Work of the Methodist Episcopal Church

The missionary work of Methodists commenced later than that of the Church of England. As mentioned earlier, the Methodist Episcopal church's leadership generally had a strong desire to evangelize and treat slaves better than other Protestant denominations. In 1808, Reverend Matthew P. Sturdevant, the first Methodist clergyman to labor in Alabama, after the constitutional provision prohibiting the importation of slaves into the several original states went into effect, reported "the names of fifteen colored members" of the Methodist Episcopal church in Alabama.[70] In many of the churches, the Christian slaves outnumbered the white membership. In 1831, specific clergymen were appointed to work among the slaves. One clergyman, Reverend Gilbert Taylor, was rejected by the Tennessee Conference to do work among slaves in North Alabama because he owned slaves. Two other missionaries were appointed to minister in North Alabama. Subsequently, "there were in round numbers about three thousand colored members in the State of Alabama."[71]

The policy of appointing clergymen to work exclusively among slaves soon came into disrepute and was temporarily discontinued for four years. Reverend Arson West remarked,

> The environment was not favorable to the organization of separate charges for the Negroes in Alabama, and progress in that line and on that plan was slow. The plan of having the whites and the Negroes in the same pastoral charge was the plan to which all were accustomed, and many of the preachers, and many of the members of both races preferred that order of things, and there was much to commend it. It was the cheaper plan, for the same preacher and the same house of worship would serve both classes. Under that plan there would be no classes of preachers of the slaves. None would be under the disparagement of being the preacher of the slaves. The Negroes generally preferred the preacher who served the white folks to the preacher who was appointed specially to their race.[72]

Another reason for the difficulty of working with slaves in Alabama was that many of the slave owners believed that "preaching to the slaves would foster insubordination, encourage abolitionist sentiments, complicate civil affairs, and hasten emancipation."[73] This sentiment was operative in other southern colonies and was carried over into the National Period. In areas where there were large numbers of slaves, the planters were especially fearful of slave revolts.

The Roman Catholic Church

The Maryland colony was rather unique in its early participation in the evangelization of slaves. It was not dominated by a strong Protestant tradition. Unlike the other colonies, many of its early settlers were Roman Catholics who played key roles in the social and political development of the colony. From its initial contact with the New World, the Roman Catholic Church accepted the institution of slavery. Prior to the English establishment of colonies in North America, the church had established a long-time tradition of involvement in the institution of African slavery. Roman Catholic priests were among the early Spanish, French, and Portuguese explorers who first came to the shores with intentions for the establishment of settlements. In 1492, Ferdinand and Isabella approved the mission of Christopher Columbus in these terms: "He is bound for certain parts of the ocean to transact business of interest both to God and to us."[74] He landed on one of the Lucayan (Bahamian) islands, prostrated himself on the ground, returned thanks to God, and planted the cross on the island which he called San Salvador.

A short time after he arrived in the West Indies, Columbus commenced a policy of genocide of the Native Americans. In some areas of the West Indies, whole tribes were completely annihilated. Nevertheless, Pope Alexander VI acknowledged the sovereignty of the Spanish kings over these new territories by three bulls issued in the year 1493, on the condition that the new land be evangelized.[75] After Columbus arrived in the New World, Spain, Portugal, and France launched aggressive policies of conquest and settlement for the exploitation of the rich natural resources and the expansion of Roman Catholicism. The Pope had given these conquerors and settlers free hand in the initial enslavement of the Native Americans for the development and exploitation of these resources. Don Charles Poulet remarked, "Soon Christianity and the European conquistadores were synonymous, and the names 'Spanish' and 'Catholic' became equally odious."[76] The expressed motif of the pope was the mission of converting the Indians to the "superior" Roman Catholic faith. This was the expressed motif used by all European Roman Catholics as they sought to justify the conquests and enslavement of the native populations. However, the natives or "Indians" were not physically able to withstand the strenuous demands required of them by these conquerors from Europe.

The Dominicans were the first to express deep concerns about the bad treatment of the Native American slaves. As early as 1510, Brother Antonio Montesino championed the cause of the Native Americans in the church of Santo Domingo in the presence of the governor and the colonists, and he was sustained in his accusations by his superior Peter of Cordova. A heated discussion followed, and Montesino returned to Spain to enlist the aid of King Ferdinand. The king merely issued orders to treat the Native Americans with kindness. In

1502, Las Casas joined the Spanish settlement in the New World and observed the poor treatment of the Native Americans, and in 1515 he journeyed to Spain to plead the cause of the natives. He obtained support in his position from the prime minister Cardinal Ximenes.[77] The Native Americans were to be treated mildly and organized into "groups of villages served by priests."[78] After realizing the insufficiency of the native slave labor force, the Roman Catholics looked to Africa for the solution to the problem.

To fill the vacuum in the labor force, the European powers entered aggressively into the Atlantic slave trade, transporting millions of African slaves to South and Central America. However, Africans were present in the Americas from the very beginnings of the European explorations of the New World. They came with the early explorers indirectly from Africa. Significantly, these Africans had been brought to Europe and introduced to Roman Catholicism before they accompanied the explorers. Some reached areas of North America that later became the United States. Hence, they reached areas like Louisiana and Florida before the English arrived to establish the thirteen original colonies.

Protestants and Catholics in Maryland

The first English contact with what later became the colony of Maryland took place in 1608 when Captain John Smith made an exploratory trip up the Chesapeake Bay. Smith had come from the Virginia settlement. He was able to make a map of the Bay which reflected the presence of an island called Winston's Island, and by the Matapeake Native Americans called "Monoponson," later called Kent Island. In 1628, William Claiborne, funded by investors from England, obtained the license to trade with the Native Americans. He chose Kent Island as the most suitable site for the trading post, which was established in 1631 as the first English settlement in Maryland. Regarding the religion of the early settlers, Frederick Emory recorded the following:

> The religion of the early settlers of Queen Anne's County was that of the English Church. Claiborne's colony on Kent Island was distinctively an Anglican settlement in contradiction to the Roman Catholic settlement in St. Mary's. We have seen that a Catholic priest, Father Altham, spent some time on the Island, but he does not appear to have established a permanent foot-hold before his coming and the little congregation passing over the mainland of Kent, Queen Anne's, and Talbot, carried with

them the seeds of their faith, which soon took root and grew in a kindly soil.[79]

Some of these early Protestant settlers were able to live a comfortable lifestyle, for Emory observed,

"The life of the well-to-do planters in Queen Anne's was exceptionally pleasant and easy-going because of the great abundance of labor. There were white servants 'held in bondage' as well as black. Many of the former were known as 'redemptioners,' that is, persons coming from Europe who pledged themselves to serve a certain number of years in payment for their passage money. In April 1671, an act was passed encouraging the importation of negroes and slaves into this province. It was not uncommon for persons to obligate themselves for a certain sum to labor for a specified period."[80]

He also noted the severe treatment of Africans who violated the laws of the settlement by running away or committed other more severe crimes, observing the following:

Convicts were also transported into the province and sold as servants. On the 25th of February, 1718, for example, Capt. John Law petitioned the Queen Anne's County Court that the Act of Parliament of March 17, 1714, providing for the transportation of convicts be recognized as affecting certain persons whom he had transported and gave a list of the persons ordered to be transported who had been convicted of divers thefts and larcenies at a court of the Western Circuit, from the counties of Dorset and Devon, held in the summer of 1718....

The laws relating to slaves were extremely severe. Thus, for example, by an Act of 1729, a negro or other slave convicted "of any Petit-Treason or Murder or willfully Burning of Dwelling Houses" might be punished as follows: "To have the Right Hand cut off, to be Hanged in the usual Manner, the Head severed from the Body, the Body divided into Four Quarters, and the Head and Quarters set up, in the most public Places of the County where such Fact was committed.[81]

Also, it was not uncommon for slavery to be passed on to future generations of Africans. Frederick Emory noted an example of this practice: "An entry in the Court Records for 1708, for example, states that Edward Hambl(e)ton, of Queen Anne's County, in the province of Maryland, in-holder, for and in consideration of the love and affection which he bore towards the children which he had or might have by his wife Elizabeth, gave to said children the "negro girle Moll and her increase, to be equally divided among them, their heirs and assigns forever."[82]

For the most part, this was the practice followed by slave holders throughout the colonies. Slaves and all of their future offspring were destined to the institution.

Another early settlement in the colony of Maryland was planned by the English Catholic peer George Calvert, first Lord Baltimore, and founded in 1634 by his son Cecil Calvert, second Lord Baltimore. The first settlers in Maryland were English Catholics accompanied by Jesuit fathers as they founded the village of St. Mary's. The early Catholic settlers were able to establish themselves in Baltimore and other parts of the colony. English Protestant settlers had entered Maryland and challenged the political rights of the Catholics which were the continuation of the political struggles from England. Something of a political revolution or civil war took place and resulted in initial victories for Maryland Protestants. Many Catholics were deprived of their possessions, and a number of Jesuit missionaries were sent back to England. However, in 1649 the Assembly of Maryland passed the famous 1649 Toleration Act concerning religion which provided that "no persons believing in Jesus Christ should be molested in respect to their religion or the exercise thereof, or compelled to adopt the belief or exercise of any other religion against their consent."[83] This opened the door for the establishment of a strong Roman Catholic presence in Maryland. Like their Protestant neighbors, the Roman Catholics found it necessary to participate in the African slave trade. Even before the Catholics lost control of the colony, when the Catholic Proprietary Governor Leonard Calvert was in power, the slave trade had its beginning in Maryland. This Catholic governor himself owned slaves.

In 1636, a biracial Roman Catholic church was established in Leonardtown, Maryland, where mass was said for whites as well as for Native Americans and African slaves. To be sure, the Jesuit priests were themselves slaveholders, calling the slaves "Priest Negroes." But these priests treated their slaves with a somewhat humanitarian type of care, unlike their Protestant neighbors. They were not willing to separate slave families, and African slaves were permitted to marry. This was a big plus factor for the establishment of a significant family life for Catholic slaves. But it must be observed that the Catholic laity held similar dehumanizing views like Protestants. Even among the clergy, there was diversity of thought regarding the nature of African slaves. In 1749, Father George Hunter expressed the opinion that "Charity to Negroes is due from all, particularly their masters. As they are members of Jesus Christ, redeemed by His precious blood, they are to be dealt with in a charitable, Christian, paternal manner, which is at the same time a great means to bring them to their duty to God and therefore to gain their souls."[84] In 1774, Father Joseph Mosley expressed a rather negative concept regarding African slaves:

> the Negroes that do belong to the Gentlemen of our Persuasion, and our own, are all Christians, and instructed in every Christian duty with care: some are good, some very bad, some docile, some very dull. They are naturally inclined to thieving, lying and much lechery. I believe what makes them worse thieves and liars, and the innate heat of the climate of Africa and their natural temper of constitution gives them a great bent to lechery. The Negroes of all other persuasions are much neglected, as you imagine, and few ever christened.[85]

Strangely enough, Father Joseph Mosley, S.J., held a negative view of Africans even after they became Roman Catholics. Although he was concerned about the moral life of the slaves, Father Mosley, like other missionaries (some holding slaves themselves), demonstrated a lack of personal interest in the social status of the slaves, but their souls were of infinite value. In some instances, a small number of Catholic churches, like some Protestant churches in the South, owned some slaves. For Protestants, slaves were provided to the priest or pastor as part of the parsonage allowance. The fact that Catholic churches owned slaves is attested by Richard R. Miller, who said,

> "The many scattered instances in which we find mentioned in these official Relations or reports of Catholic activities, indicate that the owning and working of slaves on Catholic Church-owned mission plantations and establishments was all together the order of the day. Nor were the numbers especially small in some cases. For instance, in Jesuit Relations, vol. 70, p. 245, dealing with period from 1747 to 1764, we find this statement, "finally, the Jesuits had upon their estates a hundred and twenty or a hundred and thirty slaves."[86]

Even in the hierarchy of the church, the vast majority of the bishops viewed slavery as a political issue rather than a moral one. Hence, they were not instrumental in enlightening the Catholic laity in higher views regarding the humanity of slaves. In summary, wherever Roman Catholics encountered African slaves their attitudes were, at best, condescending and paternalistic toward them in Maryland and elsewhere throughout the colonies. This factor adversely affected their success in the early evangelization of slaves.

(Endnotes)

[1] George C. Bedell, Leo Sandon, and Charles Wellborn, *Religion in America* (New York: Macmillan, 1975), 285.

[2] Ibid., 285.

[3] Ibid., 289.

[4] Ibid.

[5] Ibid.

[6] Albert J. Raboteau, *Slave Religion the "Invisible Institution" in the Antebellum South* (New York: Oxford University Press, 1978). 4.

[7] E. Franklin. Frazier, *The Negro Church in America* (New York: Liverpool University Press, 1964) 11.

[8] Du Bois William Edward Burghardt, *The Negro Church: Report of a Social Study* (Atlanta Ga.: Atlanta University Press, 1903), 5.

[9] "Negro History Bulletin," Encyclopedia of African American Education 35, no. 1 (1972).

[10] Gayraud Wilmore, *The Journal of the Interdenominational Theological Center* 16, no. Fall (1989), 84.

[11] Ibid., 87.

[12] Frederick Perry Noble, *The Redemption of Africa: A Story of Civilization* (New York: Revell Company, 1894), 18.

[13] William H. Worrell, *A Short History of the Copts* (Ann Arbor, MI: University of Michigan Press, 1945), 7.

[14] F. B.Welbourn, *The East African Christian* (Ibadan: Oxford University Press, 1965), 14.

[15] Ibid., 43.

[16] Mandour El Mahdi, *A Short History of the Sudan* (Oxford: Oxford Univ. Press, 1965), 23-24.

[17] Merl R. Eppse, *The Negro, Too, in American History* (Chicago: National Educational Pub., 1943), 24.

[18] Ibid., 24.

[19] Ibid., 24-25.

[20] Allen Weinstein, Frank Otto Gatell, and David Sarasohn, eds., *American Negro Slavery a Modern Reader* (New York: Oxford University Press, 1979), 29.

[21] T. Scott Miyakawa, *Protestants and Pioneers: Individualism and Conformity on the American Frontier* (Chicago: Univ. of Chicago Press, 1969), 174.

[22] Lester B. Scherer, *Slavery and the Churches in Early America: 1619-1819* (Grand Rapids: MI, Eerdmanns, 1975), 35.

[23] Ibid., 36.

[24] Ibid., 38.

[25] William Warren Sweet, *The Story of Religion in America* (Grand Rapids, MI: Baker Book House, 1983), 444.

[26] Ibid., 414.

[27] Ibid., 414-415.

[28] Ibid., 415.

[29] Robert T. Handy, *A History of the Churches in the United States and Canada* (Oxford: Oxford University Press, 1976), 17.

[30] William Warren Sweet, *Religion in Colonial America* (New York: Charles Scribner's Sons, 1942), 29.

[31] Handy, *A History of the Churches in the United States and Canada*, 17.

[32] Scherer, *Slavery and the Churches in Early America: 1619–1819*, 31.

[33] Ibid, 31.

[34] Bedell, Sandon, and Wellborn, *Religion in America*, 369.

[35] Winthrop S. Hudson, *Religion in America* (New York: Charles Scribner's Sons, 1965), 30.

[36] Willis Duke Weatherford, *American Churches and the Negro: An Historical Study from Early Slave Days to the Present* (Boston: Christopher Publishing House, 1957), 30.

[37] Scherer, 30.

[38] Weatherford, 32.

[39] Sweet, 416.

[40] Ibid.

[41] Winston-Salem Chronicle, May 9, 1991.

[42] Mary Burnham Putnam, *The Baptists and Slavery, 1840-1845* (Whitefish, MT: Kessinger Pub., 2012), 7.

[43] Ibid., 7.

[44] Weatherford, 119.

[45] Ibid.

[46] Ibid., 121.

[47] Putman, 24.

[48] Ibid.

[49] Donald G. Mathews, *Religion in the Old South* (Chicago: Chicago Univ. Press, 1994), 136.

[50] Ibid.

[51] Josiah Priest, *Bible Defence of Slavery: Or, The Origin, History, and Fortunes of the Negro Race, as Deducted from History, Both Sacred and Profane, Their Natural Relations, Moral, Mental and Physical, to the Other Races of Mankind, Compared and Illustrated, Their Future Destiny Predicted, Etc. To Which Is Added a Plan of National Colonization Adequate to the Entire Removal of the Free Blacks, and All That May Herafter Become Free, in a Manner Harmonizing with the Peace and Well-being of Both Races* (Detroit: Negro History Press, 1969), 34.

[52] Ibid.

[53] Ibid., 37-38.

[54] Ibid., 91.

[55] Ibid., 241.

[56] Leroy Fitts, *A History of Black Baptists* (Nashville, TN: Broadman Press, 1985), 28.

[57] Ibid., 29.

[58] Sweet., 421.

[59] Ibid.

[60] Ibid., 420.

[61] Henry Wilson, History of Slave Power in America, Volume 1 (Boston: James R. Osgood and Company, 1875).

[62] Ibid., 11.

[63] Sweet, 60-61.

[64] Hudson, 350.

[65] William Wilson Manross, *A History of the American Episcopal Church* (Atlanta: Morehouse Publishing Company, 1935), 147.

[66] Ibid., 149.

[67] Ibid., 148.

[68] Ibid., 149.

[69] Ibid., 142.

[70] Rev. Anson West, A *History of Methodism in Alabama* (Nashville, TN: Methodist Episcopal Church, South, 1893), 598.

[71] Ibid., 599.

[72] Ibid.

[73] Ibid.

[74] Charles Poulet and Sydney A. Raemers, *A History of the Catholic Church, for Use of Colleges, Seminaries, and Universities: Authorized Translation and Adaptation from the 4th French Edition* (St. Louis: Herder, 1935), 269.

[75] Ibid., 269.

[76] Ibid., 270.

[77] Ibid., 270.

[78] Ibid., 270.

[79] Frederick Emory, *Queen Anne's County Maryland:It's Early History and Development* (Baltimore: Maryland Historic Society, 1950), 134.

[80] Ibid., 54-55.

[81] Ibid., 57.

[82] Ibid.

[83] C. Joseph Nuesse, *The Social Thought of American Catholics, 1634-1829* (Westminster, MD: Newman Book Shop, 1945), 42.

[84] Ibid., 43.

[85] John Thomas Gillard, *Colored Catholics in the United States: An Investigation of Catholic Activity in Behalf of the Negroes in the United States and a Survey of the Present Condition of the Colored Missions* (Baltimore: Josephite Press, 1941), 62-63.

[86] Richard Roscoe *Miller, Slavery and Catholicism* (Durham, NC: North State Publishers, 1957), 189.

Chapter 2

PLANTATION MISSIONS AND THE EVOLUTION OF SEGREGATED WORSHIP EXPERIENCES

The early evangelistic missions of Protestant denominations as well as the Roman Catholic Church established the basis of slave entrance into the Christian faith. Most of the new converts were not able to read and write except for a few who were taught to read the Bible. The Protestant Episcopal Church as well as the Roman Catholic Church taught slaves to read or recite the catechism, the Lord's Prayer, and the Apostles' Creed as time permitted from the daily work schedule and appropriate to the church body. The work schedule for the field workers made religious instruction almost prohibitive. On some plantations the slave owners taught them, in a limited way, to read some the familiar scriptures during family devotional services. But this instruction was limited to slaves who worked in the plantation houses. However, this was the exception to the general rules on most plantations. For only a small number received the minimum instructions before laws were enacted forbidding the teaching of slaves in most southern states. However, the small number of Protestant and Roman Catholic African American converts constituted the evolution of segregated worship experience.

Secret Worship Experiences among Slaves

There were abundant reasons why slaves found it necessary to hold secret worship experiences beyond the scope of white Christians.

Slave owners who allowed the Christianization of their slaves required them to join their specific master's church denomination. They wanted to keep absolute control of slaves even over their spiritual journeys. Christian slaves were granted the opportunity to join their master's church with designated or segregated seating arrangements—the "slave pews." They had the same pastors, and their assigned names were entered in the registry of the particular church. Occasionally, the white ministers gave special messages to the slaves urging obedience to their masters as an expression of obedience to God. Such a sermon's contents included remarks like, "'Serve your masters. Don't steal your master's turkey. Don't steal your master's chickens. Don't steal your master's hogs. Don't steal your master's meat. Fix what some ever your master tell you to do.' Same old thing all de time."[1] Such messages could not be completely accepted by slaves due to their inner struggle of accepting a faith that offered no relief to their physical and mental plight. Generally, the worship experiences in biracial churches did not fulfill the longings of their suffering souls. They lacked opportunities for slaves to adequately vent their deep emotions. Emotionally, most slaves were drained by the stress and strain of daily living under a system that denied their true humanity. This fact was reinforced by a church culture that even required them to take the Eucharist after the white members had been served or at a separate time in the biracial churches. Although most of them could not read or write, they still were able to detect the disparity between the love ethic of the Christian religion and what was practiced by the ruling class. Even in denominations with congregational polity, slaves were limited in voting and other church membership privileges. As will be noted later, even free African Americans were not generally given full church membership privileges in biracial churches. They constituted a tolerated presence within the church without any consciousness of authentic brotherhood.

The failure of the biracial churches during the early period of slave conversions to Christianity resulted in the tendency of slaves to congregate secretly for their own worship experiences. These worship experiences were convened late at night and in secret locations while the masters and slave drivers were sleeping. The time and locations had to be kept secret because they were not lawful on the plantations. To worship in the "invisible church," slaves stole away to the woods, canebrakes, and remote cabins to worship the way they desired. These were very emotional gatherings, but care had to be taken to prevent the masters and slave drivers from discovering them. In some cases, these meetings were kept from non-believer slaves who might reveal them to the wrong people. It was not unusual for some slaves to serve as informants for the slave masters, hoping to gain their good graces.

Slave Preachers and Relevant Religious Worship

Slave preachers emerged partly from the unique secret worship experiences on remote areas of southern plantations. The vast majority of slaves were victims of the harsh plantation life of the south. These slaves not only carried the physical bruises from the discipline of masters, but deep internalized emotions waiting to be vented by spiritual experiences. Part of their longings for a sense of belonging stemmed from their estrangement from their native home and its worship experiences. Alex Haley's highly esteemed work, *Roots*, clearly established the fact that older family members were able to pass on some of the deeply rooted African spiritual traits to younger members in slave cabins. Much of the former African spirituality was carried over into western style Christianity with their conversion. Out of these dynamics, slave preachers soon found ready acceptance by greater numbers of slave converts than had been the case of their earlier encounter with the "white man's religion."

In order to fill the spiritual vacuum created by racist distortion of the religion, some slave and former slave preachers appeared on the plantation scene in the south and in certain northern areas where slaves were held. In order to accentuate the need for free expressions in worship, one Baptist preacher expressed:

"Son, those colored folks in those other churches, they're in white folks' churches. Any time you find our people belonging to a church where you ain't supposed to open your mouth and tell the Lord just how good you feel, then you know that ain't a church for our folks. Of course, we shout and they talk to me; they helping me when they do that, 'cause you see we worshiping the Lord together. And I'll tell you, whenever you see one of our churches, and if the Lord's in that church, then you better believe, you gonna hear some noise."[2]

In North Carolina, the first African American preacher to receive permission to evangelize his race was Uncle Harry Cowan, as he was known at that time. He was the servant of Thomas L. Cowan. His master, being present at a funeral, was so impressed with his gift to preach God's Word that he granted him "privilege papers" to preach anywhere on his four plantations. His papers were officially prepared by a lawyer. Reverend Harry Cowan, the slave preacher, became spiritually powerful and had a successful ministry of evangelism among slaves on the plantations. Therefore, his owner soon extended Reverend Cowan's preaching privileges to other nearby plantations permitted by the owners. He was able to speak the vernacular of the slaves which accounted for his success in evangelizing many of the plantation slaves.

In 1784 Reverend Harry Hoosier, better known as Black Harry, commenced a preaching tour with Bishop Francis Asbury of the Methodist Episcopal Church. He and Bishop Asbury traveled throughout the North and South seeking to convert slaves and free African Americans to the Christian faith. The expansive growth of the Methodist Episcopal Church was the results of the ministries of both Bishop Asbury and his servant and companion Reverend Harry Hoosier. During one of his preaching tours of the Eastern Shore of Maryland, Southern Methodist bishop Thomas Coke made the following comment: "I have now had the pleasure of hearing Harry preach several times, I sometimes give notice immediately after preaching, that in a little while he will preach to blacks, but the whites always stay to hear him."[3] It was not uncommon for some whites to be impressed with slave preaching.

Some of the antebellum African American preachers were rather conservative politically, seeking to please the white ruling class. They knew their "place" and sought to remain in it. Among them was Reverend Jupiter Hammon who preached a message to his fellow Christians containing the following excerpt:

"There are some things encouraging in God's word, for such ignorant creatures as we are; for God hath not chosen the rich of this world. Not many rich, not many noble are called, but God hath chosen the week things of this world, and things which are not, to confound the things that are, and when the great and the rich refuse coming to the gospel feast, the servant was told to go into the highways, and hedges, and compel those poor creatures that he found there, to come in. Now brethren, it seems to me, that there are no people that ought to attend to the hope of happiness in another world so much as we, most of us are cut off from comfort and happiness herein this world, and can expect nothing from it. Now seeing this is the case, why should we spend our whole lives in sinning against God: and be miserable in this world and in the world to come.[4]

To be sure, this sermon had strong moral and other-worldly contents, but none of it posed any threat to the master class. Seemingly, he expressed a condescending view of African American humanity which was acceptable to white Christians.

The decades from 1820 to 1860 witnessed a constant increase of pressure on the majority of African American preachers. Any time the preachers tended to challenge the existing social order, southern whites placed restrictions on them. This was especially true when slave rebellions, like the Denmark Vesey plot, developed with a degree of frequency. The extensive ministry of Reverend John Chavis, a Presbyterian minister, was hindered by legal matters in North Carolina. He was not a slave but an indentured servant. John Hope Franklin related this account: "For almost thirty years John Chavis of Raleigh, North Carolina, maintained a school in which he taught whites during the day and free Negroes in the evening, but after 1831 he confined his teaching to white children."[5] Reverend Chavis was eminently qualified as a teacher and preacher, having been the first African graduate of Princeton University and the first African American clergy in the Presbyterian church. Nathan Aaseng observed: "Whites were impressed with his orthodox Presbyterian theology, his clear and concise sermons, his understanding of Latin and Greek, and his speech which was described in a nineteenth century article as "remarkably pure" and free of black dialect and accent."[6] Although he was an extraordinary minister, a new law in North Carolina prevented him from continuing his preaching profession.

In Virginia Reverend John Jasper (1812-1901), another notable minister, appeared on the preaching scene in Richmond during the antebellum period likewise preaching to both races. He was born a slave on the plantation of the Peachy family in one of the largest slaveholding counties in Virginia. Reverend Jasper, like a few other slave preachers, was noted for his emotional and powerful funeral sermons. Reverend Isaac James made a detailed study of Reverend Jasper:

"Jasper's formal education was extremely limited. He was illiterate until after his conversion, when he was taught to spell by an old colored slave named William Jackson. For six or seven months, Jasper labored over the pages of a New York speller which the slave had somehow obtained. As soon as Jasper found himself able to make any sort of headway with his reading, he took himself to the Bible and began the studies of this book which continued until his death. Although he read other books and all through his life urged the members of his race to read everything that they could, the Bible was always the one book for him….

"The Bible became for him not only the source of all his knowledge, but the final arbiter in all of his judgments. He believed in the Bible explicitly and in later years when he expounded his famous sermon 'The Sun Do Move', it was to the Bible he clung in the face of overwhelming scientific evidence to the contrary."[7]

This was perhaps one of the most popular sermons ever preached by a slave in America. Large crowds were eager to hear him in Richmond and other parts of Virginia. William Hatcher offered the following assessment of Jasper regarding the sermon:

"The occasion on which I heard his 'astronomical sermon,' as one of his opponents deridingly dubbed it, was not at its first presentation. He had delivered it repeatedly before and knew his ground. The gleam of confidence and victory shone clear and strong on his face.

"The audience looked like a small nation. Long before the solemn janitor, proud of his place, strict to the minute, swung open the front doors, the adjacent streets swarmed with the eager throngs. Instantly there was a rush, and in surged the people, each anxious to get a seat. The spacious house was utterly inadequate to the exigencies of the hour. Many crowded the Church, disposed themselves around the pulpit, sat on pew-arms, or in friendly laps.

"Jasper's entrance was quite picturesque. He appeared in the long aisle wearing a cape overcoat, with a beaver in one hand, and his cane in the other, and with a dignity not entirely unconscious. His officers rose to welcome him, one removing his great coat, another his head piece, and yet another his cane. As he ascended the pulpit he turned and waved a happy greeting to his charge and it fairly set his emotional constituents to shouting."[8]

Through powerful sermons like this, Reverend Jasper was able to develop a strong and extensive evangelistic ministry. He baptized hundreds of converted souls in the James River. His baptismal services were so significant that one in particular was mentioned in *Richmond: Her Past and Present*, in which the author states, "Ninth Street Bridge was completed on June, 1873, and there was no celebration, except the next day, Sunday, John Jasper of the Second African Church, immersed fifty-five Negroes in the mill race at the Richmond end of the bridge. Thousands of people were present and the new structure was taxed to its utmost."[9]

His influence was so great that even two famous African Americans, Dr. W.L. Ransom, a leading clergyman in Virginia; and Dr. Carter G. Woodson, an outstanding intellectual, gave high evaluations of Reverend Jasper's rightful place in the annals of the Virginia pulpit.

Another outstanding slave preacher from Virginia was Reverend Lott Carey. The Reverend Lott Carey emerged on the scene as an outstanding slave preacher during the post-Revolutionary War era. He was born on the estate of William A.

Christian about four years after the signing of the Declaration of Independence. This was the time when liberal ideas permeated the new nation with emphasis on individual freedom and the rights of men being the current opinions of the builders of the new governmental experience in democracy. However, this spirit was not sufficient to terminate the worst violation of those democratic ideals, for slavery still held a firm grip on the social and political life of the new nation. The new humanistic ideas, however, did modify the social views of Lott Carey's Virginia slave master in Charles City, Virginia. This slave master owned Carey's immediate family including his grandmother who still internalized a strong African sentiment. It was Lott Carey's grandmother Mihala that exercised the greatest influence on Lott's formative years. The youthful Lott was nurtured in this spirit of an African heritage which became dominant in his later life as a preacher. He became virtually obsessed with the thought of millions of his African ancestors struggling without the Gospel of Jesus Christ.

In 1804, Lott Carey moved from the slave quarters in the rural area of Charles City County to the city of Richmond where his slave master sent him to work in the city as a slave laborer. He was hired by a local employer at age twenty-four as a common laborer in a tobacco warehouse. In 1807, Carey decided to attend church at the First Baptist Church of Richmond to nurture his earlier Christian orientation. He was converted by Reverend John Courtney, the pastor of the church who subsequently baptized by him. When Carey joined this church he was still illiterate, but Reverend Courtney's sermon instilled in him a deep desire for learning. Soon, he purchased a Bible and with the assistance of a young man he gradually learned to read and write. Consistent with other slave experiences, the Bible was the only textbook made accessible for slaves' intellectual hunger.

Lott Carey's desire for a more extensive learning experience led him to enter a night school taught by William A. Crane, a local white businessman who had organized it in 1815 as a school for Christian slaves and free African Americans at the "Old African Church" of Richmond. In addition to elementary subjects of reading, writing, arithmetic, and the Bible, Crane read to his students any book or newspaper article available. Carey became a good student and a hard worker, resulting in his ability to purchase his freedom. He was alert to every occasion for enlarging his knowledge. He studied Smith's *The Wealth of Nations* and other materials available to him.

Soon after his conversion experience, Lott Carey later experienced the call to the ministry. He was granted the preaching license by the First Baptist Church in Richmond. Subsequently, Reverend Lott Carey preached to slave and free African Americans throughout Richmond and surrounding areas. His preaching ability was highly recognized by a friend, Collin Teague, and even by a prominent pastor of the Presbyterian church of Richmond who said to Ralph R. Gurley: "A sermon which I heard from Mr. Cary, shortly before he sailed to Africa, was the best extemporaneous sermon I ever heard. It contained more original and impressive thoughts, some of which are distinct in my memory, and can never be forgotten."[10] Significantly, this white Presbyterian dared to refer to an African American man as "mister" at such an early time in American history.

Reverend Lott Carey labored extensively in Virginia on various preaching tours, but his spirit soon led him to place his vision on Africa, resulting partly from a lecture by William Crain on the urgency of Christian missions in Africa and the opportunity to go to Africa through the instrumentality of the American Colonization Society. Prior to making plans to go to Africa, Reverend Carey worked for a few years at the First African Baptist Church of Richmond to arouse the membership to a desire to support an African mission. This resulted, in 1815, in the organization of the Richmond African Missionary Society which became a supporting organization for Reverend Carey's foreign missionary work. Jointly sponsored by this society in cooperation with the General Missionary Convention and the American Colonization Society, Reverend Lott Carey and a small group of fellow African American Christians were able to journey to West Africa and assist in the founding of the colony of Liberia.

In immigrating to Africa, Reverend Carey and this small group went against the majority opinions of African Americans who challenged the objectives of the American Colonization Society and any other scheme suggesting transporting African Americans, whether former slaves or free ones, outside the United States. The vast majority favored assimilation into American society rather than immigration because of the harsh treatments in that society. They remained hopeful of constructive change in the United States. But Reverend Carey had lost such hope and felt more comfortable in the new freedom in Liberia. He served faithfully in Liberia until his accidental death in 1829.

In the deeper South another slave preacher served with distinction. He was Reverend George Washington Gayles who was born in Wilkinson, Mississippi, January 29, 1844, of slave parents, Perry and Rebecca Gayles. Initially, he was a house servant and as such was given special privileges. As a house servant, young Gayles was taught the alphabet by a lady who was employed as a private tutor in Mrs. Nancy Barron's family. This was done on account of his diligence. He soon gained the ability to read the Bible and the hymnbook, which attracted the young boy's greatest attention. This was the beginning of his brilliant development.

In 1867, Gayles was called into the ministry and by vigorous work became a tremendous preacher of the Word. He soon was appointed to some of the most prominent places in Mississippi. In 1869, Reverend Gayles was appointed by George A. Ames of the United States Army as a member of the board of police for the third district of Bolivia County, Mississippi. In 1870, Governor J.L. Alcon was instrumental in helping him to become justice of peace for the fifth district of Bolivia County.

Reverend Gayles did not allow these political involvements to deter him from advancing a significant ministry for the African American church. He served as corresponding secretary for the Missionary State Convention and later as its president. Later he extended his ministry into the field of journalism, enabling him to interpret current affairs in the light of divine providence. Accordingly, his varied ministry was successful in reaching the broader African American community in Mississippi.

A representative slave preacher among the Roman Catholics was "Uncle Harry" who labored with Father Badin in Kentucky as earlier as 1803. The Honorable Ben Webb Jr. remarked:

"Even among those who had been brought up in servitude, Father Badin had his trusted helpers. Conspicuous among these was Uncle Harry, an elderly Negro servant of one of the earliest, whose life was an example of the sublimeness of Christian virtue…. On the death of his master, he became the property of infant heirs; and he was left by the executor of the estate to his own choice in the selection of his employment…. He determined to go to Sault Licks, thinking he could there earn more by his labor for the benefit of the young heirs."[11]

In Sault Licks, he lived a life of piety ministering to the sick and offering prayers. After a brief period of time, "Uncle Harry" was sold to a slave master who was not a Roman Catholic. However, he was able to successfully persuade Father Badin to purchase him from the new owner. He dedicated his life to prayer and Christian service to other slaves. Ben Webb Jr. offered the following regarding the close of the life of this faithful Catholic preacher: "One morning, he was found dead sitting upright on a stool, his hands clasped in prayer, holding his beads, and his countenance irradiated with a smile."[12]

In South Carolina and Georgia, the voice of the slave preacher was heard in the person of Reverend George Liele. He was born into slavery in Virginia in 1750 to slave parents named Liele and Nancy. In 1773, he was taken by his owner Henry Sharp to Burke County, Georgia, where he was converted and expressed a desire to preach. Accordingly, he was able to persuade the white Baptists to license him into the ministry. He preached powerfully on plantations in Georgia and South Carolina. Many African American slaves were converted by the preaching of this great pioneer. Among the two most prominent were David George and Andrew Bryan. After a brief but successful preaching ministry, Reverend Liele encountered the British forces during the Revolutionary War and experienced initial hardships of persons known as Loyalists. During the British evacuation of Savannah, he left with them and settled in Kingston, Jamaica.

Reflecting the evangelistic ministry of Reverend Liele, David George was instrumental in the organization of the Silver Bluff Baptist Church in Aiken County, South Carolina. These two men established the earliest separate mission churches among African American Baptists. Significantly, these two missions remained associated with white Baptist churches.

Andrew Bryan was born into slavery in South Carolina in 1737 at Goose Creek. He was brought to Savannah, Georgia, and converted by the preaching of George Liele. On January 20, 1788, he along with a few slaves on the plantation of Jonathan Bryan, Esq., organized the First Colored Baptist Church in Savannah, Georgia. Bryan permitted them to erect a rough church building on his land at Yamacraw in the suburbs of Savannah. This little mission church encountered many interruptions from local whites who opposed the idea of a separate congregation of African slaves, which violated the custom of not allowing such a congregation without the presence of a white man. Consequently, many of the early members were taken before magistrates, imprisoned, and whipped.

With a few exceptions, members of Reverend Bryan's congregation were persecuted for their faith and desire to have worship experiences relevant to their own spiritual and emotional needs. Reverend James Sims has left us with a succinct account of their sufferings:

"Frequently, then, because the whipping of individual members by patrol on the plea of not having proper tickets-of-leave, which finally culminated in the arrest and punishment of a large part of the members, all of whom were severely whipped; but Rev. Andrew Bryan, their pastor, and his brother, Sampson Bryan, one of the first deacons, were inhumanly cut, and their backs were so lacerated that their blood ran down to the earth, as they, with uplifted hands, cried unto the Lord; and this first negro Baptist pastor, while under this torture, declared to his persecutors that he rejoiced not only to be whipped, but will freely suffer death for the cause of Jesus Christ."[13]

Subsequently, the majority of the congregation was accused of plotting an insurrection and placed in prison. Their meetinghouse was also taken from them in 1790. However, Jonathan Bryan, the plantation owner and master of these persecuted Baptists, interceded for them which resulted in their innocence and release. They were granted liberty to continue their worship any time between sunrise and sunset. Jonathan Bryan affirmed his right as a plantation owner to allow them to worship in his barn at a place called Brampton. After about two years of worship at Brampton, Reverend Thomas Burton, and elderly white Baptist preacher; and Reverend Andrew Marshall visited this little slave church and officially set them apart as a Baptist church.

There were many other African American preachers during the antebellum period who labored faithfully among their own people and served the greater cause of the expansion of Christianity. Some were mere preachers while others, who had been slaves, served as pastors and founders of churches and denominations among African Americans who desired separation from biracial churches. Some became noteworthy preachers at biracial churches. However, the separation or exodus from biracial churches and denominations was a gradual process. As previously indicated, segregation and racial prejudice were primary causes for the desire of African Americans to organize independent churches and denominations.

Biracial Churches and Racial Discrimination

For many decades, biracial churches were not able to overcome the practice of segregation and color prejudice. White lay members as well as leading pastors were all guilty of this pattern in church life. Sermons, public addresses, and academic studies were all utilized to support the practice. Theology, science, philosophy, and social studies were all utilized to train the consciences of young children to perpetuate the radical separation of the races. Accordingly, laws on the local and national levels were passed to sustain the emergence of racism. White Christians were among the professionals who promoted and took part in firming the system of institutional racism.

Out of this socio-religious milieu, African American religious leaders saw the urgency of separation from biracial churches. Prior to the actual process of separation, they offered many complaints and petitions designed to mitigate the unjust and immoral practice. Sermons, addresses, and the emerging African American press were utilized by church leaders to call for a more humane treatment of both enslaved and free African Americans based on Christian ethics and egalitarianism. As early as 1837, lengthy articles appeared in *The Colored American* newspaper, reflecting on the nature of racism in biracial churches. Although written about four decades after the beginning of the separation of African Americans from biracial churches, excerpts from one of these articles on March 4, 1837, portrayed a clear picture of the negative experiences of African American worshippers in biracial churches:

"The American Church, more favored of God than any other, is the strong hold of an unholy prejudice against color, more oppressive and fatal in its results, than any other sin. It is not only a generator of the darkness, but it is an extinguisher of the light. How many of God's little ones has it been made to offend? How many, by its influence, have been driven to infidelity, and now seem to be beyond recovery? ... Little do the ministers of Jesus Christ, and the officers and members, of our churches think, the evil they are doing, by drawing this cord of caste, in the house of God. It is the greatest stumbling block in the way of their colored brethren....

"In all the cities and large towns of the northern and middle States, there is but little more sympathy, or intercourse, between white and colored ministers, than there was between Jews and Samaritans. However pious and talented a colored minister may be, heaven is almost as accessible to a sinner, in his sins, as some of the pulpits of our white churches [to] their colored brother. I have often seen colored ministers of fair standing and talent, go into churches of their own denomination, where they were well known, and walk the whole length of these sanctuaries of their God, without having a pew open, or any Christian courtesy extended to them, more than would be to a beast of the forest. I have seen a minister of Jesus Christ, sitting in Presbytery, with his white brethren in the ministry, who, though it had been announced that full provision was made among the church members for every brother, and yet left by himself in the church, for three successive days, without dinner or tea, because no Christian family could be found in the congregation, who would admit him to their table, on account of color."[14]

More radically critical of biracial churches, Frederick Douglass, an ex-slave from Maryland, lashed out at the churches with these words: "Religion is prostituted to the support of robbery. Piety is pressed into the service of cruelty; and slaveholding, slave-buying, and slave-trading, is deliberately carried on in this land by all the leading Christian denominations; We have men sold to build churches, and babes sold to buy Bibles, and women sold to support missionaries."[15]

Knowledge of these facts increasingly made African American Christians more uncomfortable within biracial churches. They came to the realization that separate churches from these experiences of racial prejudice, cruelty, and segregation was the only solution open to them for experiences of the true mysteries of Christian faith. An article in the October 14, 1837, issue of *The Colored American* entitled "Prejudice in the Church" stated the rationale for separation from the Methodist Episcopal Church:

"In the earliest stages of Methodism, the cord of caste set loosely on the church; it was not drawn with so much rigor as afterwards. But as members increased – (and wealth and pride also) – as the Society gradually emerged from obscurity, the colored brethren began to find their situation more and more uncomfortable, until at length a circumstance occurred which broke the bonds of Christian fraternity between them, and ultimately led to a final separation…."[16]

Such prejudice and discrimination in the Methodist church was characteristic of other denominations with increasing memberships of African Americans.

The white majority community both within the churches and those from the general population had mixed emotions regarding the movement of African American churches to exit from predominantly white churches to start their own separate church movement. Outside the churches, public opinion favored the security of the existing circumstances with white control of all institutions relative to African Americans. However, with the constant increase of African American membership in white churches some white Christian leaders favored their exodus to form their independent churches.

(Endnotes)

1. Charles V. Hamilton, *The Black Preacher in America* (New York: Morrow, 1972), 38-39.
2. Ibid., 31.
3. Henry H. Mitchell, *Black Preaching* (New York: Lippincott Company, 1970), 69.
4. Charles V. Hamilton, 44.
5. John Hope Franklin, *From Slavery to Freedom: A History of African Americans* (New York: Vintage Books, 1967), 229-230.
6. Nathan Aaseng, *African-American Religious Leaders* (New York: Facts On File, 2003), 39.
7. Isaac James, *"The Sun Do Move": The Story of the Life of John Jasper* (Richmond, VA: Hunters Letter Shop, 1954), 11.
8. William Eldridge Hatcher, *John Jasper: The Unmatched Negro Philosopher and Preacher* (New York, Chicago: Revell, 1908), 123-124.
9. Isaac James, 19.
10. Ralph Randolph Gurley, *Life of Jehudi Ashman, Late Colonial Agent in Liberia* (New York: Negro University Press, 1835), 148.
11. Nathaniel E. Green, *The Silent Believers* (Louisville: West End Catholic Council, 1972), 30.
12. Ibid., 31.
13. James M. Simms, *The First Colored Baptist Church in North America: Constituted at Savannah, Georgia, January 20, A.D. 1788* (New York: J. B. Lippincott, 1888), 21.
14. *The Colored American*, Volume 1, Number 4, New York, Saturday, March 4, 1837.
15. John W. Blassingame, Ed., *The Frederick Douglas Papers, Series One: Speeches, Debates, and Interviews*, Volume 2 1847–54 (New Haven, CT: Yale University Press, 1982), 83.
16. *The Colored American*, Volume 1, Number 4, New York, Saturday, October 14, 1837.

Chapter 3

THE RISE OF SEPARATE AFRICAN AMERICAN CHURCHES

Simply stated, the rise of separate churches among African Americans was the results of prejudice, dehumanization, discrimination, and segregation within the biracial churches under the complete control of white Christians. African American members had few opportunities to experience the unique edification potentialities offered by church membership in these churches. Free African Americans as well as slave preachers were increasingly aware of this disparity within these biracial churches. Frederick Douglass, a Methodist exhorter and abolitionist, delivered an enlightening address on African American experiences in white churches, even in the North, before the Plymouth County Anti-Slavery Society, November 4, 1841:

> At the South I was a member of the Methodist Church. When I came North, I thought one Sunday I would attend communion, at one of the churches of my denomination in the town I was staying. The white people gathered around the altar, the blacks clustered by the door. After the good minister had served out the bread and wine to one portion of those near him, he said, "These may withdraw, and others come forward"; thus he proceeded till all the white members had been served. Then he drew a long breath, and looking out towards the door, exclaimed, "Come up, colored friends, come up! For you know God is no respecter of persons!" I haven't been there to see the sacraments taken since. At New Bedford where I live, there was a great revival of religion not long ago—many were converted and "received" as they said, "into the kingdom of heaven." But it seems, the kingdom of heaven is like a net; at least so it was according to the practice of these pious Christians; and when the net was drawn ashore, they had to set down and cull out the fish. Well, it happened now that some of the fish had rather black scales; so these were sorted out and packed by themselves. But among those who experienced religion at this time was a colored girl; she was baptized in the same water as the rest; so she thought she might sit at the Lord's table and partake of the same sacramental elements with the others. The deacon handed round the cup, and when he came to the black girl, he could not pass her, for there was the minister looking right at him, and as he was a kind of

abolitionist, the deacon was rather afraid of giving him offense; so he handed the girl the cup, and she tasted. Now it so happened that next to her sat a young lady who had been converted at the same time, baptized in the same water, and put her trust in the same blessed Saviour; yet when the cup, containing the precious blood which had been shed for all, came to her, she rose in disdain, and walked out of the church. Such was the religion she had experienced!

Another young lady fell into a trance. When she awoke, she declared she had been to heaven. Her friends were all anxious to know what and whom she had seen there; so she told the whole story. But there was one good old lady whose curiosity went beyond that of all the others—and she inquired of the girl that had the vision, if she saw any black folks in heaven? After some hesitation, the reply was "Oh, I didn't go into the kitchen!" Thus you see, my hearers, this prejudice goes even into the church of God. And there are those who carry it so far that it is disagreeable to them even to think of going to heaven, if colored people are going there too.[1]

Such issues existing in both the North as well as the South were discussed with deep emotion within private gatherings in slave quarters and homes of free African Americans. However, there were little or no resources for the correction of the problems. The white Christian ruling class, reflecting the social ethos of the general public, exercised their authority to control all relationships within the churches. Many civil laws were passed to support segregation and discrimination experienced by African Americans, with the church complicit in their enactment.

The African Methodist Episcopal Church

A classic example of the exercise of white authority in the church was reflected in the case of the St. George's Methodist Episcopal Church in Philadelphia near the end of 1786. Generally, the experiences of African American members of this biracial church were typical in such white-controlled churches. They were expected to stay in their "place" for the normal worship experiences. However, the African American membership of the church increased due to the extraordinary ministry of Richard Allen who formed a prayer meeting group outside the confines of the church. The presence of these new members increased beyond the normal seating area of the church. Consequently the white members, in order to maintain the traditional segregation, expanded a balcony area for the accommodation of the influx of these new members. Richard Allen had petitioned earlier for a separate congregation for these new Christians but was denied by the ruling authorities of the Methodist Episcopal Church. One Sunday morning, a group of these members arrived in the St. George's Church for special prayer which set in motion an incident that changed the course of Methodist history in Philadelphia and the new nation.

Richard Allen described the case which took place in St. George's Church, stating that when he, Absalom Jones, and a small number of other African American members arrived at the church, they were told by the sexton that they were expected to sit in the gallery. They assumed that they were to sit toward the front of the gallery above the seats they had previously occupied; they went forward. In the meantime, the service commenced as they neared the seats which they thought were for them. The elder proceeded to lead the congregation in prayer. They knelt, and Allen observed a disturbance nearby of scuffling and talking in low tones. He lifted his head from prayer and saw one of the trustees seize Absalom Jones and attempted to pull him from his knees while saying that they could not kneel there. Absalom Jones asked the trustees to wait until the prayer was over, but his request was refused. They continued their efforts to move him from the particular seat. In a last-minute attempt not to have the prayer interrupted, he said to the trustees, "Wait until the prayer is over and I will get up and trouble you no more." After the prayer ended, Richard Allen stated that the African American members briefly discussed the situation and "all went out of the church in a body and they were no more plagued with us in the church."[2]

Inspired by the formation of pioneer African American societies in Newport, Boston, and New York, Richard Allen and Absalom Jones decided to organize the Free African Society in Philadelphia. Partly to fill the spiritual vacuum created by their termination of membership in St. George's Church, they decided to organize the new society with broader spiritual, social, and economic implications. On April 12, 1787, the group adopted the following preamble of the Philadelphia Free African Society:

> Whereas Absalom Jones and Richard Allen, two men of the African race, who, for their religious life and conversation have obtained a good report among men, these persons, from a love to the people of their complexion whom they beheld with sorrow, because of their irreligious and uncivilized state, often communed together upon this painful and important subject in order to form some kind of religious society, but there being too few to be found under the like concern, and those who were, differed in their religious sentiments; with these circumstances they labored for some time, till it was proposed, after a serious communication of sentiments, that a society should be formed, without regard to religious tenets, provided, the person lived an orderly and sober life, in order to support one another in sickness, and for the benefit of their widows and fatherless children.[3]

Socio-religious considerations reflected in this preamble forced the leadership to embrace a stance of ecumenicalism, perhaps the earliest in the American religious experience. This was also partly reflective of the minimal denominational sensitivity among African Americans and religious freedom issues within the constitutional development of the new American nation. Also, lines of communication were opened between other similar societies among African Americans.

Although the Free African Society was not primarily a religious organization, it played a key role in the decision-making process of how and where its members should worship. Richard Allen was of the strong opinion that African Americans should form a separate congregation based on race but still be related to the Methodist Episcopal Church. On the other hand Absalom Jones, perhaps still nursing some negative feeling about the experiences at St. George's Methodist Episcopal Church, was of the opinion that African Americans should unite with the Protestant Episcopal Church denomination. The dialogue between the two leaders continued for a period of time. Nevertheless, the society experienced sufficient unity to serve as a significant means for the expression of freedom and protest. The issue of slavery was high on the protest agenda of the society.

Both Absalom Jones and Richard Allen brought with them a strong consciousness of past experiences in slavery to their mutual protest and strides for African American freedom. Absalom Jones was born into slavery in 1746 and resided with his mother at Sussex, Delaware, until he was about sixteen years old. At age sixteen, he was separated from his mother and siblings and brought by his master to Philadelphia to work in his store as a handyman and clerk. During his early life in slavery, he saved up small change that had been given to him by visitors in his master's house. He utilized this money to purchase a speller and a Bible in the endeavor to learn to read. In 1776, his master gave him permission to attend abolitionist and educator Anthony Benezet's night school. He was a highly motivated student and developed academically. In 1770, he had married a slave woman and later purchased both of their freedom from slavery. Jones built a small house for his wife and decided to continue to work for his former master. Apparently, his master had not been harsh toward him which influenced his decision to continue to work for him. Nevertheless, just the experience of slavery left a mark on Absalom Jones that lasted throughout his years.

The slave experience of Richard Allen began in Philadelphia. He was born February 14, 1760 to slave parents owned by Benjamin Chew, a lawyer in Philadelphia. In 1776, the decline of Benjamin Chew's law practice led to his decision to sell Richard Allen's family to a new slave master in Delaware near the city of Dover. The entire family was sold to the same slave master. Richard Allen lived as a slave on the plantation of his new master until he was about twenty years old. While residing with his parents, Richard was converted and accepted the Methodist faith tradition and fervently shared his new experience with his former companions. Shortly afterwards, Allen joined the Methodist Society in his neighborhood and began to attend the class meetings with other slaves which met in the forest near Dover under the leadership of Benjamin Wells.[4] Slaves who attended these class meetings tended to work better on the plantation than other slaves, convincing the master that religious instruction made better slaves. Hence, he granted permission for a traveling preacher, Rev. Freeborn Garrettson of the Methodist Episcopal Church to preach on the plantation. Rev. Garrettson had freed his own slaves in 1775 and had condemned slavery publicly in North Carolina and Virginia, which inspired some of his converts to free their slaves.

His influence was sufficient enough to inspire Richard Allen's master to give him the opportunity to purchase his freedom. Subsequently, Allen purchased his freedom in 1777 during the Revolutionary War. The war drastically affected his new freedom, but he was still able to preach to persons in various locations. In 1783, he moved from Dover to Wilmington, Delaware. His preaching ministry led him to New Jersey and later to Lancaster, Pennsylvania. From December 24, 1784, to January 2, 1785, Richard Allen attended the first General Conference of the Methodist Episcopal Church in the United States held in Baltimore, Maryland, where he met Bishop Francis Asbury and Richard Whatcoat who had come to America to assist in the organization of American Methodism. This conference signaled the official beginning of the Methodist Episcopal Church in America as a separate denomination. While in Baltimore, Allen attended the small meeting house, which was called "Methodist Alley," probably the Strawberry Alley Church, the cornerstone of which was laid by Asbury in 1773.[5]

Before leaving Baltimore, Richard Allen was invited by Bishop Asbury to become his traveling partner on preaching tours in the Carolinas and Georgia. He rejected the offer because the new conference had made no financial arrangements to support his traveling ministry. Later, Allen left Maryland and returned to Pennsylvania. In Philadelphia, he experienced a changing environment in state and national politics. Charles H. Wesley made the following remarks regarding this new environment:

> By 1787, the year of the meeting of the Constitutional Convention in Philadelphia, Massachusetts and New Hampshire had abolished slavery, and Connecticut and Rhode Island had adopted acts similar to the Pennsylvania Act. The Ordinance of 1787 prohibited slavery in the Northwest Territory which was later to comprise the states of Ohio, Indiana, Illinois, Michigan, Wisconsin, and a part of Minnesota. Viewed generally, at the time of the formation of the national government, slavery seemed to be a decaying institution.[6]

Generally, the legal situation regarding slavery evolved gradually from the early colonial period to developing national period in New England. As early as 1652, the Rhode Island Colony enacted the first American law declaring slavery illegal. But the same year, the Netherlands agreed to permit the exports of African slaves to the New Netherland Colony. In 1774, Rhode Island and Connecticut forbade the further importation of slaves. Hence, very early in the colonial period slavery was viewed in different ways in New England.

Nevertheless, the new environment in Philadelphia had not substantially changed the mind of the white membership at St. George's Methodist Episcopal Church when Richard Allen, Absalom Jones, and other African Americans walked out of the church to form the Free African Society, which paved the way for the establishment of two separate African American church movements. Later, Richard Allen separated himself from the Free African Society and founded the Bethel African Methodist Church. Absalom Jones continued his membership in the Free African Society and founded the St. Thomas Protestant Episcopal Church and became the Episcopal Church's first African American priest.

In 1794, the Bethel African Methodist Church in Philadelphia was dedicated. The organization of Bethel caused considerable agitation among the white Methodist members of the denomination. After a series of lively discussions, Bishop Asbury was able to ordain Richard Allen a deacon in 1799 and later elevated him to the status of elder. The new church continued to remain in the biracial denomination, which exercised control over the congregation for a period of time. Before Reverend Allen took over the leadership of the church, St. George's church sent elders to preach at Bethel. Tensions continued within the Methodist Episcopal denomination, and Bethel went on its own route as a separate and independent African Methodist Episcopal church.

However, Reverend Richard Allen was not able to attract all of the African American Methodists in Philadelphia. Some felt strongly that they should remain within the biracial denomination. To accommodate these African American Methodists, the denomination decided to assist in the establishment of a mission church which later became the Zoar Methodist Episcopal Church. On May 31, 1795, Bishop Asbury recorded in his diary that he met the Africans to consult about building a house and forming "a distinct, yet Methodist Church."[7]

About the same time of the founding of Bethel African Methodist Episcopal Church in Philadelphia, a similar movement took place in Baltimore. The leading figure in this movement was Reverend Daniel Coker (born, Isaac Wright) who was born in Frederick County, Maryland, during the latter part of the eighteenth century. Coker was the son of a white woman who after her first husband died took an African American slave in marriage. He was fortunate enough to receive a good education. At an early age Coker, who was first named Isaac Wright, escaped from Maryland to New York. In New York he came into contact with Bishop Asbury of the Methodist Episcopal Church and was inspired by the Methodist movement. Later, Coker was ordained into the ministry and returned to Maryland to minister to the needs of slaves and free African Americans. However, Reverend Coker had to keep his identity secret until he was able to purchase his freedom. For a period of time, Reverend Coker taught school in connection with Sharp Street Church and developed a plan for financial development, raising a considerable sum for the church. At one time, he had as many as 150 students. Several of them would go on to become some of the leading men of the race. Conspicuous among his students was Reverend William Douglas, who became rector of the St. Thomas Episcopal Church in Philadelphia, Pennsylvania. Perhaps his major achievement took place when he assisted in the organization of the Bethel African Church, which came to be known as the Bethel African Methodist Episcopal Church in Baltimore. African Americans in Baltimore had experienced similar racist treatment in the white Methodist churches of Lovely Lane and Strawberry Alley. Hence, they too decided to organize separate churches. When the independent denomination was founded in 1815, Reverend Daniel Coker was elected bishop but declined to serve in favor of Reverend Richard Allen.[8]

After spending some time in the development of Bethel African Methodist Church and the newly formed African Methodist Episcopal Church, Reverend Coker decided in 1820 to leave America to serve the cause of Christian missions in West Africa. Initially, Reverend Coker labored in the colony of Liberia as a representative of the American Colonization Society, but later he moved to the British colony of Sierra Leone where he organized what became one of the largest churches in Freetown.[9]

Reverend Richard Allen was not successful in his attempt to persuade Reverend James Varick of New York to join his African Methodist Episcopal Church movement. Hence, he decided to start a separate church movement for his denomination in the state. In 1819, Bishop Allen commissioned William Lambert, a licentiate of the Philadelphia Annual Conference, to labor in New York City for the establishment of a Methodist Episcopal church. His missionary work was successful, and he secured a school room on Mott Street for the initial meeting place. The society met in this location for seven years but later moved to different locations. By July 1820, the Bethel A.M.E. Church of New York constructed a new church building, and the congregation experienced significant growth.[10]

By 1820, the A.M.E. Church movement under Bishop Allen spread to Brooklyn, New York, with the founding of another church by Reverend Benjamin Culver and his brother Peter Culver. They had withdrawn in July 30, 1820, from the biracial Methodist Episcopal Church in New York. The new Brooklyn church experienced significant church growth and was able to purchase a church building for the congregation. Subsequently, the A.M.E. Church movement spread to White Plains and New Bedford, Massachusetts.[11]

In 1843, former slaves and free African Americans organized another separate church, the Waters African Methodist Episcopal Church in East Baltimore. The church became very influential in the denomination. Eight ministers from the church were elevated to the bishopric, giving it the name of the "Mother Church of Bishops." To be sure, Baltimore became the center for a growing movement toward independence in African American church life. The movement spread to the Eastern Shore, where a series of churches was founded in the direction of Norfolk, Virginia.

South of Baltimore, the African Methodist Episcopal separate movement spread to Washington, another stronghold of slavery. The Metropolitan African Methodist Episcopal Church, later called the National Cathedral of African Methodism was organized in the District. It was established by combining members from the Israel A. M. E. Church (established in 1838) with other African Methodists into a new church body in 1872 and culminated in the construction of a church five blocks from the White House in 1880.

The separate African Methodist Episcopal Church movement spread to Virginia during the early 1770s. As early as 1772, African Americans joined the Methodist movement in Portsmouth, organizing as a congregation in what was called The African Methodist Society. They worshipped on Washington Street between High and King Streets until the Nat Turner insurrection in 1831 caused sufficient fear among the whites to terminate the separate experience. They were forced to worship with the white Methodist church on Glasgow Street. Like some other biracial churches, the white members of the church decided to build a new church, leaving the African Americans in the old building. According to a church bulletin entitled "Emanuel African Methodist Episcopal Church: Reflections on a Historical Monument," the African Methodist Society, made up of both slave and free African Americans, remained in the Glasgow Street building until it was burned down in 1856. The first pastor of the church was Reverend George Baines.

> After the burning of the old church building, the members, with meager finances, organized an effort to purchase a lot on North Street and build another Church. They were successful and dedicated the new Church on

the first Sunday in November, 1857. The congregation remained within the Virginia Annual Conference of the Methodist Episcopal Church, South until 1871. After the end of the Civil War, the separatist spirit permeated the African Church inspiring its members to seek membership in the African Methodist Episcopal denomination. They joined the denomination with the name Emanuel African Methodist Episcopal Church.

The African Methodist Episcopal Church movement spread to North Carolina with the organization of several early churches. For example, the St. James AME Church, Winston-Salem, North Carolina, grew out of door-to-door class meetings which started in 1877. In 1882, the Church was formally organized and located on Chestnut Street. Later in 1892, the congregation purchased property on Seventh and Ogburn Streets and erected a weather board structure by 1904. The cornerstone was laid in 1904.[12]

The African Methodist Episcopal Zion Church

The founding of the African Methodist Episcopal Zion Church was similar to that of the Bethel African Methodist Episcopal Church founded by Reverend Richard Allen in Philadelphia. In New York City, white Methodists were also reluctant to receive the growing population of African American Christians into congregational life. The members of the John Street Methodist Episcopal Church in New York were not willing to nurture African American leadership and worked out an arrangement with an African American preacher as an assistant pastor. In this connection, William Jacob remarked:

> The black Methodists, in the meantime, were developing ministers in the white congregation who began to organize churches. They were licensed to preach but were denied ordination until the General Conference of 1800 passed a limited ordination rule for African preachers. It is recorded that progenitors of the Mother A.M.E. Zion Church, in New York, were meeting privately as early as 1780. The state law of New York had prevented Negro groups from holding open meetings since the Insurrection of 1712.[13]

The Insurrection of 1712 African Americans staged in New York City was quelled by the militia and resulted in the execution of twenty-one African Americans. Nevertheless, the white leadership sought to make a concession by allowing African American Christians to have a building of their own while still holding membership in the biracial church. However, the African American members insisted on having their own pastor. When the white members still were reluctant to support the desires of the African American members, leading members James Varick, George Collins, Christopher Rush, and Peter Williams Sr. decided to separate from the John Street Methodist Episcopal Church and organize a new church. In 1796, they withdrew and formed the Zion Chapel into the African Methodist Episcopal Zion Church.[14]

Reverend James Varick, its first bishop, was the leader of the group who founded the African Methodist Episcopal Zion Church. He was born January 10, 1750, in Newburgh, New York, of a slave mother and free father. At an early age, he joined the John Street Methodist Episcopal Church in New York City. In 1806, he was ordained as one of the first deacons in New York. After a short period of struggles with the white leadership of New York Methodists, he was finally ordained in 1822 as the first African American bishop of the independent African Methodist Episcopal Zion Church. Early in his professional career, he became a participant in the Abolitionist Movement. Consequently, his church became known as the "Freedom Church" because it served as a refuge for fugitive slaves and a platform for such abolitionists as Sojourner Truth and Frederick Douglass.[15] In 1820, several churches that separated from New York, New Haven, Long Island, and Philadelphia formed a union with Varick's "Zion Church" to establish a separate and independent denomination named the African Methodist Episcopal Zion Church.[16]

In 1827, another historic African Methodist Episcopal Zion church was founded in Rochester, New York, known as the Memorial African Methodist Zion Church. It was established by Reverend Thomas James, who evangelized some of the slave population that settled in the city. This church was the first African American church in Monroe County, New York. The church's major social ministry was serving as a stop for the Underground Railroad, utilizing the facility as a rest stop and giving some last traveling tips to the slaves before they began the last eighty miles into Canada.[17]

The St. James AME Church was founded in Ithaca, New York, in 1833 and is one of the oldest church structures and congregations of the African Methodist Episcopal Church. Ex-slaves under the leadership of Peter Webb, who was the only slave in the state of New York to buy his own freedom, founded the church. The church made tremendous contributions to the Ithaca community and participated in the Underground Railroad.

The Peoples AME Zion Church was organized in Syracuse, New York, in 1840. The roots of the congregation extend back to 1835 when Bishop Christopher Rush appointed Reverend Thomas James to Syracuse to establish a church for the African American community in the city. Consequently, he organized a group known as the First African Society with a spiritual mission as well as to assist runaway slaves and to provide a link with the Underground Railroad. In 1841, Reverend J. Wesley Loguen was appointed pastor of Peoples AME Zion Church. He worked with Reverend Samuel May, a Unitarian minister who was one of the chief agents of the Underground Railroad in Syracuse until the date of the Jerry Rescue in 1851, when he was forced to leave the City temporarily. Reverend May was forced to leave the city under the threat of federal prosecution for the key role he played in an act of defiance of the Fugitive Slave Act.[18]

In 1881, the Blackwell AME Zion Church was organized in Jamestown, New York, in the home of Catherine Harris. As the African American population in Jamestown began to grow following the Civil War, meetings in individual homes for religious purposes were started. A group of twelve people organized the church on August 31, 1881. In 1882, the church was incorporated with an advisory board from various churches in the area. The cornerstone was completed and dedicated in 1902.

The Archer Memorial AME Zion Church in Windsor, Connecticut, was organized as one of the earliest churches of the denomination in the state. Initially, it was located on Hayden Station Road. The Hayden Station community was one of the oldest communities in the state's oldest town. The small church was founded in the late 1800s by South Carolina preacher Rev. Dennis Scott White and was renamed in 1914 for Sandy Archer, a church member and a former slave who lived to be 108 years old. Rev. White initially conducted camp meetings in the summer in a beautiful pine grove near the intersection of Pond and Hayden Station Roads from 1880 until 1890. People from all over the region utilizing the train which stopped daily at Hayden Station, as well as local community residents attended the high-spirited camp meetings. Freed African Americans had begun to settle in the area in the Revolutionary War era. Some of them were given land in the community by former masters. The church's second pastor, Rev. Byron Scott, in 1915 had the church move out of its original site in the pines out to the road. The actual building was moved by horses and log rollers and local volunteers, and an addition was built.[19]

The Old Ship African Methodist Episcopal Zion Church in Montgomery, Alabama, was the first African American church established in the city. It began in 1852 as a home mission project to minister to slaves and served in that capacity for ten years. In 1835, the white Methodists of the city gave the mission a building on the corner of Church and Lee Streets. Reverend Allen Hannon became the first African American slave preacher to be appointed to the church, and he served in that capacity until 1870. He was able to keep the church united throughout the Civil War period.[20]

In 1866, the Hunter Chapel AME Zion Church in Tuscaloosa, Alabama, was organized by Rev. L. L. Clinton. This was the first African American church to be organized in the city. During the Reconstruction Period, Hunter Chapel served as a school for African American children, and Clinton became known as the "Father of Negro Education."[21] Also in Alabama, the Butler Chapel AME Zion Church was organized in 1867.

The St. James African Methodist Episcopal Zion Church, later known as the Shrewsbury Avenue African Methodist Episcopal Zion Church in Red Bank, New Jersey, was organized in 1834 with Reverend Noah Brooks as its first pastor. The St. James congregation was forced to worship at various sites in Red Bank after the Fair Haven Church was destroyed by fire in 1841. The congregation apparently worshipped with the Bethel AME Church for a period of time. On February 9, 1873, the Bethel building was destroyed by fire and the two groups worshipped for a short period of time in a building in Red Bank. The AME group desired to reestablish itself in Fair Haven, but the AME Zion group remained in Red Bank. By 1873, the congregation was able to construct a new building. The church was dedicated on December 25, 1873.

In 1822, the Clinton Memorial African Methodist Episcopal Church was organized in Newark, New Jersey. The church was founded by Reverend Christopher Rush under the direction of Bishop James Varick of New York. It was incorporated April 7, 1823, thirteen years before the City of Newark, which became one of earliest and most important industrial centers of the nineteenth century. From its inception, the church has played a vital role in the cultural development of the city.[22]

In 1875, the Rockwell African Methodist Episcopal Church resulted from a separation on the part of African Americans from the white Sugaw Creek Presbyterian Church which was located on North Tryon Street in Charlotte, North Carolina. The first church moved from a brush arbor to another brush arbor before it was able to acquire a regular church building.[23] In 1884, the Walls Memorial AME Zion Church was organized by a group of African Americans in the Little Hope area, southwest of Charlotte. Also in Charlotte, the Grace AME Zion Church was organized in 1886 as one of the oldest AME Zion churches in the city, and the Little Rock AME Zion Church was organized in 1884. In 1880, the Goler Memorial AME Zion Church was organized in Winston-Salem, North Carolina.

In 1882, the Rush Metropolitan AME Zion Church was organized in Raleigh, North Carolina. The first church was known as:

> St. Cyprian AME Zion Church, and was pastored by Rev. C. M. Mason of Mangum, North Carolina. He served the church for two years before his removal to another charge. The church was named in honor of Bishop Rush.

> The A.M.E. Zion Church, Manteo, North Carolina, was organized as the first church of the denomination in the northeastern part of the state, located at the corner of Sir Walter Raleigh and Bideford Streets in the town. It was the beginning of the African Methodist movement on the Outer Banks, North Carolina. It was the mother church for that area of the state. It was used in that location until 1940s. The organizational date of this church as the first in the area has been challenged by those who claim that the African Methodist Episcopal Zion Church in New Bern, North Carolina was the first to be organized. But Bishop Hood favored the claim of the Manteo church. On a boat hidden under the sail, a group of slaves under the leadership of General Burnside landed on Roanoke Island, Manteo, North Carolina, during the Civil War. Among the slaves was Rev. Andrew Cartwright, who at the close of the Civil War became the founder of African Methodism in eastern North Carolina. The church that was founded on Roanoke Island was named Cartwright Memorial in his honor.[24]

In 1864, the Diggs Chapel AME Zion Church was organized in Rockingham, North Carolina, by a group of freed slaves. Their former slave master gave them permission to use some of his land for the church. The church started as a brush arbor where members worshiped until a small church was built. The Diggs family sold the land for the church to Mr. and Mrs. Henry C. Wall, and the trustees of Diggs Chapel secured a half-acre of land from the Wall family. The

Diggs Chapel School was also build during the time of the brush arbor. In 1951, a new church was built and dedicated.

The Mitchell A.M.E. Zion Church was organized in Pittsboro, North Carolina, in 1867. Like many other early African American churches, this church started at a brush arbor, followed by a log cabin with a dirt floor and log benches. Shortly, the congregation was able to construct a wooden frame building before it constructed a brick building.[25]

In 1885, the Maize Chapel AME Zion Church was organized in Sylva, North Carolina. That year, a group of former slaves united in a log cabin on Black Branch, later known as Hog Rock, and organized a Methodist church. The first pastor of the church was probably Rev. Edinburg, whose heritage was traced back to Africa. The church called Black Branches was affiliated with the AME Zion Church. On March 24, 1910, the church purchased a lot on Clipper Curve Road and in 1914 erected a frame plank building.[26] In another small North Carolina town, the St. Paul A.M.E. Zion Church was organized in 1871. As early as 1868, the Mount Pleasant AME Zion Church was organized in Statesville, North Carolina.

Separate African American Churches in the Methodist Episcopal Church

It has already been noted that the early stages of African Methodist Episcopal Church development among African Americans was a slow but steady process. Bishop Francis Asbury worked closely with Reverend Richard Allen even during the early stages of the separate African Methodist Episcopal Church development in Philadelphia. Both men were present in Baltimore when the actual Methodist Episcopal denomination began as an American institution at the Christmas Conference in 1784. At this conference, preachers were elected and ordained without the direct supervision of the Church of England. However, John Wesley had ordained Reverend Thomas Coke and appointed him a superintendent (bishop) of the American work with the authority to ordain Asbury. Asbury was ordained as superintendent (bishop), giving him the authority to assist Reverend Richard Allen in the development of his separate church movement. Under Bishop Asbury, the Methodist Episcopal Church grew even after Allen's separate movement. He advanced a rather extensive missionary work among African Americans beyond the work in Philadelphia.

Even in Philadelphia, a growing number of African Americans chose not to unite with the movement of Rev. Richard Allen. Between 1790 and 1800, the

African American population increased from 2,489 to 6,880, or 176 percent.[27] A significant number of those who converted to Christianity united with the Methodist Episcopal Church and organized separate churches with the assistance of the Methodist Episcopal denomination but remained within the church body. The oldest African American Episcopal Church in the city was organized in 1794 as the Zoar Methodist Episcopal Church. The church had its origin when members of St. George's Church established a mission in what was then known as Campingtown, where a chapel was erected. It remained in this location until 1883 when economic and sociological factors made necessary the selection of a new site. Du Bois noted:

> The city had grown, and industries of a character in which the Negroes were not interested had developed in the neighborhood, and, as the colored people were rapidly moving to a different section of the city, it was decided that the church should follow, and the old building was sold. Through the generosity of Colonel Joseph M. Bennett a brick building was erected on Melon Street, above Twelfth.[28]

The Methodist Episcopal churches in Maryland had an early beginning, with the first organized Society of Methodism in America (except that at Savannah, Georgia) being formed in 1760 near Sam's Creek in Frederick County, Maryland, by Robert Strawbridge, a Wesleyan law preacher from Ireland. In 1772, a Methodist Society known as Strawbridge Alley Church was organized and named in honor of Robert Strawbridge. In 1773, Francis Asbury, with the assistance of Jesse Hollingsworth, George Wells, Richard Moale, George Robinson, and John Woodward, purchased a lot on Strawberry Alley for the brick church structure. The cornerstone was laid by Francis Asbury. A few African Americans were members of this new biracial church. In 1802, the white Methodists decided to separate and move to a new location on Wilkes Street with the name of Wilkes Street Chapel. The African American members remained at Strawbridge and organized the Dallas Street Methodist Episcopal Church, located at Dallas and Fleet Streets. In 1874, Reverend Henry A. Carroll became its first pastor. Included in its membership were Frederick Douglass and Isaac Roles, who was an agent of the Underground Railroad and helped Douglass to escape to freedom. In 1876, the church changed its name to the Centennial Methodist Episcopal Church.

Another historic African American church, Sharp Street Memorial, was organized in Baltimore as a separate movement around the same time as Bethel

A.M.E. Church and Centennial Methodist Episcopal. Bishop Daniel A. Payne affirmed the organizational date of the church to be 1787. The original membership may have been a part of Wesley Chapel, the "City Station," a group of Methodist churches located on the corner of Sharpe and Montgomery Streets with the Light Street Church serving as the head. J. Thomas Scharf stated:

> The first church building was on the corner of Sharpe and Montgomery Streets. A new church was built in 1833 on the corner of Sharpe and Barre Streets, and the old building given to a colored congregation. The General Conference of 1840 was held in the new church, which in 1860 was separated from the city station and made a distinct charge. In 1870 Wesley Chapel was rebuilt.[29]

With reference to the African American congregation, Scharf noted that the separate congregation built its first church in 1802, and rebuilt in 1860.[30]

Sharp Street Methodist Church played a key role during the antebellum period in the educational, economic, and social development of African Americans. Following the Civil War, the church provided a forum in 1864 for the discussion of the enlistment of African Americans to fight for the Union Army in the struggle for the liberation of slaves and the preservation of the Union. To be sure, Sharp Street, like other separate African American churches, provided such forums for lively discussions on various social and political issues.

The Orchard Street Methodist Church in Baltimore was organized by Trueman Pratt, an African American clergyman who began preaching and holding prayer meeting for his people in 1825. Again, J. Thomas Scharf affirmed:

> Several years after these meeting were held in Pratt's house, in Biddle Street, near Ross. In 1837 a church was erected at the corner of Orchard Street and Elder Alley, Pratt subscribing the first twenty dollars towards its construction. He continued to be a class-leader in the church until 1868, and was a member of the board of trustees until his death. In 1853 the present house of worship erected in Orchard Street, near Ross, which was dedicated on the fourth of December of that year. Jacob Gruber was the first pastor of the church.[31]

The church has been noted as one of the greatest historic churches in Baltimore.

Separate African American Churches in the Methodist Protestant Church

The Methodist Protestant Church began as a denomination in 1828 as the

Associated Methodist Churches by persons withdrawing or expelled from the Methodist Episcopal Church. These Methodists were motivated by opposition to the episcopacy and a desire for lay representation in the conference. The church was organized and renamed in 1830. A small number of African Americans became members of the church. In 1849, the St. Thomas Church was organized on March 7, under the name of Colored Methodist Protestant Israel Church, on Chestnut near Front Street by African Americans who withdrew from the African Methodist Episcopal Church. The congregation for a time worshiped at the residence of Rebecca Permylia, near North Street, Baltimore, Maryland, but later rented the basement of Warfield's Church on Courtland Street, where they remained for two years. The cornerstone of St. Thomas Church was laid in July 1850, and the church was dedicated March 7, 1852. Reverend Nathaniel Peck was the first pastor of St. Thomas Church.[32]

In July 1874, the First Colored Methodist Protestant Church also in Baltimore was organized and was located on the corner of Chew and McDonough Streets. The cornerstone was laid on July 19, 1874. Two years later, the Colored Methodist Protestant Church was organized and located on Durham Street, between Eager and Chase Streets in Baltimore.[33]

Separate African American Churches in the Protestant Episcopal Church

The Protestant Episcopal Church, later known as the Episcopal Church, was the American denomination whose heritage derives from the reformed Church of England established by law in 1559 during the reign of Elizabeth I. The Church of England contributed significantly to the political, religious, and economic plans of the Virginia Company in the founding of Jamestown in 1607. As previously mentioned, the Protestant Episcopal Church pioneered early works for the evangelization of African slaves. Sizable numbers coexisted with white members in various churches during the Colonial Period.

The first African American Episcopal church, St. Thomas, was organized, as previously mentioned, by Reverend Absalom Jones in 1792. The first church was constructed at 5th and Adelphi streets in Philadelphia and dedicated on July 17, 1794. The church played key roles in the Abolitionist Movement and the Underground Railroad. St. Philips in New York City was the second African American Episcopal in America.

Another early separate African American Episcopal church was the St. James Episcopal Church in Baltimore, Maryland, organized in 1824. The first worship service was held on June 23, 1824, in a building on Park Avenue and Madison Street. It was founded by Reverend William Levington, the first African American missionary of the Episcopal Church in the South. Shortly after his ordination as a deacon, Levington traveled to Baltimore to organize a work for the African Americans of the city.

Perhaps the most noteworthy minister of the church was Reverend George F. Bragg, who became the rector of St. James in 1891. He was born in Warrenton, North Carolina, on January 25, 1863. His family moved to Petersburg, Virginia, where he attended St. Stephen's Normal School and the Bishop Payne Divinity School. In 1881, Bragg was appointed page in the Virginia Legislature. In 1882, he founded and edited, at a youthful age, the *Virginia Lancet*, the first African American weekly published in the Black Belt of Virginia. He was an untiring advocate for the progress of African Americans in social, religious, and political areas.

Another very interesting establishment of a separate Episcopal church was the St. Mathew's Episcopal Church in Savannah, Georgia. On July 7, 1750, one of the slaves who attended Christ Church in the city was baptized by the rector, opening the door for other African Americans. In 1852, a mission on the Savannah River banks was established to serve slaves on the surrounding plantations. In 1855, the Episcopal Church organized a new mission in Savannah to serve the free urban African Americans. William Cleghorn, an African American businessman, owned a bakery in Savannah and invited Reverend Sherod W. Kennerly to open a new church. Under his leadership, the St. Stevens Episcopal Church had its beginning in the hall of Cleghorn's Bakery located at Habersham Street and Perry Lane, Savannah.

When General Sherman and Secretary Stanton met with the leading African Americans of Savannah, one was James Porter, the senior warden of St. Steven's Church. He stated that the church had an adult membership of 200 persons and was valued at $10,000. On December 26, 1871, Reverend John Robert Love, a West Indian, served St. Steven and became the first African-American rector of an Episcopal church in Georgia. He soon established a school which had 160 students.[34]

Separate African American Presbyterian Churches

White Presbyterians generally favored the separation of African American churches as a means by which they could promote missionary activities among them without having to admit them into their churches. It in real sense, the separation allowed the white body to maintain segregation and, at the same time, whitewash their Christian conscience. It would also lower the financial burden of having to expend extra funds on missions.

The first separate African American Presbyterian church movement began in Philadelphia. The church emerged out of the interest of Reverend Archibald Alexander, a white Presbyterian, and the labor of John Gloucester, an ex-slave of Gideon Blackburn, the Presbyterian missionary to the Cherokee Indians. Blackburn experienced a change in conscience regarding slavery and decided to manumit several of his slaves to be transported to Liberia, West Africa. John Gloucester came to the attention of the white Presbyterian minister, Reverend Alexander, who had formed the Presbyterian Evangelical Society of Philadelphia in 1807 with a major objective to advance missionary work among the African Americans in the city. John Gloucester, with liberal leaves from his master, was seen as a favorable candidate to lead the missionary work. Andrew E. Murray reports:

> The General Assembly of 1807 approved Gloucester's licensure, but Philadelphia Presbytery thought it best to refer the matter to a presbytery in Tennessee, where Blackburn was active. At the request of Alexander, Blackburn released Gloucester for missionary work in Philadelphia.... When Gloucester began his work in Philadelphia he faced opposition from the Negro Methodists, but through outdoor preaching and singing he managed to collect a group which could be organized into a church.... This church, First African Presbyterian Church, was formed in 1807 with twenty-two members.... Gloucester's church was aided by the Evangelical Society, which contributed funds for its first building; and by the General Assembly, which helped to support Gloucester as a missionary. When the church was formally received by the presbytery in 1811, it reported 123 members.[35]

Benjamin Rush helped Reverend John Gloucester to raise $1,500 to purchase the freedom of his wife and their four children. The freedom of his family relieved some of the emotional pressure on Gloucester, allowing him greater freedom to advance his pastoral duties. In concomitance to his pastoral work, Reverend Gloucester was able to advance a liberal educational ministry for the African Americans in Philadelphia. The school opened in Augustan Hall. At that time, there were about 12,000 African Americans in the city.

The spiritual example of Reverend John Gloucester inspired three of his sons to enter the Presbyterian ministry. One of his sons, Reverend Jeremiah Gloucester, was trained in the African School of the Synod of New York and New Jersey in 1817. In 1824, he was called to First African Presbyterian Church to succeed his father. Another son of Reverend John Gloucester, James Gloucester, organized the Siloam Presbyterian Church of Brooklyn, New York, and served as its pastor from1847 to 1851. Lastly, Stephen Gloucester, who had been born a slave in Tennessee but purchased by his father, took charge of a school in Norris Alley after the death of his brother Reverend Jeremiah Gloucester.[36]

In 1824, after the death of Reverend John Gloucester, a split developed in the First African Presbyterian Church over the call of Reverend Samuel Cornish of New York as pastor. His call to the pastorate was favored by a minority of the members. However, Reverend Cornish declined the call, and the minority who favored him withdrew from the church to form Second African Presbyterian Church under the leadership of Reverend Jeremiah Gloucester.[37]

In addition to the founding of First African Presbyterian Church and Second African Presbyterian Church, the third Presbyterian Church, Lombard Street Central Church, was organized in Philadelphia before the Civil War. This church was formed from Second African Presbyterian Church over the issue of failing to call Reverend Stephen Gloucester, who had been serving as its supply minister. Under Reverend Stephen Gloucester's leadership, the new church grew and was able to erect a church building.[38]

During the antebellum period, two other African American Presbyterian churches were organized in Pennsylvania, namely the Washington Street Church in Reading, Pennsylvania, which was organized in 1823, and the Capital Street Church of Harrisburg, Pennsylvania, organized in 1858 by African American members of the biracial Market Square Presbyterian Church.[39]

In 1822, the first separate African American Presbyterian church was organized in New York through the efforts of Reverend Samuel Cornish, founder of the first African American periodical in America. He also served as one of four African Americans on the executive committee of the American Anti-Slavery Society. He was able to organize twenty-five members, who had formerly attended First Presbyterian and other Presbyterian churches in the city, to form a new separate African American Presbyterian church. The new church adopted several different names: Church of the Covenant, Church of Hope, Seventh Avenue, and Emmanuel Church. The new church reported in the 1848 General

Assembly minutes with forty-three members under the care of Reverend Samuel Cornish, and by 1860 this number had grown to 139. [40]

In 1835, the First Presbyterian Colored Congregation of the City of Newark was organized with 37 charter members. This church was initially located on Plane Street but later moved to 13th Avenue. In 1845, an African American Presbyterian church was organized in Princeton, New Jersey, consisting of members who withdrew from the white Presbyterian church. The church was first known as The First Presbyterian Church of Color in Princeton, and later named the Witherspoon Street Presbyterian Church, under the leadership of Reverend E. P. Rogers.[41]

The separate Presbyterian church movement among African Americans expanded southward by the organization of the Fifteenth Street Church of Washington, D.C., in 1841, by Reverend John F. Cook who had been a teacher in a private school for African Americans in the city and a class leader in the African Methodist Episcopal Church. He left the ministry with the Methodists through the encouragement of Reverend John C. Smith, pastor of the Fourth Presbyterian Church. Shortly, Reverend John F. Cook was licensed by the presbytery of the District of Columbia in 1841. Subsequently, he called a meeting in his school to explain the principles of Presbyterianism to a group of African Americans with the desired purpose of forming a church. Out of this meeting 19 African Americans, inspired by a sermon by Reverend Stratton of Portsmouth, Virginia, united to form the new Presbyterian church. The church was received by the presbytery, and Reverend Cook was ordained in 1843. He served as pastor of the church until 1855.[42]

In 1853, Reverend Robert L. Galbreath, a white Presbyterian minister, encouraged the formation of a separate African American Presbyterian church in Baltimore, Maryland, which came to be named the Madison Street Church. The church was founded by some of the free African Americans in the city, which had become a tendency in church development among members of other denominations in the city. Shortly after the Civil War, the new Presbyterian church was served by Reverend Hiram Revels, who played an important part in the political life of the Reconstruction Era.[43] He was the first African American U.S. senator. He was born in Fayetteville, North Carolina, to free parents of African and Indian descent. After receiving as excellent education, he became the first African American pastor of Madison Street Presbyterian Church in Baltimore.

During the Civil War, he organized the first two African American military regiments in Maryland.

An extract from the report of the Committee on Freedmen presented to the presbytery of Philadelphia for the year ending in March 31, 1889, summarized the social, religious, and theoretical basis of Presbyterian work among African Americans:

> And here let me say the Presbyterian Church has a special work to perform among the Freedmen of the South and I might say also in the North. No church is so well calculated to correct the faults of the Negro, and to broaden and strengthen his manhood as the Presbyterian Church and no church should do more towards his elevation than this church.
>
> Secondly, the doctrine of the perseverance of the saints, as taught by the Presbyterian Church is what the Negro needs to correct his tendencies to regard religion simply as an influence, instead of a life, which was exemplified by Christ and which is to be lived as well as to be taught by his disciples.
>
> Thirdly, the government of the Presbyterian Church is what the Negro needs to teach him self-government and respect for authority and to correct his tendency to rule, one of the main errors which he imbibed from his schooling under the slave system which can only be corrected by the clear and forcible teachings of Christ.
>
> Fourthly, the great Presbyterian Church, with all its paraphernalia, its wonderful history, its martyred dead, its mines of scholarly lore—the accumulation of ages—its adherents to right and truth as taught in the Word of God, is what the Negro needs to guide him, to correct him, to steady him, to hold him from flying off into error, and to give him dignity and strength of character as well as the proper incentives for his emulation, that he may be devoted in all of the nobler qualities of his being and thus be fitted to occupy that sphere in the world's history which God and nature have decreed that he shall.
>
> But it is said it is not right for the church to expend money, in carrying on missions among a people who are of a highly excitable nature, being principally Methodists and Baptists, in their tendencies, and who therefore, do not sufficiently adhere to the Presbyterian Church to justify the outlay of money, in their behalf.

If this were true of the Negro it would not justify the position, but it is not true, it is not borne out in the history of the church; for it is not the position which the church has taken in her work among other people....

But it is not true that the Negro does not take to the Presbyterian Church. The fact that in less than twenty years the Presbyterian Church has organized by its Board of Missions to the Freedmen, six Presbyteries and a Synod among the Freedmen, embracing 237 churches, 116 ministers, and 17,480 communicants, 1349 having been received on confession of faith, this last year, also 83 schools with a membership of 11,275 does not look as if the Freedmen of the South do not take to the Presbyterian Church. The truth is, the Negro gives as hearty adherence to the church as he is encouraged to give.... But the fact that there have been organized 237 churches within the last 24 years in the South alone among the colored people, with a membership of 17,480 is sufficient argument that the churches of the North should give largely of their means to enable the Board of Missions to carry on its good work among the Freedmen.[44]

Like other biracial denominations, the Presbyterian church's report demonstrated a paternal and condescending attitude towards African Americans. This report was recorded by Reverend Mathew Anderson, the noted African American pastor of the Berean Presbyterian Church in Philadelphia, Pennsylvania.

The African Union Church

The African Union Church in Wilmington, Delaware, preceded the founding of the separate Methodist churches in Philadelphia, Baltimore, and New York. It began in Wilmington when a group of African American members of the biracial Asbury Methodist Episcopal Church withdrew to form an independent church named Ezion Methodist Episcopal Church. The group, under the leadership of Peter Spencer, left the church because they were no longer satisfied with being forced to occupy the balcony and to receive communion after the white members of the church. Hence, they left to form their own church in 1805. This was the first group of Methodists to separate from the Methodist Episcopal Church. Reverend Peter Spencer, founder of the church, was born in slavery in Kent County, Maryland, in 1782. He was supportive of the Underground Railroad and other movements for the liberation of slaves. In 1866 Ezion Union

Church, as it came to be known, united with the first Colored Methodist Protestant Church to form the African Union First Colored Methodist Protestant Church of America.

African American Baptists

Within a decade after the establishment of separate African American churches in Georgia and South Carolina, African American slaves and free African Americans separated from biracial churches to form independent churches. Virginia Baptists were next in line for the establishment of independent churches. They formed two different types of African American Baptist churches: the separate church under white leadership and the separate church under the leadership of African American pastors. Both the Gilfield Baptist Church and the Harrison Street Baptist Church in Petersburg claim priority in organizational dates. Miles Mark Fisher suggested 1774 as the organizational year for these two churches. He said that the Gilfield Baptist Church was the first church of African American Baptists in Petersburg to continue the organization of free African Americans and of race-conscious slaves who had been connected with neighboring churches before 1760.[45] The early historian of the African American church gave the later date of 1776 for the organization of the Harrison Street Baptist Church.[46]

The first African American Baptist church in Williamsburg, Virginia, was organized in 1776, the same year America declared her independence from England. Thad W. Tate related the social significance of the growing membership in the biracial church: "By the mid-1750s, most Williamsburg blacks were second- and third-generation African-Virginians who had become acculturated to the English language and customs. They had embraced Christianity and were attending services at Bruton Parish Church. As many as 980 had been baptized in the church by 1750."[47] Initially, the African Americans met in the vicinity of Green Spring, west of the city. They built a brush arbor where they sang and prayed, but that site was too inconvenient for most of the members. Hence, they decided to move to a new location at Racoon Chase, two and a half miles from Green Spring. The new location was a better place to hold their secret meetings. Nevertheless, this brush arbor still was not secretive enough to prevent the slave master from discovering the secret meetings. Robert F. Coles, the plantation owner, was impressed by the religious devotion of the slaves and agreed to let them use his carriage house in Williamsburg for worship. They moved to this location in 1776, where Rev. Moses was exhorting among the race. The group continued to worship in the carriage house until a church building could be constructed.[48]

The First Baptist Church of Richmond was organized in 1780, just one year after the capital of Virginia was moved from Williamsburg to the city. Initially, the church was biracial in membership but became an African American Baptist church in 1841 when the minority white members moved to a new location. The majority African American membership remained in the original building on 14th and Broad Streets. However, the power of the white members was demonstrated by the fact that they were able to keep the original name. According to Baptist congregational polity, the majority membership should have been able to keep the original name. By 1846, two other African American Baptist churches were organized in the city—First African Baptist Church and Second African Baptist Church.

In 1800, the First Baptist Church of Norfolk, Virginia, was organized by Elders David Briggs and Thomas Everidge as a biracial and bilingual church composed of whites; free and enslaved Africans coming from Europe, Africa, and the West Indies; and America's Eastern Shore Indians. Shortly after its organization, the First Baptist Church increased in membership sufficient to relocate from the original location on Cumberland Street to a new location in 1805 in the Borough Church, later known as Old St. Paul's Episcopal Church, which was practically abandoned by the Episcopalians. In 1816, the white members withdrew for the purpose of forming a church made up of whites only. However, a few whites chose to remain in the original church. From about 1805 to 1830 the original congregation continued to worship in the Borough Church. In 1830, the First Baptist Church moved to worship in the "Old Salt Box" on Bute Street. In 1839, a group of members withdrew and organized another church taking the name, "First Baptist Church" but later came to be known as Bank Street Memorial Church. For several decades, First Baptist Church was under the leadership of white pastors. In 1862, Reverend Lewis Tucker was chosen as the first African American pastor of the church.

Slaves in Norfolk were successful in organizing another church, the Mount Pleasant Baptist Church, shortly before the Emancipation Proclamation issued by President Lincoln. It started in the slave quarters of two men named Jacob Cargo and Elijah Lively. Both resided in the Lenox section of Norfolk County.

As was the tradition of the time, these two Christian men obtained permission of their owner to hold prayer services in their slave quarters. The first prayer service led by Jacob Cargo actually gave birth to the new mission. Subsequent meetings were held in the home of Peter Catney. By 1865, these meetings had grown rapidly, resulting in worship services having to be held in a brush arbor. It was not until the early 1870s that a church building was constructed on Birmingham and Newport Avenues in Norfolk.[49]

In 1867, African Americans Baptists organized the First Baptist Church of Farmville, Virginia, as an outgrowth of the Farmville Baptist Church. The first property, located on Main and Fourth Streets, then known as the old Baptist Church, was purchased April 16, 1867.

The separate African American church movement advanced into the North with the organization of Joy Baptist Church, originally called The African Meeting House of Boston, Massachusetts, which was chartered in 1805. On December 4, Reverend Thomas Paul of New Hampshire was officially installed as pastor of the church, an association destined to endure for a quarter century. The church became an important center for the cultural life of African Americans in Boston. The church also has the distinction of being the first independent African American church in the United States. It was founded at a time when African Americans began moving in larger numbers from their New Guinea neighborhood in northeast Boston to Beacon Hill in the eighteenth century. Subsequently, the church became well known for participating in the Underground Railroad; the center for the organization of the New England Abolitionist Society in 1832; and the appearance of prominent anti-slavery advocates Frederick Douglass, Wendell Phillips, and Charles Summer. From this humble beginning, the Baptists of Massachusetts spread through the state.[50]

In 1808, the African American Baptists of New York organized their first Baptist church. The Abyssinian Baptist Church of New York City was organized by a group of traders who came to the city from the country of Abyssinia, currently known as Ethiopia. According to tradition, these "Abyssinians" attended the First Baptist Church of New York where they were promptly ushered into the slave loft. They resented this expression of American segregated church life and walked out in protest along with Reverend Thomas Paul, a liberal white preacher from Harvard University.

Adamant in purpose, the small group of protesters pooled their resources and in June 1808 bought some property on Worth Street on which they established the Abyssinian Baptist Church. The organization of this church followed the style of other separate Baptist churches. The church was led by white ministers. It is noteworthy that the Abyssinian Baptist Church was the first Baptist church in the entire North to establish a non-segregated membership. From its inception, the church attracted people from all over New York. Many traveled by boat from nearby Brooklyn and northern New Jersey. The membership there grew rapidly. The leadership of Abyssinian observed with growing concern the influx of members from Brooklyn, then separated from New York by water without bridges. They urged these members from Brooklyn to organize their own church. In order to facilitate this request, the church sent Reverend Sampson White to Brooklyn to organize a new congregation. On May 18, 1847, he was able to help organize the Concord Baptist Church of Brooklyn. This new church became the second Baptist church to be organized in New York during the antebellum period.

One year after the founding of Abyssinian Baptist Church in New York, the African American Baptists of Pennsylvania organized their first separate church in 1809. The independent spirit was already widespread in the state resulting from the Reverends Richard Allen and Absalom Jones' movements. The church was organized on June 19, 1809. The pioneer roots of the First Baptist Church go back to the eastern shore of Virginia and to Savannah, Georgia. During the closing years of the eighteenth century, a few African Americans migrated to Philadelphia from Virginia to escape the cruel treatment of slave masters. Soon after their arrival, some of them united with the white First Baptist Church of Philadelphia. Most of the group decided that their spiritual needs would best be met in an independent church of their own. The church was organized under the care and protection of the white First Baptist Church. Beyond Virginia, the roots of the new church extend to Savannah, Georgia, where Reverend Henry Cunningham was being prepared for a fruitful ministry in a distant city. He became the first pastor of First African Baptist Church. He was influenced by Reverend Henry Holcombe to come to Philadelphia and to accept the call to the pastorate of the First African Baptist Church.

Another African American Baptist Church founded in the South before the Civil War was the Friendship Baptist Church in Atlanta, Georgia. It was organized in 1862 before General Sherman destroyed the city in his march toward the Atlantic Ocean. Its pastor was Rev. Frank Quarles, who with 25 African American Baptists received their letters from the biracial First Baptist Church of Atlanta. Unlike some other southern areas, Atlanta did not offer significant opposition to the separate African church movement. Due to tremendous poverty, the members of the church were not able to purchase property for the congregation; however, they worshiped in a house until a box car was sent down from Cincinnati, Ohio, as the first permanent residence of the church. This was unique for any church planting activity in the Confederate States of America, where all African Americans were expected to be loyal to the new government.

After the Emancipation Proclamation, Atlanta's African American population gained sufficient freedom and a sense of industry to build worship centers. The congregation expanded and relocated to a larger structure on Haynes and Markham Streets. Since the First Baptist Church was the only congregation located in the predominantly African American neighborhood on Atlanta's west side, the membership again outgrew its worship facility and erected a spacious church building in 1871-72 on West Mitchell Street. Rev. Quarles lived until 1881 and advanced his pioneering ministry in the city. The congregation increased substantially, reaching other parts of the city, which required the planting of other congregations in Atlanta.[51]

The early planting of separate African American churches in New Jersey began in 1812 when African Americans organized the First African Baptist Church at Trenton. The same year another separate church was organized at Salem, New Jersey. The New Jersey separate church movement progressed slowly until the mid-1850s. In 1856, the Kaighn Avenue Baptist Church was organized in Camden, New Jersey, which began as a prayer meeting movement under the leadership of Rev. Sampson White.

Curiously enough, William Crane, a white leather merchant and member of the First Baptist Church of Richmond, Virginia, led the way for the establishment of a separate church movement in Maryland. Before moving to Baltimore from Richmond in 1834, Crane organized in 1815 a school at the First African Baptist Church of Richmond where a slave named Moses C. Clayton attended along with several other slaves and members of the church. Soon after he arrived in Baltimore, Crane became deeply concerned over the neglect of the white Baptists of Maryland to cultivate a serious missionary cause among the

African American population. He frequently confronted white Baptists about this neglect. With determination to alter the situation,

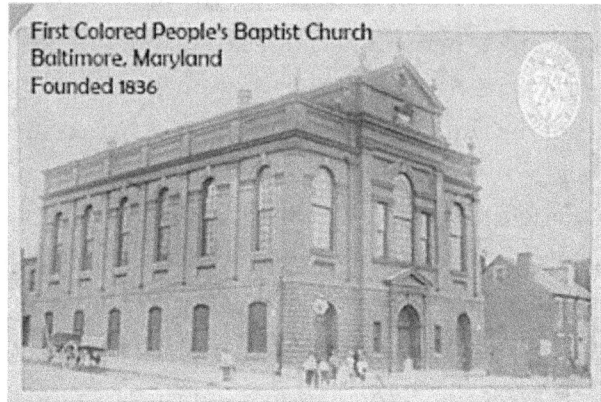

Crane communicated with Moses C. Clayton, who had gained his freedom and resided in Norfolk, Virginia, requesting him to come to Baltimore and work among his race. After arriving in Baltimore, Moses C. Clayton organized a Sunday school for the religious instruction of slaves and free African Americans in the city.

On February 20, 1836, Clayton's Sunday school was organized into the First Colored Peoples' Baptist Church. The formal organization of the church was assisted by several white ministers in the city. One year later, Reverend Moses C. Clayton was able to obtain legal status for his separate church as a Maryland corporation. In 1841, the new church joined the white Baptist's Maryland Union Association. In 1849, Reverend John Carey succeeded Reverend Clayton in the pastorate of the first church.

The next separate African American Baptist church in Maryland was established again through the cooperative strides of the Maryland Union Association and William Crane. In the early 1840s, Crane and other leaders of the association again looked to Virginia for another preacher to establish another church in Baltimore. Reverend Noah Davis, an ex-slave, took on the challenge to start the new church. He was born in Madison County, Virginia, in March 1804, to John Davis and Jane Davis, who were both slaves. Shortly after 1840, Noah Davis was able to purchase his freedom along with some other members of the family. In 1847, he came to Baltimore and organized the Second Colored Peoples' Baptist Church, which was later named the Saratoga Street African Baptist Church, Baltimore, Maryland.

In 1852, a group of members left the First Colored Peoples' Baptist Church to form the Union Baptist Church. Initially, Union Baptist Church met for worship in a small building on Lewis Street near Mullikin Street in the city. Reverend John Carey became the pastor of the new church. In 1856, Reverend Chauncey Leonard succeeded Reverend Carey in the pastorate of Union Baptist Church.

The African American Baptist movement appeared in the nation's capital in 1862. The Frist Baptist Church (Georgetown) is one of the oldest churches in Washington, D.C. The church was founded by Rev. Sandy Alexander of Fredericksburg, Virginia. He and a small group of freedmen from Fredericksburg came to the district to witness the inauguration of President Lincoln. They decided to remain in the City and to purchase some land at 29th and O Streets to establish a church. The church was originally known as "The Ark." Rev. Alexander and his followers dug the foundation of their church at night after they worked daily on wharves at Alexandria, Virginia. After the Civil War, they moved their church location to 22nd and Barton Avenue, NW. Also during the war, the church was a station for the Underground Railroad and a recruiting station for the Union Army. Several of its founders fought in major battles during the Civil War.[52]

In the deeper South, the separate church movement began in Huntsville, Alabama, with the organization of the African Baptist Church in 1820 and the Stone Street Baptist Church, Mobile, Alabama, in 1836. Mobile had the reputation of being the most liberal city toward African Americans in the state. Hence, an early separate church was established there named the Stone Street Baptist Church of Mobile. Prior to the Civil War, the church was led by Reverend J. B. Hawthorne. A split in the church resulted in the organization of the Saint Louis Street Baptist Church of Mobile. From this beginning, the separate spirit among African American Baptists slowly spread to other parts of the state.

By 1856, African American Baptists had organized another church in Alabama known as the New Prospect Baptist Church, one of the first African American churches in Anniston. An oral history of the founding of the church was given to the *Birmingham World* newspaper in 1958 by Mrs. Ella Hendrix, a 102-year-old daughter of an ex-slave. The article gave the following report of the oral history:

> This is the history of one of the first black churches in Anniston, Alabama. A church whose founders and congregations were to influence the black churches built later in the Anniston area.... The idea for a

church and the first discussion took place in secrecy as slaves were not to assemble or hold meetings. However, "Mr. Borders was pretty nice (nicer than some masters)," Pa said. These meetings were held at night. Now this was about 1856.

These meetings continued until slavery was abolished. Slave men, women, and their children were declared free. People were drifting here and there; however, some remained on the same plantations to farm and rear their children, not moving far from their past experiences. This was the slow process of motivation in and around the community of Choccolocco. Until at last, one day, there came from some of the ex-slave families, a few men who had those in-born tendencies to start a school for the children of the ex-slaves, the freeborn ones, and the ex-slaves themselves. The beginning has its origin at a corn shucking one night.

Corn shucking was a form of entertainment created out of the routine of chores common among slaves. A big pile of corn, sometimes several wagon loads, was piled in one place. All the slaves from a certain plantation would assemble on orders from their masters to shuck corn, clean the shucks, and place the corn in the barns again. This was to happen within a set number of hours in one night.

On one particular night during a corn shucking, there was a group of gentlemen: Mr. Chap Chapple, Mr. Borders, and some others. I can't recall all the names which were told my mother who then told me.

Mr. Chapple talked to the assembly at the corn shucking about a school for the children. He was encouraged by the first few anxious "yes" replies. They decided that the building would consist of ax-hewn pine logs topped with pine brush. The seats would be split wooden pegs. Everyone agreed. This bush arbor served as the church. The school was built near the site of the old grist mill known as the Morris and Downing's Mill on Choccolocco Creek.

It is this creek that gives the community its name. The name is all that remains of the Creek Indians who had been scattered throughout the region after the "French Treaty."

Mr. Chapple was the preacher. He also became the school teacher. After a few weeks of hard labor at night, the bush arbor was completed....

One blue back speller was the only book available for everyone (25-30 individuals). Rev. Mr. Chapple would first preach, then after the preaching service, school began. To supply everyone with information from the one book, he would take two or three words at a time. These he gave by syllables, like the word "baker, ba-ker." There was one word Mrs. Cunningham would spell for everyone, such as the word Constantinople, Con-stan-tin-o-ple…. This bush arbor which served as the school, and the church needed a name, so they named it Prospect Baptist Church. The church remained at its first site for nine or ten years. By this time, they decided to move the school and church closer to where the mass of the people lived in those days….

The new site was Borders Town, about two miles from the present Choccolocco community. Borders Town was a "plantation community" and at the time still retained the majority of its ex-slaves.

The organization born at the corn shucking had been in Borders Town for some twelve or fifteen years before it was moved to the present site. About 1876, a building was erected in the Choccolocco community and was given the name New Prospect Baptist Church.[53]

In Mississippi, the separate church movement in this southern state gradually developed. A sizable number of slaves worshiped in separate churches with the written permission of their masters or overseers. In reality, these were mere plantation missions. As early as 1820, an African American Baptist church was represented in the biracial Pearl River Association. The mission church was represented by delegates, "Ben, belonging to Sellers; and Bob, belonging to Mc-Graw."[54] State laws prohibited African American preachers from serving these mission churches; hence, white preachers served them by appointment. Shortly, new state laws were passed which abridged the privilege of worship on the part of the slaves. It was the white Pearl River Baptist Association along with two other associations that petitioned the state legislature to repeal "such part of said law as deprives our African churches of their religious privileges."[55]

In 1829, the white Baptists of Mississippi began to provide accommodations in their own churches for African American Baptists. The old Salem church took the lead by constructing a "shed to her meeting house" separated from the auditorium for the whites by a tall partition.[56] Furthermore, the white Baptist associations entreated their membership to take notice of any improper treatment of their members toward slaves, and to "deal with them (overbearing masters) in brotherly love, according to the gospel."[57]

The influx of African American Baptists into biracial churches resulted in a decline in the initial momentum for separate churches in Mississippi. Like movements in other states, the African American membership in these churches outnumbered the white membership. The biracial church experience remained characteristic in the state. Hence, the movement toward separate churches did not gain substantial momentum until after the Civil War.

Similarly, the African American Baptists of Tennessee made slow progress toward an independent church movement. They were less inclined to follow the driving spirit toward separation characteristic of the colonial church movement. Most of the slaves worshiped in brush arbors while others worshiped in the characteristic biracial churches, either as members or holding "after-services." It was not until 1843 that the African American Baptists were able to organize a separate church in Middle Tennessee at Columbia, the Mount Lebanon Baptist Church. Subsequently, those of West Tennessee organized the Beale Street Baptist Church at Memphis. Prior to the Civil War, the latter church was led by Reverend Morris Henderson and Reverend Scott Key.

In 1846, a separate mission grew out of the First Baptist Church of Nashville. The mission conducted its work largely as an established church, subject to approval of the white mother church. It was not until 1865 that the mission was organized into the First Colored Baptist Church of Nashville. This was the second movement for separation from biracial churches in the state. In 1875, the Braxton Chapel AME Zion Church was organized in Kingston, Tennessee, by Rev. Lewis Braxton.

Roman Catholic Separate Church Movement

The separate movement of African American Roman Catholics has roots in the segregation policy within the biracial Catholic churches during slavery in America. Like their Protestant counterparts, white Roman Catholics tended to separate African Americans within their church buildings. They held the same feelings of racial superiority as the white Protestants. Racism within the church manifested itself in reluctance on the part of white Catholics to receive the Eucharist on equal basis with their slaves and freed African Americans parishioners. Hence, the segregated covenant emerged within the Roman Catholic Church. William Osborne summarized the persistent social impact of racism in the church:

In 1871, in obedience to the wish of Pope Pius IX, and in response to the earnest plea of the American bishops at the Second Plenary Council, Father Vaughn and four other members of his recently founded Foreign Missionary Society (Josephite Fathers) arrived in Baltimore to work among the free Negroes in the United States. After being formally installed by Archbishop Spalding, Father Vaughn made a tour of Southern cities to determine the scope of his task and to raise funds. The diary he kept on the trip gives a first-hand picture of how white Southern Catholics treated their Negro co-religionists. Vaughn, who had expected the worst, was shocked. Negroes were "regarded even by priests as so many dogs," he noted. "I visited a hospital where there were a number of Negroes.... Neither the priest with me nor the Sisters in the hospital do anything to instruct them. They just smile at them as if they had no souls."

Everywhere Father Vaughn went—Savannah, Vicksburg, Natchez, Memphis, New Orleans—the situation was the same. In a Catholic cathedral he saw a Negro soldier refused communion by a white priest. There were low, backless benches marked off "For Negroes."[58]

Prior to this social experience, African American Catholics developed a consciousness of racial pride, resulting in the establishment of the first separate Roman Catholic church. On July 11, 1793, six ships arrived in the Port of Baltimore at Fells Point with a crew of between 500 and 1,000 African slaves fleeing the hostilities in the West Indies. They were a part of a French fleet from Haiti during the revolution. The refugees were all Catholics and began attending mass in the basement of St. Mary Seminary Chapel on Paca Street, under the care of the Sulpician fathers. The chapel was then known as the Chapelle Basse (parish church for colored people). In 1836, the Oblate Sisters of Providence built a chapel on Richmond Street which became the new worship location for the refugees from Haiti. In 1847, the Jesuit fathers invited these refugees to attend services in the Basement Chapel of St. Ignatius Church at Calvert and Madison Streets. The place of worship was named the Blessed Peter Claver Chapel. To be sure, there were African American Catholics in Maryland before their arrival. Approximately eight years before the Fell Point landing, in a letter to the acting Secretary of State Cardinal Antonelli, dated March 1, 1785, John Carroll, head of the Catholic missions in the newly formed United States, indicated that there were three thousand Catholic slaves in Maryland.[59]

On October 10, 1863, an old building was bought as the first permanent home of the St. Francis Xavier Roman Catholic Church, located on the corner of Calvert and Pleasant Streets. Initially, this building was a worship center for Protestants.

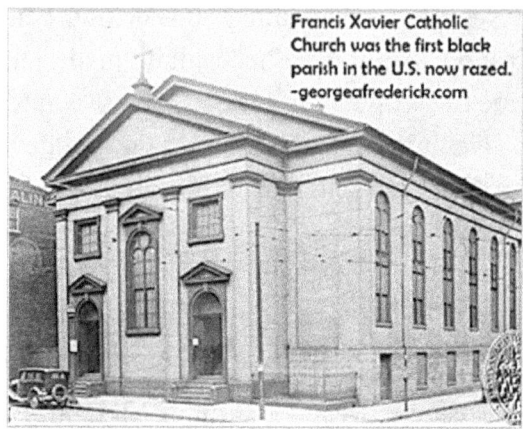

Francis Xavier Catholic Church was the first black parish in the U.S. now razed. -georgeafrederick.com

Several important political affairs had been convened in the building. On May 1, 1844, the Whig National Convention convened when Henry Clay was nominated for the presidency; four years later in 1844, the National Democratic Convention convened and nominated General Chase as its candidate for the White House. Here also was held the convention intending to carry Maryland into the Confederacy but according to chroniclers, General Ben Butler then camped on Federal Hill, interfered, and stopped the proceedings.[60] The building was purchased in 1863 for the African American Catholics of Baltimore. The first separate African American Roman Catholic church in America was then established and dedicated in the building on February 21, 1864. Father Peter Louis Miller, who had been serving the people since 1859, became the first pastor and served until 1871. Under his leadership, the parish established an orphanage, a Catholic parish school, and a night school for adults. On November 17, 1871, four Josephite priests arrived in Baltimore from Mill Hill, England, and took charge of the parish. They were the first priests ordained from a newly formed missionary society founded by Cardinal Herbert Vaughn. Father Charles Uncles, an African American priest, was ordained from St. Francis Xavier parish on December 19, 1891. This new parish played a significant role in advancing the concerns of African American Roman Catholics to the broader Catholic community. In fact, other Catholic churches emerged from St. Francis, namely St. Peter Claver, St. Barnabas, and St. Monica.[61]

The church was named in honor of St. Francis Xavier, founder and pioneer of Roman Catholic missions to persons in undeveloped areas, who was born of an aristocratic family in the kingdom of Navarre (present-day Spain) on April 7, 1506. While preparing himself for a higher spiritual career at the University of Paris, he became acquainted with Ignatius Loyola, soon stood completely under his influence, and was one of those who on August 15, 1534, bound themselves by a vow at Montmartre and formed the nucleus of the Society of Jesus. The missionary work of the Jesuits reached distant lands, winning new souls to the Roman Catholic Church.

The separate spirit of African American Catholics continued with the organization of the St. Peter Claver Parish in West Baltimore, the oldest such parish in the area. As early as 1798, St. Mary's Seminary became the sole center of worship for a group of African American Catholics newly arrived from the island of Santo Domingo. These refugees found solace in the worship services conducted by the Sulpican fathers, who had also come to Baltimore from San Domingo and spoke the native French familiar to them. Father James Nicholas Joubert experienced some difficulties in giving catechism instruction to the poorly educated group. Hence, he discussed the plight of these African American Catholics with three women: two from Santo Domingo, and one from Cuba. These women organized the first order of African American sisters in the United States, the Oblate Sisters of Providence. The church became known as the St. Peter Claver Roman Catholic Church.[62]

The new church was named in honor of St. Peter Claver, a Jesuit priest who came to the New World in the fifteenth century. He was born in 1580 in Verdu, southern Spain but later migrated to the Spanish colony of New Granada in South America where he was ordained a priest in 1616. He became very involved in relieving the suffering of slaves who were newly brought from Africa to the shores of South America. Cyprian Davis observed:

> The slaves were systematically baptized upon disembarkation. Many were suffering both psychologically and physically. The terrible middle passage, the Atlantic voyage of the slave ship, often resulted in the loss to disease of a large portion of both the human cargo and the crew. For over thirty years under the most harrowing of circumstances, Peter Claver ministered to the spiritual and bodily needs of the slaves, not only the newcomers, but those who lay ill, the prisoners, those condemned to death, the lepers, and the abandoned.[63]

He acquired the reputation as the "slave of slaves" for his dedication. Traditions about his work in South America were well known by the congregation of St. Peter Claver Roman Catholic Church in Baltimore, inspiring them to name their church in his honor. In 1888, he was canonized and thus became St. Peter Claver.

A rather small number of African American Roman Catholics actually chose to have separate churches. In September 1896, the *Catholic Review* of New York reported the number of African American Catholics in several large cities: Baltimore—35,000; Charlestown—800; Chicago—400; Covington—140; Galveston—550; Indian Territory—200; Kansas City—250; Little Rock—100; Mobile—2,500; Nashville—500; Natchez—1,700; Natchitoches—9,000; New Orleans—8,000; New York—3,000; Philadelphia—1,500; Pittsburg—1,500; Savannah—1,200; San Antonio—1,200; and Washington, D.C. —400. By that time, thirty-seven churches had been erected by African American Catholics.

The Westward Expansion: American Frontier

The migration of African Americans to the territories west of the Mississippi was a gradual process. Before the influx of significant numbers of African Americans, the early white migrants had to deal with two major barriers during the westward march—the Appalachian Range and the Rocky Mountains. First, the Appalachian Range posed challenges to settlers and traveling evangelists seeking to migrate out of Pennsylvania, Virginia, Maryland, and the Carolinas to areas east of the Mississippi River. These mountain ranges kept the early settlers confined for significant period of time to the Atlantic Coast and delayed the opening of the West. On the other hand, they provided a natural barrier from potential attackers across the mountains, the French and Indians, consequently resulting in a denser settlement of the costal lands. The Rocky Mountains posed real challenges to some of America's earliest pioneers such as Zebulon Pike and John C. Fremont and others. South Pass on the Oregon Trail and Raton Pass on the Santa Fe Trail provided passage through the Rockies for later settlers and adventurers traveling westward.

Gradually, African Americans came on the wagon trains with their white masters who were seeking greater economic opportunities and the adventures of the western territories. The western movement on the American frontier was an ongoing process that began with the first communities founded on the Atlantic seaboard in the seventeenth century and ended in the 1890s with the settlement of the Great Plains between the Mississippi River and the Rocky Mountains.

During the early national period, the impetus for settlements in the West was driven by the idea of "Manifest Destiny." The phrase was first employed by John L. O'Sullivan in an article on the annexation of Texas published in the July-August 1845 edition of the *United States Magazine and Democratic Review*, which he edited. The westward march of soldiers and settlers responded to this idea that the design of Providence was on the side of American expansion on the frontier. Religion on the American frontier was slow to become organized, even among the white frontiersmen. Initially these white men, some with families, who migrated from the thirteen original colonies across the Appalachian mountain ranges were rugged and demonstrated very little interest in organizing churches. Later, a more cultured class migrated westward, bringing with them stronger tendencies for cultural refinement, religious sentiments, and economic development. These white settlers gradually began to organize churches as various settlements grew in population. African Americans and Native Americans were gradually evangelized and joined some of their churches.

Historian John Hope Franklin gave an informative summary of the early struggles of African Americans during the westward migration. He remarked:

> For thirty years before the Civil War, Negroes were migrating North and West from the South. Not only were slaves running away, but free Negroes were looking toward the North Star in the hope of finding greater opportunities and better treatment. They went to cities in the Northeast in large numbers, and also to the Old Northwest along with white immigrants from Europe. Between 1850 and 1860, for example, Michigan's Negro population jumped from 2,500 to 6,700; Iowa's more than tripled; and California increased from 962 to 4,086. The reaction to this wholesale Negro migration was not pleasant. Northern whites had shown no unusual hostility to Negroes who were already in their midst, but they did not welcome the crude, rough type which came from the South. Indeed, they hoped to keep the West free not only from slavery but of the Negro as well.[64]

Generally, a clash developed between the pro-slavery southern settlers and the anti-slavery settlers of the northern areas of the West which eventually led to intense sectionalism and the establishment of the Mason-Dixon Line.

The emerging sectionalism did not prevent the gradual evangelization of African Americans in the West. As territories gradually became states, white Christians in the new states demonstrated an evolving interest in slaves and free

African Americans. Initially, they were brought into the biracial churches. The vast majority united with Baptist and Methodist churches. However, Roman Catholicism had deep roots in the West prior to the movements for statehood in western territories.

Baptist Separate Movement in the West

The westward expansion of African American Baptists of the late antebellum and early years of freedom continued in Indiana through the ministries of Zachariah Bassett and his two sons. They were natives of Greene County, North Carolina. In 1844, the family moved from North Carolina and settled in a Quaker settlement in Park County, Indiana. It was here that Reverend Zachariah Bassett first began to preach in the West, having organized a little church with persons who followed him from North Carolina.

Reverend Miles Bassett, the eldest son, was ordained in 1865 to preach in Indiana. He served the Second Baptist Church of Shelbyville for nine years, and the congregation grew rapidly during his administration. Later, Reverend Miles Bassett became pastor of the Second Baptist Church of Rising Sun, Indiana, and at the same time by unanimous consent of this church, he supplied alternately the churches in Carrollton, Kentucky; and Madison, Indiana. He later became the founder of the Eastern Indiana Baptist Association.

The youngest Bassett son, Reverend Richard Bassett, was ordained in New Albany in August 1867, and served the pastorate of the Shiloh Baptist Church of Rising Sun, Indiana. Subsequently, he was called to the pastorate of the Corinthian Baptist Church of Indianapolis.

The first African American Baptist church in Indianapolis was organized in 1846 by Elder Charles Shachel, who came from Cincinnati as a missionary. He started preaching and gathering up some African Americans who had joined the Methodists along with a few others and organized the Second Baptist Church in Indianapolis. The church grew slowly and experienced some internal difficulties. In 1851 the building was burned, leaving the church with the burden of having to sell part of the land owned by them in order to build a new one.

In 1857, Reverend Moses Broyles became the pastor of Second African Baptist Church. He was born a slave in Maryland, sold at an early age, and taken to Tennessee by his master. He was later sold to a Kentucky master named Broyles who allowed him to be taught to read and attend debates with white students in the local schoolhouse. Emma Lou Thornbrough remarked: "While yet a slave Moses had read the New Testament five times and the entire Bible twice. He had also read the Constitution of the United States, Benedict's History of the Bible, and some of the writings of Alexander Campbell. When he was fourteen years old, Moses' master promised him that he would free him in 1854."[65] In 1851, he was allowed to start missionary work among African American slaves. The few that responded were organized into the new mission.

Another African American Baptist pioneer in the westward expansion of the churches was Reverend George Washington Dupree. He was born a slave July 24, 1826, in Gallatin County, Kentucky. As a slave, he was hired out to various white businessmen. He was converted to the Christian faith and expressed an early desire to preach. During his preaching career, Reverend Dupree ministered at Buck Run Church and other churches in counties such as Woodford, Franklin, Scott, Jessamine, Fayette, and Owen. In 1851, he received the call to the pastorate of a Baptist church at Georgetown. In 1853, he organized a church at Old Big Springs in Woodford County. In 1861, Reverend Dupree organized at Versailles the first ministers and deacons' meeting ever held by African American Baptists in the Southwestern states. In 1867, he extended his ministry further by assisting in the organization of General Association of Colored Baptists of Kentucky. In 1871, Reverend Dupree was elected moderator of the association. He remained in that position until his death in 1881.[66] By 1869, the association reported fifty-five churches with a membership of about 13,000.

The General Association of Colored Baptists of Kentucky consisted of African American Baptist churches that predated its organization. As early as 1790, the First Baptist Church of Lexington, Kentucky, was organized as the first African American Baptist church west of the Allegheny Mountains. The first pastor of the church was Reverend Peter Duerett, also known as "Brother Captain," who was born of slave parents in Caroline County, Virginia, in 1733. The owner of his parents decided to move to Kentucky and, desiring not to separate the wife from the husband, traded another slave for "Brother Captain" and brought them with him to Kentucky.[67] Among other historic Baptist churches organized during the early westward expansion of separated churches were: The Colored Baptist Church later known as the First Colored Baptist Church in Louisville, Kentucky; the Fifth Street Baptist Church organized in 1845; the First Baptist Church in Frankfort, Kentucky organized in 1833; First Baptist Church, Eminence, Kentucky, organized in 1865; the First Baptist Church, Danville, Kentucky, organized in 1846; the First Baptist Church, Versailles, Kentucky, organized in 1853; the Mt. Gilead Baptist Church, Fayette County, Kentucky, organized in 1790; the Second Baptist Church, Mays Lick, Kentucky, organized in 1788; and the First Baptist Church, Covington, Kentucky, organized In 1864.

The First African Baptist Church in St. Louis, Missouri, was the beginning of the separate African Baptist movement in Missouri, being founded in 1825 by Reverend John Berry Meachum who was born of slave parents. His father was a Baptist preacher, but the religious status of his mother is not known. Probably, she was influenced by the religious life of her husband. Without doubt, Reverend John Berry Meachum was nurtured by the religion of his father. During his early life, Reverend Meachum developed several employment skills, such as carpenter, cabinet maker, and cooper.

His master decided to migrate to the West, seeking greater economic opportunities and brought the highly skilled slave laborer with him to Kentucky. While in Kentucky, young John earned sufficient funds to purchase his freedom and the freedom of his father. Shortly, he married a slave woman and started a family. He was not willing to be separated from his wife when her master decided to move to St. Louis. Hence, he also moved to St. Louis in 1815. Early after his arrival, he was able to purchase the freedom of his wife and children.

While actively pursuing his regular employment, Meachum met two white Baptist missionaries, Mason Peck and John Welch, who encouraged him to work with them among the African Americans in St. Louis. They were able to open a Sunday school in the village of St. Louis, which soon increased from fourteen to ninety students. The students were taught to read, Bible lessons, and had worship experiences. By 1825, these students were organized into a religious group under the leadership of John Berry Meachum. However, the social expectations of the time required the oversight of a white man, and this was fulfilled by John Peck. In 1825, he was ordained and organized the group into the First African Baptist Church of St. Louis. In 1827, the church occupied its first meeting house located at Third and Almond Street.

While developing the First African Baptist Church, Reverend Meachum continued his labors to help slaves to become free. In 1836, he purchased about twenty slaves and trained them in good employment skills. His purpose was not ownership of the slaves but to prepare them to gain their freedom. Soon they were able to purchase their freedom and worked with Reverend Meachum in the shipping business on a steamboat.

His educational ministry was hampered by the Missouri law which prohibited the instruction of slaves. In order to circumvent the law, Reverend Meachum held his school activities in the basement of the First African Baptist Church. However, the local authorities discovered the basement school, disrupted its operation, and threaten to jail him if he continued to evade the law. Consequently, he decided to equip one of his boats with a library and anchored it in the middle of the Mississippi River, which was federal property beyond Missouri jurisdiction. He provided free ferry transportation for needy slave and free youths to attend the "Freedom School" on the steamboat. [68]

In 1846, a group of members of the First African Baptist Church withdrew and organized the Second African Baptist Church of St. Louis. The church later became known as the Central Baptist Church. The new church was under the leadership of Reverends Richard Sneether and J.R. Anderson, two former students of Reverend Meacheum's Freedom School. On October 24, the new mission was formally set apart as a regular Baptist church. The Second Baptist Church opened with twenty-three charter members.[69]

The African American Baptists of Minnesota organized their first church in 1863. The Pilgrim Baptist Church became the oldest and largest church of the race in Minnesota. It had its inception when Robert T. Hickman, a slave, was licensed as a preacher. He and about fifty other slaves escaped by way of the Underground Railroad, settled in St. Paul, and organized the church.[70]

In 1867, the Pleasant Green Baptist Church was organized in Kansas City. It was founded by a group of southern migrants who arrived prior to the development of heavy industry in the area. The first pastor of the church was Reverend I. H. Brown, who led the members in worship services in a small building which was once an ice house. The church later erected a large frame building. Packing house workers and their families made up the majority of the membership. In 1892, Reverend George McNeal was elected the new pastor, and he led the church to construct a new building at Fourth and Oakland Streets.[71]

A key factor in the expansion of African American Baptists in the West was the organization of the Baptist General Association of the Western States and Territories, organized in 1873. It facilitated the penetration of independent ideas among increasing numbers of African Americans in the West. In 1874, the Jefferson City Colored Baptists hosted the General Baptist Colored Convention of Missouri, Kansas, and adjoining states and territories. That convention was held with its objective being, "the evangelization of the colored people of the west, and taking measures toward their education." Delegates were drawn from a wide range of associations as indicated in the statistical report provided at the Pleasant Green Baptist Church, Kansas City, Missouri, September 21, 1887. States represented were California, Colorado, Illinois, Indiana, Iowa, Kansas, Michigan, Minnesota, Nebraska, Ohio, Wyoming, and the province of Ontario.[72]

To be sure, the westward movement of African American Baptists continued to advance slowly into other areas of the West. It gained tremendous momentum after the Civil War. In fact, the end of the war marked the beginnings of the rapid expansion of African American churches throughout the nation.

The A.M.E. Zion Church Expansion in the West

African American Methodists were early in the westward movement of establishing separate churches. For example, the opening of the Good Tidings Church in Omaha, Nebraska, was the first launching of the AME Zion church in Nebraska. In 1881, the first AME Zion church was organized in Arkansas. The first AME church in Cincinnati, Ohio, was the St. John AME Zion Church, followed by the organization of the St. James AME Zion Church.

The African Methodist Episcopal Zion Church reached California as early as the 1880s. In 1887, the First African Methodist Episcopal Zion Church, later called The First Zion Cathedral, was organized in Los Angeles under the leadership of Reverend Tillman Brown who came from San Francisco to organize a mission in the city. The church moved to several places before a new structure was built on Pico and Paloma Streets, and the cornerstone was laid in 1906. Initially, the African Methodist Episcopal Zion Church movement was little more than an experiment in California. The denomination had only three churches in the state, namely, "Big Zion" in San Francisco and two small missions in San Jose and Pasa Robles, California.[73]

The A.M.E. Church Expansion in the West

In 1864, the St. James African Methodist Episcopal Church of Minneapolis, Minnesota, was organized as the first African American church of any denomination in the Northwest area. The Native American Sioux were living in the region when the first whites arrived in the 1600s. French fur traders and missionaries settled the area. At various times, parts of Minnesota were held by France, Spain, and Britain. Some of Minnesota became part of the United States after the American Revolution; the rest followed with the Louisiana Purchase.

In 1851 the Sioux were forced to sign treaties that opened most of Minnesota to whites, enabling them to form growing settlements. In 1858, Minnesota became a state. By that time, sufficient numbers of African Americans were in the area to form an independent church movement.

In 1847, the Quinn Chapel African Methodist Episcopal Church was organized as the first African American church in Chicago. The church was named in honor of Reverend Paul Quinn, who was the primary moving force for the expansion of the African Methodist Episcopal Church in the West. Born in India, he came to the Unites States, joined the AME Church and became a missionary and circuit rider for the denomination. In the context of a hostile environment, he planted churches in territories such as St. Louis, Louisville, Cincinnati, and other parts of the West. Reverend Quinn was challenged by Morris Brown to "go west and build up the Church." In 1840, he was selected by the General Conference to be a missionary to the section West of Ohio. The subsequent General Conference of 1844 elected him a bishop after hearing his report showing tremendous success in the organization of forty-seven churches.[74]

The African Methodist Episcopal Church began in Indianapolis with the organization of the Bethel AME Church in the downtown district. The church, located at 414 W. Vermont Street, adjacent to the revitalized Central Canal that dates back to the pre-Civil War era. The congregation met in various sites until the current church was constructed in 1867. It was founded in 1836 by William Quinn as Indianapolis Station A.M.E. Church, known as Bethel A.M.E. Church later in the nineteenth century. It was active in the Underground Railroad movement for assisting slaves in their passage to freedom in Canada. Bethel was the first African American church in the city of Indianapolis, owned and operated by and for African Americans.[75]

The First African Methodist Church in Kansas City, Kansas, located in the junction of the Missouri and Kansas Rivers, was organized in 1859, the same year the city was incorporated. Interestingly enough, the African American Methodist and Baptist movements were jointly founded in Kansas City. The First AME Church and First Baptist Church had their joint beginnings in the small Indian village of Wyandotte populated by some six hundred Wyandotte Indians who had migrated to Kansas from Ohio. The Indians gave refuge to three African American families who had come from the South. Through the kindness of the Indians, they were able to sustain themselves when Kansas Territory was coming into statehood. Native Americans inhabited the region long before the first white settlers arrived. Gold-seeking Spaniards were the first Europeans to enter the area in 1541; in the late 1600s French explorer claimed the land. The United States acquired most of Kansas as part of the Louisiana Purchase in 1803. In the mid-1880s, the nationwide debate over slavery led to a series of disturbances and killings that earned the territory the nickname of "Bleeding Kansas." In 1854, a bill passed the United States Congress to establish the territories of Nebraska and Kansas. In 1861, Kansas became a state, supporting the Union cause during the Civil War.

Two ministers—Reverend Joe Strater, a Baptist; and Reverend Buchanan, a Methodist—gathered the African American families together and held prayer meetings in their homes beginning with Dinah Smith who lived near the edge of the Indian village later identified as the southwest corner of Fifth Street and State Avenue where an historical monument was jointly erected. This small group of worshippers eventually grew in numbers and separated in 1864 into the Baptist and Methodist churches.[76] Subsequently, the Allen Chapel AME Church in Salina, Kansas, was founded in 1882.

A similar story of African American church expansion took place in Kansas City, Missouri, with the founding of a Baptist and a Methodist church. Like Kansas, Native Americans lived in Missouri long before the first white French explorers Marquette and Joliet arrived in 1673. France claimed the entire Mississippi Valley after La Salle's voyage down the river in 1682. The United States acquired the area in the 1803 Louisiana Purchase. In 1812, Congress created the Missouri Territory. By 1815, fighting between Indians and settlers ended in treaties that followed further white settlements. Most new settlers were slave owners from the South, which caused problems when Missouri requested statehood. After three years of controversy, the Missouri Compromise of 1820 allowed Missouri to enter the Union as a slave state in 1821. During the Civil War, bitter fighting and division took place in the state.

In the context of the aftermath of tremendous tensions, a small group of African American Christian worshipper met from house to house in an area known as Straggler's Camp, located on the south bank of the Missouri River with the presence of Reverend Clark Moore, a local Baptist preacher from Leavenworth, Kansas; and Reverend John Loving, a Methodist preacher from Quindaro, Kansas. The two preachers held an organizational meeting at the camp in October of 1863. Reverend Moore gave each convert the opportunity to express choice of denominational preference during night worship experiences. Out of this choice was born a Baptist and a Methodist church in Kansas City, Missouri, namely, the Allen Chapel AME Church and the Second Baptist Church.[77]

The St. John AME Church was the first organized church for African Americans in Nebraska. It was founded in 1865 in North Omaha. The first pastor of the church was Reverend W.T. Osborn, who also was the first African American minister in Nebraska. The first meeting was held in a private residence on Capital Avenue and Ninth Street in downtown Omaha. After worshipping there for a brief period of time, the congregation moved to Douglas and 15th Streets until the summer of 1865. Afterwards, it located on 22nd Street in Omaha.[78]

Union Bethel AME Church of Great Falls, Montana, was one of the first and longest used church buildings for African Americans in Montana. Montana, a state in the then-northwestern United States, was not admitted as a state into the Union until 1889. Initially, it was the home of many Native American tribes before the arrival of whites. The Lewis and Clark expedition of 1803-06 was the first recorded visit by whites in the area. The discovery of gold at Gold Creek in 1852 swelled the white population, as well as lawlessness. To better control the area, Congress created the Montana Territory in 1864. Conflict between whites and Indians peaked in the 1870's; "Custer's Last Stand" was fought at Montana's Little Bighorn River in 1876.

The "Providential Manifest Destiny" of African Methodism reached Washington with the ministry of a young minister, Reverend A.M. Taylor, who was sent out to explore the possibility of a church in Tacoma, Washington in 1826. Initially, he established a class, then a prayer meeting, which met in an upstairs room in a building at 14th and Tacoma Avenue. Later, a room on the ground floor was secured, and here the society met and worshipped until the body was properly organized as a church. The first property was located at the southwest t corner of G Street and 14th. Organized in 1889, the church became known as the Allen African Methodist Episcopal Church.[79]

The Westward Spread of the Roman Catholic Church

The Roman Catholic presence in the West predates that of Protestants. Roman Catholic explorers, both white and African American, came to various western regions at very early dates. John Hope Franklin said:

> Africans came as explorers, servants, and slaves.... As the Spanish and Portuguese moved into the interior of North America, Negroes assisted

in the undertakings. They were with [Hernando de] Alarcon and [Francisco Vazquez de] Coronado in the Conquest of New Mexico. They accompanied Narvaez on his expedition of 1525 and were with Cabeza de Vaca in the exploration of the southwest part of the present United States. One of the outstanding Negro explorers was Estevanico, who opened up New Mexico and Arizona for the Spaniards.... Negroes were with the French in their exploration of the New World. In the Canadian expeditions, Negroes were with the Jesuit missionaries. When the great conquest of the Mississippi Valley was undertaken by the French in the seventeenth century, Negroes constituted a substantial portion of the pioneers who settled in the region.[80]

Unfortunately, those early settlers made no attempts to establish Christian churches in the West.

To be sure, the Roman Catholic Church experienced tremendous difficulties in its attempt to be effective in the conversion of African Americans outside Maryland and Louisiana. They encountered prejudice and sometimes violence from the majority Protestant settlers. Religious persecution particularly in Maryland caused African Americans to settle in the Atlantic seaboard and Kentucky. Nathaniel E. Green remarked:

> We find the first black Catholics coming into Kentucky, prior to statehood, around 1785. This was during a time when the population was increasing in the Kentucky area at a fantastic rate. These pioneers came from the Carolinas, Pennsylvania, Virginia, and Maryland to settle in Kentucky, bringing with them some slaves. Most of them were [of] Scottish, Irish, English, German, and French lineage. Blacks, who were Catholics, came to Kentucky from Maryland, primarily with their masters who were fleeing religious persecution there.[81]

Beginning in 1774, there were several settlements of Catholics who sought to escape the intolerable conditions in Maryland—at Pottinger's Creek, Harden's Creek, Bardstown, and Froman's Creek. Many of these settlers brought slaves with them to Kentucky. Some of the Catholic bishops were instrumental in advancing missionary work among the slaves. Father Charles Nerinckx was the founder of the sisterhood of The Little Society of the Friends of Mary, at the Foot of the Cross, a community of nuns which was the first attempt at sisterhood, and who opened a school at Loretto, Kentucky, which became an asylum "for old age, and decrepit and useless slaves."[82] In 1869, St. Augustine's Roman Catholic Church, under the pastorate of Father John L. Spalding, later Bishop of Peoria, was erected for the African American Catholics in Kentucky.[83]

Nathaniel E. Green also cited an account from Webb's book entitled *Catholicity in Kentucky*, regarding early Catholic settlements in the area of Bardstown: "One such settlement was an Irish group at lower Cox's Creek, afterwards better known as Fairfield, about seven miles from Bardstown. This group has been there almost from the beginning of the century. The Celtic tongue was almost exclusively spoken by the families of the colonies. He tells in a footnote of the first black child brought to the settlement. "The first slave property to come into the colony is said to have been a Negro boy-child of five years of age, bought by a Mr. Tuell at a public sale of an insolvent debtor's estate. In connection with this Negro boy, I remember to have heard an amusing anecdote related by the late Daniel Dwyer Sr., at the time, nearly half a century ago (around 1834), a leading grocer in Louisville. I was his guest and seated at his own table when he related the incident: "These Irish settlers on Cox's Creek," said Mr. Dwyer, "had been my customers for many years. It pleased them to deal with a countryman who could speak their own mother tongue, Patrick Tuell by name, who bought of me a pretty large bill of goods. His instructions were that the goods should be delivered to his Negro wagoner, who would call for them the following morning. Since you must have observed it, Mr. Webb, I need not tell you that what is known as the brogue of my country is in my case ineradicable. Though it is something of which I am not ashamed, and have no right to be ashamed, I am not a little sensitive to this mimicry by those who have it not. Well, on the following morning after I had closed my business transaction with Mr. Tuell, a Negro fellow, some twenty years of age, entered the store, and with as honest a Tipperary brogue as ever fell from tongue, asked for his "master's groceries." I had but one idea, and that was, that black rascal was trying to imitate my own manner of speech. Picking up an axe-helve, I made after him, and he, frightened at my demonstrative attitude, backed out of the store and leaped into the wagon that was standing in the middle of the street.

Turning to me before he could reach the saddle horse of his team, with a most piteous look, he asked, in native Irish, what he had done to offend me. I was utterly confounded, you may be sure, and the weapon I held dropped to the pavement as from a nerveless hand. Questioning the boy, I found that he had been brought up from childhood in his master's family, where he had only naturally contracted the brogue which I had regarded as mere mimicry, but had learned with the other children, to understand and speak the Celtic of the family's daily intercommunication.[84]

It was not uncommon for a slave to speak languages other than English.

After emancipation at the end of the Civil War, many African Americans spread westward. When they came to realize that the promised "forty acres and a mule" was not forthcoming from the government and that they had to work hard for little or no pay, African American leaders voiced the disappointment of the masses by urging migration as the solution to the ills that beset them. Beginning in 1869, there was a movement of freed African Americans from the Atlantic seaboard states. In 1871, the beginning stage of organizations were designed to facilitate their migration from the South Central states to the fertile lands of the West, especially Arkansas and Kansas. Accounts of freedom and plenty went back to inspire others to migrate. It was reported that 60,000 African Americans went to Kansas alone, with others following to Arkansas and other western states or territories. Even in 1879 the "Negro exodus" was still taking them from Louisiana. Roman Catholics were very much a part of this migration. John T. Gillard reported, "Certainly there must have been a considerable number among the 98,000 reported ready to move west from Louisiana at that time, and of whom a large number actually did go to Kansas."[85]

The number of African American Catholics in Louisiana and other parts of the country at the time of the emancipation was relatively small. Again, John T. Gillard reported in summary:

In 1810, which was the apogee of "Colored Louisiana," there were only 42,245 colored in the whole State, and from current complaints of Church authorities it is certain that not all of these were baptized Catholics. Any population figure for colored Catholics must use this as a starting point. Thenceforth the greatest increases in the State's population were American and definitely not Catholic; consequently, any increase in the number of colored Catholics would have to come from the normal source of births and limited purchases by Catholic masters. Even if by these means the number of colored Catholics doubled, it would be the utmost which could reasonably be allowed. In 1954 Archbishop Blanc placed the total Catholic population of his archdiocese, which comprised all southern Louisiana, at 95,000. At that time, the Negro formed but 40 per cent of the territory's total population, so allowing a generous proportion of more than 50 per cent of the Catholic population to be colored, it would still give only 50,000 colored Catholics for the southern part of the State where Catholics were concentrated. For the northern half of the State, 12,500 is a very liberal figure. Consequently, 62,500 colored Catholics is the top limit for any Louisiana figure based upon the facts in the situation. Adding 15,000 for the number of colored Catholics in Maryland and a generous 22,500 for the rest of the country, the highest figure that can be allowed for the number of colored Catholics in the United States at the time of the emancipation is 100,000.[86]

Hence, at no time did the African American presence in biracial Catholic churches increase dramatically enough to encourage the white Catholics to desire a separation within the church. This was also a contributing factor to the small number of separate African American Roman Catholic churches in the West as well as in other parts of the country.

In summary, a surprising number of African Americans, many who were former slaves, opted to withdraw from biracial churches and organize separate churches. Often they were opposed, especially in the South, by the white church community. Nevertheless, they prevailed in forming separated churches on the East Coast and the westward expansion to the North and Southwest.

(Endnotes)

[1] *The Post*, December 31, 1989, 4.

[2] Charles Harris Wesley, *Richard Allen, Apostle of Freedom* (Washington, D.C.: Ass. Publ., 1935), 52-53.

[3] William Douglass, *Annals of the First African Church: In the United States of America, Now Styled the African Episcopal Church of St. Thomas*, Philadelphia, in Its Connection with the Early Struggles of the Colored People to Improve Their Condition, with the Co-operation of the Friends, and Other Philanthropists, Partly Derived from the Minutes of a Beneficial Society, Established by Absalom Jones, Richard Allen and Others, in 1787, and Partly

from the Minutes of the Aforesaid Church (Philadelphia: King & Baird, Printers, 1862), 15.

4   Wesley, 12-13.

5   Ibid., 33.

6   Ibid., 47.

7   Ibid., 83.

8   George F. Bragg, *Men of Maryland* (Baltimore, MD: Church Advocate Press, 1914), 39-40.

9   Howard D. Gregg, *History of the African Methodist Episcopal Church: The Black Church in Action* (Nashville, TN: AMEC Sunday School Union, 1980), 88-89.

10 Ibid., 40.

11 Ibid., 89.

12 *Winston Salem Chronicle*, February 13, 1992, B9.

13 William Jacob Walls, *The African Methodist Episcopal Zion Church: Reality of the Black Church* (Charlotte, NC: A.M.E. Zion Publ. House, 1974), 26.

14 Ibid., 26-27.

15 Ibid., 45.

16 Ibid., 76.

17 *The Star of Zion*, May 12, 1988, 2.

18 *The Star of Zion*, February 14-28, 1990, 21.

19 *The Star of Zion*, September 23, 1982, 1.

20 *The Star of Zion*, October 1, 1987, 60.

21 *The Star of Zion*, May 13, 1982, 2.

22 *The Star of Zion*, January 8, 1987, 1-2.

23 *The Star of Zion*, May 24, 1990, 3.

24 *The Star of Zion*, October 15, 1981, 1-2.

25 *The Star of Zion*, August 10, 1989, 9.

26 *The Star of Zion*, September 28, 1989, 12.

27 William Edward Burghardt DuBois, *The Philadelphia Negro: A Social Study:*

Together with a Special Report on Domestic Services by Isabel Eaton (New York: Schocken, 1967), 17.

28 Ibid., 198.

29 J. Thomas Scharf, *History of Baltimore City and County: From Its Earliest Period to the Present Day, including Biographical Sketches of Their Representative Men* (Philadelphia: Lewis H. Everts, 1881), 579.

30 Ibid., 580.

31 Ibid., 580-581.

32 Ibid., 584.

33 Ibid.

34 *The Herald*, Savannah, Georgia, February 14, 1990, 13.

35 Andrew E. Murray, *Presbyterians and the Negro: A History* (Philadelphia, PA: Presbyterian Historical Society, 1966), 32-33.

36 Ibid., 34.

37 Ibid., 35.

38 Ibid.

39 Ibid.

40 Ibid., 37.

41 Ibid., 37-38.

42 Ibid., 28-29.

43 Ibid., 39.

44 Report of the Committee on Freedom, *Philadelphia Presbytery*, March 31, 1889, 118-124.

45 Miles Mark Fisher, *A Short History of the Baptist Denomination* (Nashville, TN: Sunday School Publishing Board, 1933), 39.

46 Carter Godwin Woodson, *The History of the Negro Church* (Washington, D.C.: Associated Publishers, 1921), 85.

47 Thad W. Tate, *The Negro in Eighteenth-century Williamsburg* (Williamsburg, VA: Colonial Williamsburg Foundation, 1965), 73.

48 First Baptist Church, Williamsburg, VA, "How Our Church Began," 12.

49 *Journal and Guide*, September 25–October 2, 1985, 8.

50 *Bay State Banner*, September 25, 1986, 7.

51 *Atlanta Daily World,* February 14, 1993, 7.

52 *The Afro-American,* September 27, 1852, 20.

53 *Birmingham World,* October 15, 1988, 1.

54 Jesse L. Boyd, *A Popular History of the Baptists in Mississippi* (Jackson, MS: Baptist Press, 1930), 30.

55 Ibid., 70.

56 Ibid.

57 William Audley Osborne, *The Segregated Covenant: Race Relations and American Catholics* (New York: Herder & Herder, 1967), 23.

58 Christopher J. Kauffmann, ed., *U.S. Catholic Historian* (Baltimore, MD: United States Catholic Historical Society, 1986), 1.

59 Annual Edition, 1924-1925 *First Colored Directory of Baltimore City,* 4.

60 *The Baltimore Afro-American,* October 8, 1988, D8.

61 *The Baltimore Afro-American,* October 22, 1988, C6.

62 Cyprian Davis, *The History of Black Catholics in the United States* (New York: Crossroad, 1992), 23.

63 Franklin, 234.

64 Emma Lou Thornbrough, *The Negro in Indiana a Study of a Minority* (Indianapolis: Indiana Historical Bureau, 1957), 157.

65 *American Baptists, the Official Newspaper of the Colored Baptists of Kentucky,* February 26, 1988.

66 Frank M. Masters, *A History of Baptists in Kentucky* (Louisville, KY: Baptist Historical Society, 1953), 342.

67 Alberta D. Shipley, ed., The History of Black Baptists in Missouri (Kansas City, MO: Missionary Baptist State Convention of Missouri, 1976), 22-23.

68 *Twin Cities Courier,* June 20, 1985, 6.

69 *The Call,* Kansas City, Missouri, August 11-17, 1989, 23.

70 Shipley, 31.

71 *The Star of Zion,* February 12, 1987, 2.

72 Gregg, 55-56.

73 *Daily Challenge,* July 22, 1991, 3.

74 *The Call,* April 13, 1989, 19.

[75] *The Call*, June 23, 1989, 10.

[776] Ibid.

[77] *Northwest Dispatch*, August 9, 1989, 11.

[78] Franklin, 46-47.

[79] Nathaniel E. Green, *The Silent Believers* (Louisville: West End Catholic Council, 1972), 19.

[80] John Thomas Gillard, *Colored Catholics in the United States: An Investigation of Catholic Activity in Behalf of the Negroes in the United States and a Survey of the Present Condition of the Colored Missions* (Baltimore: Josephite Press, 1941), 70.

[81] Ibid., 73.

[82] Green, 22-23.

[83] Ibid., 103.

[84] Ibid., 98-99.

[85] Ibid., 103.

[86] Gillard, 98-99.

Chapter 4

THE INSTITUTIONALIZATION OF AFRICAN AMERICAN CHURCHES

African American Christians followed the general flow of denominationalism among white Christians in America. For the most part, African American churches grew out of the early trend of inclusion of slaves and free African Americans in biracial churches based on the emerging style of evangelism. The decision to branch out and start separate African American churches did not negate the trend to accept the denominational exposure of the specific local churches. However, African Americans never accepted the radical denominational fever of white Christians. An ecumenical spirit prevailed among them, allowing close interdenominational cooperation. Especially in the rural South, where most of the population resided, members of specific denominations freely attended other denominational churches. This was especially true among Baptists and Methodists. Some of these churches held worship services on one or two Sundays per month. Urban churches, for the most part, held worship services every Sunday of the month. Beyond denominational lines, African Americans were accepted as authentic brothers and sisters of the Christian faith.

REV. E. C. MORRIS, D.D., HELENA, ARK. PRESIDENT, NATIONAL BAPTIST CONVENTION, MEMBER BOARD OF DIRECTORS NEGRO YOUNG PEOPLE'S CHRISTIAN AND EDUCATIONAL CONGRESS.

Bishop Christopher Rush

First Bishop of the African
Methodist Episcopal
Zion Church

Frederick Douglas

REV. W. M. ALEXANDER, D.D., BALTIMORE, MD.,
(BAPTIST.) COR. SEC'Y LOTT CAREY FOREIGN
MISSIONARY CONVENTION, TREAS-
URER N. Y. P. C. AND E. C.

MISS NANNIE H. BURROUGHS, LOUIS-
VILLE, KY., (BAPTIST.) COR. SEC'Y
NATIONAL BAPTIST WOMAN'S CON-
VENTION, MEMBER BOARD OF DI-
RECTORS N. Y. P. C. AND E. C.

WILBERFORCE UNIVERSITY, WILBERFORCE, OHIO, (A. M. E. CHURCH.)

GROUP OF COMMISSIONERS NEGRO Y. P. C. AND E. C.
1. Rev. C. F. Sams, Deland, Fla.; 2. Rev. R. J. Buckner, M. D., Birmingham, Ala.; 3. Rev. R. E. Wall, D.D., Columbia, S. C.; 4 Rev. J. L. Frazier, Mobile, Ala.; 5. Rev. D. J. Jenkins, Charleston, S. C.; 6. Prof. A. J. Wade, West Side, Miss.; 7. Prof. R. E. Huson, A.B., Selma, Ala.; 8. Dr. D. H. C. Scott, Montgomery, Ala.; 9. Rev. R. J. Daniels, Deanwood, D. C.; 10. Rev. P. W. Jefferson, D.D. Beaufort, S. C.; 11. Rev. Robt. Mitchell, D.D. Frankfort, Ky.; 12. Rev. Ezekiel Smith, New York, N. Y.; 13. Rev. F. M. Gordon, Cave Spring, Ga.; 14. Rev. G. W. Smith, Yazoo City, Miss., 15. Rev. J. E. Beard, Prosperity, S. C.; 16. Rev. E. M. Pegues, Greenwood, S. C.; 17. Mr. C. H. Bullock, Brooklyn, N. Y.; 18. Rev. J. M. Walton, Greenville, Miss.; 19. Rev. George A. Sisco, Indianapolis, Ind.; 20. Rev. D. G. McDaniel, Greenville, S. C.

The African Methodist Episcopal Church

The genesis of denominationalism among African Americans began with the organization of the African Methodist Church in 1815. By that time, the decision had been made to separate completely from the biracial Methodist Episcopal Church but to maintain the denominational doctrines and basic structure of the Church. African American Methodists never entertained any significant differences with their white denominational leaders over doctrinal, structural, or judicatory issues in principle. However, they differed radically when these issues assumed the social tendencies of racial discrimination and separatism. Almost from the beginning of the separation of members of Bethel African Methodist Church from St. George's Methodist Church, tensions soon developed between Reverend Richard Allen's members and the biracial denomination. The impetus for self-determination and freedom was early implied in a report of a committee appointed by Richard Allen to make a public statement about the new movement. On November 3, 1794, the report was published in the spirit of what Bishop Arnett described as a "Declaration of Independence" of the African Methodist Episcopal Church.[1]

In his review of this public statement, Charles H. Wesley observed: "This public statement provided for the acceptance of the rules, government, and discipline and articles of faith of the Methodist Episcopal Church. They agreed that they would continue in union with and subject to the government of the Bishops of the Methodist Episcopal Church in all ecclesiastical affairs except in the right to the church property."[2]

Richard Allen
-episcopalarchives.org

The trustees of the separate church were to be given control of all temporal matters. The internal affairs and property issues drove the new movement toward complete separation. Again, Richard Allen led the Bethel movement to seek legal independence by incorporation of the "Trustees and members of the African Methodist Episcopal Church called Bethel Church." On August 23, 1796, they applied to the attorney general and the Supreme Court of Pennsylvania for the issuance of Articles of Association under the incorporation laws of the state. With the legal incorporation of the Bethel Church, the road to larger independence was paved. Nevertheless, two other crucial issues had to be resolved regarding the actual ownership of church property and the control of the pulpit at the Bethel Church. By 1805, these issues grew into heated controversy resulting in a unanimous vote on the part of Bethel's membership to seek an amendment to the charter. On March 24, 1807, the so-called "African Supplement" legally amended the charter providing that "while the Elder of the Methodist Episcopal Church could nominate a person to preach at Bethel, this could be done only with the agreement of a majority of the trustees, and any nomination made without their concurrence was to be regarded as void."[3] Also, the ownership of the property was granted to the Bethel Church.

Two elders from the Methodist Episcopal Church decided to test the charter amendment regarding the control of the Bethel Church. In 1813, Rev. Robert R. Roberts insisted on preaching and taking charge of Bethel. When advised that he should try to negotiate with the congregation, he replied that he "did not come to consult with Richard Allen or the trustees but to notify the congregation that on the next Sabbath he would be present and take charge."[4] Upon his arrival, the congregation prevented him from entering the pulpit. Again on December 31, 1815, another elder from St. George's Church made a similar attempt but was rejected by the Bethel members. He did not accept the reaction of Bethel's members and decided on January 1, 1816, to apply to the Supreme Court of the state for a writ of mandamus to restore the Bethel pulpit to him. The attorneys for the Bethel Church pleaded to the court "that neither Burch nor any other elder of the Methodist Episcopal Church had any right to the pulpit contrary to the wishes of the congregation, and that any grant of a right to him could be withdrawn at their pleasure."[5] The court decided in favor of the Bethel Church. Bishop Asbury saw clearly the implications of their successful incorporation. He remarked in his journal, "The Africans of this town desire a church which, in temporals, shall be altogether under their direction, and ask greater privileges than the white stewards and trustees ever had a right to claim."[6] Hence, the emerging 1816 independent denominational movement was no surprise to the white Methodist leadership.

On April 9, 1816, a group of sixteen African American Methodists met in Philadelphia to officially organize the African Methodist Episcopal Church. The leading figures were Richard Allen, Daniel Coker, and Stephen Hill. George F. Bragg remarked that Daniel Coker was really the "brain" of the organizational meeting who provided the intellectual components for the new denomination.[7] The group adopted the following resolution for the establishment of the connectional movement: "Resolved, that the people of Philadelphia, Baltimore, and other places who may unite with them shall become one body under the style of the African Methodist Church of the United States of America and that the book of Discipline of the Methodist Episcopal Church be adopted as our Discipline until further orders, except that portion relating to Presiding Elders."[8] Daniel Coker was elected as bishop of the new denomination immediately following its formation. This gave him the distinction of being the first African American in America to be elected a bishop. However, Coker declined the election on the next day, paving the way for Richard Allen to become bishop of the African Methodist Episcopal Church. According to oral tradition, color consciousness played a role in Daniel Coker's decision. Bishop Daniel A. Payne remarked:

> "On the 9th of April, 1816, an election took place for bishop, and Daniel Coker was elected on account of his superior education and talents. An objection was immediately made by the pure blacks, led by Jonathan Tudas, a friend in council with Richard Allen. This objection was on account of his color, his mother being an English woman and his father a pure African. Daniel Coker, being a man of high feeling, resigned on the spot in favor of Richard Allen…."[9]

The first Annual Conference of the African Methodist Episcopal Church was held at Bethel African Methodist Episcopal Church in Baltimore, Maryland, in 1817. One year after the new denomination was organized, delegates from Philadelphia, Baltimore, and other areas on April 12, 1817, met in the home of Samuel Williams to open the conference. Bishop Richard Allen presided over this Baltimore Annual Conference. The Discipline of 1817 recorded that "on April 11, 1816, Richard Allen was solemnly set apart for the Episcopal office by prayer, and the imposition of the hands of five regularly ordained ministers, at which time the general convention held in Philadelphia did unanimously receive the said Bishop Allen as their Bishop, being fully satisfied of the validity of his Episcopal ordination."[10] Hence, Richard Allen came to Baltimore bearing the full authority of Bishop. The Discipline of 1817 also made provisions for the election of future bishops and the establishment of a General Conference. The authority to publish materials, such as the Discipline, Minutes, and other official documents was delegated to Bishop Allen. Also, he was given the authority of ordination, appointment of pastors and missionaries, and the general episcopal rights of a bishop. Accordingly, he ordained Rev. Edward Waters, a future pastor of the Bethel Church of Baltimore, as a deacon. Later, Reverend Waters became the third bishop of the African Methodist Episcopal Church.

The 1817 conference in Baltimore was not really a general conference of the African Methodist Episcopal Church. It did assume similar authority to a general conference. Actually, the first general conference of the new denomination was held in Philadelphia on July 9, 1820. Bishop Allen presided at this conference, which he referred to as a convention. He delivered the opening address of the conference in which he enumerated the administrative challenges of the denomination, namely, the revision of the Discipline; the establishment of the duties and privileges of the bishop, elders, and deacons; and the powers of the General Conference. These topics were fully evaluated during the five-day session of the conference. One major decision at the conference was the passing of a provision which denied membership to any slaveholder, including the few African Americans who held slaves. This principle had already been stated in the 1817 Discipline that no person would be received into the denomination "as a member, who is a slaveholder, and any who are now members, that have slaves and refuse to emancipate them after notification being given by the preacher having charge, shall be excluded."[11] Hence, the denomination committed itself to the fundamental beliefs in human freedom and self-determination by denying membership to anyone of contrary beliefs and practices. This was a radical move since most of the denomination's membership resided in slaveholding states.

After the General Conference, Bishop Allen envisioned the unification of all separated African Methodist Episcopal American churches. On August 11, 1820, Bishop Allen traveled to New York City to meet with separated African Methodist church leader with the objective of uniting them under his leadership. From 1800 until 1819 they had existed as separate from the John Street Methodist Episcopal Church in the city. However, they had remained within the biracial Methodist Episcopal denomination. By 1819, they had become uncomfortable with the episcopal restraints placed upon them by the Methodist denomination. Bishop Allen hoped to utilize this dissatisfaction to his advantage by offering them a viable option of uniting with an African American Methodist denomination. After lengthy discussions, the New York African Methodists decided not to unite with Bishop but to organize their own independent denomination.

With persistent determination, Bishop Allen called another meeting to persuade the New York group to unite under his leadership. The meeting again resulted in another failure for Bishop Allen because the representative majority of the African Methodist Episcopal Zion Church was of the opinion they desired more freedom than what was offered by him. Charles H. Wesley remarked, "They refused to recognize and to accept him as their bishop and to place themselves under his government. Several of the members who were present agreed to go with him. Among them was a man of influence named William Miller. Through his efforts, part of the membership of Asbury Church joined in forming an African Methodist Episcopal church in New York City."[12]

In 1824, the General Conference of the African Methodist Church met in Philadelphia, Pennsylvania. The responsibilities of Bishop Allen had increased to point that he needed someone to assist him. Hence, the conference elected Reverend Jacob Matthews as Assistant Bishop. Among the principle challenges of the two episcopal leaders were to make plans for the expansion of the denomination into new territories and the development of administrative policies for effective denominationalism. With limited time and resources, they aggressively sought to meet the challenges set before them. Bishop Allen envisioned the leadership of the denomination as an extension of his pastoral role at Bethel. He had to share his time and energy with his growing church as well as the new emerging denomination. As bishop, he was given the broad responsibility of serving as the chief executive officer and representative of the entire denomination. Hence, the assistance of Reverend Jacob Mathews was indispensable for any substantial success of Bishop Allen's episcopal leadership. Both men worked untiringly to meet the challenging tasks of leadership.

To be sure, the denominational development of the African Methodist Episcopal Church was a gradual process. With the adoption of the episcopal form of church governance, a hagiocracy emerged ranging from the authority of the bishops, General Conferences, and Annual Conferences. Among the early conferences were the Baltimore Annual Conference, organized at Bethel in 1817; the Philadelphia Conference, organized in 1816; the New York Conference, organized in 1822; the New England Conference, organized in 1852; the Ohio Conference, organized in 1830; the Canada Conference, organized in 1840; the Indiana Conference, organized in 1840; the South Carolina Conference, organized in 1865; and the Kansas Conference, organized in 1875; District Conferences (the General Conference of 1852 established the first three Episcopal districts and instituted the Bishop's Council); Quarterly Conferences; and Church Conferences. The Book of Discipline specified the functions and authority of the conferences, human resources, and departments. Among the leading human resources were bishops, presiding elders, itinerants, department presidents, missionaries, missionary bishops with authority limited to their mission territory, presidents of educational institutions, and pastors, deacons, deaconesses, and trustees of local churches.

Bishop M.H. Davis, in his episcopal address to the General Conference of 1944, offered a rather detailed account of the structure and operation of the African Methodist Episcopal Church. He noted, with developmental notes on each, the *Christian Recorder*, the Missionary Department, the Sunday School Union, the Finance Department, Church Extension Society, *Southern Christian Recorder*, *Western Recorder*, and the *African Methodist Episcopal Review*.

In 1852, the Christian Recorder was established in Philadelphia by authority of the General Conference meeting in New York. Among some of its earliest editors were Bishop J.P. Campbell, Bishop B.T. Tanner, and Bishop B.F. Lee. The publication was under the control of the Publication Board with a wide circulation and annual subscriber's list of 5,500. The *Christian Recorder* grew out of the initial publication of *African Methodist Episcopal Church Magazine*, May 1841, with George Hogarth of Brooklyn, New York, serving as editor. In order to increase its circulation, the editor recommended that new subscriptions be budgeted annually to several pastors and be reported to their annual conferences along with other items.

During the Philadelphia Conference of 1855, the Committee on Missions recommended that the denomination establish a Home and Foreign Missionary Society with the purpose of sending missionaries to Africa and other parts of the world. Bishop Davis noted the complexity experienced by the newly named Board of Missions, revealing the political problems of serving under foreign governments. In 1944, the denomination had missionary ministries established in North America, South America, the West Indies, the West Coast, and South America.

With reference to the development of the Sunday School Union, Bishop M. H. Davis noted:

"The Sunday School Union of the African Methodist Episcopal Church has had an interesting history. It was first organized by the late Bishop

C.S. Smith and in securing a charter there was a serious omission that enabled one of his successors to revise that charter and make the Board of Managers self-perpetuating. This cost the African Methodist Episcopal Church more than $30,000.00 and wrought unpleasant criticism to those who entered into litigation to have the charter changed. This also brought the department back under the control of the African Methodist Episcopal Church, as it should be."[13]

Regarding the Financial Department, Bishop Davis observed, "The Financial Department is among the oldest in the African Methodist Episcopal Church. In matters of finance it ranks first. The department was established with a view of centralizing the funds of the General Conference in a given department and thereby, facilitating the discharge of the obligations of the connection."[14] He noted further: "Throughout all the years the Financial Department has carried forward its obligations in a most business-like manner. Business procedure has been accentuated since the adjournment of the General Conference that ordered and directed that the Financial Department should employ a certified public accountant to audit the books and accounts of this department."[15] Both the Pension Department and the Church Extension Society operated under the auspices of the Finance Department.

Through the years, the African Methodist Episcopal Church has developed as a premier religious organization among African Americans. Its structure, leadership, and church growth strategies have advanced the denomination toward a world leadership position in missions, evangelism, education, and social action for the race. Lincoln and Mamiya summarized the advancement of the denomination:

> "The supreme legislative body of the A.M.E. Church at the national level is the General Conference, which meets once every four years. Participants include the bishops, general officers, heads of colleges and seminaries, armed forces' chaplains, and ministerial and lay delegates from all the annual conferences. The General Conference conducts its business through some 30 committees and is responsible for electing general officers (for example, editors, publishers, secretaries of departments, treasurer, historiographer), establishing the budget, receiving reports from various agencies, determining organizational structures and regulations, assessing the work of the bishops, and electing new bishops.

"Below the General Conference are four other major denominational divisions. The Council of Bishops constitutes the executive branch of the church, assuming oversight of superintendence of the entire church between quadrennial sessions of the General Conference. A judicial council functions as an appellate court to hear appeals from any decision affecting any member or minister within the church. The Board of Trustees is responsible for church property. The budget and programs of the church are administered by the General Board whose eleven vice presidents each chair one of the standing commissions: Finance and Statistics, Pensions, Publications, Minimum Salary, Church Extension and Evangelism, Missions, Higher Education, Research and Development, Christian Education, Social Action, and the Lay Commission. Each commission in turn is responsible for one or more departments that actually implement the programs."[16]

The African Methodist Episcopal Zion Church

The African Methodist Episcopal Zion Church evolved from a small church in New York envisioned by Peter Williams in 1796 as an African chapel which was organized and incorporated as the Zion Church on September 8, 1800. In 1801, the name of the church became "The African Methodist Episcopal Church in New York City." James Varick was given the credit as the principle founder. The numbers of independent minded African American Methodists grew, and other churches were organized in Long Island; New Haven, Connecticut; New Jersey; Philadelphia; and eastern Pennsylvania. After many struggles in their relationship with the biracial Methodist Episcopal Church, these churches decided to organize an independent denomination in 1820. The founders' address to the members of the African Methodist Episcopal in America established the rationale for the new emerging denomination:

"BELOVED BRETHREN: We think it proper to state briefly that, after due consideration, the Official Members of the African Methodist Episcopal Zion and Asbury Churches in the City of New York have been led to conclude that such was the relation in which we stood to the white Bishops and Conference, relative to the ecclesiastical government of the African Methodist Church or Society in America, so long as we remain in that situation our Preachers would never be able to enjoy these privileges which the Discipline of the white Church holds to all its Members that are called to preach, inconsequence of the limited access our brethren had to those privileges, and particularly in consequence of the difference of color. We have been led also to conclude that the usefulness of our Preachers has been very much hindered, and our brethren in general have been deprived of those blessings which Almighty God may have designed to grant them, through the means of those Preachers whom He has from time to time raised up from among them, because there has been no means adopted by the said Bishop and Conference for our Preachers to travel through the Connection and promulgate the Gospel of our Lord Jesus Christ; and they have no access to the only source from whence they might have obtained a support, at least, while they traveled. Under these circumstances they believed that the formation of an itinerant plan and the establishment of a Conference for the African Methodist Preachers of the United States, who are not yet attached to any Conference of that nature, would be essential to the prosperity of the spiritual concerns of our colored brethren in general, and would be the means of advancing our Preachers (who are now in regular standing in connection with the white Preachers of the Methodist Episcopal Church), whenever it should be found necessary for the advancement of the Redeemer's kingdom among our brethren, to bring forward for ordination those who are called of God to preach the Gospel of our Lord, which may be done from time to time, according to the best of our judgment of the necessity thereof, and not according to the method which is natural to suppose our white brethren would pursue, to determine upon the necessity of such ordination. We are under strong impression of mind that such measures would induce many of our brethren to attend divine worship, who are yet careless about their eternal welfare, and thereby prove effective in the hands of God in the awakening and conversion of their souls to the knowledge of the truth.

"And whereas, Almighty God, in His all-wise and gracious providence, has recently offered a favorable opportunity, whereby these Societies may be regularly organized as an evangelical African Methodist Church, we have therefore resolved to embrace the said opportunity, and have agreed that the title of the Connection shall be the African Methodist Episcopal Church in America; and we have selected a form of Discipline, with a little alteration from that of our Mother Church, which selection were commended to you, for the Discipline of our Church, hoping that the great Shepherd and Bishop of souls, the all-wise and gracious God, will be pleased to approve of the above measures and grant that we may obtain and preserve those privileges which we have been heretofore deprived of; that thereby we may unite our mutual efforts for the prosperity of the Redeemer's kingdom among us, and for the encouragement of our colored brethren in the Ministry.

"Earnestly soliciting your prayers and united endeavors for the same, we remain yousr affectionate brethren and servants in the kingdom of our ever-adorable Lord.

ABRAHAM THOMPSON,

JAMES VARICK,

WILLIAM MILLER"[17]

The leadership of James Varick was affirmed in the Quadrennial Address of the bishops to the General Conference in 1892 in the following:

"The Afro-American Church is the one great developing and elevation agency, in comparison with which all others sink into insignificance. There is one name connected with this movement of which comparatively little is now said, which coming generations will rescue from the obscurity in which we have permitted it to rest. Our children's children in their search for information respecting this movement which has done so much to develop the race will find the name of James Varick, and will discover that to him is due the credit of starting a Church organization for the race. We know more of Father Rush, because our immediate predecessors were all acquainted with him and have told us more about him. We know still more about Clinton and Jones, and their praises hang upon our tongues. But we have only to read between the lines of the meager history which has come down to us to realize that the idea of a great Afro-American Church was conceived in the mind of James Varick, and that he of all the men of his day, build most wisely. His skillful hand is seen in the Act of Incorporation, drawn up in1801, which secured the independence of the Church, and yet, while it protected the Church property from the encroachments of the white bishops, he managed to hold their friendship, or at least avoid their open hostility."[18]

To be sure, James Varick cooperated with other leaders in the founding of this free African Methodist movement, but his name was elevated above the other pioneers. He was elected first bishop during the Annual Conference, according to the Discipline of the African Methodist Episcopal Zion Church, and consecrated on Sunday morning, July 30, 1822. Following his consecration as bishop he, assisted by elders Abraham Thompson and Leven Smith, ordained six deacons: Christopher Rush, James Smith, James Anderson, William Carman, Edward Johnson, and Tillman Cornish. Bishop Varick presided over the next five annual conferences of the New York Conference until his death in 1827.[19] The new denomination adapted the structure, style, and doctrines of the white Methodist Episcopal Church with minor alterations. Provisions were made for Christian freedom and self-determination beyond racial lines. However, the denomination was still faced with challenges from African Methodists who did not favor joining the new group. Accordingly, Walls noted:

> "There were those who wanted to be a Negro unit within the Methodist Church. There were still others who felt sympathy with black groups in other areas, such as the A.M.E. Bethel Church and the African Union Church of Wilmington, Del., and preferred to see a union of them all. The small faction, 61 of the 751 colored members that preferred the Mother Church withdrew and settled on remaining in the Methodist Episcopal Church."[20]

Gradually, the African Methodist Episcopal Zion denomination structured itself in terms of boards and conferences, namely, the Board of Bishops (during the initial stages called superintendents, organized in 1860 after years of strife over assistant superintendents, three bishops were elected on equality; Joseph J. Clinton, Peter Ross, and William H. Bishop), General Conference (the legislative body of the denomination, authorized to elect bishops and general officers, and assign them to their field of operation, appoint the connectional boards, and regulate all spiritual and temporal affairs of the denomination), Annual Conference, Quarterly Conference, District Conference, and Local Church Conference. The denomination recognized the importance of pastors and itinerant preachers and exhorters. These ministers were expected to be motivated by the spirit of evangelism and advance the growth of the denomination.

Initially, the New York Conference served as a General Conference. The Second Annual Conference of the denomination was the Philadelphia Conference, which convened on June 13, 1829, at Wesley Church in the city, with Bishop Christopher Russ presiding. During this conference, Bishop Russ appointed

Reverends Edward Johnson to Wesley Chapel in Philadelphia; Jacob Richardson to the charge of the Western District of Pennsylvania; and David Smith and Richard Smith as missionaries.[21] In 1845, Bishop Russ organized the New England Conference in the Elm Street Church in Harford, Connecticut. This church emerged out of a split in the African Relief Society, organized in 1827, when two groups pulled out to form the Elm Street Church (later known as the Metropolitan A.M.E. Zion Church) and a Congregational church. In 1849, the fourth conference was organized by Bishop Russ with the assistance of Bishop Galbraith, known as the Allegheny Conference, which was separated from the Philadelphia Conference. The General Conference of 1848 separated the Allegheny Conference as well as the Genesee Conference from the Philadelphia Conference.[22]

In 1849, Bishop Russ organized the Fifth Annual Conference (also initially known as the Genesee Conference), separating from the New York Conference. Its first session was held in Auburn, New York. When the conference was organized there were twelve preachers and two lay delegates in attendance. At that time, the African American population was small in the region. The name was changed to Western New York Conference in 1897, while Bishop A. Walters presided.[23] Other early conferences were organized. The Canada-Michigan Conference, for example, was to serve the mission work in Canada and the expansion of the denomination in Michigan. The conference was later named the Michigan Conference, and the Canadian churches were connected with the New York Conference. In 1859, the Southern Conference was organized in Washington, D. C., later renamed the Baltimore Conference until in 1872 its name was again changed to the Philadelphia and Baltimore Conference.[24] In 1864, Bishop Joseph Jackson Clinton organized the North Carolina Conference. There were only twelve members of the conference including the bishop. It initial session served similar to a school where men were taught how to plant churches in other parts of the state.

The denomination experienced rapid church growth in North Carolina following the Civil War. In 1882, the Central North Carolina Conference had 100 ministers and 20,000 members. From North Carolina, the work of the denomination expanded to other areas of the South. Bishop Hood reported that four conferences were:

> "…set off by the North Carolina Conference, as follows: The Tennessee, Virginia, South Carolina, and Central North Carolina. Out of the

Central North Carolina the Western North Carolina has been formed; out of the South Carolina the Palmetto has been formed; and out of the Tennessee Conference the West Tennessee and Mississippi and the East Tennessee, Virginia, and North Carolina; and out of the West Tennessee and Mississippi, the South Mississippi, making in all nine Conferences that have sprung from the North Carolina Conference."[25]

In 1865, Bishop J.J. Clinton organized the Louisiana Conference with fifteen preachers. The earlier work in the area had been personally superintended largely by the Bishop. Soon after Bishop Clinton organized the North Carolina Conference, he went by sea to New Orleans which, like New Berne, had been captured by the Federal forces.[26] It was the last conference of the denomination formed in the South before the end of the Civil War.

The organization of the Kentucky Conference not only reflected denominational growth but also tensions within African Methodism. It was organized in 1866 by Bishop Sampson D. Talbot in the Center Street Church in Louisville, Kentucky. At the first session of the conference, there were 1,841 members present. By the second conference session the membership had increased to 3,253. However, Bishop Hood reported that "an unfortunate matter at the third session of the Conference created schism, which, together with some trouble in Tennessee and Georgia, resulted in the formation of the Colored Methodist Episcopal Church."[27] The conflicts were of such significance that Bishop Hood recorded the following detailed report furnished by Reverend E. H. Curry:

"A SKETCH OF THE ORGANIZATION OF THE KENTUCKY ANNUAL CONFERENCE

The Kentucky Annual Conference was organized June 6, 1866, in Center Street Church, in the city of Louisville and the State of Kentucky, by Right Rev. Sampson Talbot, General Superintendent of the African Methodist Episcopal Zion Connection, assisted by Superintendent Joseph J. Clinton. The membership of the Conference was made up of men of no experience in the itinerant work, and without a basic knowledge of the polity of the Church. They were sent to their appointments in many places without a church edifice, nay, without members; nevertheless, they went trusting in God for success. The superintendent left and was seen no more until the next Annual Conference, and the only guides left to instruct the Conference were Rev. W. F. Butler and Rev. W.H. Miles.

The latter was appointed general missionary and supported from Center Street Church by the Daughter of Conference, or least in part.

At the reassembling of the second Annual Conference William Haywood, Bishop, general superintendent, presided. Rev. W. F. Butler was removed from Center Street Church, and succeeded by Rev. W.H. Miles. Hence some feeling of unpleasantness sprang up between those two divines. The superintendent, however, left again, to be seen no more until the sitting of the third Annual Conference, at which Rev. J.W. Loguen, general superintendent, presided. Then began the scene of trouble in the Conference, and the Rev. W.H. Miles tendered his resignation, which was finally received. This created quite a feeling, and many of the leading men of the higher rank left, until the Conference was left with only seven elders all told, and many of the churches followed in rapid succession; yet there were a few who dared to hold on to Zion, and continued to struggle against all opposition. Rev. Richard Bridwell, Samuel Elliott, Rev. A. Bunch, Samuel Shurman, Leroy Brannon, J. B. Stansbury, William T. Biddle, with one other man, were all the elders left in the Kentucky Conference. One year later showed a gradual decline in both churches and communicants. This rigor in the Conference discouraged the churches and ministers, and all the more because the ministers being returned to their former charges it was easy for them to confuse the minds of the people by trying to carry them into the Colored Methodist Episcopal Church, and that by the same men who led them into the Zion Connection at a date still fresh in their memory.

One year later, reports showed the following churches lost: Falmouth, Ky.; Millersburg, Ky.; Carrollton, Ky.; Flemingsburg, Ky.; Owingsville, Ky.; Glasgow, Ky.; Sharpsburg, Ky.; Elkton, Ky.; Frankfort, Ky.; Burkesville, Ky.; Greensburg, Ky.; with Center Street Church of Louisville, Ky. But there were a faithful few who still stood up for Zion.

The next event worthy of special mention was the appointment of Right Rev. S.T. Jones, D.D., to the Third Episcopal District, which gave new life and impulse to the Kentucky Conference. The work settled to a firmer base during the twelve consecutive years of his administration, not-withstanding there was some dissatisfaction in the Board of Bishops and among leading men about organic union with the Methodist Episcopal Church, and the Conference being told by those in authority that the union would be consummated in the near future, it was hard for them to tell what they were. This had much to do in shaking their faith in the firmness and stability of Zion Connection. But the fight ended, and the faithful few were seen doing what they could to build up Zion. The Kentucky Conference carried the standard of Zion into Indiana, Illinois, and Missouri, and organized the Arkansas Missouri Annual Conference."[28]

The magnitude of this conflict in the Kentucky Conference reflected the general growth pains of the African Methodist Episcopal Zion Church.

Similar to the Kentucky Conference, the Tennessee Conference experienced growth pains as denominations competed for churches in pioneer regions. The conference was organized at Knoxville by Bishop J.J. Clinton. Again, Bishop Hood offered a long but informative account of the struggles of the conference:

"The Tennessee Conference was organized at Knoxville, Ten., October 6, 1868 by Bishop J.J. Clinton. The first two annual sessions were held in the above named city. Elder J.W. Loguen, who was afterward made bishop, organized the first African Methodist Episcopal Zion church in the State at Knoxville….

When Bishop S.D. Talbot took charge of the district in 1870 the African Methodist Episcopal Zion Church was the most influential church in all the territory named above. There was no opposition to our onward march. During Bishop Talbot's administration hundreds were added to the church. The bishop added, comparatively speaking, a new set of ministers to the Conference. Many of the original members had transferred, and some had joined other denominations that had been created….

Rev. James A. Zachary, Robert R. Russell, Thomas Warren, Joseph Pugh, J.P. Jay, Henry Tipson, John N. Brown, D.W. Wells, W.H. Ferguson, and James D. Rogers were among those who composed the Conference when Bishop S.T. Jones took charge in the fall of 1872.

There was no advancement during these two years in the rural districts. The larger towns held their own. When Bishop. J. W. Hood, D.D., came to the district he found the work in a dormant state. This was not without cause. Rev. D.W. Wells, with over six hundred members, had rebelled and gone out of the connection in Knoxville. The Conference had never completely recovered from the shock. Several small charges followed in the wake of the Knoxville rebellion. Bishop Hood, however, was not discouraged.... He won the confidence of both clergy and laity. The waste places of Zion began to rebuild, and in two years' time the membership nearly doubled itself, new churches sprang up, and confidence was once more established on the part of the people....

The Weekly Watchman, a Conference journal issued weekly by the Conference, is the most promising sheet in the connection aside from the Star of Zion. It was founded January 1, 1891, by Rev. W.H. Ferguson, A.M., at Athens, Tenn. The paper has had much to do with informing and molding public sentiment in favor of our Church. It was through its columns the donation that opened the Greenville High School was obtained.... The Tennessee Conference represents one hundred thousand dollars' worth of church and school property. The Conference was divided in 1892."[29]

With the end of the Civil War, the denomination organized other conferences. In 1866, Bishop J.J. Clinton organized the Virginia Conference with about twenty-five preachers present. He organized the South Carolina Conference in 1867 with the assistance of Reverends W.J. Moore, F.B. Moore, and Thomas Henderson from the North Carolina Conference. When Bishop Clinton organized the Georgia Conference, he felt confident that the denomination would prosper in the State. However, the work encountered difficulties because two other Methodist denominations exerted strong influences in key areas of the state, as the Methodist Episcopal Church held Atlanta and the African Methodist Episcopal Church held Savannah. The next year, Bishop Clinton organized the Alabama Conference in the State Street Church in Mobile, Alabama, on April 3, 1867. This conference became very large, almost the size of the North Carolina Conference. Next, Bishop Clinton organized the California Conference on Wednesday June 10, 1868. This fulfilled the denomination's "manifest destiny" evangelistic strides in the West. He organized the Florida Conference in 1869; the West Tennessee and Mississippi Conference in 1871; and the New Jersey Conference in 1874. To be sure, Bishop Clinton became well known as a great denominational organizer within the African Methodist Episcopal Zion Church.

The organization of conferences continued, especially at the close of the Civil War, as the African Methodist Episcopal Church expanded its mission of planting churches in other parts of the United States and in foreign lands. These conferences played vital roles in superintending the growing churches of the denomination. They were very influential in the decision-making process of the General Conferences. This was especially true with the rapid development of new churches in the South where the vast majority of African Americans lived.

As previously inferred, the General Conference of the denomination represents the legislative branch with the authority to elect bishops and other denominational officers, define policy, and establish boards, departments, and commissions. The operational machinery of the denomination included the Board of Bishops, 12 Episcopal Districts, 142 Annual Conferences; general officers, including a Secretary-auditor, Secretary of the Department of Finance, General Manager of the Department of Finance, General Manager of the AME Zion Publishing House, Editor of *The Star of Zion*, Editor of *The AME Zion Quarterly Review*, Connectional Officers of the Woman's Home, and Overseas Missionary Society; departments including Department of Overseas Missions and Missionary Seer, Department of Brotherhood Pensions and Ministerial Relief, Christian Education Department, Department of Church School Literature, Department of Church Extension and Home Missions, Department of Evangelism, Director of Public Affairs, Department of Health and Social Concerns, Judicial Council, and the Connectional Lay Council. To be sure, this current operational machinery evolved historically with the utilization of human, economic, and physical resources.

The Colored Methodist Episcopal Church

The genesis of the Colored Methodist Episcopal Church must be traced back to persistent ideological trends, segregation, and racism in the Methodist Episcopal Church, South. The biracial yet predominantly white Methodist Episcopal Church, South originated in 1844 when the Methodist Episcopal Church agreed at its General Conference to become a bisectional denomination. The Methodist Episcopal Church, South was formally organized at Louisville, Kentucky, in 1845. However, the northern unionists in the church were dissatisfied and declared the action unconstitutional, and when the next General Conference met in Pittsburg in 1848, they declared the act null and refused to accept the southern fraternal delegates. The two bisectional denominations fought legal battles over property, churches, and institutions. These issues greatly disturbed the African American Methodists who were faithful to the Methodist Episcopal Church in both regions of the nation. Such disturbing developments were in response to sectionalism, the slavery controversy, and the southern anti-unionists, which caused the Civil War. During the Civil War and Reconstruction, African

Americans in the South existed as separate conferences, districts, and churches within the Methodist Episcopal Church, South.

These developments created the matrix out of which the Colored Methodist Episcopal Church was born, with the General Conference being organized at Jackson, Tennessee, on December 15, 1870. The historical statement from the bishops of the denomination expressed the internal developments within the Methodist Episcopal Church, South which led to the move on the part of the African American members:

> "At the General Conference of the Methodist Episcopal Church, South, at Memphis, Tennessee, May, 1870, it was found that five Annual Conferences had been formed among us, and that an almost universal desire had been expressed on our part that we might be organized into a separate and distinct Church, which was acquiesced by the Bishops of the Methodist Episcopal Church, South, and recommended to said Conference in their address; whereupon by our request, the Bishops of the Methodist Episcopal Church, South, together with A.L. Green, Samuel Watson, Edmund W. Sehon, Thomas Whitehead, R.J. Morgan, and Thomas Taylor were appointed by said Conference to aid in organizing our General Conference at the time and place specified above.
>
> "At the succeeding sessions of our Annual Conferences, delegates were elected to attend our General Conference, in according with the Discipline of the Methodist Episcopal Church, South.
>
> It was further determined by the acts of the General Conference of the Methodist Episcopal Church, South, 1866, that should the time arrive when we should be formed into a separate and distinct organization, all property which was intended for the use and benefit of the Negro constituency of said Church, and held by the trustees of the Methodist Episcopal Church, South, should be transferred to trustees appointed by said Negro constituency, to be held forever for their use and benefit."[30]

The cooperation of the bishops of the Methodist Episcopal Church, South in facilitating the successful organization the Colored Methodist Episcopal Church, later named in 1954 the Christian Methodist Episcopal Church, was rather remarkable during such a volatile time in American history.

Leaders of the 1870 General Conference of the denomination organized several committees for defining the structure of the church: Committee on Church

Organization, Episcopacy, Discipline, Books and Periodicals, Itinerary, and Boundaries. Rev. I. H. Anderson chaired the Committee on Church Organization and made the following report:

> "Whereas the Methodist Episcopal Church in America was the name first given to the Methodist Church in the United States: and,
>
> "Whereas we are a part of that same Church, never having seceded or separated from The Church; but in the division of the Church by the General Conference in 1844 we naturally belonged to the South, and have been in that division ever since; and now, as we belong to the colored race, we simply prefix the word "colored" to the name, and for ourselves adopt the name, as we are in fact a part of the original Church, as old as any in America; therefore be it Resolved,
>
> 1. That our name be the 'Colored Methodist Episcopal Church in America.'
> 2. That while we thus claim ourselves an antiquity running as far back as any branch of the Methodist family on this side of the Atlantic Ocean, and while we claim for ourselves all that we concede to others of ecclesiastical and civil rights, we shall ever hold in grateful remembrance what the Methodist Church, South, has done for us; we shall ever cherish the kindliest feelings towards the Bishops and General Conference on giving to us all that they enjoy of religious privileges, the ordination of our deacons and elders; and at this conference our bishops will be ordained by them to the highest office known in our Church…
> 3. That we request the bishops to organize our General Conference on the basis of the Discipline of the Methodist Episcopal Church, South, in its entire doctrine, discipline, and economy, making only such verbal alterations and changes as may be necessary to conform it to our name and the peculiarities of our condition."[31]

The conference elected Rev. William Henry Miles, a reserve delegate from the Kentucky Conference; and Rev. Richard H. Vanderhorst of the Georgia Conference as the first bishops of the Colored Methodist Episcopal Church.

They were consecrated into the office of bishop by Bishops Thomas Payne and William H. McTyeire of the Methodist Episcopal Church, South.

Currently, the Christian Methodist Episcopal Church operates through eleven Episcopal Districts, nine located in the United States and two in Africa. Each of these Episcopal Districts consists of designated geographical regions presided over by a bishop elected by the General Conference. Several connectional departments under the authority of a General Secretary execute the ministries of the denomination, including Christian education, discipleship, evangelism, and missions. The official organ of the church is the *Christian Index*. The denomination has a theological school named the Phillips School of Theology operating within the Interdenominational Theological Center in Atlanta, Georgia and sponsors four liberal arts colleges, namely, Lane College in Jackson, Tennessee; Paine College in Augusta, Georgia; Miles College in Birmingham, Alabama; and Texas College in Tyler, Texas. The worldwide membership of the Church is approximately 1,000,000.

Unification Movements in African Methodism

During the initial stage of independent African American denominational development, Bishop Richard Allen of the newly formed African Methodist Episcopal Church sought the unification of African American Methodists into one denomination. He offered to provide ordination services for African American Methodist church leaders which would make them independent of the Methodist Episcopal Church. It would also allow them to be free from the encroachment of white clergy over their pulpits. As previously mentioned, however, his attempts in New York City resulted in a disappointing failure.

The first substantial overture for African American Methodist union of the African Methodist Episcopal Church and the African Methodist Episcopal Zion Church came soon after the emancipation of slaves at the twelfth session of the African Methodist Episcopal Zion General Conference in 1864. The dialogue was soon terminated "after some points of disagreement were never resolved."[32] After the failure of union between these two denominations, the African Methodist Episcopal Church turned its attention to the possible union with the Colored Methodist Episcopal Church in 1900. The idea of such union was first introduced by Rev. M. T. Jamison, the fraternal messenger to that General Conference. The General Conference responded by appointing a commission of eighteen members to study the prospect of union. In the General Conference of the Colored Methodist Episcopal Church in 1902 in Nashville, Tennessee, a similar commission was appointed. The two commissions met in Israel CME Church, in Washington, D.C. on October 7, 1902, and drew up articles of agreement to be submitted to the next two General Conferences. In 1904, the articles of agreement were presented to the General Conference with an introductory statement:

> "We believe that we voice the sentiment of the General Conference when we assert that we are prepared to stand by the articles as signed by our Commissioners and recommend them to your most favorable consideration. We have been marching around in the wilderness long enough. Let us go into the Promised Land of Oneness. The sentiment hopefully in this meeting should be formulated in definite favor of Organic Union and should be irresistible that it will obliterate what little pessimism there may be."[33]

The Report proceeded to state the rationale for the "Organic Union":

1. Because our doctrines are so similar and the small difference in polity can easily be adjusted.
2. Because in a very large measure we cover and visit the same areas, and thusly prevent overlapping of areas.
3. A big factor would be for economic reasons in running machinery of the church.... We cannot afford the luxury of separation in these days of escalation of prices and high cost of doing business.
4. It could be a great advantage in increased efficiency and add to the crystalizing sentiment politically in favor of our race.

Then, finally, that which should have been first, I sincerely believe we would please our Master if we be One. A divided church cannot as it ought, lift a broken, suffering and frustrated world.[34]

In 1938, Bishop Lynwood Westinghouse Kyles, senior prelate of the African Methodist Episcopal Zion Church, renewed the proposed the unification of African American Methodists. In the opening session of the 117th Annual Conference at Hood Memorial AME Zion Church, he said, "the greatest obstacle in the way of unification of the Methodist Episcopal denominations has been the colored communicants of the great white churches of America."[35] He added that "the effort to achieve union by compromising the rights and cramping the spirit of racial minorities is out of harmony with Christian principles."[36] After criticizing the efforts to unify the biracial Methodist Episcopal denominations, the Bishop proceeded to recommend "unification of all colored Methodists denominations and building of a great colored church in America'" as a haven for colored Methodists discriminated against in other churches."[37] The conference passed a resolution to make several thousand copies of the Bishops' Episcopal Address to be distributed throughout the African Methodist Episcopal Zion Church. News of this development was received by other African American Methodists.

By 1943, the idea of organic union of African American Methodism was introduced to the episcopal leadership of the two largest Methodist denominations. In a semi-annual meeting in Nashville, Tennessee, Bishops Cameron Chesterfield Alleyne, W.J. Walls, and B.G. Shaw representing the Bishop's Council of the African Methodist Episcopal Zion Church met the Bishop's Council of the African Methodist Episcopal Church to negotiate ways and means to achieve the union of the two denominations. They presented a statement from their council approving the union which was approved in principle by the African Methodist Episcopal bishops. Each denomination authorized the appointment of a joint commission of twenty-two members to complete the details. The African Methodist Episcopal bishops specified that its representatives would include eight bishops, one general officer, and one layman.[38]

Again, a long period of time transpired before the issue of "Organic Union" was seriously considered by the leadership of black Methodist denominations. On March 14, 1985, Dr. J.H. Winston published a detailed report on the strides of the denominations for union. His report covered decades of General Council and Bishops meetings to implement such a union:

> "During the early part of this century, the idea of merger was conceived by the AME, AME Zion, and CME churches. The concept was essentially allowed to wither and remain dormant until the last decade when the concept of church union was revived in the General Conference of the CME and AME Zion churches. At a meeting in Washington, D.C., about two years ago, positional papers on various church departments and operation were presented by the bishops. A Joint Commission on Church Union was appointed with members from each denomination being selected. In September of 1983, the Joint Commission on Organic Union held its first formal session in Charlotte, North Carolina. The position papers were presented to each committee by the Bishops and discussions, conclusions and approaches to the merger (union) process

suggested. Additional steering committee meetings subsequently met in Atlanta, Georgia, the last being in January of 1985 to plan for a March meeting of the entire Joint Commission in March of 1985 in St. Louis, Missouri.

"The concept of church union is a noble pursuit whose time has long since passed. There are many similarities of both denominations and their union would have many advantages as well as some minor areas of differences. Some advantages are:

1. The union would bring together a total membership of about 3,000,000.
2. Unification in areas of education could more effectively strengthen our educational institutions and emphasize and adequately support areas of priority.
3. Unification could effectively combine and expand publications so as to make materials more meaningful and inclusive.
4. Combining of Episcopal Districts could strengthen effectiveness in advocating and fostering human rights.
5. Unification and combination could effectively aid in development of doctrinal principles. In keeping with the church in a living and changing world….

"I will openly suggest that we initiate without undue delay during our pre-union or courtship the following efforts:

1. In our local churches to encourage frequent (joint) visitations and fellowship, as well as public service projects such as feeding programs, clothing drives, tutorial programs for general testing (exit exams etc.).
2. Joint district conferences (at least some part of the district conferences) where similarities can be emphasized…projects of common interest fostered such as Black on Black crime.
3. Initiate cooperative session for the purpose of fraternization and familiarization of similarities and differences so as friendly objectivity in solutions may be undertaken."[39]

This informative report was offered by H.H. Winston Jr., M.D., President, Lay Council of Central Alabama Conference and member of the Joint Commission on Organic Church Union. It provided sufficient information and clear rationalization to convince all reasonable African American Methodists to move forward with the union. Clearly, the two denominations expended a considerable amount of time and utilized significant resources to bring about the finalization of the union. Nevertheless, the movement for "Organic Union" still has not materialized.

The failure to succeed in "Organic Union" did not hinder the spirit of cooperation among African Methodists. Specifically, they joined or at least cooperated with several other like African Americans denominations, the broader ecumenical movement transcending racial, ethnic, doctrinal and geographical lines. Soon after the organization of the National Council of Churches in 1950 (an organization of U.S. churches to facilitate unity in fellowship, witness, and service); the Fraternal Council of Churches, U.S.A, Inc., an association of predominantly African American churches organized in 1952 on the model of the National Council of Churches; Consultation on Church Union (discussions concerning merger among several U.S. denominations, 1962); and the World Council of Churches, constituted in 1948, they visited and later cooperated with these organizations which fostered the spirit of ecumenism. However, the vast majority of their work was fostered through the Fraternal Council of Churches because white Christians in the larger ecumenical organizations seemingly lacked a serious commitment to end racism in their local churches and to come to terms with the theological significance of the Civil Rights revolution.

Leadership Crises in African Methodism

Generally, the African American community has always looked to their churches to provide productive spiritual and social leadership. For the most part, the churches measured up to these expectations. But there have been some incidents of failure on the part of church leaders within African Methodism as well as other African American churches which damaged the image of the church among members of the community. Some churches and denominations have experienced conflicts among the clergy, criminally minded individuals, congregational splits, and leadership struggles in civil and ecclesiastical courts. Again, like other African American denominations, African Methodism has experience these crises in leadership. Much of the crisis may be attributed to deviant personality issues, greed, lust for power, and misunderstanding of the biblical mandate for leadership. One or more of these issues were causative of crisis situations in Methodism.

A significant leadership issue was that of Ira Toussaint Bryant and the operation of the AME Sunday School Union. He was elected in 1908 as Secretary-Treasurer to administer the affairs of the department. In that position, he gained tremendous economic power and operated the Union, assuming almost exclusive administrative rights. When a replacement for his position was elected in 1936, Bryant refused to turn over the Union to E.A. Selby on the claim that the General Conference had no right to replace him. This action resulted in a four-year civil court battle between him and the episcopal leadership of the denomination. The court decided in favor of the episcopacy and required Bryant to turn over the position to E.A. Selby.

During the four years of civil court litigation, tremendous bitterness resulted between Ira Toussaint Bryant and the bishops. In 1943, the *Baltimore Afro-American* published the following article by John Jasper entitled "Bryant-Bishops Feud Enters Eleventh Year Long Court Battle Could Have Been Settled by Compromise Years Ago," describing this crisis in denominational leadership:

"The AME legal redress committee's request for a chancery court decree requiring Ira Bryant to surrender the charter for the Sunday School Union is a purely technical matter. Since the Federal Court recognized the new corporation headed by E.A. Selby and ousted Bryant it follows as a matter of course that Bryant shall have to surrender the charter. The Bryant-Selby feud for the control of the AME Sunday School Union, a $200,000 property, has been in court since 1932.

"Here is the history of the case: 1908—Ira T. Bryant elected secretary of the Sunday School Union printing plant by the AME General Conference; plant worth $2,000; 1912-1916—Re-elected; 1918—Union incorporated under independent trustees; 1932—General Conference ousts Bryant; names E.A. Selby to succeed him. Bryant declines to step down; says plant is now worth $250,000; Lower court upholds Bryant's right to continue in office; 1937—Court of Appeals sustains the lower court's decision; 1938—Federal Court hears charges that Bryant has misused union's funds; 1940—AME General Conference at Detroit declines to seat Bryant as a delegate and elected a new board of trustees for the Sunday School Union; Federal Court names receiver, ousts Bryant, and prepares to turn plant back to new trustees; 1941—Bryant appeals ruling of court; U.S. District Court of Appeals affirms decision of the U.S. District Court, ousting Bryant from control of the AME Sunday School Union and orders return of $250,000 plant to the church; 1942—Bryant opens new Sunday School Union across street. His Tennessee corporation charter not revoked, claims building belongs to him; 1943—AME

Bishops seek chancery court decree ordering Bryant to surrender charter and dissolve his corporation....

"Spectators who have followed the expensive and lengthy court proceedings over a decade declare that seldom has a case been fought in lower court with more bitterness.... Writing about the role of Ira Bryant as a purifier in the church, May 28, 1932, the late Kelly Miller said that Bryant's organ, *The Allenite*, is also the financial organ of the church and the church's greatest critic. 'If half the scandals in high places and in low places which it exposes were true, they were enough to make the church blush with shame,' Kelly Miller said. 'And yet *The Allenite* was continued by the support of the very denomination which it denounced.... The bishops and pastors who were denounced should have been put out of the church or Bryant should have been put behind bars.'"[40]

This comment by Kelly Miller reflected public opinion regarding the general atmosphere of negativity existing within the leadership of the denomination.

Another classic example of a crisis situation in African Methodism was described by the *Afro-American Newspaper* as the "Battle of Bishops." It was a severe struggle within the African Methodist Episcopal Church regarding the question of leadership over the church's First Episcopal District. In 1947, the *Afro-American* described the "Battle of Bishops Enters New Phase":

"Bishop S.L. Greene, restrained by court order from assuming authority over two conferences of the AME Church's First Episcopal District, jumped the gun on his blocker, last week, with an unusual legal move. With the Rev. David H. Sims's injunction suit against him still being heard in U.S. District Court here, Bishop Greene on Friday carried the battle to the Third Circuit Court of Appeals. In his petition, Bishop Greene, through his attorney, Ray Pace Alexander, says the restraining order imposed by District Judge George A. Welch had disrupted the affairs of the Church and 'virtually paralyzed its functioning.'

"The bishop, assigned to the Philadelphia and Delaware Conference after the Rev. Mr. Sims was expelled from the bishopric by the Special General Conference last November, asks the higher court for an immediate hearing to dissolve the restraining order.

"The restraining order, normally effective for ten days, was issued by Judge Welsh on Dec. 2 and extended five times during the two months the injunction case has been in litigation.

"Twice disrupted by physical scuffles—once between two ministers and then two lawyers—the case was scheduled to be resumed Monday before Judge Welsh.

"Bishop Green's petition to the Court of Appeals complains that Judge Welsh has enormously confused and complicated the issues involved.

"The prolonged court battle, with its postponements, is affecting the morale of the entire congregation, Bishop Green asserts, particularly the 100,000 members in the First Episcopal District which the Rev. Mr. Sims formerly headed.

"The question of whether he or the Rev. Mr. Sims is the presiding official for the conference is a matter for the 'ecclesiastical court' of the church, not civil courts to decide, Bishop Green contends."[41]

During the struggle in the Federal courtroom, "the Rev. George Sims, brother of the ousted bishop, The Rev. David H. Sims, charged into the confrontation on the side of Rev. Mr. Curry, and after being restrained from violence by spectators, challenged the Reverend Mr. Clark to come out in the corridor and settle things."[42]

During the cross examination in court, Bishop Sims denied "that he had benefitted financially from the transaction involving the purchase of Paradise Lakes Development in New Jersey by the First Episcopal District several years ago," and, "there was not anything 'wrong' in depositing conference funds to his personal bank account even though the Church Discipline said otherwise."[43] The complaint had been referred to the Senior Bishop by Bishop Sims' divorced wife.

In New York, the Supreme Court Justice dismissed all claims of Rev. David H. Sims and his associates and "ruled the Rt. Rev. R.R. Wright to be the duly-appointed bishop of the New York Conference, AME Church."[44] They were also restrained from interfering with the property or conduct of any churchman within the conference. Particular emphasis was stressed that they could not prevent the Rev. J. A. Portlock from performing his duties as the newly-appointed pastor of Bethel AME Church, New York. It was not until 1956 that the General

Conference reconsidered Rev. David H. Sims' case and, in 1960, restored him to the episcopacy. In 1960, he was assigned to the Fourteenth Episcopal District in West Africa. Subsequently, he was assigned in 1962 to the Eighth Episcopal District (Mississippi and Louisiana).

In 1940, a lawsuit was filed against Bishop M.H. Davis relative to an economic issue with the administration of Kittrell College in North Carolina. B.B Martin, Kenneth Jones, and several other members of the Second Episcopal District filed the suit in North Carolina Superior Court claiming that the bishop was improperly utilizing $166,000 in stocks left by B.N. Duke to the college and that Bishop Davis was using the college for his own personal benefit. The restraining order was signed by Judge W.C. Harris of the Superior Court. However, Bishop Davis challenged the decision during several years of legal involvements. Finally, the Vance County Superior Court in Henderson, North Carolina, settled the matter by ordering Bishop Davis and eleven trustees to replace $42,804 of the endowment fund for the school. However, the judgment absolved all the defendants of any criminal intent. In delivering the judgment, Judge John J. Burney declared: "I don't think any of these gentlemen intentionally did anything wrong."[45]

Several other significant civil court proceedings involving African Methodist Episcopal bishops resulted from a variety of administrative issues. In 1948, a suit filed in the Fulton County (Georgia) Superior Court which ordered Bishop W.A. Fountain and W.A. Fountain Jr., president of Morris Brown College, to show why a charter granted to them should not be rescinded. It had been issued to authorize them to borrow money for the college. However, the real issue in the disturbance in Georgia was broader than mere money matters. It involved some disagreements between Bishop W.A. Fountain and Bishop R.R. Wright. In New Jersey Rev. Mattie E. Jackson, pastor of the St. Peters African Methodist Church of Rutherford, charged Bishop D. Ward Nichols, prelate of the First Episcopal District with mishandling conference funds. These cases posed tremendous challenges to the denomination. However, the AME Church had sufficient strength to overcome the negative developments and emerge as a leading movement among African American churches.

African American Baptist Denominations

Unlike African American Methodism, African American Baptist denominations did not evolve from the leadership style of an episcopal hierarchy. The autonomy of local Baptist churches was a fundamental doctrine of the denomination from the very beginning. This belief evolved from their radical opposition to established religions with popes and bishops exercising authority over the churches and their adherence to democratic ideals. Hence, they were uncompromising in their adherence to local church autonomy. This played a significant role in the restrictions placed on denominational leadership. Baptists organized their associations, state conventions, regional, and national conventions merely as cooperative organizations for local churches to extend their home and foreign ministries.

Initially, local Baptist churches decided to organize associations as their first attempt at cooperation with other Baptist churches. The earliest separated associational movement of African American Baptists evolved out of the independent church movement of the Ohio African American Baptists. Reminiscences of the early history of the Baptists of this state will show how a mixture of a missionary motif with a general desire for racial progress gave birth to their first associations. To begin with, the evolution of cooperative movements among Ohio's local African American churches encountered opposition from the larger community. African Americans were not initially welcomed in Ohio, and what few were there during the antebellum period already were Christians and holding membership in white churches. Nevertheless, pioneer African American preachers were able to begin a cooperative movement among the churches and, subsequently, organize church associations.

In 1834, the Providence Baptist Association was organized at the Providence Baptist Church of Berlin Crossroads, Ohio. This was the first such independent association to be organized by African American Baptists. Among the organizers of the Providence Baptist Association were Reverends William Bryant, Jonathan Cradic, T.W. Frye, Benjamin Sales, Jeremiah Walker, Lewis Wright, J.B. Steptoe, P.H. Williams, and Kendall Carter. These were the pioneers of the associational movement among African American Baptists. Not only did they concern themselves with the organization an association for missionary and educational purposes, but also the Providence, the Middlerun, and the Union Anti-slavery Baptist Associations merged the focus of the sociopolitical development of the race.

The Union Anti-slavery Baptist Association was organized in 1843. Initially, it was composed of about 13 churches, having a total membership of about 1,000. By 1872, the association had 68 churches with a membership of about 4,567. The Union Anti-slavery Baptist Association was divided to form the Western Union

Anti-slavery Baptist Association and the Eastern Union Anti-slavery Baptist Association.

At the time of the initial division of the Union Anti-slavery Baptist Association, an agreement was made by the leadership of the new association that every four years a union meeting should be held. In 1878, the first union meeting was held in Columbus, Ohio. The delegates of this union meeting laid the groundwork for the subsequent organization of the Ohio Baptist State Convention in 1896.

Following the leadership of Ohio's African American Baptists, the Baptists of Illinois organized the Wood River Baptist Association of Illinois in 1838. By this time, the associational movement gained momentum. In 1865, The Baptists of Louisiana organized their first association, followed in rapid succession by other states.

Against the background of the associational movement, African American Baptist leaders soon sought even wider cooperative movements among their churches. They saw that expanding needs for the education, sociopolitical uplift of the race, and dreams of foreign missions necessitated the organization of state conventions which would facilitate cooperation among the associations. The African American Baptists of North Carolina were the first to bring the vision of cooperative programs to fruition with the organization of the General Baptist State Convention in 1866. Other states followed such as Alabama in 1866, Virginia Baptist State Convention in 1867, Arkansas in 1869, and soon the Missionary Baptist State Convention of Georgia.

As early as 1840, African American Baptists sought even greater cooperative opportunities beyond state lines. They were anxious to unite as many Baptists as possible to struggle for the advancement of the race and the spread of the kingdom of God. This was quite remarkable given the sociopolitical situation existing before the Civil War. Notwithstanding that reality, African American Baptist leaders organized the American Baptist Missionary Convention in 1840. Those who lived in New England and some other Atlantic states met at the Abyssinian Baptist Church of New York to organize this pioneering regional convention. A constitution was drawn up to reflect the nature and purpose of the convention.

Initially, the convention's growth was inhibited by both internal and external pressures. Internally, certain leaders felt that the convention placed too much emphasis on missions at the expense of local pastors. Externally, a prevailing agitation in the mind of whites was the antislavery proclivities of the convention's leading ministers. Hence, some of these ministers were proscribed in many instances. Nevertheless, the heroic among them still struggled courageously to advance the program of the American Baptist Missionary Convention.

The original motion to organize district associations was offered by Rev. William Troy in 1867. At that time, he was pastor of the Second Baptist Church in Richmond, Virginia. The motion prevailed, but its execution was delayed. It was not until 1872 that the motion gained attention within the report of the Executive Board of the convention. Still, the convention desired a more detailed study of the proposal for the organization of district auxiliary conventions. The report was referred to a special committee to develop a broader program for the district auxiliary conventions sufficiently expansive to embrace all of the United States, resulting in the creation of the Consolidated American Baptist Convention.

In 1873, the African American Baptists of the West organized the General Association of the Western States and Territories; and in 1874 the East organized the New England Baptist Missionary Convention. The growth of these two regional bodies soon overshadowed that of the parent body of the Consolidated American Baptist Convention, resulting in its rapid decline. The final meeting of the convention was held in Lexington, Kentucky, in 1878.

Prior to 1878, the major challenge to the success of the Consolidated American Baptist Convention came from the organization of the New England Baptist Missionary Convention. Most of the larger churches and ablest leaders among African American Baptists were members of the new convention in New England. Hence, this district convention was able to live on as a separate convention after the decline of the Consolidated American Baptist Convention. The new convention experienced rapid growth in membership. Many independent churches were organized by the pioneer leaders of the New England Baptist Missionary Convention.

To be sure, the developers of the New England Baptist Missionary Convention's constitution were careful to reflect a broad and progressive scope of ministry. Provisions were made for the convention to foster and maintain home and foreign missionary work, establish and maintain educational institutions, and to establish other agencies necessary for the development of the convention. This was perhaps the first time that African American Baptists organized, although with limited national scope, a comprehensive denomination.

Increasingly, the desire of African American Baptists to advance a progressive missionary enterprise led to efforts to organize a national body dedicated to foreign missions. With the demise of the old Consolidated American Baptist Convention, a vacuum had been created in the cooperative movement among African American Baptists. This factor limited their strides in home and foreign missions. Foreign missions had been a driving force for cooperation among them, extending back into the antebellum period. Hence, momentum within local churches was sufficient to cause their leaders to organize the Baptist Foreign Mission Convention.

The strides toward the organization of the Baptist Foreign Mission Convention gained a degree of urgency with the work of Rev. William W. Colley, a missionary to Africa appointed by the Foreign Mission Board of the Southern Baptist Convention. Upon his return from Africa, Rev. Colley possessed a strong determination to arouse his fellow African American Baptists to the urgent needs for missionary work in Africa. The Baptist brethren of Virginia employed him to canvass the United States to organize a general denominational convention among the race. He traveled extensively and wrote many letters to church leaders urging African American Baptists to meet in Montgomery, Alabama, on November 24-26, 1880, for the purpose of organizing a national convention to fill the vacuum created by the failure of the Consolidated American Baptist Convention. They responded positively and met in the First Baptist Church of Montgomery to organize the Baptist Foreign Mission Convention.

The developmental years (1880-1895) of the Baptist Foreign Mission Convention were characterized by growing pains. Its initial progress was rather slow. However, the brilliant missionary mind of Rev. W.W. Colley was sufficient to unite the majority of the African American Baptists in the cause of foreign missions. With its emphasis on foreign missions, the home mission strides of local churches still lacked a national vehicle for successful missions. Moreover, the strong New England Baptist Convention elected not to join the Baptist Foreign Mission Convention.

Again, African American Baptists made attempts to create a vehicle of national scope for effective denominational ministries. In 1886, Rev. William J. Simmons called together clergy and laymen to meet in St. Louis, Missouri, for the purpose of organizing the American National Baptist Convention. He was elected the first president of the new convention. The new convention cooperated with the white Southern Baptist Convention in promoting foreign missions.

Again, the new convention failed to attract churches across the nation to join its membership.

In 1893, another organization of African American Baptists proposing to be national in scope was founded in Washington, D.C. The new convention was named the National Baptist Educational Convention. The main objective of this convention was to provide for an educated ministry in the leadership of African American Baptist churches. This was the first attempt by African American Baptists to direct in a unified way the educational policy of their churches. The leading person in the organization of the new convention was Rev. W. Bishop Johnson, pastor of the Second Baptist Church, Washington, D.C. The idea for such a convention grew out of his earlier strides in Christian education. He had (in 1885) organized the Sunday School Lyceum movement in the United States. With the organization of the National Baptist Educational Convention, Rev. W. Bishop Johnson and Rev. P.F. Morris of Virginia federated all schools controlled and managed by African American Baptists, making them a part of the educational machinery of the denomination. He gathered educational data and statistics from these institutions and showed their number, location, and property value. This afforded the local churches information on the relative strength of the denomination. Obviously, this new convention specialized in raising large sums of money for the support of schools among African American Baptists.

Again, the long stride for national cooperation among African American Baptists continued into the 1890's. In a meeting at Washington, D.C., several leading preachers repeated the question about a united Baptist organization with national scope and a comprehensive purpose. The new convention was called the Tripartite Union consisting of the New England Baptist Missionary Convention, the Baptist Foreign Mission Convention, and the National Baptist Educational Convention. The effort failed to gain national support. However, the groundwork was prepared for the final organization of a national denomination.

Out of the spirit of the Tripartite Union emerged a successful attempt to organize a national denomination. On September 24, 1895, a committee report was adopted to organize the National Baptist Convention. Subsequently in 1895 at Atlanta, Georgia, the Foreign Mission Convention, the National Baptist Educational Convention, and the American National Baptist Convention consolidated to form a new national convention with Rev. E.C. Morris of Helena, Arkansas, as president and Mr. W.H. Stewart as secretary. The result of this meeting was the formation of the National Baptist Convention of America. Finally, the dream of a truly national denomination was realized among African American Baptists.

The primary concern of the National Baptist Convention of America was to facilitate a comprehensive home and foreign missionary program. While the African mission was still very much a concern of the leaders, the convention also advanced a lively interest in missionary work in America. Provisions were made for the cause of education and the publication of literature designed to meet the special needs of African Americans. In order to facilitate a practical structure for these objectives, the organizers of the convention decided to work through specialized boards. Hence, they organized a Foreign Mission Board, a Home Mission Board, an Educational Board, a Baptist Young People's Union Board (B.Y.P.U.), and a Publishing Board. These boards represented the basic denominational structure of the convention.

In the early 1900s, the constitution was revised for the first time to reflect the extensive growth and development of the National Baptist Convention. In a special report issued in 1906 by the Department of Commerce and Labor, Bureau of the Census on Religious Bodies, a significant growth in the convention was reported: In 1890 there were 1,348,989 members in the continental United States; and in 1906 the number had increased to 2,261,607 members. A large percentage of African Americans were united with the National Baptist Convention by 1906. This was a period of unprecedented growth among Baptists. Following the Reconstruction Period, Baptists had constructed large church structures to accommodate the increasing numbers of new members. Hence, certain constitutional provisions were made for this great growth in the denomination.

Some of the essential revisions in the constitution were as follows: first, the representation fees of messengers, district associations, or conventions were increased to reflect the new economic needs of the growing denomination; second, new regulations were established for life membership; and third, positions and eligibility requirements were established for new officers with the convention reserving the right to try such officers, particularly officers of the Executive Board, and dismiss them. This was perhaps the closest Baptists had ever come to the establishment of a judicatory outside the local congregation. The Executive Board was given authority to create from its own body an executive committee consisting of nine members. Also, provisions were made for the organization and government of subsidiary bodies to the convention.

The greatest challenge that the National Baptist Convention faced centered in the organization and administration of its various boards. A succinct summary of the actual organizational time frame of the boards will set the background for the later leadership crisis in the convention. Like other African American denominations, effective leadership skills were slowly developed for board executives. In 1895, the oldest Board established was the National Baptist Foreign Mission Board, located in Louisville, Kentucky. By and large, the new board was a continuation of the old Foreign Mission Convention of America. The initial officers were Rev. John H. Frank, chairman; and Rev. L.M. Luke, corresponding secretary.

The next board to be organized was the National Baptist Publishing Board. In 1896, the convention made plans for the organization of this Board. Rev. R.H. Boyd, who had played a significant part in the development of the concept, was appointed general secretary of the National Baptist Publishing Board, with Rev. C.H. Clark serving as chairman. By 1898, the new board had become operational and located in Nashville, Tennessee. It was the largest African American publishing enterprise in the United States. The board was given the exclusive right of publishing Sunday school literature and other publications for the National Baptist Convention. By 1911, the Board had property, machinery, and stock estimated at $350,000 and employed about 150 clerks, stenographers, and skilled workers. This board gradually became the economic power basis of the National Baptist Convention, which later became problematic. Specifically, Rev. R. H. Boyd and the National Baptist Publishing Board gradually pursued an independent path from the convention's leadership, which resulted in a leadership crisis in the Baptist denomination.

Correspondingly, the Educational Board of the National Baptist Convention was organized about the same time as the Publishing Board. In 1895, it was located in Washington, D.C., with Rev. W. Bishop Johnson serving as corresponding secretary. Actually, this Board was a continuation of the old National Baptist Educational Convention previously led by Rev. W. Bishop Johnson. By 1911, the board had moved its headquarters to Nashville and elected Rev. T. J. Searcy as chairman and Rev. A.N. McEwen as its corresponding secretary. This Board was designed to federate all African American Baptist schools in the United States, except the eight owned by the American Baptist Home Mission Society, and to establish and operate a national theological seminary in Nashville, Tennessee. In 1911, the Board made plans for the erection of a $50,000 building for the theological seminary. That same year, Rev. Sutton E. Griggs was elected corresponding secretary of the Educational Board.

In 1899, the National Baptist B.Y.P.U. Board was organized with Rev. N.H. Pius as chairman and Rev. E.W.D. Isaac as secretary. The board was also located in Nashville, Tennessee. By 1911, the board had elected Rev. P. James Bryant as its chairman. Over a ten-year period, the board had led in the organization of 7,600 local B.Y.P.U. societies and thirty-eight state societies, plus 320 B.Y.P.U. district conventions.

The last Board to be organized during the formative period of the National Baptist Convention was the National Baptist Benefit Association Board, organized in 1903 and located in Helena, Arkansas. The initial officers were Rev. C.B. Brown, chairman; and Rev. W.A. Homes, corresponding secretary. The purpose of this board was to pay death claims of Baptist ministers and laymen who became members of the association. Its function was similar to that of a small benefit insurance company. Later, some local churches established similar associations, such as the First Baptist Relief Association of the Colored Peoples' First Baptist Church, Baltimore, Maryland.

The leadership of the National Baptist Convention demonstrated creative and visionary guidance for structuring a denomination well on the way of becoming one of the largest structured organizations among African American Christians. However, like African American Methodism, Baptists soon witnessed a crisis situation in denominational development. Severe tensions that developed within two of its boards led to subsequent splits from the convention.

The first significant tension emerged from the administration and development of the Foreign Mission Board. Several clergymen of national prominence prepared statements designed to sway the sentiment of the delegates of the forthcoming 1897 session of the National Baptist Convention with their unique persuasion of operational policies to be presented on the convention's program. In September 1897, the convention met with the Ebenezer Baptist Church of Boston, Massachusetts. The initial business session began with a debate among the clergymen. The debate centered around several key and somewhat emotional issues: (1) the advisability of the removal of the Foreign Mission Board from Richmond to Louisville; (2) the use of American Baptist literature and cooperation with white Baptists in general; and, (3) the primacy of foreign missions as a greater emphasis for the convention. The majority of the ministers demonstrated an independent spirit, favoring separation from white Baptist bodies. However, several clergymen from Virginia and North Carolina favored the primacy of foreign missions and cooperation with white Baptists.

Through heated debates, it became obvious that the delegates of the National Baptist Convention could not hope for consensus of opinions. The minority faction of the delegates decided to hold a caucus session in Boston to evaluate the relative strength of their idea and to plan a strategy for the realization of their goal of cooperation with white Baptists. There was sufficient enthusiasm generated at this caucus session to motivate the disengaged National Baptist brethren to call a subsequent meeting at Shiloh Baptist Church in Washington, D.C., on December 16, 1897, for the purpose of developing a new conventional strategy. Out of this meeting, the Lott Carey Baptist Home and Foreign Mission Convention was organized, named in honor of Rev. Lott Carey, the first African American Baptist missionary to Africa. This was the preliminary organization formed December 16, 1897. The convention was subsequently confirmed September 8 and 9, 1898, by large delegations from North Carolina, Virginia, the District of Columbia, Maryland, Pennsylvania, New Jersey, New York, and the New England states. The relative strength of this new convention surprised the National Baptist Convention and angered its leadership.

Nevertheless, the leadership of the new convention persisted. In 1899, the annual meeting of the Lott Carey Home and Foreign Mission Convention was held at the First Baptist Church in Baltimore, Maryland, with Rev. J.C. Allen serving as host pastor. At this meeting, the first idea of a woman's auxiliary was conceived, and the next year the auxiliary was organized. Several decades later in 1943, the convention organized the Lott Carey Laymen's League.

Soon after some tensions subsided between the two conventions, several attempts were made to bring back the leadership of the Lott Carey Home and Foreign Mission Convention into the National Baptist Convention. Rev. W.M. Alexander reported to the Lott Carey constituency that the time was ripe to bring the two bodies into an organic relationship. Rev. C.S. Brown, president of the Lott Carey body, received the idea with cautious optimism, noting that attitudinal and operational changes must be met on the part of National Baptist leadership. Within two years, agreements were negotiated and an organic relationship between the two bodies emerged. The cooperation was restricted primarily to the foreign mission programs of the two conventions. Specifically, the Lott Carey Convention enrolled as the First District Convention of the

National Baptist Convention, USA. The compact remained undisturbed until internal discord erupted over the ownership of the National Baptist Publishing Board. The crisis developed into some significant changes in cooperative strides among African American Baptists.

To be sure, the greatest rift within the National Baptist Convention during its formative years came in 1915, centering in Rev. R. H. Boyd's claim of exclusive leadership rights over the National Baptist Publishing Board. He claimed that the original constitution of the convention did not contain a clear provision for the establishment of the board and that the board was actually organized with little or no help from President Elias Camp Morris and other officials of the convention. This was the basis of his claim of an independent legal status of the board from the National Baptist Convention's official structure. Actually, the economic power of the Board played a significant role in the independent spirit of Rev. R.H. Boyd.

The severe internal struggles over the ownership of the National Baptist Publishing Board led to bitter clashes among convention leadership. There were discussions, arguments, and investigations made as to the rightful ownership and control of the board. However, the board refused to obey the directives of the convention, which led ultimately to a lawsuit in civil court between those who followed Rev. R.H. Boyd's claim of independence for the Publishing Board and the leadership of the convention. In 1915, Judge Smith of Chicago, Illinois, in open court, pronounced the Boyd group a "rump" convention and dissolved an injunction which they had taken out against President Elias Camp Morris and other officers of the National Baptist Convention, USA.

Disappointed with the court's decision, the Boyd group decided to organize a new convention named the National Baptist Convention of America. Initially, they called the new body the National Baptist Convention, Unincorporated, organized on September 9, 1915. Again, the leadership of National Baptist Publishing Board affirmed its independence of any convention, based on its establishment as a legal entity by the State of Tennessee on the 15th day of August 1898, and reserved the right to affiliate with any convention it so desired. This was done to counter the opinion of a few delegates of the new convention who were somewhat doubtful of the ethics of the Publishing Board's leadership. Nevertheless, the National Baptist Convention, Unincorporated, evolved with a close relationship with the National Baptist Publishing Board.

During the early development of the National Baptist Convention, Unincorporated, negotiations between the leadership of the convention and the Lott Carey Home and Foreign Mission Convention emerged to promote a cooperative program. Since the National Baptist Convention, Unincorporated, did not have an initial foreign mission program, its leadership sought to channel the foreign mission work through the Lott Carey Convention. Subsequently, the Lott Carey Convention acquiesced, and in 1924 a formal compact was agreed upon by the two conventions.

Soon after 1924, failed attempts were made to unite all three national conventions into a "tripartite union." The failure of these attempts at union was perhaps the greatest of all among the African American Baptists of the twentieth century. One major result was the slow progress of both of the National Baptist Convention, Unincorporated, and the Lott Carey Home and Foreign Mission Convention. However, the National Baptist Convention experienced steady growth and development.

It was not until the leadership of Rev. Wendell Clay Summerville, executive secretary of the Lott Carey Convention, that the group specialized in foreign missions and experienced growth as an Atlantic regional convention. Its foreign mission program extended to several different foreign colonies and nations. Likewise, the National Baptist Convention, Unincorporated, organized its own Foreign Mission Board and Educational Board, under the leadership of Rev. J.C. Sams, which resulted in some growth of the denomination.

Again, growth pains of the National Baptist Convention, USA, were exposed through the issue of tenure during the administration of Rev. J.H. Jackson. He had led the convention for a considerable period of time and had risen to great power and prestige, so much so that the majority of the convention's leaders wanted him to remain in office beyond the normal period of service. However, some strong leaders desired new leadership and pressed for the appointment of a committee on tenure. On Thursday, September 4, 1956, the question of tenure was strongly debated at the seventy-sixth annual session in Denver, Colorado. Rev. E.C. Smith was called to make the report of the tenure committee. The majority report was not in favor of tenure for the presidency, resulting in tremendous controversy within the convention. However, Rev. J.H. Jackson was able to remain in office as the president of the convention.

The next major conflict within the National Baptist Convention, USA, was more political in nature. In 1954, the Supreme Court of the United States ruled that the segregation of public schools was unconstitutional. It was a time of socio-political unrest in the South as whites were challenged to reevaluate their long-standing policies toward African Americans. The pressures of the Supreme Court's decision pressed hard on both white and African American churches. White churches were not prepared to accept African Americans in their midst, nor in their schools. They were willing to violate basic Christian ethical principles, even to the point of violence, to circumvent the court's decision. Hence, the National Baptist Convention, USA, the largest organized body of African Americans, was not exempted from taking positions of leadership during the social upheaval.

To be sure, the leadership of the convention found tremendous difficulties on deciding how best to address the new circumstance. Several debates took place in the convention regarding ways and means of addressing the need for progress in the civil rights of all African Americans. In 1956, a symposium was held to relate to the critical challenge: "National Baptists Facing Integration-Shall Gradualism Be Applied?" President J.H. Jackson, the dominant figure in the convention, favored gradualism in civil rights with an emphasis on working with the NAACP. Several other leading clergymen addressed the issue. Rev. C.K. Steele of Florida spoke of the bus boycott in Tallahassee and took a position against gradualism. Rev. T. J. Jemison also spoke of his experience in the Baton Rouge Boycott in 1953, and he strongly favored a more aggressive approach of the convention in the civil rights struggle. Another prominent clergyman, Rev. Thomas Kilgore, spoke in unprecedented terms against gradualism as an appropriate position for the convention.

After the symposium, Rev. J.H. Jackson presented Rev. Martin Luther King Jr., president of the Montgomery Improvement Association and pastor of the Dexter Avenue Baptist Church in Montgomery, to address the convention. King initially congratulated President J.H. Jackson for his support of the boycott movement. Rev. Martin Luther King Jr. spoke on the subject, "Paul's Letter to American Christians." Clearly, his address was a tremendous challenge to gradualism in civil rights. After the address, a significant atmosphere of tension existed between Reverends King and Jackson.

The urgency of the challenge of civil rights prompted several clergymen to challenge the presidency of the National Baptist Convention, USA. President Jackson had already lost favoritism of some leaders over the issue of tenure. A small minority of delegates to the convention favored the candidacy of Rev.

Gardner C. Taylor as a progressive-minded leader to meet the urgent crisis in America. Some of his followers challenged the election process, which resulted in disorder in the annual session meeting in Kansas City. The crisis in the convention became so severe that both sides of issue of the election process elected to obtain legal representation. After consultation with a local judge, it was decided that all delegates who had registered with the convention and those registered who were of the Taylor group would have to be certified by both groups. Both sides agreed to the legal counsel of the judge, and the election process progressed. Rev. J.H. Jackson received the majority vote and continued in the presidency of the convention.

Nevertheless, the victory of Rev. J.H. Jackson, in a fair and legal election process, did not calm the troubled waters of the convention. On September 11, 1961, a national news release was issued which electrified African American Baptists throughout the nation. In effect, the news release was a call issued by Rev. L.V. Booth, pastor of Zion Baptist Church in Cincinnati, Ohio, to organize a new national convention based on democratic principles dedicated to Christian objectives. Among the clergy who responded to the call were those who had supported the failed candidacy of Rev. Gardner C. Taylor for the National Baptist Convention, USA presidency. Some who attended the organizational meeting of the Progressive National Baptist Convention were still reluctant about such a major division within the denomination at such a critical period in the struggles of African Americans.

Nevertheless, about twenty-three African American preachers moved beyond their initial reluctance and responded positively to the call for a new convention. On November 14-15, they convened the organizational meeting of the Progressive National Baptist Convention at the Zion Baptist Church in Cincinnati. Only a small number of delegates and states participated in the organizational process. However, these progressive-minded leaders were eager to organize a convention that would take on the crisis of the African American experience with unconditional seriousness. They were keenly aware of the new opportunities afforded the African American Baptist church to be relevant to the theological, social, and political issues of the Civil Rights movement.

The following persons were elected as officers of the new Progressive National Baptist Convention of America: Rev. T. M. Chambers of California, president; Rev. L. V. Booth of Ohio, vice president; Rev. J. Carl Mitchell of West Virginia, secretary; Rev. Louis Rawls of Illinois, treasurer; A.J. Hargett, director of publicity; and the Honorable William W. Parker, attorney. These men were able to lead the convention through slow but significant progress. Soon, other national clergy leaders like Reverends Martin Luther King Jr., Ralph David Abernathy, Harold A. Carter, Nelson H. Smith, Fred C. Lofton, Thomas Kilgore, T.R. Washington, William A. Jones Jr., and Gardner C. Taylor united with the new convention. They saw clearly that the growth of the new convention would tend to add support to the civil rights movement.

Like other conventions, the Progressive National Baptist Convention organized boards and auxiliaries necessary to carry on the work of the organization. It became a strong supporter of the NAACP, the SCLC, the Baptist World Alliance, the North American Baptist Fellowship, and the protest movement against South African apartheid. Additionally, the convention has contributed to several institutions of higher learning, including Central Baptist Theological Seminary, Howard University School of Divinity, Morehouse School of Religion, Morris College, Shaw University, and Virginia Union University. The convention established a cooperative relationship with the American Baptist Churches, USA, in a special program called the Fund of Renewal Program.

In 1988, another national Baptist convention was organized in Dallas, Texas, named the National Missionary Baptist Convention of America, resulting from controversy concerning the Sunday School Congress and the National Baptist Publishing Board. Rev. S.M. Lockridge, pastor of the Calvary Baptist Church of San Diego, became its first president, and Rev. F. Benjamin Davis, vice president of ecumenical affairs. At its annual meeting in San Antonio, Texas, the convention leadership declared its intent to organize a Sunday school congress under its control, thus effectively ending its ties with the National Baptist Publishing Board and congress under the Boyd family. In September 1989, the new convention convened in Chicago with its host church, Antioch Missionary Baptist Church, under the pastorate of Rev. W.N. Daniel. The estimated attendance of the convention was approximately 8,000 delegates.

President S.M. Lockridge provided the social and theological purpose of the National Missionary Baptist Convention, suggesting the need for the continuous spiritual development of African Americans; to equip them to meet the challenges of contemporary life, and to create more effective programs to encourage African American entrepreneurship, education, and economic empowerment for minorities. Like other denominations, the new convention organized boards and departments to carry out these objectives.[46]

The Afro-Christian Convention: Congregational Christian Churches

African American Congregational Christian churches emerged in 1865 from the missionary work of the American Missionary Association. The earliest African American Congregational churches were organized by white Congregational ministers who came to the South after the Civil War as missionary teachers to work in schools and colleges that had been started by the American Missionary Association. The first Congregational Christian church with an all-African American membership was the Providence Church of Norfolk, Virginia, dedicated on June 4, 1854. The membership consisted of both slaves and free African Americans who had worshiped in the balconies of white Christian churches in Virginia. The first pastor of the church was white, and white Congregational Church leaders gave guidance in organizing the church.[47]

Similar to the other separate African American churches, African American Congregational Christian churches remained initially within the biracial Congregational Christian Church, Southern District. Generally, the biracial Congregational Christian Church was a movement growing out of the "Restoration Movement" of the early nineteenth century with the goal of Christian unity and the reestablishment of simple New Testament Christianity. It was a reform movement designed to restore the church to its original biblical state. Adherents of the movement rejected creeds and ecclesiastical organizations, calling their churches just "Christian churches." Their history of the church evolved similar to the Disciples of Christ.

Soon after the end of the Civil War, African American Christian churches were organized in various locations in North Carolina and Virginia. In 1866, the North Carolina Colored Conference, originally called the Western North Carolina Conference, was organized in Raleigh, North Carolina, with Rev. William M. Hayes serving as its first president. The conference included African American Christians from North Carolina and Virginia. J. Taylor Stanley observed: "The Rev. W.B. Wellons, the Rev. J.W. Wellons, and the Rev. H.B. Hayes, white ministers of the General Christian Convention, ably assisted the 'colored brethren' in organizing churches of their own and in the organization of colored conferences, in keeping with the cardinal principles of the Christian platform."[48] By 1875, African American churches had organized three conferences, namely, the Western North Carolina Conference, the Eastern North Carolina Conference, and the Eastern Virginia Colored Christian Conference. In 1887, the

Georgia-Alabama Colored Christian Conference was organized and became affiliated with the Afro-Christian Convention. The Georgia-Alabama Conference consisted of several congregations in western Georgia and eastern Alabama. In 1912 the Pennsylvania, New Jersey, and New York Christian Conference was organized and united with the Afro-Christian Convention.[49]

In 1957, most of the African American Congregational Christian churches were relating directly to the biracial denomination. During the same year, the dream for church union was realized at a joint meeting of the General Council of Congregational Christian Churches and of the General Synod of the Evangelical and Reformed Church, where they formed the United Church of Christ. After four more years of negotiation, the new denomination was formed with the adoption of its constitution at the General Synod in Philadelphia. The new constitution established the denomination as an integrated body. The inclusiveness of the denomination was to reflect its designation as the United Church of Christ.[50]

Holiness and Pentecostal Denominations

From the early evolution of the Christian church, there have always been movements within the church designed to emphasize the need for deep spirituality among believers. Hence, the organization of the Holiness and Pentecostal movements was not a digression from the spirituality of Christians but attempts at reaffirmation and actualization. Actually, the Holiness movement, which predated Pentecostalism, originated in the United States in the 1840's and 1850's as an endeavor to preserve and propagate John Wesley's teachings on entire sanctification and Christian perfection. The pioneers of the movements were convinced that the mainline denominations had become disconnected from the biblically-based spirituality of early Christianity and had admitted unregenerated individuals into their respective memberships. The Holiness movement experienced significant growth from about 1888 to 1935, becoming international and developing into many sectarian bodies with strong Pentecostal emphases.

African Americans responded to the new trends of Holiness and Pentecostal beliefs because they shared a similar belief that the mainline denominations of African American denominational churches had become devoid of the emotional content of the Christianity. They felt that the mainline churches had acculturated religiosity with the materialistic class of white American denominations. G.S. Wilmore described: "The period between 1890 and the Second

World War was one of the luxuriant growth and proliferation of many forms of black religion in the United States and Africa that challenged the bourgeoisification of the mainline denominations."[51] He saw the evolution of "Black Holiness and Pentecostalism from southern folk religion pressure-cooked in the teeming ghettos of the North, mixed in fascinating combinations with some of the black consciousness and nationalistic" tendencies emerging among African Americans.[52]

In reality, the roots of Pentecostalism extended deep into the general biracial Holiness movement among Methodists after the Civil War with an emphasis on "entire sanctification." With the emergence of the Holiness movement began a strong evangelical and fundamentalist theological emphasis stressing the fact that the church and the sacraments were not necessary for salvation, which is a direct work of the Spirit. They stressed a commitment to what was called the "foursquare gospel"—Jesus as Savior, sanctifier, healer, and coming-again Lord. Again, these teachings were the logical deduction from John Wesley's doctrine of Christian perfection which greatly defined Methodism and the later Holiness and Pentecostal movements among American Christians.

Specifically, the origin of African American Pentecostalism must be traced by the Rev. William J. Seymour, a former member of the Methodist Episcopal Church, born in Centerville, Louisiana. In 1895, he moved to Indianapolis, Indiana, and again moved in 1900 to Cincinnati, Ohio, where he came under the influence of Martin Wells Knapp, a former Methodist minister who had formed an independent Holiness school and mission. Later, Rev. Seymour joined the Church of God and was ordained into the Holiness ministry. In 1906, he was invited by Rev. Neely Terry, an African American woman preacher of the Nazarenes, to move to Los Angeles, California, to preach in her pulpit, resulting in his call to become the pastor of a newly formed African American Holiness congregation affiliated with the predominantly white Southern California Holiness Association.

During a Pentecostal revival meeting, Rev. Seymour preached a sermon with emphasis on the Pentecostal experience, resulting in some worshipers actually experiencing glossolalia (speaking in tongues). Soon, he experienced the same spiritual occurrence. Those who had such experiences decided to congregate and rent a building on Azusa Street, the former site of First African Methodist Episcopal Church of Los Angeles. The congregation consisted of African Americans, Hispanics, and Euro-Americans. Rev. William J. Seymour designated the congregation "Pentecostal" and in 1907, formally incorporated the Azusa Street Apostolic Faith Mission of Los Angeles, California, which soon became nationally renowned. The mission witnessed steady growth resulting from Rev. Seymour's preaching and publication of his periodical called the *Apostolic Faith*. To facilitate the growth of the movement, he published in 1915 the Doctrines and Discipline to guide those who remained in his movement.

However, internal dissent soon interrupted the growth of the Azusa church movement. As early as 1907, J.D. Young, Charles Harrison Mason, and J.A. Jeter arrived at the Azusa church to experience the spiritual awakening of the revival movement. Young and Mason believed that they received the baptism of the Holy Spirit, but Jeter did not share their experience. Evidently, these men reflected the divided opinions existing within the revival movement. When these three men went to Memphis, they discovered the widespread division operative within Pentecostalism.

Later in 1907, the General Assembly of the Church of God in Christ met in Jackson, Mississippi, to discuss the divisive issue. The assembly decided to withdraw the right hand of fellowship from Mason and all others who held the Pentecostal doctrine of speaking in tongues. Mason left the assembly with a large portion of its delegates and reorganized as the First General Assembly of the Pentecostal Church of God in Christ. A lawsuit developed between the divided assemblies, resulting in the court decision to allow the followers of Mason to keep the charter and the name, "Church of God in Christ." The denomination grew rapidly under the episcopate of Mason, who remained as the bishop until his death in 1961. In its beginning as a denomination, the church reported ten congregations in Tennessee, Mississippi, Arkansas, and Oklahoma, with Bishop Mason serving as the "Chief Apostle" as well as elder. By 1948, over 14,000 delegates of the denomination took part in the dedication of Mason's Tabernacle in Memphis, Tennessee, as the world headquarters. It became the largest African American Pentecostal denomination in the United States, according to the *1992 Yearbook of American Churches*. As early as 1964, the denomination reported 4,150 churches with a membership of 419,466 members in the US, Africa, and the West Indies. By 1992, the denomination under the leadership of Bishop Louis H. Ford, reported millions of members with jurisdictions in all fifty states and fifty-four foreign countries.[53] The growing church took on a denominational structure similar to other bodies governed by the Episcopal form of government. In establishing the Episcopal form of government, the denomination differed from other Pentecostal bodies.

After the division, the opposing group reorganized into the Church of Christ (Holiness) USA, under the leadership of Bishop Charles Price Jones. Initially, the Church of Christ (Holiness) USA was founded by Rev. Jones, a former Baptist minister, who left the Baptist denomination because of his emphasis on sanctification through the Holy Spirit. It was initially designed as an interdenominational body. But in 1998, it became a full-fledged Holiness denomination.

In 1932, the Church of Christ (Holiness) U.S.A. faced a division over the polity of Episcopal leadership. Rev. Justice Bowe of Hot Springs, Arkansas, opposed that polity, expressing belief in congregational polity. Hence, he organized in the Church of God in Christ Congregational. The new body differed only with the parent body over the issue of polity and conscientious objection to war. The new denomination experienced relatively slow growth.

These were some of the pioneer movements among African American Pentecostalism. By the 1960's, the Holiness and Pentecostal movement became characterized by internal division and the proliferation of new denominations. Among them were the African Universal Church founded in Jacksonville, Florida, in 1927, by Archbishop Clarence C. Addison; the Alpha and Omega Pentecostal Church of America, Inc., organized in 1945 by Rev. Magdalene Phillips; Apostolic Assemblies of Christ, Inc., founded by former members of the Pentecostal Churches of the Apostolic Faith; Apostolic Church of Christ, Inc., founded in Winston-Salem, North Carolina, by Bishop Johnnie Draft; Bible Way Church of Our Lord Jesus Christ Worldwide, Inc. organized by Elder Smallwood E. Williams in 1957 out of a dispute within the Church of Our Lord Jesus Christ of the Apostolic Faith; and the Bible Way Pentecostal Apostolic Church founded in 1960 by Rev. Curtis P. Jones, a minister in the Church of Our Lord Jesus Christ of the Apostolic Faith headed by Bishop Robert Clarence Lawson. Significantly, The Church of the Lord Jesus Christ of the Apostolic Faith, under the leadership of Bishop S. McDowell Shelton, Apostle and General Overseer, advanced an international radio broadcast which claimed to be the only "real church" proclaiming "the whole truth." With headquarters in Philadelphia, Bishop Shelton, with his emphasis on "Jesus only" theology, constantly lashed out at other church leaders whom he believed to be false prophets leading a multitude of members to hell because of their false biblical teachings. He was even reluctant to recognize the legitimacy of other Holiness, Pentecostal, and Apostolic denominations. These noteworthy movements were among many other Holiness, Pentecostal, and Apostolic denominations among African American Christians.

Among the many innovations of the African American Holiness and Pentecostal movement was the restoration of the music of the pioneer African American churches. With the Americanization and adaptation of African American mainline denominations to European hymns and gospels, the Holiness and Pentecostal churches preserved the traditional Negro Spirituals of antebellum churches. To be sure, the spirituality and general worship experiences of antebellum Christianity were enhanced by these new sects and denominations. Revivalism was very much alive with the advance of these rapidly growing groups.

(Endnotes)

[1] Charles Harris Wesley, *Richard Allen, Apostle of Freedom* (Washington, D.C.: Ass. Publ., 1935), 52-53.

[2] Ibid., 80.

[3] Ibid., 136-137.

[4] Ibid., 140.

[5] Ibid.

[6] Ibid., 87.

[7] George F. Bragg, *Men of Maryland* (Baltimore, MD: Church Advocate Press, 1914), 39-40.

[8] Wesley, 152.

[9] Daniel Alexander Payne, *Recollections of Seventy Years* (New York: Arno Press, 1969), 100-101.

[10] Wesley, 155.

[11] Ibid., 176-177.

[12] Ibid., 179.

[13] The Episcopal Address Presented by Bishop M. H. Davis to the Thirty-second Quadrennial Session of the General Conference of the African Methodist Episcopal Church at Philadelphia, May 1944, Published by Order of the Conference of the Methodist Episcopal Church, 44.

[14] Ibid., 44-45.

[15] Ibid., 45.

[16] Charles Eric. Lincoln and Lawrence H. Mamiya, *The Black Church in the African American Experience* (Durham, North Carolina: Duke University Press, 1990), 55.

17 William Jacob Walls, *The African Methodist Episcopal Zion Church: Reality of the Black Church* (Charlotte, NC: A.M.E. Zion Publ. House, 1974), 49-50.

18 J. W. Hood, *One Hundred Years of the African Methodist Episcopal Zion Church* (New York, NY: A.M.E. Zion Book Concern, 1895), 162.

19 Walls, 94.

20 Ibid., 71.

21 Ibid., 126.

22 Ibid., 130.

23 Ibid., 131.

24 Ibid., 282.

25 Ibid., 298-299.

26 Ibid., 312.

27 Ibid., 328.

28 Ibid., 329-330.

29 Ibid., 336-337.

30 Jno J. Tigert and John Wesley, *The Doctrines of the Methodist Episcopal Church in America: 1974 Bicentennial Edition* (Memphis, TN: Christian Methodist Episcopal Publishing House, 1976), 4-5.

31 Joseph Andrew Johnson, *Our Faith, Heritage and Church* (Place of Publication Not Identified: Publisher Not Identified, 1975), 38-39.

32 *The Star of Zion*, January 12, 1984, 12.

33 *The Star of Zion*, October 6, 1983, 1-2.

34 *The Star of Zion*, October 6, 1983, 2.

35 *The Afro-American*, Baltimore, Maryland, June 25, 1938, 11.

36 Ibid., 11.

37 Ibid.

38 *The Afro-American*, Baltimore, Maryland, February 23, 1943, 1.

39 *The Star of Zion*, March 14, 1985, 6.

40 *The Afro-American*, Baltimore, Maryland, March 23, 1943, 6.

41 *The Afro-American*, Baltimore, Maryland, January 28, 1947, 6.

42 *The Afro-American*, Baltimore, Maryland, December 21, 1946, 36.

43 Ibid.

[44] *The Afro-American*, Baltimore, Maryland, January 28, 1947, 3.

[45] *The Afro-American*, Baltimore, Maryland, June 29, 1943, 1.

[46] *The Philadelphia Tribune*, September 5, 1989, 4B.

[47] J. Taylor. Stanley, *A History of Black Congregational Christian Churches of the South* (New York: United Church Press for the American Missionary Association, 1978), 49.

[48] Ibid., 49-50.

[49] Ibid., 58.

[50] Ibid., 138-139.

[51] Gayraud S. Wilmore, *Black Religion and Black Radicalism an Interpretation of the Religious History of Afro-American People* (New York: Orbis Books, 1986), 152.

[52] Ibid., 152.

[53] *The Chicago Defender*, November 28, 1992, 13.

Chapter 5

EMANCIPATION, CHURCH GROWTH, AND NEW AFRICAN AMERICAN RELIGIOUS MOVEMENTS

The issuance of President Abraham Lincoln's Emancipation Proclamation and the fall of the Confederate States of America radically altered the economic and social milieu of African Americans. First, with the proclamation, the Union effectively denied the Confederacy slavery as a secure economic base and opened the doors for slaves to flee the plantations and find freedom behind the military lines of the Union armies. This was the beginning of a major demographic shift in the African American population, perhaps exceeding the effectiveness of the Underground Railroad. Secondly, the fall of the Confederate States of America, which had established in its Constitution the legal perpetuation of the institution of slavery, effectively altered the social and economic environment of the remaining slaves and subsequent freedmen as well as what John Hope Franklin called in his book *From Slavery to Freedom* the "quasi-free Negroes."

At the end of the Civil War, the economic and social environment was changed for both white southerners as well as African Americans. It had been the bloodiest and most destructive war fought on American soil, leaving staggering numbers of victims on the battlefields primarily located in the southern region of America. The solidarity and efficiency of the plantation system was destroyed. Wealthy southern community leaders saw their plight altered through their failed investment in Confederate currency. John Hope Franklin described:

> "At the end of the war scores of visitors from the North and other parts of the world swarmed over the South, and their descriptions of the prostrate South all dwell upon the widespread devastation suffered by the Confederacy. Fields were laid waste, cities burned, bridges and roads destroyed. Even most of the woefully inadequate factories were leveled, as if to underscore the unchallenged industrial superiority of the North."[1]

The traditional poor whites and the newly created poor white element of southern society wandered over the lands as refugees without secure housing facilities and local resources for rebuilding.

To be sure, these circumstances altered the relationship between white southerners and African Americans. Southern whites bemoaned the end of total control over their former slaves and blamed them for their new economic plight. Much of their paternalistic feeling toward African Americans turned into bitterness. A resurgence of terrorist organizations such as the Ku Klux Klan and Knights of the White Camellias took place with devastating consequences for African Americans. Hadley Cantril reported, "During the Reconstruction Period after the Civil War, the lynching of freed slaves was conducted with new vigor. Wholesale 'nigger hunts' were organized and scores of Negroes were rounded up and killed in bunches. As late as the decade between 1889 and 1899, there were 1,875 lynching reported."[2]

More significant than the new southern white experience was the radical economic and social shift of African Americans. However, they did not respond to their new circumstances with violence and hatred but with tempered hopefulness and a rugged determination for survival in freedom. Slaves had not been prepared physically, economically, and psychologically for emancipation. Upon their entrée into freedom, Rev. J.W.E. Bowen observed:

> "No other people ever had more disadvantages to contend with on their issue into freedom. They were seduced, deceived, misled. Their habits of industry were destroyed, and they were fooled into believing that they could be legislated into immediate equality with a race that, without mentioning superiority of ability and education, had a thousand years' start of them. They were made to believe that their only salvation lay in aligning themselves against the other race, and following blindly the adventurers who came to lead them to a new promised land. It is no wonder that they committed great blunders and great excesses."[3]

Even more pointedly, Rev. M.C.B. Mason reported, "A generation ago, he had practically nothing. He started out with scarcely a name—poor, ignorant, degraded, demoralized, as slavery had left him.... Without a home, without a foot of land, without the true sense of real manhood, ragged, destitute, so freedom found him.... Under these peculiar circumstances and amid these peculiar difficulties he began life for himself."[4] Out of this abject poverty, some freedmen were forced to return to the plantations with promises of meager financial compensations. Others wandered and relocated in their quest for survival in emancipation.

African American church leaders, with the assistance of some northern philanthropic minded preachers and teachers and the Freedmen's Bureau, sought with great determination to meet the spiritual, economic, psychological, and economic needs of the freedmen dispersed within the South. Most of the leaders came from the ranks of African American churches. Some were educated southerners who had never been slaves; and, others were basically illiterate freedmen. They were highly challenged by the fact that the ex-slaves were about 90 percent illiterate and by the efforts of the former master class and its allies to restore the race controls of slavery through Black Codes and strict rules on employment, vagrancy, and residence.

Church leaders found a positive ally for the protection of African Americans in the Freedmen's Bureau, the shortened name of the U.S. Bureau of Refugees, Freedmen, and Abandoned Lands (1865-72), established during Reconstruction to act as a welfare agency for freed slaves in the South and led by Major O.O. Howard. The bureau assisted by furnishing supplies and medical services, establishing schools, supervising contracts between freedmen and their employers, and managing confiscated or abandoned lands. John Hope Franklin remarked:

"Within four years the Bureau had issued twenty-one million rations to white and Negro freedmen.... It assisted in the settlement of some thirty thousand persons who had been displaced by the war. After passage of the Southern Homestead Act of 1866, the Bureau hoped to assist Negroes in obtaining farms under its terms. The lands that were opened up were, for the most part, inferior and unattractive. Although the Bureau would provide free transportation to the new lands and one month's subsistence, Negroes had no means to support while they developed the land. With the exception of a few locations in Florida, Louisiana, and Arkansas, the lands remained unsettled. The 'forty acres' were most unattractive—and there were no mules.[5]

Even with some of its apparent failures, the Freedman's Bureau was still utilized by church leaders to provide for the survival of African Americans in emancipation.

The next form of assistance came from northern churches and philanthropic individuals. Even before the close of the Civil War, white churches of the North became involved in relief work among African Americans by establishing Freedmen Societies as early as the end of 1862. Subsequently, Freedmen's Relief Associations were in every section of the North. The United Presbyterians of Ohio formed a Freedmen's Society in 1863; while the same year the Baptists, the United Brethren, and the Reformed Presbyterians formed their own societies. In 1865, the Protestant Episcopal Church formed a Freedmen's Society, and the same year the Congregationalists began their large work among African Americans and called upon their churches to provide substantial support for the cause. The Methodist Episcopal Church formed in 1866 their Freedman's Aid Society. To the disdain of some southern churchmen, these societies made the work among freedmen "the great benevolent enterprise of the church."[6] Indirectly, these societies aided the expansion of Christianity among African Americans.

Kletzing and Crogman summarized the assistance of biracial churches to the freedmen:

> "In education and evangelism among the Negroes, the various religious bodies have been especially active. Among these bodies the Congregationalists claim to have spent $11,000 for the Negro, and spend now nearly $400,000 a year. The Methodists have spent since emancipation $6,000,000, and are now spending annually through the Freedman's Aid and Southern Educational Society $350,000; The Presbyterian Board of Missions for Freedmen in twenty years have spent $2,400,000, and in addition to this contribution founded Lincoln University, Pennsylvania, in 1859. The Baptists [have spent] since 1865, $3,000,000; the Southern Presbyterian Church, $55,000, between 1878 and 1894; [and] the Christian Church, $100,000."[7]

Even in these biracial churches, their African American minority memberships contributed financially toward the assistance for the Freedmen.

Church Growth among African American Baptists

The church growth among African American Baptists, as well as among other African American denominations, must be viewed in the context of the general demographics and statistics in the United States. Kletzing and Crogman reported: "In 1800 the slave population was over 900,000; in 1830 it had reached about 2,000,000; in 1840 it was estimated to be about 2,500,000; and in 1850 it was about 3,000,000. In 1860 the aggregate Negro population in the United States was about 4,500,000, of which about 4,000,000 were slaves. Nearly 3,000,000 of the slaves were in the rural South."[8] The African American population increased from three-quarters of a million to nearly ten million in the period of 120 years from 1790 to 1910, and of this increase, approximately one-half was in the four decades between 1870 and 1910. The African American population of the South in 1910 numbered 8,749,427, and amounted to 89 percent, or approximately nine-tenths of the total African American population of the United States. At the date of the first census in 1790, Virginia's African American population of 305,493 greatly exceeded that of any other state. Two-fifths of the total African American population of the nation resided in Virginia. Other densely populated states in excess of 100,000 were Maryland, 111,079; North Carolina, 105,547; South Carolina, 108,895; and Georgia, 29,662. Of the states reporting African American population of at least 200,000 in 1910, all were southern. Georgia ranked first in African American population in 1910; Mississippi, the second most populous state; and Alabama, the third most populous state.[9]

With the large population of freedmen in the South, a southern evangelistic strategy was aggressively advanced in rural and, to a certain degree, in urban centers of the southern states. Although trained clergy leadership was rare among African American Baptists, their preachers were still the undisputed leaders in the communities. Part of their success may be attributed to Spirit-filled preaching, revivals or "protracted meetings," and the ability of local pastors and evangelists to convince large numbers of African Americans of their unique "call" into the ministry. Much of the culture of the "invisible institution" was brought into the worship experiences of the churches. The local autonomy of Baptist churches and the ability to advance upward in leadership positions without initial educational skills proved to be very attractive to the freedmen. The free socialization of these churches gave them a new sense of personal worth or self-actualization. Hence, African American Baptist churches, like other denominations, were able to begin the long process of humanizing a dehumanized population.

By 1890, there were 1,348,989 African American Baptists in the United States as reported by the National Baptists. Although the largest population still resided in the rural South, Baptist churches were rapidly being planted in northern and western states. There were 12,533 African American Baptist churches, valued at $9,038,549. The Free Baptist movement, a small group distinguished from regular Baptists, reported 5 churches in 1890 with 271 members and church property valued at $13,300. The Colored Primitive Baptists in America reported 323 churches, with 18,162 members; and, the value of their church property was $296,539. These statistics were reported in the Department of Commerce and Labor, Bureau of the Census, 1906. Comparatively, the 1906 statistics reflect extensive increases in all Baptist groups except the Free Baptists. The National Baptist Convention reported 18,534 churches; 2,261,607 members, and church property valued at $24,437,272. This was a 47.9 percent increase over the 1890 report, representing 50.4 percent of the total number of African American organizations in the United States. Also, National Baptists reported the largest membership among other denomination representing 61.4 percent of the entire membership of African American organizations, as also reported by the Bureau of the Census, 1906.[10]

Similarly, the Sunday school movement among National Baptists experienced tremendous advances. One of the earliest Sunday schools among African American Baptists was organized by Rev. Moses Clayton in 1834, later evolving into the Colored Peoples First Baptist Church of Baltimore, Maryland. The movement spread rapidly to other African American churches. The aim of the Sunday schools was to provide general rudimentary as well as specifically religious education. The National Baptist Publishing House was organized largely to provide literature for Sunday schools. In 1901, Rev. R.H. Boyd, secretary and manager of the National Baptist Publishing House, reported that the publishing house had filled 43,051 orders for Sunday school literature and other religious supplies and had sent out in the Sunday School Department 5,509,000 copies of periodicals.[11] In 1905, National Baptist leaders organized the Sunday School Congress which also experienced rapid growth. By 1906, they reported to the Bureau of Census 17,478 Sunday schools, with 924,665 students. The total number of Sunday schools among African Americans was 34,681 nationally; while, the National Baptists reported 51.6 percent of all existing Sunday schools. Sunday schools and Baptist Training Unions played key roles in the Christian education of African American Baptists.

African American Baptist church growth continued to increase rapidly in the early twentieth century. With rapid population increases and expanding educational opportunities for the laity as well as the clergy, churches developed greater venues for the evangelization and edification of African Americans. Various statistical reports reflect Baptist church growth. In 1922, there were 3,116,325 National Baptists with 21,113 churches, 19,423 ministers, 20,099 Sunday schools, and 1,305,087 Sunday school students. There were 13,362 members of the Free Will Baptists with 170 churches, 294 ministers, and 90 Sunday schools. Primitive Baptists had 15,144 members with 336 churches, 600 ministers, and 88 Sunday schools with 3,607 students.[12] In 1926, the statistical report reflects Baptist growth in sixteen large American cities: Fort Worth, 15,896; Houston, 33,960; Richmond, 54,041; Dallas, 24,023; San Antonio, 14,341; Louisville, 40,087; Nashville, 35,633; Kansas City, 30,719; Atlanta, 62,769; New Orleans, 100,930; Birmingham, 70,320; Washington, 109,966; Baltimore, 108,322; Memphis, 61,181; St. Louis, 69,854; and, Norfolk, 43,392.[13] In 1936, there were 23,093 National Baptist churches; 7,547 in urban areas, 15,546 in rural areas; with 3,782,464 total membership—1,872,909 in urban areas, and 1,909,555 in rural areas. The Colored Primitive Baptists had 1,009 churches, 353 located in urban areas and 656 located in rural areas, with a total membership of 43,897, with 18,414 located in urban areas and 25,483 in rural areas.[14]

In 1947, the United American Free Will Baptist Church experienced some significant growth when the Free Will Baptist Church of America, Inc. of Missouri and the Original Free Will Baptist Church of North Carolina merged to expand the ministry of the denomination. The western union, with 100,000 members, was led by Rev. E. W. Warfield; and the Southern region with 7,000 members was led by Rev. W.W. Askew, General Moderator. With the merger, the United American Free Will Baptist Church had 32 conferences, 498 ministers, and 75,000 members. The denomination owned church property valued at approximately $1 million.[15] Nevertheless, the merger did not constitute the body as one of the larger African American Baptist denominations.

By the end of the twentieth century, African American Baptists of three major denominations had firmly established the lead in the number of churches and members in the United States. Baptist churches passed through many crises such as church and denominational splits, sects and cults, civil court battles, societal racism, competing political ideologies, the civil rights revolution, the new morality, and the rise of secular humanism without any serious setbacks in membership growth. They struggled to meet the challenges of denominationalism, family life, evangelism, economic development, education, and global expansion. Toward the end of the twentieth century and the beginning of the twenty-first century, some particular social forces such as poverty, dysfunctional family life, the drug culture and street violence, the criminal justice system, and the emerging sexual culture showed serious signs of impacting church growth, especially in inner city communities. The rise of megachurches may prove to offset some of these challenges.

Church Growth among African American Methodists

The various African Methodist Episcopal denominations' church growth closely approximates that of Baptists. To be sure, the African Methodist Episcopal Church and the African Methodist Episcopal Zion Church experienced the largest growth among African Methodism during the late nineteenth and early twentieth centuries. The two denominations were quick to evangelize and educate the freedmen in cooperation with the Freedmen's Bureau and Methodists from the North. They also benefitted from a significant exodus of African Americans from biracial Methodist churches in the South. Sometimes the two denominations competed for the membership of these African American Methodists who decided to leave the Methodist Episcopal Church, South. Concomitantly, both denominations spread further southwest and to the western states where a sizable number of freedmen resided. In these areas, they planted new churches and organized annual conferences.

As early as 1890, the African Methodist Episcopal Church reported 2,481 churches with a membership of 452,725. By 1906, the denomination had grown to 6,647 churches with a membership of 494,777; and, 6,285 Sunday schools with 292,689 students. Similarly, the African Methodist Episcopal Zion Church reported 1,704 churches in 1890 with a membership of 349,788. In 1906, the denomination had grown to 2,204 churches, but the membership had declined to 184,542; but it had 2,092 Sunday schools with 107,692 students. This brief decline in membership may be attributed to internal challenges and the competition between the two major African Methodist Episcopal denominations.

The third largest African Methodist Episcopal denomination was the Colored Methodist Episcopal Church, later known as the Christian Methodist Episcopal Church. As previously mentioned, this denomination was organized out of the biracial Methodist Episcopal Church, South. The majority of the African American Methodists who had opted not to unite with either of the two independent Methodist denominations were residing in the South. In 1860, they were slaves who had come from plantation missions or segregated congregations in Southern towns numbering about 207,766. They were not organized into a denomination until 1870. After the separation the Methodist Episcopal Church, South became all white and highly racist. Hence, none of the African American churches remained in the denomination after the organization of their own denomination. However, a significant number of northern African American Methodists elected to remain in the Methodist Episcopal Church, North. Harry V. Richardson offered several reasons for the decision of some northern African American Methodists to remain in the Methodist Episcopal Church: "The Negroes who joined the M.E. Church after the Civil War did so for several reasons; first, because of the educational and other services rendered to the freedmen; secondly, because they wanted to be part of the main body of Methodism, rather than in the separate all-black churches which in reality were segregated Methodist churches."[16]

Nevertheless, the majority of African American Methodists, especially in the South, became members of the Colored Methodist Episcopal Church. By 1890, there were 1,759 churches with 129,383 members of the separated denomination. In 1906, the denomination had increased to 2,381 churches, 172,996 members, and 2,328 Sunday schools with 92,457 students. By 1947, the denomination had decreased to 2,063 churches, but it increased in membership to 269,915, with 632 urban and 1,431 rural congregations.

The rural nature of the membership in the Colored Methodist Church reflected the general conditions of most other African American denominations. Most African American denominations faced challenging problems in rural areas, especially in the South. Among the challenge were: 1. Lack of an educated ministry; 2. Migration of lay leaders to urban areas; 3. Decrease in agricultural economic opportunities with the tenant farming system; and, 4. Inadequate educational opportunities in the segregated school systems. Jessie P. Guzman addressed some of these issues:

"Forty-three and seven-tenths percent (43.7) of the Negroes of American in 1930 were in cities. The rural church membership constituted 64.7 per cent or nearly two-thirds of the Negro church members, while 54.3 per cent of the Negroes live in the rural districts. Almost half of the Negro population, 48.6 percent, lived in the cities in 1940, but the Church has not made adequate provisions to cope with the problems of church membership, although the average city church has 219 members and is twice as large as the average church in rural districts, which has 109 members. The largest portion of non-church Negroes is in the cities.... In hundreds of communities the churches have been abandoned and sold, because the few people left have been unable to support or carry on the work of the church. The great demand for trained preachers is so great and the number so few that the rural churches have most inadequate leadership."[17]

Nevertheless, urban African American churches tended to increase in membership even in the context of great social, political, and economic challenges. Many of the most talented ministers migrated to urban areas. The episcopal systems of African American Methodism tended to make appointments to larger churches on the bases of ministerial skills.

To be sure, African American Methodism was also challenged by internal controversies. Several small denominations grew out of the African Methodist Episcopal Church and the African Methodist Episcopal Zion Church. As early as 1907, the Independent AME Church denomination was organized in Jacksonville, Florida, by twelve elders who withdrew from the African Methodist Episcopal Church. But in 1940, the new denomination had only 12 churches with 1000 members. Even earlier in 1885, the Reformed Methodist Union Episcopal Church was organized at Charleston, South Carolina, among persons withdrawing from the same denomination. By 1942, the new denomination had 43 churches with 3,000 members. The African Methodist Episcopal Zion denomination experienced similar problems. As early as 1869, the Reformed Union Apostolic Church was formed at Boydton, Virginia, by Elder James R. Howell of New York, a minister of the denomination. In 1950, the new denomination had 55 churches with a membership of 1200. In 1929, the Kodesh Church of Immanuel was formed by Rev. Frank Killingworth from among a group withdrawing from the denomination. In 1936, the new denomination had 9 churches with a membership of 562.[18]

Two other denominations of African Methodism emerged which did not evolve out of existing African American denominations, namely, the African Union Colored Methodist Protestant Church, U.S.A. and Canada; and the Congregational Methodist Church. The former denomination was formed in 1805 out of the Methodist Episcopal Church. It became a denomination in 1813. In 1890, the denomination had 40 churches, with 3,415 members. By 1906, it had grown to 69 churches, with 5,592 members. By 1947, it had decreased in the number of churches to 45 churches but increased in the number of members to 4,239. The majority of its members, 2,384, lived in urban areas while 1,855 lived in rural areas. The Congregational Methodist Church was organized in 1852, by a small group in Georgia who withdrew from the Methodist Episcopal Church, South. The separation was caused by a rejection of the episcopacy and itinerancy and by a desire that each local church should have the right to call its own pastor rather than receive one appointed by a bishop of the Methodist Episcopal Church, South. In 1887, the denomination faced a severe crisis resulting in a sharp decline when two-thirds of members withdrew to join the Congregational Church. However, its doctrine remained largely Methodist. In 1890, it had only 9 churches with 316 members.[19] Fortunately, the Congregational Methodist Church was able to recover from the crisis, and by 1968 it reported 223 churches and 308 ministers.

The Growth Phenomenon of Pentecostal and Apostolic Churches

To a certain extent, church growth among Pentecostal and Apostolic churches was paradoxically hindered and propelled by the splintering of the various denominations at the turn of the century. Increasingly, the twentieth century was characterized by the birth of new denominations, mostly splintered bodies from Holiness and Pentecostal movements. As previously mentioned, the influence of the revivals and camp meetings gave impetus to the splintering of both white church bodies and late nineteenth century African American Holiness and Pentecostal churches from which other Pentecostal and Apostolic denominations emerged rapidly, beginning initially as small sects. Even within some traditional denominations,

Pentecostalism penetrated with divisive tendencies. Principally, it clashed with the bourgeoisie culture within these churches. African American churches had become increasingly susceptible to this emerging culture.

Elmer T. Clark has offered an insightful method of classification for the emerging Pentecostal and Apostolic Churches: 1. Perfectionist or Subjectivist sects, including the previously mentioned African American Methodist groups; 2. Charismatic or Pentecostal sects, including the Pentecostal Assemblies of the World; the United Holy Church of America; the Church of God in Christ; the Free Zion Church of Christ; the Church of God (Holiness); the Churches of the Living God; the Apostolic Overcoming Holy Church of God; the House of Prayer; the Father Divine's Peace Movement; the National David Spiritual Temple of Christ Church Union; the Latter House of the Lord for All People and the Church of the Mountain, Apostolic Faith; the Sought Out Church of God in Christ and Spiritual House of Prayer, Inc.; Triumph the Church and the Kingdom of God in Christ; the House of God, the Holy Church of the Living God, the Pillar and Ground of the Truth; House of Prayer for All People;, and the Christ's Sanctified Holy Church, Colored; 3. Communistic sects including at least one African American sect called Church of God and Saints of Christ ("Black Jews"); and 4. Legalistic or Objectivist sects, including the Commandment Keepers or Black Jews, The African Orthodox Church, the African Orthodox Church of New York, the Colored Primitive Baptists; and the United American Free Will Baptist Church. Most of these bodies, influenced by revivalism and Pentecostalism, were organized by charismatic individuals or groups separating from existing denominations or sects.

An early proponent of the Black Jewish movement was William Christian, born a slave in Mississippi in 1856, who organized the Church of God, utilizing the motto "Christian Workers for Fellowship" in 1889. Before venturing out on his new religious path, he had been active as a Baptist minister but left the denomination after a dispute with another Baptist minister. It was under a brush arbor in Caine Creek, near Wrightsville, Arkansas, where he began preaching his version of Christianity. According to his preaching, African Americans are the descendants of the lost tribes of Israel. He firmly believed in the truth of the new movement, feeling that it was based on the faith "laid down in the Bible."[20] However, only a few African Americans joined the Church of God.

In 1892, Rev. William Sanders Crowdy (born 1847 in Maryland of slave parents, but migrated to Oklahoma), appeared on the African American religious scene during the early stages of the sectarian movement. He had a vision of new religion, called the Church of God and Saints of Christ, while plowing an Oklahoma field in Kansas. He came to believe some new ideas spreading among a few nationalistic minded African Americans that the original Jews were black people. Within a year he moved to Kansas City, initially finding employment as a hotel cook for the Santa Fe Railroad. In 1896, he decided to proceed with the organization of a new religion in Lawrence expressive of Judeo-Christian concepts. Wynia-Trey expressed the probability the new organization began while he was preaching in the streets of Lawrence and gained a large following of more than 2,000 of the total 10,000 African American population in the city.[21] The new church movement adopted Jewish holidays and worshiped in tabernacles but utilized both the Old and New Testaments. Reverend Crowdy organized the Church of God and Saints of Christ in the following Kansas communities: Abilene, Arkansas City, Chanute, Coffeyville, Dodge City, Emporia, Enterprise, Florence, Garden City, Lawrence, Junction City, Girard, Leavenworth, Lyons, Manhattan, Ottawa, Peabody, Salina, Strong City, Topeka, Valley Falls, Wamego, and Wichita. The new movement reached its peak in 1936, but by 1988 declined to about 100 churches.[22]

The twentieth century witnessed an avalanche of small sectarian denominations which challenged the structure and theology of traditional denominations. They impacted the traditional ecumenical spirit of these denominations, especially among Baptists and African Methodists. Also, the early sectarian denominations became culturally and theologically foundational for the establishment of later denominations influenced by the wave of revivalism. Among the earliest twentieth century African American sectarian movements were the Church of God, Sanctified Church (1901); the Triumph the Church and Kingdom of God in Christ (1902), the Christ's Sanctified Holy Church (1903), the Church of the Living God, Pillar and Ground of the Truth, Which He Purchased with His Own Blood, Inc. (1903), the First Born Church of the Living God, (1903), the Christ Sanctified Holy Church (1904), Free Christian Zion Church of Christ (1905), the Apostolic Faith Mission Church of God (1906), the Fire Baptized Holiness Church of the Americas (1908), the Apostolic Faith Church of God (1909), the Apostolic Faith Churches of God, Inc. (1909), the Christ Holy Sanctified Church of America, Inc. (1910), the Church of God, Holiness (1914), the Church of God by Faith, Inc. (1914), the Churches of Christ (Holiness), Inc. (1915), the Church of God (Apostolic), Inc. (1915), the Apostolic Overcoming Holy Church of God in Christ, Inc. (1916), the House of God, the Holy Church of the Living God, the Pillar and Ground of Truth, House of Prayer for All People (1918), and the Bible Church of God, Inc. (1919). To be sure, the first two decades of the twentieth century set the precedent for the birth of a multiplicity of African American sectarian denominations.

The Church of God (Sanctified Church) founded in 1901 in Columbia, Tennessee, by Elder Charles W. Gray and John C. Brown. It was the result of a schism within the movement of Bishop C.H. Mason over the issue of Pentecostalism. The founders of the new movement became firm adherents to the theological belief in "holiness through sanctification by the Holy Spirit" and established the new denomination on this commitment. However, it remained faithful to the Holiness movement of the Church of Christ (Holiness) U.S.A, differing only with the appointment of ministers. The church has the authority to appoint its own ministers. Another schism emerged in 1927 that resulted in Elder Gray establishing the Original Church of God (or Sanctified Church).[23]

In 1902, the Triumph the Church and Kingdom of God in Christ was founded in Georgia by Elder E.D. Smith, emphasizing sanctification and the second coming of Christ. In 1940, the denomination had about 400 churches with a membership of approximately 30,000. The second coming of Christ had become a powerful theme within both white and African American sectarian movements. It had a powerful influence on Elder E.D. Smith.[24]

The Christ's Sanctified Holy Church was organized in 1903 by members who had withdrawn from an African Methodist Episcopal Church in West Lake, Louisiana. Initially, the church became a member of the biracial Christ Sanctified Holy Church which organized it as its extended ministry to African Americans. However, Dempsey Perkins, A.C. Mitchell, James Briller Sr., and Leggie Pleasant organized the new denomination known by two names—the Colored Church South (its original name) and the Christ Sanctified Holy Church Colored—as a denomination in 1904. It placed special emphasis on the doctrines of the Holy Trinity and sanctification.[25] In 1948 the denomination, operating through an annual conference, had 28 churches with a membership of 831.

Also in 1903, the Church of the Living God, the Pillar and Ground of the Truth, Inc. (Lewis Dominion) was organized by Mary Magdalena Lewis Tate in Dixon, Tennessee. She led the denomination to adopt the doctrine of holiness with related principles of conversion, sanctification, water baptism, and baptism of the Holy Spirit as evidenced by glossolalia. She believed that the name of the church was divinely inspired. In 1908 she, initially chief apostle of the church, was ordained to the bishopric by the elders of the church, thus becoming the first know African American woman to become a bishop in a denomination. Subsequently, the church fell victim to several splits. One of the splits was the House of God, Which Is the Church of the Living God, the Pillar and Ground of Truth Without Controversy, also known as the McLeod Dominion, led by Mrs. Mary Frankie Lewis Tate in 1931. After the death of Bishop Tate of the original body, the Church's General Assembly established the office of chief overseer with a triumvirate rule in 1931, with each member overseeing sixteen of the existing forty-eight states of the United States. Subsequently, the denomination became associated with the United Churches of the Living God, the Pillar and Ground of the Truth, Inc. By 1995, the denomination had about 20 churches with a membership of approximately 2,000.[26]

In 1905, the Free Christian Zion Church of Christ was organized at Redemption, Arkansas, by a group of African American ministers originally associated with various denominations. They maintained the general polity of African Methodism. By 1944, the denomination consisted of 37 churches with about 5,838 members.[27]

In 1906, the Apostolic Faith Mission Church of God was organized by F. W. Williams who attended the Azusa Street Revival in Los Angeles and received the baptism of the Holy Spirit under the leadership of William Joseph Seymour. He returned to the South and attempted to organize a branch of the Apostolic Faith Mission in the state of Mississippi. However, he was not successful and decided to go to Mobile, Alabama, to conduct a revival. Strangely enough, he was able to convert a complete congregation of Primitive Baptists to the revival spirit evolving from the Azusa Street Revival. Subsequently, he successfully organized the Apostolic Faith Mission and became its first bishop, embracing the doctrines of Oneness and Apostolic in 1915. He broke ties with William J. Seymour and incorporated a new denomination on October 9, 1915. The new denomination adopted an emphasis on foot-washing with communion, divine healing, and baptizing in the name of Lord Jesus Christ. Herein was the later emphasis on the "Jesus only" in African American sectarian movements. The Jesus Only movement was a major schism within the growing Pentecostal movement. Richard Kyle remarked:

> "It grew out of the 'Pentecostal Unitarian' question, also called the 'Oneness' or 'Jesus Only' issue. Out of this controversy a movement developed which challenged the traditional Christian doctrine of the Holy Trinity. This movement spread rapidly among the Pentecostals, eventually forming about twenty-five religious bodies, the largest being the United Pentecostal Church. The Oneness message had a particular ap-

peal among black people and eventually claimed about one-fourth of all Pentecostals.[28]

In 1982, the denomination had 16 membership churches.[29]

Also in 1906, the Pentecostal Assemblies of the World, Inc. was organized as a racially mixed body in Los Angeles, California, and was the oldest major Apostolic and Pentecostal denomination proclaiming the Jesus Only doctrine. These Pentecostals held the belief that Jesus was Himself the Father God. They maintained a strong emphasis on the doctrines of holiness and sanctification. Bishop Garfield Thomas Haywood of Indianapolis, Indiana, a strong proponent of the Oneness doctrine, was the first prominent African American leader of the denomination. The denomination emphasized speaking in tongues like other Pentecostals but differed from them by its emphasis on its Oneness doctrine. The churches took the radical position that speaking in tongues was a necessary sign of salvation and that baptism in Jesus's name was equally a requirement for salvation. Moreover, they maintained that they were the only people who will go to heaven. Among the social activities denied to their members included theater attendance, dances, mixed bathing, cutting of women's hair, unwholesome radio programs and music, and watching television.[30] By 1993, the Pentecostal Assemblies of the World had become a major African American denomination with 1,000,000 members in 1,600 churches in the United States.[31]

In 1908, the Fire Baptized Holiness Church of the Americas developed from the emphasis of the Fire Baptized Holiness Church which was organized in 1898 in Anderson, South Carolina. The new denomination was founded by Bishop and Mrs. W.E. Fuller. The church placed strong emphasis on holiness and baptism in the Holy Spirit. It became a national association of Fire Baptized Holiness churches, and in 1968 had a membership of 9,008 in 53 churches in the United States.[32]

The year 1909 witnessed the organization of two African American sectarian movements— Apostolic Faith Church of God and the Apostolic Faith Churches of God, Inc. The Apostolic Faith Church of God evolved from the Azusa Street Revival in Los Angeles, under the leadership of William Joseph Seymour and Charles W. Lowe. However, the organizational date of the new denomination has not been clearly formulated. When Charles W. Lowe initially separated from Seymour's movement, he kept the same name but eventually changed it to the Apostolic Faith Church of God and True Holiness. Around the same time, Apostolic Faith Churches of God, Inc. was organized by William Joseph Seymour in Handsom,

Virginia; some time later, the denomination united with six other organizations to create a fellowship convention.[33]

Again in 1910, two more African American sectarian denominations were organized—Christ Holy Sanctified Church of America, Inc., and King's Apostolic Holiness Church of God, Inc. The former was organized and chartered by Judge and Sarah King in Keatchi, Louisiana. As early as 1907, the group had conducted informal meetings in Mansfield, Louisiana. Sarah King had been introduced to the doctrines of sanctification and holiness by a white missionary who came to Louisiana after having been released from membership in the Methodist Episcopal Church of Chincoteague Island, Virginia. Later, Judge King was also converted to the same doctrines, and together they organized the denomination. By 1995, the denomination had more than 250 churches located primarily in the South. During the same year, the King's Apostolic Holiness Church of God, Inc. was founded through the results of the founding of the oldest African American Pentecostal and Holiness church in Baltimore, Maryland, organized in 1907. It became the headquarters church for the new denomination. By 1995, the denomination had 17 churches.[34]

A prominent African American minister in the Church of God in Christ movement was Bishop Virgil Moses Baker, founder of the historic "Mother Church" Baker Temple Church of God in Christ. He was born June 24, 1880, near Pine Bluff, Arkansas. He attended school in Arkansas, and after graduation he studied at Branch Normal College, later known as Arkansas A&M College (currently, the University of Arkansas in Pine Bluff). During Baker's early twenties, he was called to the ministry and began his first mission in Missouri in 1912. Subsequently, he organized more than fifty churches in western Missouri and became a pioneer figure in religious circles in Kansas, Missouri, Iowa, and Nebraska. Baker's prominence in the denomination was instrumental in his later elevation to the bishopric of Western Missouri of the Church of God in Christ.[35]

Similarly, the early twentieth century African American Pentecostal and Holiness movement spread with the founding of several other denominations: the Churches of God, Holiness, founded in 1914, grew to about 42 churches with 25,600 members in 1967; Churches of God (Holiness), Inc., founded in 1915; the Full Gospel Pentecostal Missionary Association, also founded in in 1915; the Apostolic Overcoming Holy Church of God, Inc., founded in 1916; the Bible Church of God, Inc., founded in 1919; and, the Church of Our Lord Jesus Christ of the Apostolic Faith, also founded in 1919. All of these denominations hold in common the basic beliefs in Holiness and Pentecostalism.

With the organization of these early twentieth century African American Pentecostal and Holiness denomination, the latter part of the century witnessed the proliferation of many more like minded denominations with minor doctrinal innovations. Between 1920 and the 1970s, some of the following Pentecostal, Apostolic, and Holiness denominations were organized, some remaining small but others with significant church growth trends: the National David Spiritual Temple of Christ Church, organized in 1921; the Mount Sinai Holy Church of America, organized in 1924; the Churches of Christ Holiness unto the Lord, Inc., organized in 1926; the House of God, Which Is the Church of the Living God, the Pillar and Ground of Truth, Inc., organized in 1926; the Apostolic Holiness Church of America, organized 1927; the New Bethel Church of God in Christ (Pentecostal), organized in 1927; the Original Church of God (or Sanctified Church), organized in 1927; the United House of Prayer for All People, organized in 1927; the Way of the Cross Church of Christ, International, organized in 1928; the Free Church of God in Christ in Jesus' Name, Inc., organized in 1928; the House of God, Which Is the Church of the Living God, the Pillar and Ground of Truth Without Controversy (Keith Dominion), organized in 1931; the Churches of God in Christ Congregational, organized in 1932; the Federated Pentecostal Church International, Inc., organized in 1934; the Latter House of the Lord Apostolic Faith, organized in 1936; the Apostolic Faith Churches of God in Christ, Inc., organized in 1936; the Apostolic Church of Christ in God, organized in 1940; the Apostolic Faith Church of God, Inc., organized in 1952; the Original Glorious Church of God in Christ, Apostolic Faith, Inc., organized in 1952; the United Way of the Cross Churches of Christ of the Apostolic Faith, Inc., organized in 1952; the Universal Christian Spiritual Faith and Churches for All Nations, organized in 1952; the Holy Temple of Jesus Christ Church, Inc., organized in 1954; the Pentecostal Churches of Apostolic Faith, organized in 1957; the Bible Way Pentecostal Apostolic Church, organized in 1960; the Deliverance Evangelistic Church, organized in 1961; the United Church of Jesus Christ Apostolic, Inc., organized in 1961; the True Vine Pentecostal Churches of Jesus, organized in 1961; the Free Gospel Church of the Apostle's Doctrine, organized in 1962; the Pentecostal Miracle Deliverance Center, Inc., organized in 1962; the True Fellowship Church of America, organized in 1964; the First United Church of Jesus Christ (Apostolic), Inc., organized in 1965; the Shrine of the Black Madonna of the Pan African Orthodox Christian Church, organized in 1969; the Church of God in Christ, International, organized in 1969; the Apostolic Assemblies of Christ, Inc., organized in 1970; the National Tabernacle of Deliverance, Inc., organized in 1972; and, the Redeemed Assembly of Jesus Christ, Apostolic, organized in 1979.

The multiplicity of these organizations reflects a tremendous divisive tendency of the Pentecostal, Apostolic, and Holiness Church movement. In fact, many of them were the expressions of strong preachers who interpreted Christianity on their own personal views of the Bible. Most of them had little or no exposure to the fundamental doctrines of the Bible and hermeneutics. Initially, their membership consisted basically of the rural and urban poor population, but a few were later able to attract higher class African Americans throughout the United States. Hence, some of the sects and denominations under better trained leadership and aggressive missionary strategies experienced tremendous growth and development before the beginning of the twenty-first century.

The African American Apostolic faith denominations were Pentecostals that emphasized the return to apostolic Pentecostalism. They believed that they were in continuance of the early church's tradition handed down by the original New Testament apostles. They strongly resisted the emerging secular humanism and biblical criticism of many liberal theologians and Christian churches. Holiness and Pentecostalism became foundational pillars of all the African American denominations and sects utilizing the name Apostolic.

The Coming of Cults in the African American Religious Experience

If the rise and expansion of African American sects challenged the mainline denominations, the cults represented a radical departure from basic Christian beliefs and practices. Just how to classify these new religious movements has been difficult because definitions of the term "cult" vary. The *Twenty-first Century Webster's Family Encyclopedia* defines the word "cult" as "a religious worship of a supernatural object or of a representation of it." To be sure, a cult is a religious body with specific worship forms, or the veneration of a god, closely resembling a sect. Sometimes, "sect" and "cult" are used interchangeably. Sociologists like J.M. Yinger tend to distinguish a cult from a sect by analysis of belief systems and rituals of such religious groups, distinguishing them by their small size, localization, dependence upon a leader with a magnetic personality, and beliefs and rites that deviate widely from the norms of society in general, and those of traditional religions in particular. Richard Kyle devised classifications of cults as fringe religions, alternative religions, or new religions. A social and historical study of the various cults influencing African Americans directly or indirectly will certainly reflect a rather wide deviance from established norms.

The influx of African Americans and foreign immigrants into urban ghettos complicated their experiences of various racial and ethnic groups, especially in a competitive environment for jobs, education, and affordable housing. African Americans who arrived in the urban ghettos of northern cities were largely denied access to labor unions and forced to compete with the immigrants from Europe seeking advantages which were not available in their native countries. Until World War II the industrial workforce of the United States consisted of these European immigrants. Unfortunately for African Americans, these immigrants adopted the existing racial attitudes of white America. James Boggs, in his article "A Black View of the White Worker" suggested:

> "With this view of the land to which they were coming, it was only natural that these workers accepted the attitude toward black people held by the whites already here. It is true that these workers waged many militant struggles against the American capitalists, but these struggles were always limited by the workers' acceptance of racist policies by which the blacks were kept beneath them and by the fact they themselves were willing to keep the blacks down as a basis for their own elevation."[36]

Often, violence erupted in the competition for opportunities in the cities. A.D. Grimshaw, in his 1959 doctoral dissertation at the University of Pennsylvania, entitled, *A Study in Violence,* identified thirty-three major interracial disturbances in the United States between 1900-1949.[37] To be sure, African Americans were the greatest victims of these riots.

In such volatile environments, the poverty-stricken and dehumanized African Americans of the ghettos reached out to any new form of religion that would tend to give them emotional, spiritual, and social relief. Some believed that organized churches had failed to offer them any substantial relief. Gayraud S. Wilmore saw several contributing factors which led to the failure of these churches to meet the needs of these African Americans: 1. The large number of churches that had an inadequately trained ministry and limited resources for work among this increasing population; 2. The African American churches of the1920s and 1930s retained a basically rural orientation insufficient to meet the challenges of urban environments; and, 3. The overall dysfunctional nature of the mainline churches between the two wars weakened the total impact on African American religion in the urban community by reducing the economic and political viability of individual congregations and shattering the institutional solidity of the historic denominations.[38] Hence, the organizers of African American cults were quick to realize the gullibility of these oppressed people seeking survival.

Prominent among charismatic cult leaders of the 1920s and 1930s were such strong personalities such as Marcus M. Garvey (1887-1940), Rev. M. J. Divine ("Father Divine," 1876-1965), Bishop Charles Emmanuel Grace (1882-1960), and Elijah Poole, renamed Elijah Muhammad (1897-1975). Each cult leader capitalized on the gullibility of many poor urban African Americans and offered them new and often exciting alternative religious experiences. Marcus M. Garvey, an immigrant from Jamaica, in 1914 decided to establish the Universal Negro Improvement Association in order to improve the predicament of urban African Americans. In an effort to change the psychological marks of oppression on African Americans, Marcus Garvey offered a message of the African heritage based on the affirmation of a black God. Randall K. Burkett observed about Garvey's doctrine of God: "While Garvey was thus content to have his followers remain within any [black-led] religious organization, whether Protestant or Catholic, Christian or non-Christian, he was not willing for them to retain the religious ideals or conceptualizations of another race. In the first place, he specifically and emphatically rejected the conceptualization of God as white."[39] In this connection, Marcus Garvey once remarked:

> "If the white man has the idea of a white God, let him worship his God as he desires.... We, as Negroes, have found a new ideal. While our God has no color, yet it is human to see everything through one's own spectacles, and since the white people have seen their God through white spectacles, we have only now started out (late though it be) to see our God through our own spectacles.... We Negroes believe in the God of Ethiopia, the everlasting God—God the Father, God the Son and God the Holy Ghost, the one God in all ages. That is the God in whom we believe, but we shall worship Him through the spectacles of Ethiopia."[40]

Clearly, the movement of Marcus Garvey had both religious and socio-political implications. Harold E. Charles remarked:

> "The basic tenets of Garveyism were: economic autonomy, political empowerment, Black liberation theology, and cultural affirmation. Included in each of these were systematic, programmed activities that mobilized the masses of our people into a self-respecting entity. Amidst all

of the pomp and ceremonies, UNIA members were highly trained and disciplined to carry out the philosophy and opinions of their great teacher and leader."[41]

There was also tremendous growth of the organization among African Americans. At the apex of its existence, the UNIA had 1,100 chapters throughout North, Central, and South America, Africa, and Europe with approximately five million members.

To affirm the religious nature of his message, Marcus Garvey was instrumental in the foundation of the African Orthodox Church in New York City in 1921. Actually, the church was founded by George Alexander McGuire for the purpose of providing African Americans with an Episcopalian type of church polity. Together, Marcus Garvey and George A. McGuire sought to establish a firm relationship between the Universal Negro Improvement Association and the new African Orthodox Church. One problem they faced was the difficulty of recruiting African American members of other denominations to work with an organization so closely aligned with the African Orthodox Church and the new theology of Marcus Garvey. Moreover, Garvey envisioned the return of African Americans to Africa, perhaps reminiscent of the antebellum colonization society, to create an independent state. But in 1927, his scheme was interrupted by accusations of financial fraud which resulted in his deportation from the United States. Nevertheless, Garvey's theological influence remained partially intact within the continual African Orthodox Church movement.

The next African American cult leader was home-grown—Father Major Morgan J. Divine, or "Father Divine," allegedly born, George Baker—with the establishment of his Peace Mission Movement in 1919. The *Richmond Afro-American*, January 2, 1965, reported that he was born on a Wayne County farm in Georgia. However, many researchers affirmed that there is no certainty about the actual place of his birth, but apparently Reverend Divine grew up in the South where he was later seen as a traveling preacher in Americus, Georgia, in 1912; and Valdosta, Georgia, in 1914. Initially, he became a member of the First Born Church of the Living God, in Brunswick, Georgia. His early preaching was likely influenced by the perfectionism of the Holiness Movement in the South. He left the South as a young man and relocated in Baltimore, Maryland, where he continued his preaching ministry and taught Sunday school in an African American Baptist church. While in Baltimore, Father Divine met Father Samuel Morris, an itinerant minister who called himself "the Father Eternal." Father Morris organized his own church and made Father Divine his "messenger" or second person in charge. Apparently, Father Divine gained his concept of personal divinity from Father Morris before he left Baltimore.

When Father Divine left Baltimore, he went back South to Valdosta, Georgia, to start his own movement where he was able to attract a small following among both whites and African Americans. In 1919, he migrated to New York and started a religious community located in an eight-room house in Sayville, Long Island. Here, Father Divine gave real birth to his cult which led the congregation to view him as divinity. His popularity spread as he provided housing and food for his followers and preached to them lengthy sermons. Subsequently, he and his movement were harassed, including judicial and civil suits, in efforts to make them leave the area. After several months, he moved his headquarters to Harlem where he officially adopted the name "Father Divine" and attracted a large following of both whites and African Americans. Many of them exercised faith in his divinity and had their lives transformed by their relationship with him, some describing their experiences as conversions similar to Christian conversion. During his daily messages to his followers, which he published in his newspaper, the *New Day*, Father Divine stressed personal morality and the ethical side of religion. His members were forbidden to drink alcohol, smoke, gamble, or own life insurance. In order to solidify his position of the one granting divine favor, he instituted the free messianic banquet table in the Peace Mission where he sat with his followers to enjoy a plentiful variety of food. He proclaimed his own immortality and that of his faithful followers if they kept faith in his divinity.

After Father Divine's influence extended beyond the poor ghetto residents to more affluent African Americans and whites, he was able to obtain a large financial base which resulted in the founding of other missions, hostels, restaurants, stores, and other businesses in every major city on the East Coast of the nation, the Mid-west, on the West Coast, and to a lesser extent in the southern states. His cult attracted millions in America and extended as far as England. In 1936, the *Afro-American* reported that ten million peoples of both races internationally believe that Father Divine, a miraculous preacher, is God in person.[42]

The tremendous economic power and influence of Father Divine caused him to become a victim of criticism on the part of African American church leaders and the investigation of his wealthy headquarters in New York for suspicion of tax evasion. However, the IRS was never successful in bringing a case against him. In fact, Father Divine claimed that he had the power to bring down violent retribution on persons who opposed his movement. Still, his extensive missions and claim to divinity were grounds for the opposition of mainline churches. However, Bishop R.A. Ransom of the CME Church startled the sixty-second annual session of the Washington and Philadelphia Conference when he lauded Father Divine for having a program for "feeding and clothing the people" and calling Jesus the "greatest socialist of all time."[43] Nevertheless, the majority of African American church leaders strongly opposed the work of Father Divine, especially his claim to divinity.

The next major cult leader to proclaim divinity was Bishop Charles Immanuel Grace, or "Sweet Daddy Grace" (1883-1960) as his followers affectionately called him. His original name was Marcelino Manuel da Graça and was from Cape Verde Islands, a possession of Portugal at the time. He migrated to the United States as a seaman around 1900 and settled in New Bedford, Massachusetts, where others Portuguese immigrants settled. Later, he was instrumental in helping other members of the family to migrate to New Bedford. In 1919, Daddy Grace was ordained into the ministry, and in 1924 he opened a small mission in West Wareham, Massachusetts. While on a visit in Harlem, New York, he conceived the idea of organizing a religious sect. According to the *Grace Magazine*, the official organ of the religious sect, he formed the first House of Prayer for All People in 1924 in West Wareham in a poverty-stricken area of the city.

Subsequently, he moved to Charlotte, North Carolina, in 1926 where he preached and baptized a small number of converts. It was in Charlotte that Daddy Grace laid the real foundation of his House of Prayer for All People in the Brooklyn area, which was "the slum-ridden, crime infested section of the city," thus becoming a later tendency on his part to serve in such areas of other cities.[44] After firmly establishing his movement in Charlotte, Daddy Grace baptized approximately 1000 converts annually, utilizing fire hoses. While in New York City, he was arrested for preaching a false doctrine under an old law in the city. A prominent part of his service was the healing ministry during the baptismal services, inviting anyone to come who wanted to be healed.[45] Following the establishment of the House of Prayer for All People, he organized churches in several other North Carolina cities including Winston-Salem, Greensboro, and Wilmington. When he traveled to Virginia, large crowds of oppressed men, women, and children flocked to him during his ministry in Norfolk and Newport News. Similarly, in the ghettos of major cities like Savannah and Augusta, Georgia; Jacksonville and Miami, Florida; and Los Angeles, California, Daddy Grace succeeded in establishing Houses of Prayer for All People, never referring to them as churches.

The worship services of the House of Prayer for All People were based on the traditional Holiness and Pentecostal denominations. Their services included Bible study, exhortations, brass bands, ecstatic dancing, and shouting. Bishop Grace preached against crime and adultery, urging his followers to respect law and order in the community. Also, he advised them to seek gainful employment and to work hard and faithfully. Members of the movement were inspired to obey him because "he gave humble folks status—something to hold on to…the poor, the down-trodden, the neglected, a new self-identity." His teachings positively impacted the communities by curbing crime, violence, and juvenile delinquency.[46]

Like Father Divine, Daddy Grace's ministry was highly criticized by both the religious and secular communities. He was often arrested and compelled to appear in court, but he successfully defended himself which added to his fame and resulted in the myth of his invincibility as a special man of God. He was successful in having approximately three million persons to worship him as divinity, and they contributed to his ministry approximately $25 million.

After the death of Daddy Grace, which brought a great crisis in the House of Prayer, Bishop Walter McCollough was successful in becoming the leader of the House of Prayer for All People. Initially, the election of Bishop McCollough was contested in court by a group that finally left the movement to found the True Grace Memorial House of Prayer for All People. The petition of Bishop McCollough's group claimed that the new body had no right to utilize the original name of the body organized by Daddy Grace. However, the new group filed the following claim entitled "Declaration of Independence and Separation":

> "We the undersigned, presently members of the religious society or church known as the United House of Prayer for All People of the Church on the Rock of the Apostolic Faith, founded by the late Bishop Charles M. "Daddy Grace," do hereby make the following declaration and announcement: 'For reasons hereinafter stated and because the present leaders of said church have departed and deviated from the true doctrine and principles of said church, we shall retain and worship in according with the true faith and doctrine of the said United House of Prayer, as taught by Bishop Grace, but we do hereby separate ourselves from the aforementioned church as now constituted under the leadership and control of Bishop Walter McCollough or said church as having any authority or control over our church property, money, ministers, affairs and religious doctrine…. We do hereby adopt as the official and chartered name of our branch of the United

House of Prayer for All People of the Church on the Rock of the Apostolic Faith, the following, "The True Grace Memorial House of Prayer for All People," which has been duly incorporated and registered under the laws of the District of Columbia."[47]

Despite the continuance of the breakaway movement, the sect or cult under the leadership of Bishop Walter McCollough continued to grow when he added several innovative additions to the program. He modernized the buildings, constructed a senior citizens center in Washington, D.C., opened day care centers and apartments for members, and opened the McCollough Seminary in Richmond, Virginia, for ministers of the movement. Gwendolyn Daniels of the *Charlotte Post* remarked, "Not only is Bishop McCollough recognized and highly respected by his church community, but he has also been recognized by several presidents, governors, and mayors. Most recently, he received recognition from President George Bush."[48]

Another cult movement within the African American community was the Nation of Yahweh founded by Yahweh Ben Yahweh, born in 1935 in Enid, Oklahoma, where his father was a pastor in the Church of God in Christ. He earned his undergraduate degree in psychology at Phillips University in Enid and after serving in the United States Air Force, he graduated from Atlanta University with a graduate degree in economics. In order to continue his spiritual journey, he founded the Modern Christian Church in Atlanta, Georgia, in 1970. After a brief period of time, he came under the influence of Black Hebrew ideas, incorporated an idea of personal divinity, and organized the Nation of Yahweh Movement founded in Miami, Florida. He taught aggressively against the rule of white people, suggesting that Yahweh's original people were black. He urged African Americans to accept their rightful leadership position in the world under the black God, Yahweh.

Soon the cult spread from Miami to other parts of the South. In 1989, the Nation of Yahweh purchased the Barclay Hotel in Atlanta, Georgia. The Barclay became the cult's first hotel outside of South Florida when four sect members formed a Georgia corporation, B&W Ltd., and bought the 11-story, 73-room building for $1.8 million. The growing wealth of the Nation of Yahweh soon caught the attention of the government when the cult's spiritual leader Yahweh Ben Yahweh and fifteen of his lieutenants were arrested and charged with racketeering. Several leading religious leaders called for him to be released from jail, the most prominent being the Nation of Islam leader Louis Farrakhan who launched a nationwide petition drive for his release. Farrakhan stated, "I am obligated to stand and support my brother because he has truly done beautiful works; all that he has done has been nothing but good….

Every time one of our people stands up and does good for our people the white man wants to kill that person; they did it to Marcus Garvey, Martin Luther King, Malcolm X, etc. They are trying to do the same to Yahweh Ben Yahweh and myself."[49] Even with support like this, the Nation of Yahweh was not able to appeal to the masses of African Americans. Hence, it never gained a sustainable presence in the nation sufficient to challenge mainline denominations.

However, the strong sects and cults did pose a real challenge to the mainline churches. They forced them to review and articulate their fundamental doctrines in order to regain some of the members lost to the cults. One major failure of mainline churches was their inability to articulate these fundamentals to the lower class of African Americans concentrated in the poverty-stricken areas of major cities. Church leaders were more readily concerned with communicating middle class values. Many were not able to speak the language of the streets. Cult leaders came into the streets and convinced the common people that they knew more about their plight.

(Endnotes)

[1] John Hope. Franklin, *Reconstruction: After the Civil War* (Chicago: University of Chicago Press, 1961), 2.

[2] Hadley Cantril, *The Psychology of Social Movements* (New York: John Wiley & Sons Incorporated., 1963), 80.

[3] D. W. Culp, *Twentieth Century Negro Literature* (Naperville, IL: J. L. Nichols, 1902), 31.

[4] Ibid., 34.

[5] Franklin, 37.

[6] William Warren Sweet, *The Story of Religion in America an Interpretation* (New York: Harper & Brothers Pub., 1950), 319-320.

[7] H. F. Kletzing, *Progress of a Race: Or, the Remarkable Advancement of the American Negro* (Naperville, IL: J.L. Nichols, 1900), 425.

[8] Ibid., 115.

[9] Department of Commerce Bureau of the Census Negro Population 1790-1915 (Washington: Government Printing Office, 1918), 22, 25, 31, 35.

[10] Ibid., 137.

[11] J. W. E. Bowen and I. Garland Penn, *The United Negro: His Problems and His Progress*; Containing the Addresses and Proceedings the Negro Young Peoples Christian and Educational Congress, Held August 6-11, 1902 (Atlanta, GA: D. E. Luther Publishing, 1902), 527.

[12] *Journal of the National Baptist Convention*, December 6-11, 1922, 77.

[13] *Journal of the Forty-sixth Annual Session of the National Baptist Convention*, September 8-13, 1926, 285.

[14] Jessie P. Guzman, *Negro Year Book: A Review of Events Affecting Negro Life, 1941-1946* (Tuskegee Institute, AL: Department of Records and Research, 1947), 111.

[15] *Baltimore Afro-American*, December 9, 1947, 8.

[16] H. V. Richardson, *Dark Salvation: The Story of Methodism* (Garden City, N.Y: Anchor Press/Doubleday, 1976), 271.

[17] Guzman, 117-118.

[18] Ibid., 259.

[19] Ibid., 113.

[20] *Chicago Defender*, February 11, 1989, 67.

[21] *Chicago Defender*, October 29, 1988, 43.

[22] Ibid., 43.

[23] Wardell J. Payne, *Directory of African American Religious Bodies: A Compendium by the Howard University School of Divinity*; Edited by Wardell J. Payne ; Prepared under the Auspices of the Research Center on Black Religious Bodies, Howard University School of Divinity, Washington, D.C (Washington: Howard University Press, 1995), 164.

[24] Guzman, 113.

[25] Payne., 160.

[26] Ibid., 165-166.

[27] Guzman., 257.

[28] Richard G. Kyle, *The Religious Fringe: A History of Alternative Religions in America* (Downers Grove, IL: InterVarsity Press, 1993), 163.

[29] Payne, 157.

[30] Kyle, 164-165.

[31] Payne, 181.

32 Ibid., 169.

33 Ibid., 153-154.

34 Ibid., 160, 178.

35 *The Call*, Kansas City, Missouri, June 30-July 6, 1989, 20.

36 Jack Rothman, ed., *Issues in Race and Ethnic Relations: Theory Research and Action* (Ithaca, IL: Peacock Publishers, 1979), 244.

37 Charles F. Marden and Gladys Meyer, eds., *Minorities in American Society* (New York: Van Nostrand Reinhold Company, 1962), 253.

38 Gayraud S. Wilmore, B*lack Religion and Black Radicalism an Interpretation of the Religious History of Afro-American People* (New York: Orbis Books, 1986), 161.

39 Randall K. Burkett, *Garveyism as a Religious Movement the Institutionalization of a Black Civil Religion* (Metuchen, NJ: Scarecrow and the American Theological Library Association, 1978), 46-47.

40 Ibid., 47.

41 *Chicago Defender*, August 29, 1987, 18.

42 *The Afro-American*, January 11, 1936, 10.

43 *The Afro-American*, May 4, 1935, 16.

44 *The Afro-American*, February 13, 1960, 4.

45 *The Afro-American*, January 23, 1960, 1.

46 *The Afro-American*, February 13, 1960, 4.

47 *The Richmond Afro-American*, August 25, 1963, 1-2.

48 *The Charlotte Post*, October 4, 1990, 9A.

49 *The Call and Post*, September 19, 1991, 1B.

Chapter 6

THE CHRISTIAN MISSIONS OF AFRICAN AMERICAN DENOMINATIONS

The beginning of the missionary spirit among African Americans is a remarkable adventure against seemingly unprecedented odds. Given the radical nature of slavery in Colonial America, it seems almost inconceivable that such a people even in the early stages of their conversion to the Christian religion would have dreams of giving their full attention to their native land with desires of converting the inhabitants of Africa. The African American slaves and free blacks were themselves beneficiaries of the missionary nature of Christianity. From its inception, Christianity by nature has been a missionary religion. Its worldwide expansion resulted from strong and vital missionary strides. Even during the early stages of European exploration, various Christian nations were driven partly by a desire to convert the known world to the faith. Roman Catholic explorers sought to introduce the Christian faith on the West Coast of Africa in their strides to reach India for oriental trade. They had minimal success on the fringes of West Africa from which most of the slaves were brought to the New World. A few Africans were converted and brought to Europe as servants. After Columbus made his contacts with the Americas, some few African Roman Catholics arrived in various parts of the lands in company with the European explorers.

With the entrance of Protestant England in the colonial expansion of European powers, the dawn of missionary activity became a real possibility among the African slaves transplanted to North America. Initially, there was very little concern, as mentioned earlier, on the part of British Protestant slave owners in the evangelization of their free labor force. Slowly, Protestant denominations began to respond to the fundamental missionary and evangelistic nature of Christianity and commenced the conversion of some of their slaves. Fortunately, the spirit of missions gradually entered the Christian consciousness of a few of these African slave and free black converts which ignited a desire to share their newfound faith in the context of severe oppression with their brothers and sisters in Africa.

The Lure of Africa
With the beginning of separated denominational developments among African American churches, two strong motivating forces—Christian education and

the stories of white Protestant missionaries—inspired African American Christians to reach out beyond the limits of home missions. Gradually, they set their sights on Africa and beyond. A few pioneer African American Baptist and Methodist missionaries decided to labor in West Africa with the financial assistance of white missionary associations. Reverend Lott Carey was the first African American Baptist to respond to the lure of African missions. He was jointly assisted by southern white Baptists, the Richmond African Missionary Society, and the American Colonization Society. Just a short period before Lott Carey reached Sierra Leone and later Liberia, West Africa, another African American missionary, Daniel Coker, a devout Methodist churchman of Baltimore, organized a group on board a ship, under the auspices of the American Colonization Society in 1820 headed for Liberia, West Africa. The ship landed in West Africa, just before the ship on which Lott Carey and his little "missionary church" group arrived. Initially, the journeys of both of these groups were opposed by the majority of African American church leaders who were strongly against the objectives of the American Colonization Society. Nevertheless, these two African American missionaries set the stage for the subsequent organization of foreign missionary societies, regional conventions, and denominational boards for the advancement of Christian missions.

African American Baptist Foreign Missions

With the missionary work of Reverend Lott Carey in focus, African American Baptists entered the African missionary fields with determination to promote evangelism, education, medicine, and economic development for the African people. Lott Carey's work in Liberia focused on all four of these missionary objectives. Before his departure from Virginia to Liberia, he worked with the First African Baptist Church of Richmond and organized the Richmond African Missionary Society in 1815, which for several years contributed between $100 and $250 for the African mission. William Crane, a white Baptist deacon who taught Lott Carey and inspired him to become a missionary, was elected to the dual role of president and secretary of the society. He reported on the work of the Richmond African Missionary Society to the triennial session of the General Missionary Convention at Philadelphia in May 1817, and the convention unanimously adopted the following resolution:

> "Resolve, that the said letter be noticed on the minutes of the Convention, and that the Board, if they find it practicable, be advised to institute an African Mission, conformable to the wishes of the said African

Mission Society; and the corresponding Secretary of the Board that the corresponding Secretary of the Board be requested to communicate this resolution with an encouraging affectionate letter to that society."[1]

This action set the stage for the beginning of Baptist missionary work in West Africa. Ironically, Baptist missionary work started in the same region where slaves had been extracted.

Clearly, the formation of the Richmond African Missionary Society was not sufficient to satisfy Lott Carey's attraction to the lure of Africa that was inspired by his grandmother Mihala. She had told him prophetically: "Son, you will grow strong. You will lead many, and perhaps it may be you who will travel over the big seas to carry the great secret to my people."[2] After Carey became a Christian minister, memory of her challenge was sufficient for him to feel a strong lure from Africa, compelling him to board the ship *Nautilus* on January 23, 1821, and set sail for West Africa. In 1822, Lott Carey and his little missionary church organized aboard the *Nautilus* began the African mission at Cape Montserado. Upon his arrival, the new settlers organized a colonial government with Lott Carey serving as a medical officer, teacher, preacher, and organizer of the Providence Baptist Church of Monrovia, Liberia. The Providence Baptist Church was the first Baptist church in Africa and one of the earliest denominational movements on the continent.

After the death of Reverend Lott Carey, African American Baptists began to take a greater interest in foreign missions. Several pioneer African American Baptists went to West Africa to advance the African mission. Among them were Reverends A.W. Anderson, John Lewis, Hilary Teague, and John Day. Gradually, the African mission attracted the attention of other African American church leaders. To be sure, the evolution of African missions became a strong motivating factor for the actual organization of associations and conventions among them. The primary objective of most organized movements was to spread the Gospel of Jesus Christ to millions of Africa's son and daughters groping in spiritual darkness from the lack of salvation in His Name. To this end, much of the economic strength of the associations and conventions went to the support of an African mission.

The American Baptist Missionary Convention, organized in 1840, came into being as a result of many calls and requests from Africa for missionaries and means to continue the African mission commenced by Rev. Lott Carey and other pioneer Baptists. Hence, the African mission was a very strong appeal on the new convention. Due to the limited economic means, however, the convention was forced to cooperate with white missionary organizations in the support of an African mission.

Whatever the degree of involvement, however, the leadership of the American Baptist Missionary Convention took pride in their missionary work. Rev. Rufus Perry, corresponding secretary, mentioned this in his report to the convention:

"We have been laboring in the field of missions thirty-one years. But till our consolidation with our Southern brethren at Richmond, Va., in 1867, our labors were confined to the North and West Coast of Africa. Now our field is the world and we are only detained mostly in the South, for the time being, by the great demand for our work, and by our limited resources.... During the past year we have labored more or less in Canada, and in eighteen different states."[3]

This report reflected the growing tendency on the part of African American Baptists to move beyond a parochial vision of Christian missions to a more global one. To be sure, they wanted to expand their missions to other areas of Africa but at the same time, pursue missionary objectives in other parts of the world.

In 1873, African American Baptists in western states organized the Baptist African Missionary Convention of Western States and Territories primarily for the support of African missions. Apparently, they were not willing to focus their missions beyond the limits of Africa, perhaps partly because the local churches established a policy of sending their own missionaries to Africa while receiving credit through the convention. Statistics regarding the extent of the missionary programs of the convention were not documented.

By 1877, the missionary work of African American Baptists in Africa had all but died out. In the report to the Consolidated American Baptist Convention, the leadership complained:

"The zeal for Missionary work in Africa, that characterized our Convention, some fifteen years ago, has all but died out. Our Convention ought to support a missionary in Africa. Indeed, there ought to be a foreign department to the Convention, offered or managed by a Foreign Board, to take entire charge of the Haitian Mission, and to found a Mission in Africa, or cooperate with those already established. We are too great a body, and too deeply concerned in the enlightenment of Africa, to be indifferent in regard to missionary work there...."

"Though of American birth and education, we are nevertheless sons of Africa. God has ordained it…. England is circumscribing the continent of Africa, with commercial posts, and acquiring the territory. God signals the intelligent men of our race, to begin to occupy the land, lest the African soon become as a wandering Jew, without Judea, and without Jerusalem.[4]

Again, the urgency and primacy of the African mission were expressed in this report to the convention. They were not content with the meager support of African missions on the part of white Baptists. Also, they were aware of the relationship between African American missionary involvement and the socio-political interests of Africans. It was believed that white missionaries would not respect the culture and dignity of the African people. In 1879, the Consolidated American Baptist Convention was supporting the missionary work of Rev. C.H. Richardson in Africa. By then, the Foreign Mission Board apparently had been organized to coordinate the African mission. Upon his arrival in Victoria, Cameroon, Rev. C.H. Richardson in the company of a few other missionaries traveled into the interior of Africa and established a mission station at Bakunda. The local king of the area received them cordially and gave them the assurance of protection and aid in their work. Rev. Richardson was able to preach regularly and organize a school. By orders of the king, the natives were required to assist in the construction of the school, and the youth of his dominion had to attend the school. Just before the king's death, he advised his subjects: "Hear what the missionaries teach you, for I believe they bring you a message from God, for he has sent a multitude of people to bring me to him, and I have seen them."[5]

Also, in 1878, the African American Baptists of Virginia, being foremost in mission work since the founding of two missionary societies—the Richmond African Baptist Missionary Society and the Petersburg African Baptist Missionary Society—raised money and sent Rev. Solomon Crosby to Africa. He was sent to Africa to work with Rev. W.W. Colley at Abeokuta in connection with the Foreign Mission Board of the Southern Baptist Convention.

Similarly, the African American Baptists of South Carolina made independent attempts to develop African missions. They sent Rev. Harrison N. Bouey who organized a significant work in Liberia. He organized two churches, two associations, and so aroused a missionary spirit that it subsequently led to the organization of a national Baptist convention back in the United States. He spent several years working in Royesville with the Gola tribe and built a road in the area. He was so impressed by the possibilities of expanding the African mission that he felt compelled, upon his return to the United States, to encourage African American Baptists to organize a national Baptist convention.

Another strong proponent of a national convention for expanding the African mission was Rev. W.W. Colley. Having worked successfully with the Foreign Mission Board of the Southern Baptist Convention, he felt that the time was ripe for greater involvement of African Americans in the African mission. In the early 1880s, the Foreign Mission Board had lost some of its momentum in Africa, gradually ending its work largely caused by the germination of the spirit of African nationalism. Africans became increasingly aware of the racism expressed by white missionaries, which prevented them from relating positively to African heritage and aspirations.

With the advancement of the National Baptist Convention, USA, and the Lott Carey Home and Foreign Mission Convention, the African American Baptist missionary enterprise took on a new momentum. More money and personnel were utilized in the development of the African missions. Many of the national leaders became highly motivated to do something significant for the motherland. In 1902, Rev. L.G. Jordan, Corresponding Secretary of the National Baptist Foreign Mission Board, delivered a major address on the needs of Africa to the Negro Young People's Christian and Educational Congress in Atlanta, Georgia, emphasizing the fact that African Americans were responsible for the evangelization of Africa:

> "If the Negro of America will but feel his responsibility and undertake the evangelization of Africa in God's name, unborn millions of Africa's sons will witness a transformed continent.... From that great black continent can be carved states or empires, from her cradle will come sons and daughters to rule and reign in the name of Christianity. Negroes of America, God calls you to duty; He calls you to service and He calls you now.[6]

It goes without saying that African American missionaries were better equipped spiritually and psychologically to meet the needs of African missions because they shared the same heartbeat of worldview.

In 1883 Rev. W.W. Colley, along with five other missionaries, was sent to establish a stronger missionary program in Liberia. By December 1883, they settled in the Vey country, near Monrovia, to organize two missions, Bendoo and Jundoo. However, they were hindered by diseases and tribal wars. Subsequently, the African mission advanced slowly in Liberia. However, the Foreign Mission Board of the National Baptist Convention sent twenty-six missionaries to Africa to revitalize the African mission. Near the turn of the century Rev. J.C. Jackson, who became the father of missions among African American Baptists, was sent to Cape Town. He was able to convert significant numbers of Africans who went back to their homes in the interior carrying the Gospel of Jesus Christ. He used this methodology of starting churches throughout South Africa.

By 1925, major changes in the political climate of Africa radically hindered the work of African American missionaries in Africa. Some six European nations had come to Africa to establish colonial governments. These colonial administrators did not want African American missionaries to serve in their areas of concern due to fear that they might cause political unrest among the native Africans. Many mission doors were closed to African American missionaries, leaving the only possibility of expanding the missions through the utilization of nationals as missionaries. This issue came to focus at the Foreign Mission Conference at Le Zoute, Belgium, in 1925 which convened to consider the significance of cooperation in African missions. Several African American missionary organizations were represented to urge that missionary doors would be opened to them. Hence, the conference appointed a "Committee on American Negroes and Africa" which made the following report:

> "The Conference with the information at its disposal, believes the following to be a true statement of the facts relative to this report.
>
> 1. Although there are not legislative restrictions specifically directed against the American Negro, most African Governments are either opposed to or place difficulties in the way of the sending of American Negroes to Africa.
>
> 2. Opposition to the sending of American Negroes to Africa is due mainly to three factors:
>
> (a) The unrest caused by the so-called Pan-African and Garvey Movements.
>
> (b) The antagonism to Government of certain American Negroes in Africa in past years with resulting serious disturbances in some cases.
>
> (c) The failure of certain American Negroes in Africa in past years.

3. Most of American Negroes consulted, owing to the effect of one or more of the reasons above named, do not think the present time auspicious for pressing upon the Government such a general change in policy as would mean the sending of a large number of American Negroes to Africa in the immediate future, although strongly believe that efforts should be made so that the number of such missionaries may be gradually and steadily increased.

4. There are at present working in various parts of Africa American Negroes of the highest character and usefulness, whose fine spirit and devoted work will in the course of a few years greatly increase the respect in which American Negro missionaries are held and make the securing of permission for the entrance of additional colleagues easier.

5. There is a natural and laudable desire on the part of American Missionary societies, both white and Negro, to send additional African Negroes as Missionaries in Africa—thereby giving the educated Negro an outlet for his zeal to render unselfish service, and aiding in what would seem a natural and important way [to further] the cause of African evangelism and education."[7]

The report on American Negroes and Africa was considered by some of the leading churchmen of Christianity. Every part of Africa was represented by able and experienced missionaries. Belgians, British, French, Swiss, Swedes, Portuguese, black and white Americans, native Africans, and representatives from all Christian nations joined with great candor in the consideration of the report. After a very exhaustive evaluation, the Foreign Mission Conference at Le Zoute adapted the following resolution:

"1. That the Negro of America should be permitted by Government and encouraged by Missionary Societies to play an increasingly important part in the evangelization and education of Africa, and that the number of their missionaries should be increased as rapidly as qualified candidates are available for needed work, and as their representatives already in the field still further succeed in gaining for their people and their societies that public confidence which is so essential.

2. That every practical form of assistance and support should be given in the spirit of Christian friendship and fellowship as to colleagues of the same missionary status by White missionaries to qualified American Negroes working in Africa, who show themselves worthy of confidence, and that the same spirit of co-operation should be expected by White missionaries from American Negro Missionaries.

3. That Governments should be supported in requiring that American Negroes, wishing to enter Africa for missionary purposes, should go out under the auspices of recognized and well-established standing, and that owing to the difficult and delicate inter-racial situation in Africa, exceptional care should be used in the selection of men and women of strength of character and a fine spirit of co-operation, who can meet the same tests as White missionaries.

4. That in the interest of comity and co-operation American Negro Missionary societies not now represented in Africa should work as far as possible through well-established societies already in Africa, and that they should consider particularly the needs of un-evangelized districts.

5. That when Missionary Societies of established reputation are unable to secure the admission to Africa of American Negroes needed for important work, and qualified to perform it, the matter may properly be taken up with the International Missionary Council for use of its friendly offices.

6. In adopting these resolutions the Conference recognizes that the above recommendations are not an ideal or complete solution of these questions, but believes that they represent the 'next step' which may be wisely taken, and that they should, in the providence of God, gradually bring about a highly significant and increasingly important contribution by the Negroes of American to their distant kindred in Africa.[8]

The report of the Conference positively impacted the work of both African American Baptist and Methodist sending agencies in their efforts to establish viable missionary programs in Africa. To be sure, African Methodist missionaries faced the same challenges in their quest for open doors of serviced in the African missionary enterprise.

Early Missionary Strides of African American Methodists

Like Baptist, the African American Methodist pioneer missionaries focused their attention on the evangelization of their kindred in Africa. Also, their first pioneers to Africa came under the auspices of the American Colonization Society. This society provided transportation to West Africa for both missionary minded groups. Rev. Daniel Coker, the first elected bishop of the African Methodist Episcopal Church, and his small missionary group traveled to West Africa in 1820. Like Lott Carey, he experienced great hardships in the evolving colonial experience of Liberia. More likely, Lott Carey and Daniel Coker were contemporaries in the volatile social and political experiences of Liberia. In an early letter, Daniel Coker urgently informed:

> "We have met trials; we are but a handful; our provisions are running low; we are in a strange, heathen land; we have not heard from America, and know not whether provisions or people will be sent out; yet, thank the Lord, my confidence is strong in the veracity of his promise. Tell my brethren to come; fear not; this land is good; it only wants men to possess it. I have opened a little Sabbath-school for native children. Oh, it would do your heart good to see the little naked sons of Africa around me. Tell the Colored People to come up to the help of the Lord. Let nothing discourage the Society or the Colored People." [9]

Unfortunately, help for the early African mission did not come from the African Methodist Episcopal Church as requested by Rev. Daniel Coker. This may be attributed to two reasons: 1. Lack of an organized missionary department for overseas missions in the African Methodist Episcopal Church. During its early developmental stage, the denomination focused its missionary emphasis on home missions and limited missions in Canada and the nearby West Indies; 2. The general negative climate in Philadelphia and other northern cities, especially among leading African American churches, toward the objectives of the American Colonization Society prevented any substantial support from being forthcoming to this early African mission. The American Colonization Society was organized by a New Jersey Presbyterian minister in December 1816 with the support of strong political leaders in government dedicated to settling of emancipated slaves from the South and free black volunteer immigrants to Africa. Among the leading opponents of the emigration scheme was Frederick Douglass, an African Methodist Episcopal exhorter and abolitionist.

In his address delivered in New York City, on May 11, 1849, entitled "Slavery, the Slumbering Volcano," to an audience of approximately twelve hundred in Shiloh Presbyterian Church, Frederick Douglass reiterated the earlier hostility held by African Americans of the North toward the American Colonization Society:

> "Of all the assaults which we have experienced during the last twenty years, none have been more subtle and plausible than those emanating from the American Colonization Society. Under the garb of philanthropy and religion its efforts to degrade us have been as various as they have been grievous. Of the history of that Society you have already been well informed, and with its origin you are equally familiar. It is, as you are aware, the joint product of slaveholders of the South and negro haters of the North, and fitly bears the image of both parents. Embodying all the malignity of the slaveholders, and all the negro-hating spirit of the Northerner, it is our vigilant and bitter adversary.... It is now, as it has ever been, a most deceitful and cunning scheme against the peace and freedom of the coloured people of the land."[10]

Similarly, Bishop Richard Allen addressed a letter to the *Freedom's Journal* on November 27, 1827, stating, "I have for several years been striving to reconcile my mind to the colonization of Africans in Liberia; but there have always been and there still remain great and insurmountable objections against the scheme."[11] As previously mentioned, Rev. Lott Carey was able to receive some support for his Liberian mission from white Southern Baptists and the Richmond African Baptist Missionary Society.

Neither Reverends Lott Carey nor Daniel Coker was characterized by philosophical passivity in relations to a defense of the new settlers in Liberia. They were not reluctant to fight the native Africans who attacked the community. Reverend Coker participated also in the affairs of government in the colony. After a short period of time, he decided to leave Liberia and work in the British colony of Sierra Leone. In Sierra Leone, he settled down to rear a family and establish a viable mission among the African Americans, slaves liberated by the British navy, and the native Africans. He organized a mission church in Freetown and became its first pastor. By 1852 the church where the congregation worshiped, constructed with stones, was still standing as one of the largest churches in the city. After his death, the members of the church placed a memorial tablet in memory of his ministry in

Sierra Leone. His family highly respected the dedication and work of this African American Methodist missionary. One of them became a successful trader with the natives in the interior and was able to endow the church in memory of his father.[12]

Apparently, the African Methodist Episcopal Church did not take any interest in African missions until the Philadelphia Conference in 1822, approving a request from Charles Butler to be ordained as deacon and elder and sent as a missionary to Africa. However, the conference failed to execute its unanimous resolution to send Charles Butler to Africa. It was not until after the organization of Parent Home and Foreign Missionary Society in 1844 that the denomination was in an organizational position to consider the establishment of an African mission. Rev. J.R. Frederick was sent to organize a new missionary work in Sierra Leone, West Africa. He did not come to a vacant missionary field since the London Missionary Society, under the leadership of Rev. W.A.B. Johnson, had firmly established missionary work in Bullum, Quia, and Sherbro counties, Sierra Leone. In 1836, an independent church, Zion Chapel and School, had been established in Freetown, Sierra Leone. In 1885, Zion Chapel, of the Countess Connection, negotiated with the Executive Committee of the Parent Home and Foreign Missionary Society for union with the denomination. Rev. John Richard Frederick was sent out as their agent to complete the establishment of the requested relationship. In March 1887, the trustees and members of Zion Chapel changed the name to The Zion African Methodist Episcopal Church.

After this successful transaction, Rev. J.R. Frederick advised the African Methodist Episcopal Church that "the king of the of the Small Scarcies River, and several chiefs, have invited the African Methodist Episcopal Church to establish a mission church and school within their boundaries, and have also by deed ten acres of land for that purpose."[13] The donated land was located in town of Ro Manga, near the Small Scarcies River. In 1887, the property was secured to the denomination by deed. Subsequently, Rev. J.R. Frederick reported to the denomination that he had sent a missionary by the name of Moses D. Davies to establish the missionary work in Ro Manga. He gave the missionary some detailed instructions on how to undertake a successful mission in the area:

> "The Lord has been pleased to open for us the way for the extension of mission work in the direction of Small Scarcies River.... By virtue of the authority invested in me as the representative of the mission of the A.M.E. Church at Sierra Leone and Liberia, on the west coast of Africa, I hereby appoint you as a missionary, subject to the approval of the Parent

Home and Foreign Missionary Society of the A.M.E. Church, to enter upon this most important work, fully believing that the Holy Spirit has directed us, and that by the aid of this same spirit you will be instrumental in the hand of the God of Missions in accomplishing much good in this dark corner among heathens and Mohammedans, who are waiting to receive the message of pardon and peace trough Christ, our Saviour....

"You are appointed as a schoolmaster and exhorter, and at the same time to render any and every service necessary to the advancement of the missions.... You are aware that there are mixed tribes to be found in that part of the country—Timneh, Susu, and others—yet the Timneh is the commonly spoken language of the people.... At present there is a great barrier between you and them, which will, in a measure, be removed by an acquaintance with the language.... Study the people as well.... Let them feel that you love them, if you are able to gain their confidence and bring them to Christ. Never forget that while you are studying them, they are studying you to.... Let the people see the image of Christ reflected in your life and conversation. You are sent out as a missionary, and not as a leader, to seek for souls, not for your own interest....

"You will be stationed at Ro Manga, but you are expected to itinerate through the country as often as opportunities offer. Wherever you go, sow the seed. One very important object we would wish you to keep always before you and to be instilled into the minds of the natives is a spirit of independence. We entreat, and actually beg you, to instruct and train the people to the principle of self-support. This is one of the great aims of the A.M.E. Church, to which you are connected.... Do all you can to inculcate a spirit of self-support.

"You have no authority to introduce any foreign rites or ceremonies. Don't let the people think that our religion is cumbersome. Plain reading and expounding God's word with singing and prayer is what we would recommend. Avoid everything like interference with their long-established customs. We strongly emphasize the importance of nationalizing converts to Christianity. Beware of the Sierra Leone traders you meet with on the river...."[14]

These instructions reflected the religious and cultural tenants of the African Methodist Episcopal Church's missionary enterprise. The early African missions were the introductory stages of an ever-expanding missionary program in Africa.

Similarly, the African Methodist Episcopal Zion Church did not establish an antebellum missionary work in Africa. The initial interest of the denomination in establishing a foreign mission program was expressed in a resolution in the minutes of the New England Annual Conference in 1851: "Resolved: That a committee of three be appointed to draw a plan for establishing a Home and Foreign Missionary Society in the New England Conference District."[15] However, the denomination did not take action on the initial interest of the New England Annual Conference in foreign missions in Africa until Rev. Andrew Cartwright, a member of the Virginia Conference, expressed an earnest desire to establish a missionary work in Africa. At the Virginia Annual Conference in November 1875, he approached Bishop Hood, who had been strongly opposed to the work of the American Colonization Society in Africa, and Bishop Hood granted approval for Rev. Cartwright to go as the denomination's pioneer missionary to Africa. However, before Bishop Hood granted his approval, he sought to clarify his position regarding African missions:

> "There is much excitement at this time on the subject of the colonization of our people in Africa. The colonization society, the old and untiring enemy of our race, is usually active at this time. I have ever been opposed to the scheme of this society. It has done more to impede the progress of our people than any other agency except slavery, and caste prejudice…. I would not be understood as opposing the evangelization of Africa."[16]

He made it clear that he was supportive of any person with the missionary spirit to go to Africa and start an African mission.

In 1876 Rev. Andrew Cartwright, along with his wife and two daughters, landed in Monrovia, Liberia, to begin an African mission. They commenced their missionary activities at the New Commer Settlement of Brewerville, Liberia in 1878. Eliza Ann Gardner, a strong missionary minded person, influenced the New England Conference to provide funds for the support of the African mission. Rev. Cartwright sent such positive reports back to the denomination that it moved the 1880 Annual Conference of the African Methodist Episcopal Zion Church to take permanent action for the support of African missions. William J. Walls credits Rev. Andrew Cartwright with the following major accomplishments: "His pioneer work in Africa led to the first organization of a connectional mission board, a missionary society in 1880, and eventually the Foreign Missions Department."[17] The new Foreign Missions Department was successfully established as the Home and Foreign Missionary Board of the AME Zion Church of America. It was strongly assisted by the Women's Home and Foreign Missionary Society.

By 1888, the African mission of Rev. Andrew Cartwright had experienced the organization of AMEZ Mission School in Liberia, with about a hundred male and female students. In their evaluation of the African mission, the denominational leaders acknowledged the need for more funds to support the mission and qualified African American missionary preachers to evangelize, enlist, and educate native Africans to expand the mission of the AME Zion Church.

The Globalization of African American Missions

With the organization of various foreign missions conventions and boards, African American denominations expanded their foreign missions work beyond Africa to global missionary enterprises. To be sure, Africa still remained a principal focus of the denominations, but the unprecedented global challenges of the twentieth century inspired African American church leaders to engage the emerging challenges of war, economic developments in the so-called Third World, communism, Pan-Africanism, the expansion of Islam, and other religious and socio-political changes in the world.

RUSSIA

Unique among African American missionary activity, the Lott Carey Baptist Foreign Mission Convention established a missionary program in Russia during the early twentieth century during the advancement of the Communist mind. The encounter of Communism and Christian theology was one of the most significant events of the age. Both required of the Russian people a commitment and a unique way of life. At the dawn of the 1900's, the evolution of the Communist mind was expressed in two revolutionary movements: Bolsheviks and Mensheviks. The former became the dominant Communist movement under the leadership of Vladimir Ilyich Ulyanov Lenin.

The intellectual origins of the Communist movement must be approached as an interaction of Marx's ideas and the political and intellectual setting of pre-revolutionary Russia in which they took root. In 1903, the Bolsheviks emerged from the Russian intelligentsia to give fervor to a revolutionary spirit. They came at a time when Russia was just beginning to experience the change and dislocation which accompany the initial stages of industrialization. Under the leadership of Lenin, the Bolsheviks were able to infuse into the Russian mind the moral imperative of revolution. Lenin, like Marx, was dedicated to the anticipated revolution as a moral absolute, as a sort of purgative judgment day which would extirpate all the evil in the old way of life and usher in the millennium.

Unfortunately, the Russian intelligentsia linked Christianity with the ills in Russian society that should be destroyed by a revolution. Hence, the Lott Carey Convention found itself working in a country which was experiencing the initial stage of its revolt against Christianity. Radical changes within the political and social life of the Russian people overshadowed, to a degree, the significance of the small Russian mission. Nevertheless, the convention was still able to maintain minimal contacts within Russia for a period of about two decades.

Rev. M. W. Martens was the convention's pioneer missionary to Russia. He contributed significantly to the convention's educational work at Bessarabia. The Bessarabia mission school experienced grave difficulty in its encounter with the Communists. New requirements were constantly presented to the mission school. One of the greatest success stories of the Russian mission was a report on the evangelistic work of Rev. Martens. In a letter addressed to Rev. I. Neplash, the Lott Carey Convention's Russian agent in the United States, from a woman member of the Russian church in Kharkov the capital of southern Russia, the work of Rev. Martens was appraised: "The Lord wonderfully blessed us during the time when Bro. Martens was here. God used him mightily. During the two weeks of his work here, about two hundred souls were thoroughly converted. The grace of God was pouring on the hearts of the people. Seeing that, the church was revived. We do not remember anything like it in our city."[18]

After about two decades of the firm grip of Communism on the Russian people, the Lott Carey Convention terminated its Russian mission. However, the precariousness of the socio-political climate did not completely deter at least minimal success in Russia before the termination of the mission. The historic Russian Orthodox Church, although suppressed by the Communist government, and the Protestant converts by the Lott Carey Mission continued to provide a Christian witness in Russia.

Liberia

In 1915 Dr. E.D. Hubbard, a native of Mississippi, indicated his desire to go to Africa and serve as a missionary. Initially, he worked in Africa under the auspices of the newly organized National Baptist Convention of America, Unincorporated. He sailed for Liberia and did his first mission work near Careysburg. After clearing away trees, he erected a temporary building for a mission station. There he labored very hard to build a school, the Hubbard Mission School. However, his work with the newly organized convention was not sufficiently supported financially.

Subsequently, Rev. E.D. Hubbard visited the Seuhn Mission of the National Baptist Convention, USA, Inc., and made application to the Foreign Mission Board to work under the auspices of the older and better established convention. He became one of the principal missionaries at Seuhn, where a tremendous agricultural mission was advanced to feed the national students. His outstanding missionary work in Liberia was terminated by his death in 1932.

In the meantime, Rev. James Edward East had returned to the United States from Africa and had been elected corresponding secretary of the Foreign Mission Board. To this office he brought a wealth of experience from the foreign field. In this position, he supervised the missionary program of the National Baptist Convention in Liberia and other parts of the continent. The convention faced some tremendous challenges which he detailed in a report in 1925:

> "Circumstances have altogether changed in recent years. Africa has been gobbled up by some six European nations. The world has watched carefully the progress of the American Negro; the wonderful strides he has made in civilization, the rapid way he has reduced his illiteracy since the Civil War, the thousands of professional men, lawyers, doctors, teachers and businessmen that have developed within the last half century, the vast amount of real estate and wealth he has acquired, the number of wonderful institutions he has built; and this progress of the black man has made the white world tremble as they question themselves, 'What will happen if all of Africa awakens as the black man of America?'

> "First, a great discussion was held by the European nations as to what steps should be taken to keep the black man of Africa from coming to America, being educated in our schools and getting ideas of freedom and desires for equal opportunities for happiness and livelihood. Everything possible was done to discourage native Africans from coming to this country. Then the next step was taken to prohibit people of color from America, especially those who represented religious institutions and went as leaders of the people. We are now at the point where with the exception of Liberia, a Negro Republic, with about 360 miles of coastline, all of the 'dark continent' is practically closed to Negro missionaries who go out under independent Negro Churches such as the Baptists, A.M.E., and A.M.E.Z."[19]

European colonial powers were keenly aware of the danger of social and religious contacts between African American Christians and native Africans. They carefully considered: 1. The cultural advancement of African Americans would inspire native Africans to critically evaluate their situation in Africa; 2. African American Christians demonstrated leadership ability in the administration of their schools where African nationals were being educated; 3. Native African students were being influenced by the spirit of African nationalism taught in the independent African American colleges and the African American press, which would ultimately challenge white supremacy in colonial Africa; and 4. The risk that African American missionaries may teach and preach the social gospel of ideas of self-worth, self-sufficiency, and self determination to native Africans.

Such encounters and social teachings would tend to make the administration of colonial power difficult in Africa. The ethnographic considerations of colonial powers taught by political theorist and even white missionary organizations, were directly contrary to the needs of native Africans. Leslie Rubin and Brian Weinstein observed the following regarding the institutionalization of European control in Africa:

"In Africa, a European minority ruled with an ideology and the threat of force based on the machine gun. The ideology proclaimed that Africans were inferior culturally, mentally, and physically, because they were less developed materially and technologically. The fact that some African peoples did not write their languages was chosen as one mark of inferiority…. Africans were called uniformly 'preliterate' even though in the nineteenth century a high percentage of Europeans were preliterate too."[20]

To be sure, African American missionaries did not hold any dehumanizing ideology of the African peoples. In fact, African American churches and schools were instrumental in the upsurge of African nationalism. Although the primary goal of the missionaries was to preach the Gospel, the social gospel element of their preaching and teaching were motivational for the rise of African nationalism. Ndabaningi Sithole observed:

"We have had to quote at length in order to show that the Christian Church has created in Africa, at least in some part of Africa, a strong Christian consciousness that transcends the usual barriers of race and color, and this Christian consciousness is based on the love of God and the love of our fellow-men. It is based on a strong sense of human justice. The story of African nationalism would be incomplete if this Christian awareness was ignored since it is this awareness that is an integral part of the creativeness of African nationalism."[21]

Liberia represented an example of the ability of Africans to rule their own government and institutions.

However, Rev. James Edward East was practical in his evaluation of the political sensitivity of missionary work beyond Liberia. His strategy under the circumstances was to develop a model to be duplicated. Political sensitivity was advanced for missionary activity in other parts of the continent. He said: "One of the most effective weapons we can use to break open the doors in other parts of Africa and have those European governments to open their doors and let us in, is to put on a very effective, sound missionary program for the redemption of Liberia."[22]

In 1924, the Foreign Mission Board of the National Baptist Convention, USA, Inc., sent Miss Sarah C. Williamson to Africa to take over the Seuhn Mission Station in Liberia. In 1925, she was able to report to the board that there were almost a hundred students, including day school students from Fortsville and Hartford, attending the Bible Industrial Mission of the Seuhn Mission. She organized the girls of this school into girl reserve clubs patterned after the YMCA in the United States.

In 1928, Miss Ruth Occomy was commissioned by the Foreign Mission Board to serve as a medical missionary to work at the Carrie V. Dyer Hospital of Monrovia. She worked as a yokefellow for the missionary Dr. A.F. DeWitt, a dental surgeon in the hospital, which was the first missionary hospital erected in Liberia, and the first in Africa erected by African American women. It was erected by the National Baptist Convention Women's of the National Baptist Convention, USA, Inc. The hospital was established as a medium of hospitalization and life-saving for the natives, citizens of Liberia living in Monrovia, and missionaries of the various stations in the Republic of Liberia.

Miss Mildred Griffin was another missionary sent by the Foreign Mission Board to work in the Seuhn Industrial Mission of Monrovia. She witnessed a significant increase in the student body of the school. Her work was highly valued at the mission in Liberia. Also, Miss Naomi Crawford was sent by the board to work as a nurse in the Carrie V. Dyer Memorial Hospital in Monrovia. She, along with Miss Susan Harris, contributed greatly to the medical mission of the convention.

Also during the nineteenth century, the Lott Carey Baptist Convention continued to develop its missions in Liberia. As previously noted, the Liberian mission represented African American Christians' earliest contact with Africa. Liberia has the distinction of being the oldest independent republic on the continent. Officially, it is a Christian state although religious freedom is guaranteed throughout the nation. Islam and Christianity are the two main religions. Various native religions are also present, especially in rural areas.

The Lott Carey Baptist Convention has shared the Liberian mission field with other Christian denominations. Early in the twentieth century, the Roman Catholic Church opened its missionary work in the republic. As of recent years, there are approximately 20,000 members, 7,000 pupils in elementary schools, and 5,000 students in Catholic high schools and colleges. Other church bodies in Liberia are: Assemblies of God, American Protestant Episcopal Church, Evangelical Lutherans, National Baptist Mission, and the Church of the Lord (Aladura).

The Lott Carey Baptist Convention opened its first substantial mission in Brewerville, Liberia, under the leadership Rev. J.O. Hayes, a native of North Carolina, who offered himself for the mission field almost immediately after the convention was founded in 1897. Prior to his affiliation with the convention, he had been serving in Liberia under the auspices of the Baptist Foreign Mission Convention since 1881. Initially, his mission was hindered by the persistence of native religions. However, he was able to open a school for the training of boys who came into the towns from the interior of the country.

In 1909, the Lott Carey Baptist Convention sent Rev. and Mrs. W.H. Thomas to work in Brewerville. Rev. W.H. Thomas extended the mission of the convention into a pioneer phase of Liberian journalism. He opened the only printing press among the African American Christians in Liberia. The intellectual development of the people of the republic was greatly enhanced by the *Watchman*, a monthly paper which was organized at the mission. He completed the Alexander Chapel, which was used as church, Sunday school, and day school. He was able to convert the king of Bhulah, and he baptized the king along with thirty-three other natives.

Consistent with its basic philosophy of cooperation, the Lott Carey Baptist Convention established a cooperative program with other bodies doing missions in Liberia, especially the Liberian Baptist Convention. The cooperative program resulted in joint missions at the Ricks Institute, which became one of the leading institutions. The convention contributed significant funds for the operation of Ricks Institute.

Not only did the Lott Carey Baptist Convention support programs of evangelism, Christian education, and vocational education, but it also made early strides in medical missions. In 1912, Rev. C.C. Boone, a veteran missionary to the Congo, was appointed by the convention to serve at Brewerville. He had completed medical training at the Leonard Medical School of Shaw University in Raleigh, North Carolina, before arriving on the African mission field. He worked successfully as a medical doctor in the hospital at Brewerville.

The expansion of mission projects in Liberia evolve slowly, but the Lott Carey Convention was able to maintain a station at Careysburg. By 1948, the Lott Carey Mission School at the Brewerville Station became one of Liberia's five fully accredited high schools. Some of Liberia's leading citizens graduated from this school, including Counselor Angie Brooks, once President of the General Assembly of the United Nations (1969); Her Excellency Eugenia Stevenson, Consul General of Liberia to the United States of America; Honorable David Thomas, Ambassador to the Cameroons; and Counselor Joseph W. Garber, former Attorney General of Liberia. To be sure, the Brewerville station became the leading mission for the convention and the headquarters for all of its work. As early as 1933, Rev. W.H. Thomas reported the enrollment of 192 students from native tribes in the school.

The Lott Carey Baptist Convention enjoyed continual development and expansion in its work in Liberia until interrupted by political unrest during the 1980s, which erupted into a civil war. In 1980, Samuel Kanyon Doe staged a successful coup d'état, brutally murdering President William R. Tolbert. The civil war made missionary expansion virtually impossible. The administration of President Samuel Kanyon Doe was characterized by mismanagement, inflation, corruption, and the suppression of the free press. However, the leadership of the mission work had of necessity to remain neutral regarding the revolution.

Another political crisis erupted when Charles Taylor led a movement to overthrow the Doe administration in 1989. Charles Taylor, a former member of President Doe's government who fled Liberia after he was accused of embezzlement, invaded the republic with only 150 men. Within a short period of time, he was able to recruit 14,000 fighting men from the Gio and Mano tribes, organizing this new fighting force around a new revolutionary movement called the National Patriotic Front of Liberia. The Taylor forces were able to occupy the Lott Carey Mission in Brewerville as a military post. Fierce fighting between the National Patriotic Front of Liberia and the government's forces caused major damages to the Lott Carey Mission.

Subsequently, the Liberian Council of Churches put forward a three-point proposal, calling for an immediate cease-fire, a roundtable conference, and assurance of internal security. However, the fighting parties did not agree on the peace talks. The failure of the peace proposal made the invasion of Monrovia inevitable, resulting in fierce battles being fought on the streets of the city. The street-to-street battles continue until the Economic Community of West African States decided to intervene in the civil war. About six thousand troops from Nigeria, Sierra Leone, Ghana, Gambia, and Guinea arrived in Liberia in 1991. Fortunately for the Lott Carey Baptist Convention, they liberated the Liberian mission from rebel hands. By 1992, the convention made plans for the restoration of the mission which progressed rapidly once civil order was restored to the republic.

The missionary activities of the African Methodist Episcopal Church in Liberia were also seriously affected by the civil war. During the Forty-First Session of the General Conference, a resolution was published regarding the effects of the war and the position of the denomination toward the new administration. It clarified the religious and social considerations of the denomination, proclaiming:

> "In consideration of the fact that the present and future status of the work of the African Methodist Episcopal Church in Liberia, West Africa and the Welfare of the Liberian African Methodists have been placed in question, as a result of the Coup D'état which occurred in Monrovia, Liberia, on April 12, 1980, AND

> "In consideration of the fact that the events following the overthrow have also led to distorted reporting, the circulation of misinformation by the white press, and subsequent declarations of condemnation and the threatened withdrawal of church support and resources by some American and European-based Christian Denominations, And

> "In consideration of the fact that several Liberian A.M.E. clergy and laypersons have been arrested and are presently facing life-imprisonment and death sentences as a result of their high-ranking positions in the government of deposed President William R. Tolbert;

> "It is hereby proposed that the 41st Session of the General Conference convening in New Orleans, Louisiana, June 18-25, 1980, representing approximately two million people of color around the world:
> 1. Draft and convey a formal expression of concern, neither condemning nor condoning the recent political developments in Liberia, but conveying our prayers and support for peace, unity and harmony in the Republic of Liberia; AND

2. That the A.M.E. Church reaffirm a passionate commitment to the spread of the gospel of Jesus Christ, to the support, growth and development of the A.M.E. Church in Liberia, and to the educational, economic, and social development and upliftment of the people of the Republic of Liberia; AND

3. That a plea for mercy and clemency for A.M.E.'s imprisonment by the new government be drafted and presented to Master Sargent Samuel K. Doe, Head of State and Chairman of the People's Redemption Council, along with a general plea for an end of all bloodshed and executions of former government officials; AND

4. That a special delegation be sent to accompany the reassigned or newly assigned bishop of the 14th Episcopal District to the Republic of Liberia to: (A) personally convey the above-listed items to Chairman Doe, (B) to convey personally the encouragement, support, goodwill, love and concern of A.M.E.'s around the world to the clergy, laity and youth of the A.M.E. Church in Liberia, and (C) to assist the presiding bishop in establishing or reestablishing relationships and laying the groundwork for the continued expansion and progress of the work of the African Methodist Episcopal Church in Liberia; AND

5. That an expression of appreciation and thanks be conveyed to Chairman Doe and the members of the People's Redemption Council for allowing such an able delegation to represent the A.M.E. Church of the Republic of Liberia in the 41st Session of the General Conference of the A.M.E. Church."[23]

This resolution demonstrated the keen awareness of the denomination concerning the precariousness of foreign missions programs in volatile social and political environments.

Denominational leaders were challenged to be faithful advocates of Christian moral values and at the same time be sensitive to the dangers of missionaries and program development on foreign fields. Often, this seemingly required neutrality or passive acceptance of human rights violations on the part of foreign governments.

Haiti

From the outset of its founding, the Lott Carey Convention expressed a missionary interest in Haiti. Rev. C.S. Brown, the convention's president, expressed his desire for the convention to open mission work in Haiti and made it a special feature of his annual addresses in 1914, 1915, and 1916. In 1916 the convention began, with the appointment of a committee on Haitian missions, its work in Haiti in cooperation with the Baptist pastors and private school teachers who were supplementing their small salaries by doing mission work on the island.

The pioneers of the conventions' Haitian missionary projects were Rev. Lucius Hippolite, pastor and teacher in Port-au-Prince; Rev. Jeannes Jacque, the only Baptist pastor in Cape Haitien; Rev. Delfort Eustache, pastor of several churches in North Haiti; Rev. De Lattree, pastor in St. Marc; Miss Alice Pierre-Alexis, teacher and interpreter on behalf of the natives; Rev. Dumay Pierre-Alexis, pastor in North Haiti and supervisor of several stations; and Rev. L. Ton Evans. These missionaries afforded the convention a good start in Haiti. In 1925, President C.S. Brown communicated the special interest of the Lott Carey Convention in Haiti:

> "We have a peculiar interest in Haiti, because it is the only Negro Republic in the Western World, and because the people are inclined to be Baptist. By mutual agreement, the American Baptist Home Mission Society has consented to assist in the evangelization of Haiti. We feel that this marks a new day in the work among the two and a half million Haitians. We are deeply interested in the political as well as the spiritual welfare of Haiti, and cannot bring ourselves to believe that the United States means to crush by force the aspirations of the Haitian people and deprive them of the right to govern themselves—a freedom for which their forefathers fought, bled, and died."[24]

In this statement, Rev. C.S. Brown was referring to a past United States intervention in Haitian economic and political affairs. In 1915, a revolution had taken place resulting in the overthrow and assassination of President Vibrun G. Sam. U.S. President Wilson decided to send U.S. Marines and impose military occupation, establishing Haiti for all practical purposes as a United States protectorate. The entrance of the U.S. into Haitian political issues was based primarily on economic considerations with regards to investments in the Haitian National Bank and Haitian National Railroad.

In 1929, the convention's president recommended that a commission be sent to Haiti to make a study of the missionary enterprise. The commission made the following report in 1931, representing a telescopic view of the missionary enterprise as well as the social and political situation in the 1930s:

"Your Commission deputized to visit the Republic of Haiti sailed on the 17th of February, 1931, and landed at Port-au-Prince, the Capital, on Sunday morning, February 22, where we were received by our alert Superintendent, Dr. Boaz A. Harris, accompanied by Rev. Mr. Kennedy pastor of St. Paul A.M.E. Church of Port-au-Prince, at whose church we attended Divine Service, after which we dined at the Palace Hotel and then set out for St. Marc, the headquarters of our Superintendent, sixty-two miles away, located in the central part of the country.…

"On Wednesday, in company with Dr. Boaz A. Harris and Congressman Marc Cemiron, we returned to the Capital, Port-au-Prince, and visited the President, Stenio Vincent, and also President of the Congress, Honorable J. Jolibois. The President, in response to our addresses, pledged his protection of our Society in the prosecution of the work in which we are engaged in the country and welcomed us to the Republic on behalf of all the people. He further stated that about 85% of the population of Haiti was backward morally, intellectually, and spiritually.…

"It appears that the mind of the elite and ruling class of the country is gradually undergoing a change as to their attitude in respect to the education and advancement of the masses. From this we see that Haiti welcomes religious organizations and educational groups that will labor unselfishly among either caste of their population, since the national bands of social difference on account of caste prevent them from the necessary contact for mutual uplift, which is essential to the development of the entire people. It is evident from the present intellectual status and religious life of the country that Haiti has shared, to a great degree, similar sentiments and opinions of the antebellum thought of our own Southland—that public education and advanced culture belong only to the aristocrats; but now caste and class are yielding to the floodtide of modern light, due to scientific progress in quest of truth, social contact, commercial preference and achievement.…

"Roman Catholicism is the dominant religion and is the recognized State church. Other religious groups are the A.M.E. Methodist, the Wesleyan Methodist, the Episcopal, the Adventist, and the Baptist. It is conceded by the well-informed that apart from Roman Catholicism, the Baptists are the strongest denomination in the country; and it is boldly asserted by those of other persuasions that the door of hope for the Haitian people morally and religiously lies largely in the doctrines and democratic principles of the Baptists and that full amplitude is seen in the plans of operation laid by the heroic struggles of our Superintendent to reach all classes. But the task is a gigantic one and can be accomplished only by men of initiative and vision….

"At St. Marc is located the Shiloh Baptist Church, with a membership of 150 and a thorough-going day school, with Miss Eva Kenol as Principal, with several Assistants. The people are poor and have little to give for the support of the church and school, but do what they can for the religious education of their children.

"Fonds-des-Negres in the South represents a large field of service with Brother Christian Coicou serving as preacher and teacher. The natives are kind and anxious to know the truth. At this point Dr. A.W. Brown, of Richmond, Va., performed the first baptismal serviced for the organization of a church.

"On the Island of La Gonave there are 14 Stations, directed by the native chiefs or preachers, under the supervision of Dr. Harris; these serve as an Advisory Board to the Superintendent, somewhat in the capacity of Deacons.

"The church at Marc Sucrin is the most outstanding on the island…. The house of worship has a seating capacity of about 1,000, with a sheet roof; there is also a flourishing day school with Prof. Black as Principal. This is known as the Eastern-Central Station of the island…."[25]

The commission made several recommendations, and the convention increased its work in Haiti. By 1932, Mrs. Boaz A. Harris was able to report that 3,000 natives had been led to Christ under the work of Rev. B.A. Harris. In 1937, the Haitian report reflected 7 churches and 23 other stations under Rev. Harris's supervision with a membership of more than 1,500; 2 pastors and missionaries; and 34 other preachers. The number of converts to Christ increased to more than 4,000 in 1962. The Lott Carey Convention experienced tremendous success in Haiti, but not without some difficult challenges.

As early as 1974, the Lott Carey Convention noted that an event of a precipitous character erupted regarding language problems and numerous other difficulties. The political climate in Haiti slowly changed subsequent to the death of

His Excellency Dr. Francois Duvalier, president of the Republic of Haiti, who had inspired the Lott Carey Convention's work for a period of fourteen years. The new president, Jean-Claude Duvalier, created a political situation in Haiti which caused problems leading to the reversal of the convention's earlier success story. Hence, the convention temporarily suspended its work in Haiti.

The beginning of the twenty-first century witnessed a resurgence of interest in missionary work in Haiti. Rev. Marcus G. Wood, pastor of the Providence Baptist of Baltimore, Maryland, visited Haiti and encouraged the Lott Carey Baptist Foreign Mission Convention to restore its mission in Haiti. Consequently, Dr. David Emmanuel Goatley, executive secretary of the convention met with some of the leaders of the former Lott Carey Convention-sponsored churches, consisting of 28 congregations and 39 schools with approximately 9,000 students. The meetings were positive and the convention restored its missionary work in Haiti. The convention has been especially effective in its service as a relief agency during the devastating situation caused by the January 2010 earthquake. It channeled thousands of dollars in relief aid for the numerous Haitian victims.

South Africa

During the early years of the of the twentieth century, the Lott Carey Baptist Convention and the Foreign Mission Board of the National Baptist Convention set their focus on South Africa as an important field for African American missionary activity. European missionary organizations had already arrived, but African Americans were needed to give a sound social gospel message relevant to the hopes and aspirations of the native people. The theological, political, and social values of European Christianity were not conducive for to the freedom and brotherhood the Christian faith of the African American experience offered the millions of natives in the Republic of South Africa.

The Republic of South Africa occupies the southern extremity of Africa, the second largest continent in the world. To the northwest lies Namibia (southwest Africa), with Botswana and Rhodesia to the north, Mozambique to the northeast, and Swaziland to the east. South Africa's official languages are Afrikaans and English; the principal African languages are Xhosa, Zulu, and Sesotho. European Christianity is the principal religion of the Republic, with the politically influential Dutch Reformed Church attracting about 55 percent of the white population. Only a fifth of the population belongs to the African Separatist Church, although the movement is rapidly growing.

Some time near the turn of the century, the National Baptist Convention sent Rev. J.C. Jackson, who became the father of African American missions in South Africa, to work at Cape Town. At this time, Cape Town was a great city that attracted people from other areas to work on the docks of the seaport city. Many of these workers were converted by Rev. J.C. Jackson and carried the Gospel to their homes in the interior of the nation. This was his method of starting churches throughout South Africa. The nationals who came to hear him, principally from Middledrift, were instrumental in organizing new churches in South Africa.

Significantly enough, Rev. J.C. Jackson was also able to lead a Roman Catholic to join in the National Baptist Convention's missionary endeavor in Africa. Namely, Rev. J.I. Buchanan was converted by the powerful preaching ministry of this missionary and started a strong church in Middledrift, South Africa. He also attempted to start a school in Middledrift but died in 1907before his dream was realized. After his death, the natives attempted to organize the school.

Another African American Baptist missionary of note was Rev. James Edward East, who was born January 27, 1881, in Huntsville, Alabama. He was converted at an early age and became interested in African missions. Hence, he entered the Missionary Training Institute at Nyack, New York, in 1904, and later became a student in the Virginia Seminary of Lynchburg, Virginia. While attending Virginia Seminary, he met and married Miss Lucinda Thomas. After they graduated, they went to South Africa to serve as missionaries. For eleven years, Rev. East and Mrs. East served faithfully on the foreign field before returning to the United States in 1920, leaving behind a church with 600 members at Rubula, South Africa.

As early as 1899, the Lott Carey Convention began a limited work in South Africa. Rev. John Tule, the convention's pioneer missionary, noted his extensive evangelistic travel and health issues as he sought to advance the mission. Hence, he urged the convention to employ some native preachers whom he had baptized and ordained to assist in the mission. Also, he desired that the convention would construct a small chapel centrally located for his missionary work.

However, the changing political situation in South Africa during the early 1900s compelled the Lott Carey Convention to reevaluate its initial missionary contact in the republic. By 1915, state law provided that "colored people including missionaries shall not emigrate" into the country. In order to maintain its contact in the country, the convention was compelled to cooperate with the South African Baptist Union, which was confirmed in 1916. The South African Baptist Union was composed of pastors and laymen of white and "colored" churches. This mixed race union was so organized in order to be recognized by the state. Native churches would not be recognized by the state unless they were commissioned by the South African Baptist Union. In fact, the union actually took charge of the Lott Carey Convention's mission stations which had been previously opened and operated by missionaries employed by the convention.

Complications associated with the political situation in South Africa and the organic union with the South African Baptist Union led the convention's officials to limit its work there and focus more on the Liberian mission. Progress in South Africa remained slow for about a decade. Early in 1926, the convention expressed renewed interest in its South African mission. One of its veteran missionaries, Rev. B.F. Mdodona, gained the approval of the British Baptist Union of South Africa to serve freely under the Convention's board. He proceeded to organize the Lott Carey Baptist Home Mission Society of South Africa with some forty affiliating branches. In 1931, he baptized 422 natives of the Zulu tribe of South Africa.

In the early 1930s, the Lott Carey Convention established mutual cooperation with the National Baptist Convention's missionaries in South Africa. This resulted in greater success in missionary activities. Rev. B.F. Mdodona presided over an association of 77 mission stations, representing a constituency of 152,978 members and 297evangelists; the British government of the Union of South Africa at Pretoria recognized him as the head of the Baptist denomination, with headquarters at the Taleni Baptist Mission in the district of Idutywa. Baptist organizations under his authority included six divisional associations: the Regular Baptist Christian Association; the Amoci Divisional Baptist Association; the Regular Baptist Territorial Association; and the Zulu Baptist Christian Divisional Association.

With the emerging development of the socio-political system of apartheid, the Lott Carey Baptist Convention again experienced grave difficulties in its South African mission. International reactions to the new political situation led to the government's decision to expel several international bodies. Subsequently, South Africa seceded from the British Commonwealth and became an independent republic in 1961.

By 1964, the Lott Carey Convention was dealing with an intense and potentially explosive situation in the republic. Dr. W.C. Somerville, executive secretary-treasurer of the convention, reported the next world holocaust would take place in Africa. He affirmed: "It is my candid opinion that within the next ten years South Africa will be the scene of mankind's greatest massacre and blood-bath."[26]

Again, the convention's mission was negatively impacted, resulting in a tendency to simply provide educational opportunities for native South African medical students to be educated in the Unites States. New momentum for the convention's mission was not substantially regained until the election of Nelson Mandela as president of the Republic of South Africa.

Congo (Zaire)

Another early twentieth-century mission of the Lott Carey Convention was the work of Rev. C.C. Boone at Mpalabala, Congo (currently Zaire). He was the convention's pioneer preacher and physician. He and his wife established a mission house, a chapel for preaching, and industrial school rooms—compliments of the Missionary Union of Boston. In 1902, he reported a large number of natives in his congregation. His work was sponsored jointly with the Lott Carey Convention and the Missionary Union of Boston.

Again, the Lott Carey Convention experience political problems in the Congo similar to later ones experienced in South Africa. The Belgian government was reluctant to allow African American missionaries to work in the Congo. By 1947, the convention could do only limited work in the country. In 1964, Rev. W.C. Somerville evaluated the challenges:

> "Of the 37 countries that have become independent since 1956, it is the Congo… suffering the greatest pains of a new birth.

> "The conflict and dissensions in the Congo must be traced directly to the Belgian Government who for seventy-five years robbed and looted the Congolese people of their moral and material possessions without giving anything valuable in return.

> "As a result of the Belgian brigandage and plunder, approximately one million people have died from hunger and starvation since independence in 1956. Since the murder of Patrice Lumumba, who had been duly elected president by the majority of the Congolese; and, since it is generally believed that Lumumba's death resulted from a conspiracy in which the so-called "civilized" leaders participated, there has been nothing but vengeance and hatred spread throughout the Congo regions.

> "Presently the Congo is a loose association of some 200 hundred tribes, with various differences. The present head, President Joseph Kassavubu of the Central Government, does not have grassroots support. As these words are written, the current Premier Cyrille Adoula has resigned and

Moise Tshombe, the deposed Katanga leader, who had been in exile in Spain and Brussels, has returned to the Congo and President Kasavubu has requested him to form a new cabinet.

"One of the tragedies of this new development is that Tshombe is reported to be hostile towards both the United States and the U.N. It is rumored that the Chinese Communists seem to be behind the current unrest, and are ready to assist in the outright takeover of Africa's richest country."[27]

The evaluation was made in response to an earlier appeal from the people of Zaire for greater African American missionary work in the country. Sebastian B. Kiambu communicated the appeal to Rev. W. C. Somerville in 1963. But the convention decided not to extend its work in the country due to the social and political unrest. For several decades, the work in the Congo did not progress.

INDIA

In 1926, the Lott Carey Baptist Convention extended its missionary work to India. Currently the Union of India, the seventh largest country in the world forms a natural subcontinent with the great Himalayas to the north and is flanked by the Arabian Sea and the Bay of Bengal. Its neighbors are China and Nepal to the north, Pakistan to the northeast, and Burma to the east. Its official language is Hindi, but English is used as an associate language for many official purposes. About 83 percent of the population is Hindu, and 11 percent are Muslim. There are also Christians, Sikhs, Buddhists, Jains, and other minorities. Christianity has about fourteen million followers in India.

The Lott Carey Convention decided to enter this vast field of labor to extend Christianity in the nation. Its pioneer representatives were Manmatha Nath Biswas and Mrs. Sukoda Banerjee with her assistants. Missionary work was established in Calcutta. In the late 1940s, the convention established a school in the slums of Delhi. The school provided educational opportunities for young Indian children and offered evening courses for adults. The school became one of the leading institutions of social service in Delhi.

Two significant events in the advancement of the convention's mission in India transpired in 1949. One was the official establishment of an Indian office of the Lott Carey Baptist Convention under the leadership of Rev. Joswant Harnam Nelson, located in Delhi. Secondly, the Indian office gained an associated status with the National Christian Council, which opened the doors of greater missionary operations in India. As a result, Rev. Nelson was able to bring the St. Hugh's Church at Chakrata under the Lott Carey Convention's Indian office; the church was located in the hills of the Himalayas near Dehra Dun in the state of Uttar Pradesh. Formerly, the church belonged to the Church Missionary Society of England.

A significant turn of events in Christian missions transpired in August 1947, when the British's Indian Empire was partitioned on religious lines between India and Pakistan. This event signaled the independence of India and the end of the so-called "white man's burden." A powerful Indian leader emerged in the person of Prime Minister Jawaharlal Nehru. The change in the government in India caused major changes in the policies of the major foreign mission boards. In fact, some of the boards actually recalled their missionaries and abandoned their mission buildings. Hence, Rev. John Nelson urged the Lott Carey Baptist Convention to increase its missionary operations in India. Upon the closure of the Church Missionary Society's work at Tundla in 1949, the convention expanded its work there and opened a Sunday school and a daily school for the children of Tundla.

The mission schools in India were later named the Somerville Schools in honor of the leadership of the convention's executive secretary Rev. Wendell C. Somerville for his tremendous interest in the education of Indian children. Ecumenically, the school employed Christian, Hindu, and Muslim teachers to educate Indian children of these faith traditions.

By 1961, the Lott Carey Baptist Convention was doing work in Delhi and other regions of India. It expanded its mission to lepers, the untouchables, the naked, and the starved of the Union of India. Medical missions became a signature program of the convention's Indian Mission. Large sums of money have been donated by African American Baptist churches for the support of medical missions in the country.

Nigeria

Nigeria is the most populous of all African nations, constituting more than seventy million inhabitants who make up about a sixth of the total population of the continent. The Nigerian people, previously organized in the Yoruba, Hausa, Bornu, Fulani, Ibo, and other states won their independence from the United Kingdom in 1960 as a federation of four regions. The British had been in Nigeria since 1553, but it was not until 1861 that they took over the settlement of Lagos and constituted it a colony. At the Berlin Conference of 1885, when the colonial powers carved up Africa among themselves, the British were given carte blanche to take over Nigeria. In 1951, a constitution gave Nigerians a token measure of self-government but not enough to satisfy the Nigerian people. They succeeded in getting the British government to introduce still another constitution, in 1954, under which the Federation of Nigeria came into being. Again, it was in 1960 Nigeria became an independent federal state within the British Commonwealth, and in 1963 it became a federal republic.

The Lott Carey Baptist Convention began its missionary work in Nigeria in 1961 under the leadership of Rev. Charles Ebong. By 1963, the Lott Carey mission had been organized into the Wendell Baptist Convention of Africa with its headquarters in Uyo, Nigeria. In 1964, three new congregations embraced the Baptist faith and joined the Wendell Baptist Convention of Nigeria. The largest of the three congregations was the Ediene Ikot Obio Imo Baptist Church, under the leadership of Rev. B.S. Usanga. These three congregations constituted the nucleus of the convention's work in Nigeria.

The Wendell Baptist Convention of African constructed an educational facility to accommodate forty girls; a dispensary to meet the medical needs of students and the nearby community; and facilities for Bible schools in each of its church districts. Further missionary developments were interrupted by the outbreak of the Nigeria-Biafra Civil War. Since independence, Nigeria had been troubled by tribal conflicts among the country's three major peoples: the industrious, largely Roman Catholic Ibo who predominated in the East; the urbanized Yoruba of the West, and the Moslem Hausa of the North.

In 1967, the Nigerian federal government was overthrown and a military government was set up. This was followed by a period of violence in which thousands of Ibos were murdered and more than one million were forced to flee from the North to the eastern region. Subsequently, the eastern region seceded from the government and proclaimed itself the Republic of Biafra, which ushered in a lengthy and bloody civil war. It was not until January 1970 that Biafra capitulated to the authority of the federal government.

The civil war drastically affected the Lott Carey Convention's mission in Nigeria. It closed the schools and cut off reliable communication between the convention and its Wendell Baptist Convention of Africa. When the war ended, the convention opened its schools under the leadership of Rev. C.E. Ebong. The Lott Carey Secondary School in the eastern region became one of the best schools in Nigeria. Similarly, the Wendell Baptist Mission Dispensary was meeting the medical needs of about four thousand Nigerians by the end of 1970. Also, the Wendell

Baptist Convention of Africa was able to open a nursery school in the southeastern state of Nigeria. By 1972, seventy churches were active members of the convention. Later, Nigeria became one of the convention's leading missions.

Kenya

Kenya represents the first involvement of the Lott Carey Baptist Convention in East Africa. In 1985, the potential for the convention's missionary involvement in the country was brought to the attention of Rev. W.C. Somerville by Rev. Hezron K. Cheruiyot. The convention sought to construct a substantial mission in the country. The focus of the mission was the development of churches and schools. The convention donated funds for the support of the Kenyan mission. By 1987, there were six Lott Carey stations in Kenya with about a hundred students enrolled in its secondary school, and the convention also operated a "Science and Carpentry Workshop."

Nyasaland (now Malawi)

The Republic of Malawi, formerly Nyasaland, is located in East Africa, lying west and south of Lake Malawi and bordered by Tanzania to the north, Mozambique to the east and south, and Zambia to the west. The people are almost entirely Bantu-speaking native Africans. About 75 percent of the people are Christians with the balance professing Islam or practicing native religions. In 1859, the British missionary Dr. David Livingston visited Malawi. An attempt by the Portuguese to siege the south was defeated, leading to the establishment of a British protectorate in 1890. Shortly thereafter, the area became known as Nyasaland. In 1953, the country entered the Federation of Rhodesia and Nyasaland, but the association with white-dominated Rhodesia was an uneasy one and lasted until 1963. In 1964, Nyasaland became the independent state of Malawi.

The missionary work in Malawi began by the National Baptist Convention's relationship with John Chilembwe. As early as 1896, the seed was planted for the beginning of service on the part of nationals in the foreign mission program. Joseph Booth, a friend of Africa, brought John Chilembwe to the United States from East Central Africa. The story of this young African boy will highlight further the rationale for the indigenousness of Christianity. He was born some time in the late nineteenth century in East Central Africa (Malawi). He was a member of the Yao tribe, known as a strong and aggressive people. He was expelled from the Pedo-Baptist Mission (a Baptist group that believes in the baptism of infants) in East Central Africa because he had read in the Gospel of Matthew that Jesus was baptized in the Jordan. The word for baptism in John Chilembwe's native tongue is *ambezu*, the meaning of which was equivalent to the Greek word *baptizo*. When this young African boy fastened the concept in his mind that baptizing meant dipping, a covering up, submerging in water; he refused to have water sprinkled on his head. Hence, he was expelled from the mission.

Fortunately Joseph Booth, an Englishman, met John Chilembwe and baptized him in the Zambesi River. They became friends, and Booth decided to bring him to the United States. Soon after their arrival in New York, Joseph Booth introduced the young boy to Rev. L.G. Jordan, secretary of the Foreign Mission Board of the National Baptist Convention, USA, Inc., who expressed interest in the education of John Chilembwe. Early in 1898, Rev. Jordan took him to Roanoke, Virginia, where Rev. William W. Brown was the pastor of the High Street Baptist Church. The two ministers decided to introduce the African boy to Professor Gregory Willis Hayes, president of Virginia Theological Seminary and College in Lynchburg, Virginia, who spiritually adopted this African youth. In the meantime, the African American Baptists of Philadelphia and Rev. William W. Brown decided to sponsor John Chilembwe's educational expenses at the Virginia Theological Seminary and College (currently, Virginia University of Lynchburg). Professor Hayes schooled the African student in the self-help philosophy of the institution in relationship to African American struggles in the United States. This philosophy had a powerful influence on Chilembwe.

In 1899, John Chilembwe returned to his native land after graduating from Virginia Theological Seminary and College. Just prior to his departure, he was ordained into the Gospel ministry. He was accompanied by Rev. Charles S. Morris on his voyage back to Africa. Rev. Morris was given an assignment by the Foreign Mission Board of the National Baptist Convention, USA, Inc. to take over the general supervision of the National Baptist Convention's work in Africa, and Rev. John Chilembwe was to set up his own mission in Malawi. By 1900, he had established a small church and school. His mission was originally named the Afawa Providence Industrial Mission. He was assisted by Rev. L.N. Cheek and Miss Emma Delany.

The work of the new mission grew rapidly. Chilembwe and Cheek divided between themselves the tasks of teaching and evangelizing. The team approach to missions continued between the missionaries for about two years. Sewing and other classes were instituted. After two years, John Chilembwe had the sole responsibility for the work of the mission.

Soon after 1910, the native converts of John Chilembwe were implicated in the Bambata Rebellion in British Central Africa. In 1906, a Zulu tribal military force rebelled against British oppression. The uprising was, however, crushed by the British military power. This signaled the beginning of grave troubles for John Chilembwe and the Afawa Providence Industrial Mission. The nationalistic tendencies of Chilembwe's earlier teaching in Virginia arose in him, prompting his involvement in the struggles of his people against the British. In 1915, he led a conspiracy that resulted in a revolt against the authority of the colonial power. Again, the revolt was crushed by the military power of Britain. His church was destroyed by the British, and he and about forty of his leaders were killed in the revolt, and the mission closed.

Subsequently, the British troops made several indiscriminate attacks against several other missions for their role in the Chilembwe revolt. This was followed by a general onslaught by Nyasaland settler groups on all missionaries in the protectorate. It was not until 1926 that the Afawa Providence Industrial Mission was allowed to reopen under the auspices of the Foreign Mission Board, which indicated the depth of bitterness the British held toward the revolt.

In the meantime Dr. Daniel S. Malekebu, a member of the same tribe, had finished his training at the Meharry Medical College in Nashville, Tennessee, and returned to East Central Africa. He was born in Malawi about 1890 and attended a mission school there sponsored by the Foreign Mission Board. As one of the first students and early converts, he was baptized in 1902; consequently, his parents refused to provide food for him because he had taken on the customs of "strangers." Before the revolt, he had assisted John Chilembwe at the mission. Later, he founded the African Baptist Congress, an organization patterned after the National Baptist Convention. The congress included churches in South Africa, Northern and Southern Rhodesia, Nyasaland, East Africa, and Portuguese East Africa. In 1952, more than 1,000 churches were members of the African Baptist Congress with an approximate membership of 300,000.[28] He died in 1978, and his death was a great loss to the medical mission in Malawi.

Several smaller African American denominations established missionary work in Kenya and other parts of Africa. Among them was the Pentecostal Assemblies of the World, Inc.

During the year 2000, Suffragan Bishop Michael Hannah and Bishop James W. Gaiters, the Bishop of Mission of the denomination, traveled to Nairobi and participated in the baptism of 140 pastors in the name of Jesus Christ. This signaled the recruitment of new pastors and churches into the denomination, which emphasized the importance of being baptized in the name of Jesus only in order to receive the Holy Ghost. Similar Pentecostal emphasis has been introduced by other Holiness and Pentecostal denominations in Kenya. Generally, Africans in other parts of the continent have responded favorably to Pentecostalism.

Guyana

The Lott Carey Baptist Convention began its missionary work in the South American country of Guyana while the nation was still a British colony. In 1964, Dr. A. Carlyle Miller petitioned the Lott Carey Baptist Convention to look with favor in accepting the educational and missionary program which he had initiated and carried on for several years. The convention accepted the challenge and opened its missionary work. Dr. Miller was a trained medical doctor and Christian minister. The Guyana mission was a cooperative program between the Convent Avenue Baptist Church of New York and the convention.

On May 26, 1966, Guyana won its independence from England and the new republic became known as the Cooperative Republic of Guyana. The independence of the Republic afforded the Lott Carey Baptist Convention new doors of opportunity for an expanded involvement. In 1970, Dr. Miller renovated the Lott Carey Mission in Campbellville and opened a Head Start school with an enrollment of 127 students. Later, the missionary work was expanded into the field of agriculture. He acquired from the government five hundred acres of land for development. By 1977, the mission had constructed a cottage hospital at Long Creek, known as the Carlyle Miller Health and Cottage Hospital.

Canada

The early history of Canada was dominated by France. Until about 1760, Canada was known as New France. Some historians believe that Africans came to New France almost as early as the French pioneers. Actually, the first known African to come to New France was Oliver Le Jeune, a slave who began his quest for freedom in response to the claims of Christian freedom taught by a Jesuit missionary named Paul Le Jeune in 1632. This suggests that early Africans who came to New France were Roman Catholics. Likely, others Roman Catholic slaves accompanied the French as they explored the vast region of Louisiana en route to New Spain.

Between the years of 1628 and 1760, slavery evolved slowly in New France. Several reasons have been suggested for the slow evolution of slavery in the region. Initially, Native Americans were utilized as slaves, similar to the practice of the

Spanish and Portuguese in South America, but their labor was not adequate for the demands of the Frenchmen, especially because they were not able to overcome the diseases of the French. However, Africans in the West Indies proved their ability to survive diseases and to become productive. This awareness attracted a few Frenchmen, but the supply and demand for slave labor in New France remained very small.

The second reason for the slow growth of slavery in New France was the legal difficulties in establishing it as an institution. It was very difficult to obtain legal clarity from France regarding African slavery. The French monarchs showed very little interest in such an institution in the colony. The primary concern of the French Crown was with how slavery developed in the West Indies.

It was not until the British came to power in Canada that slavery gained significant momentum for its institutionalization. Principally, the new momentum resulted from the influx of some white loyalists from the rebellious British colonies who came to Canada and brought with them the spirit of slavery as an institution. Some brought their slaves with them.

The rise of the abolitionist movement in the United States—and to a certain extent in Canada—ushered in a new era of migration of African Americans to Canada. The Underground Railroad became a means for the practical promotion of emancipation of slaves from the United States to Canada. The harsh reality of slavery pushed many fugitives to seek security and freedom in Canada. The passage of fugitive slave laws and the growing abolitionist movement prompted rather large numbers of slaves and some free blacks to migrate to the land of freedom. The latter group migrated because slave catchers resorted to enslaving free blacks who could not prove they were actually free. No African American was safe in the United States unless he or she could prove freedom with legal documentation.

African American churches and abolitionist societies soon became involved in the migration of the oppressed to Canada. Once in Canada, African Americans who had experienced evangelization on Southern plantations found it necessary to organize their own churches in Canada since there were no plantations in the country. Unlike antebellum America, there were no plantation missions. Principally, Baptist and Methodist churches were organized in the prevailing styles after a brief period of biracial worship experiences in Canadian churches. Although Canada did not have the developed institution of slavery, racism and discrimination were still factors that kept African Americans from enjoying the full degree of freedom as the majority population. They were never completely welcomed in the biracial churches on the basis of equality and Christian brotherhood.

With the rise of separate churches, African Canadian Christians began a movement of church development based on race. There is no strong indication that they were forced out of their biracial churches. Apparently, African Americans in Canada were influenced by their previous experiences in the United States. They were well aware of the separate independent church movement of African American Baptists and Methodists.

One of the earliest African American Baptist preachers to arrive in Canada was Rev. William Wilks, who was born in the Congo and first came to Canada from the United States in 1818. Initially, he landed at Amherstburg in1818 and traveled to Colchester a year later. He bought forty acres of land and built a church for African American Baptists in Canada, located north of the shore of Lake Erie. On the first Friday in October, he was ordained by the white Canadian Baptist ministers, and the First African Baptist Church of Colchester was officially organized in 1821.[29] The new church remained small with only thirty-six members in 1830, rising to its zenith of ninety in 1845 after which internal problems developed and the church declined. The internal difficulties signaled the fate of the church.

Another pioneer African American Baptist preacher was Rev. Washington Christian, a native of Virginia, who migrated to Toronto. Prior to his arrival, he had been ordained by the Abyssinian Baptist Church of New York City in 1822 and subsequently set himself to the task of aiding his brethren in Toronto and elsewhere. He organized the first Baptist church ever to be instituted in Toronto and the first African American institution in Toronto. Initially, the church did not have a meeting house and worshiped outdoors and in various homes. In 1827, it leased St. George's Masonic Lodge for a house of worship. The following year, a small chapel was constructed on Lombard Street in Toronto.

In 1841, the First Baptist Church of Toronto erected a new church on the corner of Victoria and Queen Streets. The property was donated to the church by the family of Squire McCutchen. On March 28, 1841, the church occupied its new site. Rev. Washington Christian thus led the church to realize a tremendous growth materially. He remained pastor until his death on July 3, 1850.[30]

Internal difficulties within the First Baptist Church of Toronto soon erupted in the congregation after the church move to a new site. The property was left in the hands of a board of trustees elected for life who usurped unreasonable authority over the deacons and pastor. The result of this controversy was the organization of a new church in 1855. This new church became known as the Colored Regular Baptist Church and was located on the corner of Terauley and Edward Streets. Both congregations sought to maintain the status of the First Baptist Church of Toronto. They appealed to the Haldimand Association for such recognition. The association recognized the members of new congregational location as the First Baptist Church of Toronto.

After the division within the First Baptist Church of Toronto Rev. William Mitchell, a native of North Carolina, served as the pastor of the congregation recognized by the Haldimand Association. He came to Toronto in the late 1850s, pastored at First Baptist Church for a brief period, then left for England on a fundraising tour. While in England, Rev. Mitchell wrote and published a book entitled *The Underground Railroad from Slavery to Freedom*.

Still another pioneer African American Baptist preacher moved to Canada to extend the Christian witness to his people. His name was Edward Mitchell (1794-1872). He was a native of Martinique, West Indies. The president of Dartmouth College observed the outstanding possibilities in this man and brought him to Hanover, New Hampshire, to be educated. After graduation in 1828, he was ordained in 1831 and preached for five years to white congregations in New Hampshire and Vermont. Subsequently, he migrated to Canada where he spent the rest of his life preaching to African Canadians in Eaton and Magog, Canada.

The year 1841 ushered in a new era in the development of missions in Canada. Several significant events began to transpire which affected the spread of African American Baptists in Canada. First, larger numbers were migrating from the United States to Canada. Second, the black Baptists of Amherstburg organized the first cooperative venture, the Amherstburg Baptist Association. This association assimilated most of the separate Baptist churches formed prior to 1841 and contributed to the subsequent organization of other separate African American Canadian Baptist churches. The boundaries of the association were racial not geographical. The association became international through its member churches on of the Canadian-American border. It also overlapped areas in Canada previously influenced by Baptist associations organized by white Canadian Baptists. This development sparked signs of racial friction within the Baptist movement in Canada.

With the development of their first cooperative venture, the African Americans in Canada later saw a need to become more involved in the political affairs of the race. Hence, they organized the Canadian Anti-Slavery Baptist Association. This new association became involved in the abolitionist movement. Previously in

1833, slavery was abolished throughout the British colonies by an act of Imperial Parliament, passed on August 28, 1833, to take effect on August 1, 1834. The legal authorities in Canada had already virtually ended slavery. The Canadian Anti-Slavery Baptist Association sought to end slavery throughout is sphere of influence.

In Nova Scotia, the free Christians were particularly inclined toward activism. Rev. Richard Preston, a strong African American Baptist leader, organized in1842 an Anglo-African Mutual Improvement and Aid Association. One of his earliest strategies was to appoint a committee responsible for political action. Under his leadership, the African American Baptists in Nova Scotia and New Brunswick were able to exert significant political influence. One reason for this was that there was a large concentration of African Canadians in the area. At one time, they outnumbered the white Canadian population of Nova Scotia.

In 1846, Rev. Richard Preston organized yet another politically oriented organization in Canada, the Abolitionist Society. For a brief period, this organization cooperated with the existing biracial abolitionist groups. The group parted ways with the biracial societies due to some religious and sociological differences with "the mainstream of general Baptist development in the province."[31] Subsequently, Rev. Preston decided to establish the separate African United Baptist Association to serve the general purpose of the older Amherstburg Association. Nova Scotia shared with Ontario the distinction of a sizable African Baptist presence. As early as 1840, there had been seven such congregations in Nova Scotia with 273 members; in 1897, there were twenty-two churches and 2,440 members; and, by 1970, the numbers had increased to more than ten thousand in Nova Scotia.

Similarly, the African American Baptists in Canada were interested in other matters affecting the race. Almost from the beginning of the separate church movement, they involved themselves in the educational and social uplift of the race. They participated in the organization of local schools and temperance societies. Good schools were a high priority, and apparently they were influenced by the temperance movement and moral reform in the United States. They were strongly aware of the necessity of these strides for the advancement of the race.

Generally, the growth and development of African American Baptists in Canada took place wherever there was a significant population suitable for church planting. Prior to the 1860s, such churches were organized in various cities and small towns throughout southeastern Canada. After the end of the Civil War in the United States, church growth became slow since the influx of fugitives ended. In fact, some of them returned to the United States. This was a serious blow to the separate church movement. By the end of the century, they sought closer ties with the African American Baptist denominations in the United States.

Foreign missions programs have contributed a vital part of the program development of African American denominations. The mainline denominations as well as smaller churches, like the Pentecostal and Holiness bodies, have directed much of the human, economic, and spiritual resources to address the challenges of missions throughout the world, especially in so-called third world countries. The missionary initiatives developed initially from their focus on Africa and grew into global missions. To be sure, African American Christians have demonstrated a substantial commitment to world evangelism and socio-political causes expressed by peoples globally.

(Endnotes)

[1] *Proceedings of the Baptist General Convention*, 1817, 134.

[2] J. E. East, *Lott Carey, Pioneer Missionary, Files of the Lott Carey Baptist Foreign Mission Convention*, Washington, D.C., 2.

[3] *Report of the Fifth Annual Meeting of the Consolidated American Baptist Convention*, 1871, 14-15.

[4] *The Triennial Report or Thirty-Seventh Annual Report of the Consolidated American Baptist Convention*, 1877, 30-31.

[5] Ibid., 8-9.

[6] J. W. E. Bowen and I. Garland Penn, *The United Negro: His Problems and His Progress*; Containing the Addresses and Proceedings the Negro Young Peoples Christian and Educational Congress, Held August 6-11, 1902 (Atlanta, GA: D. E. Luther Publishing, 1902), 310.

[7] *Annual Report of the Corresponding Secretary*, Lott Carey Baptist Foreign Mission Society, U.S.A., 1925-1926, 25-26.

[8] *Proceedings of the Fifth Annual Session of the Lott Carey Baptist Home and Foreign Mission Convention*, 24.

[9] George F. Bragg, *Men of Maryland* (Baltimore, MD: Church Advocate Press, 1914), 39-40.

[10] John W. Blassingame, ed., *The Frederick Douglas Papers, Series One: Speeches, Debates, and Interviews*, vol. 2 (New Haven, CT: Yale University Press, 1982), 149-150.

11 Charles Harris Wesley, *Richard Allen, Apostle of Freedom* (Washington, D.C.: Ass. Publ., 1935), 219.

12 Bragg, 40.

13 Daniel Alexander Payne, *Recollections of Seventy Years* (New York: Arno Press, 1969), 489.

14 Ibid., 489-490.

15 David Henry Bradley, Sr., *A History of the A. M. E. Zion Church: Part II, 1872-1968* (Nashville, TN: Parthenon Press, 1970), 232.

16 William Jacob Walls, *The African Methodist Episcopal Zion Church: Reality of the Black Church* (Charlotte, NC: A.M.E. Zion Publ. House, 1974), 375.

17 Ibid., 375.

18 *The Lott Carey Herald*, Volume 18, September 1925, 155.

19 J. E. East, *Forty-Fifth Annual Report of the Foreign Mission Board of the National Baptist Convention*, Inc., September 9-14, 1925, 6.

20 Leslie Rubin and Brian Weinstein, eds., *Introduction to African Politics: A Continental Approach* (New York: Prager Publishers, 1874), 33.

21 Ndabaningi Sithole, *African Nationalism* (Cape Town: Oxford University Press, 1959), 56.

22 J. E. East, Forty-Fifth Annual Report of the Foreign Mission Board of the National Baptist Convention, Inc., September 9-14, 1925, 8.

23 *The Combined Minutes of the Forty-First Session of the General Conference of the African Methodist Episcopal Church*, June 18-28, 1980, 317-318.

24 *The Lott Carey Herald*, 133

25 *Annual Report of the Corresponding Secretary of the Lott Carey Baptist Foreign Mission Society of the U.S.A.*, 1930-1931, 19-25.

26 *Annual Report of the Corresponding Secretary of the Lott Carey Baptist Foreign Mission Society of the U.S.A.*, 1964, 4.

27 *Annual Report of the Executive Secretary of the Lott Carey Baptist Foreign Mission Convention*, 1964, 4.

28 C.C. Adams and Marshall A. Talley, *Negro Baptists and Foreign Missions* (Philadelphia, PA: Foreign Mission Board of the National Baptist Convention, USA, 1952), 56.

[29] Robin W. Winks, *The Blacks in Canada* (Montreal, McGill-Queens University Press; New Haven: Yale University Press, 1971), 1.

[30] Ibid., 31-32.

[31] Ibid., 340.

Chapter 7

THE RISE OF AFRICAN AMERICAN DENOMINATIONAL SCHOOLS

African Americans have been challenged with the radical demands for education in American social settings from their first encounters with Euro-Americans. Initially, they had to learn several critical survival skills: 1. The necessity of adjusting to severe treatments by slave captains on the ships with limited food and space for ordinary human existence; 2. Physically and psychologically forced instruction for acceptance of the "breaking-in" period of the West Indies; 3. Passive acceptance of dehumanization and the requirements of new language skills for acceptance by slave owners; 4. Mastery of new labor skills as required by their masters; 5. The evolving violent opposition to schools for African Americans; and, 6. Acceptance of what some have labeled the "miseducation of the Negro." During the early days of slavery, it was against some colonial and later southern state laws to educate African Americans. In fact, many questioned the educability of transported Africans, believing that they were biologically, intellectually, and inherently inferior. All of these factors and many more impacted the educational experiences of African Americans during the antebellum period of American history.

Antebellum Education of African Americans

Initially, some attempts were made on the part of the dominant white Protestant churches to offer some basic education in the Bible and practical skills for adjustment to the new environment of transplanted Africans.

Booker T. Washington

This form of education was thought to be essential for the development of "good slaves" and some emancipated African Americans. Such schools were sponsored and controlled by a small number of white Protestants.

Among the earliest church groups to become involved in the education of Africans Americans was the Society for the Propagation of the Gospel in Foreign Parts. It sought to raise the standard of living among both whites and African Americans by suggesting to slave owners that their slaves should be given time to study the Bible and to learn to read and write. In the New England colonies, the society was active in promoting the education of the race by sponsoring schoolmasters for the instruction of slave children. As early as 1740, the famous preacher George Whitfield, himself a longtime slaveholder, proposed to the society an idea of establishing a school for the race in Pennsylvania. In 1762, the society maintained a school for African Americans in Newport, Rhode Island, with thirty in attendance. Even in the South, the society advocated the education of African Americans. In 1752, Rev. Thomas Thompson taught a school for the race in Baltimore, Maryland. John Hope Franklin stated: "In several instances, they taught slaves themselves and in one notable instance they fostered the establishment of a school for Negroes in Charleston in which the teachers were Negro slaves owned by the society."[1] This was especially significant because it took place in South Carolina at such an early period. Despite some restrictions, slaves were being taught in various parts of the

South either by church organizations or individual white Americans. Such famous Protestant leaders as Roger Williams, Cotton Mather, and John Eliot were strong advocates of education for African Americans. Similarly, the Quakers of the North were pioneers in the education of African Americans. Hugh Victor Brown stated: "The Quakers in the North were actively interested in freedom first, religion afterward and, in the South, through some Quaker owned slaves, under the influence of their northern brethren, they later set them free or transported them to Africa. Quaker schools for Negroes in North Carolina existed as early as 1731."[2] It was not until the rise of serious slave rebellions that serious restrictions were placed on the education of the race in the South.

In the middle colonies where humanitarian considerations were stronger, George Fox encouraged Quakers in these strong areas, as well as some southern locations, to give religious instruction to slaves and teach them the Gospel. In fact, Quaker schools for the race existed in North Carolina as early as 1731. As early as the 1700s, many other colonists were teaching slaves and emancipated African Americans. By the middle of the century, several classes in the rudiments were established for them. Significantly in 1722, one individual offered to teach "his poor Brethren the Negroes to read the Holy Scriptures…without any Manner of Expence [sic] to their respective Masters or Mistreses [sic]."[3]

During the late 1700s and early 1800s, white American denominations became increasingly interested and involved in the education of African Americans, especially in the North. This resulted partly because of the end of slavery in northern states and the increase in the population of free African Americans. Some of them who had escaped to freedom were very interested in obtaining educational skills for their adaptation to the new environment. Hence, they enrolled in some northern schools, some church-related, where they could satisfy their hunger for education.

White Denominational Schools for African Americans

Admittedly, African American masses were dependent on white Christian denominations for educational opportunities. As previously mentioned, African American churches made small attempts to educate the race before the Civil War, but these efforts reached only a minority of African Americans. Broader educational opportunities for them were provided, especially after the Civil War, by white denominations which had the material and human resources necessary to meet the challenges of African American education on a large-scale basis. Not only were they better equipped for providing adult education and religious education, but these denominations were uniquely equipped to provide higher education for African Americans. With the unprecedented challenge of mass education following the Civil War, most established white Christian denominations quickly took on the task of establishing schools, seminaries, and colleges for African Americans. Moreover, it will be seen that they provided foundational work for the later African American church's strides in education.

Horace Mann Bond offered a succinct appraisal of initial white denominational involvement in African American education:

> The great denominations worked through the special agency of missionary boards that established specific "Societies" for the Freedmen, or devised sub-committees to organize and conduct the work. The American Missionary Association was recognized by the Congregationalist Church as its official agency, in elevating the Freedmen. A sum of $250,000 was immediately raised. Added to assistance from the Freedmen's Bureau, the Association was enabled to become the most vigorous of all the church societies promoting education on all levels. Hampton, Howard, Fisk, Atlanta, and Talladega were among its early foundations.[4]

The American Missionary Association was organized prior to the Civil War in 1846 by amalgamating a group of evangelical associations which shared a powerful concern for "equal brotherhood in the family of Christ" primarily for the education of African Americans. Wesley A. Hotchkiss stated that such a concern was so radical that it expressed itself in a militant but legal abolitionism.[5] As early as 1861, the American Missionary Association shifted its major resources to the South to establish schools for the Freedmen beginning with a school at Fortress Monroe, Hampton, Virginia, with Mrs. Mary Peake, an African American teacher. General Butler encouraged this work among the homeless and destitute "contrabands." The school was known as the Butler School and was the forerunner of the Hampton Institute, also organized by the American Missionary Association with Gen. Samuel C. Armstrong as its first principal. The American Missionary Association rapidly extended its work in the South and West during the Civil War when schools were opened in twelve states including Kansas, Missouri, and the District of Columbia. By 1880, the association supported eight chartered institutions, twelve high and normal schools, and twenty-four common schools in the South, with approximately 7,207 students and 163 teachers. From the beginning of its work, some

150,000 students had been educated in these schools.[6] Hence, the Congregationalist Church linked its establishment of church-related schools for African Americans to a rather radical missionary organization.

After the Civil War, the National Council of Congregational Churches decided to establish one school of higher learning in each of the larger states of the South; normal and graded schools in principal cities; and common and parochial schools in smaller towns and country areas. Under this broad plan rose Hampton Institute, Atlanta University, Berea College of Kentucky, Fisk University in Tennessee, and Talladega College in Alabama. Out of Fisk University emerged the famous Fish Jubilee Singers which captured and promoted indigenous African American music.

Initially, the Methodist Episcopal Church cooperated with the Freedmen's Bureau and certain interdenominational attempts to provide educational opportunities for African Americans. However, by the close of the Civil War, some leaders of the denomination came to realize that the scope of need and a particular approach demanded a separate church organization that would be financed and controlled by the Methodist Episcopal Church. Influential Methodist leader Dr. J.M. Walden offered the following statement to his colleagues for discussion and decision:

> Since the organization of the Western and Northwestern Freedmen's Aid Commission, the membership of the Methodist Episcopal Church have been aiding these societies in prosecuting their work in behalf of the freedmen. We have met to consider whether this cooperation shall be continued, or whether the times and work requires the organization of a Society to be controlled entirely by members of our own Church.[7]

Following this dialogue, the denomination organized the Freedmen's Aid Society of the Methodist Episcopal Church which opened in Trinity Methodist Episcopal Church, Cincinnati, Ohio, on August 7, 1866. The Society was organized by ministers and laymen for the relief and education of the freedmen. It was structured to operate in connection with the official Missionary and Church Extension Societies of the Methodist Episcopal Church.[8] Subsequently, that society gave extensive support to African American schools. It directed most of its support to schools in the South. By 1867, the Society reported 59 schools in ten states with 52 teachers and approximately 5,000 pupils; and in 1869 there were 60 schools with 105 teachers and approximately 10,000 students.[9] Later, the Methodist Episcopal Church gained the reputation of supporting more African American colleges than any other denomination.

Like the Methodist Episcopal Church, the Presbyterian Church in the U.S.A. entered cooperative relationships for the support of African American education. Initially, it operated a college in Tennessee relate to the Board of National Missions. Later, it operated another college related to the Board of Christian Education. The denomination established Stillman College, originally called Tuscaloosa Institute, in 1876. The primary purpose of the school was to train ministers for the African American Presbyterian churches. Later, it expanded the program to include liberal arts education. In 1899, the assembly approved a plan to admit young men to study who were interested in the gospel ministry, and also girls over fourteen years of age who commuted daily.[10]

The Protestant Episcopal Church entered the mission of support of the education of the Freedmen as early as 1865. Both northern and southern members of the denomination began drives to awaken the denomination to its obligation to render aid to the Freedmen. An organization was established to be known as The Protestant Episcopal Freedmen's Commission to Colored People. In 1865, the name was changed to Commission on Work among Colored People, and again to Commission on Negro Work. By 1900, the later commission had received some appropriations from the Board of Missions toward its proposed work. In 1904, the commission was dissolved and the work was completely turned over to the Board of Missions. By the end of 1905, the Board decided to organize a small autonomous body of twelve churchmen to specialize in African American works, called The American Church Institute for Negroes. The emphasis of the institute was on the development of sound education and Christian character.

The following schools were among those originally supported by the American Church Institute for Negroes: St. Paul's College in Lawrenceville, Virginia; St. Augustine's College in Raleigh, North Carolina; Voorhees Junior College in Denmark, South Carolina; Fort Valley College, High and Industrial School in Fort Valley, Georgia; St. Agnes School for Nurses in Raleigh, North Carolina; Bishop Payne Divinity School in Petersburg, Virginia; Gaudet Normal and Industrial School in New Orleans, Louisiana; Hoffman St. Mary's College in Manson, Tennessee; and St. Mark's Industrial School in Birmingham, Alabama.

The Seventh Day Adventist Church did not become extensively involved in African American education until 1895 with the establishment of Oakwood College in Huntsville, Alabama. The denomination purchased 565 acres of land near the city for the location of a training school for African Americans. The purpose of the school was for the training and development of leaders for the service of God and the church. The denomination sought to fulfill its post-emancipation responsibility to the race. Earlier mission schools organized in other parts of the South necessitated the establishment of Oakwood College.

The Evangelical Lutheran Church played a significant role in early African American education. White Evangelical Lutherans held many extensive dialogues before a final decision was made to accept the challenge of education for Freedmen. In 1877 Pastor H.A. Preus, president of Norwegian Synod of the Synodical Conference, raised the question of "the desirability of directing work among the heathen and perhaps among the Negroes and Indians of our country."[11] Subsequently, the Synodical Conference appointed a Board of Missions with the responsibility to begin the work. Pastor J.F. Doescher of Yankton, Dakota, was appointed as the missionary to work among African Americans with instructions to explore the South for the establishment of Lutheran churches in African American settlements. In 1902, the Synodical Conference broadened the mission to include the training of African Americans for missionary work. Earlier, the Immanuel Conference of North Carolina, composed of white and African American missionaries, had appointed a committee which was instructed to work with Synodical Conference officials toward the possible establishment of a school. The necessity for training African Americans for missions and other church work was readily seen by the conference.

Lutheran leaders produced a detailed statement expressing the rationale for the education of African Americans and the variety of difficulties generally encountered. The following excerpts from the statement reveal existing attitudes and cultural differences among Lutherans as well as other whites, especially in the South:

1. The number of white Christians wiling to serve as missionaries and teachers among Negroes is acutely meager.

2. A Negro pastor or teacher is more familiar with the racial characteristics ideals, objectives, and peculiarities of his race, and also in better position to rightfully discern their tendencies, attitudes, aptitudes and deficiencies, and for that reason can apply the Word of God more adequately and effectively to their moral and spiritual needs.

3. A Negro has the advantage over the white "stranger" and can more readily gain the confidence and good will of his people and thus make his labors among them more satisfactory and fruitful.

4. The racial hatred in the South has manifested itself to such an extent that a white man's success among the Negro population is greatly curtailed and jeopardized.

5. White pastors and their families are looked down upon and despised because they are trying to help the Negro, and often suffer undue hardship. Because of this antagonism and hatred on the part of whites they frequently have no friends or few social contacts....

6. Some white people have gone so far as to persuade the Negroes to turn against the white missionaries and his family by perverting their minds with false propaganda and libelous accusations.

7. Some Negro preachers have become jealous or envious of the white missionaries....

8. It was emphasized that the majority of Negroes do not trust any white man, because of the experiences of slavery days.... Some were told that it was a sin to listen to a white man's sermons.

9. It would cost the Church less to use Negro pastors and teachers, and this would not impair the work if the "right kind" of Negroes were properly prepared and trained. It was contended that Negroes can and do live cheaper than a white man primarily because the cost of housing, food, and clothing, auxiliaries, etc. is less.... Furthermore, it would enable the Negro churches to become self-supporting much more quicker and be less dependent on the white church....

10. It was asserted that the Lutheran Synodical Conference must make haste to prepare more church workers in the shortest possible time because of the tragic moral and spiritual conditions prevalent everywhere. Prominent leaders of the Negro race were cited as deploring the sad state of affairs among their people. These leaders stated without hesitation that many Negro preachers were either ignorant or incapable of adequately discerning the truths of Holy Writ.... Booker T. Washington is supposed to have said that fully two thirds or three fourths of the Negro preachers in certain deep-South rural communities of that day were neither spiritually nor morally fit to preach the Gospel to others or to be spiritual leaders....

11. Another pertinent reason was the language question. Practically all the instruction in the white Lutheran preparatory schools and seminaries was in the German and other foreign languages and most of the theological material was written in these languages.... Hence it was argued that a Negro college and theological seminary in the

South in which the English language would be the medium of instruction would be more advantageous.

12. Another reason advanced was that the climate of the North, in which all of the Lutheran Synodical Conference schools were located, was too rigorous for most Negroes and would discourage many prospective students from attending there. Also the cost of transportation and the distance would prove a financial burden to most Negroes.

13. It was contended that a school for Negroes in some Southern state could be operated and maintained at a lower overhead cost for buildings, fuel, board, utilities and upkeep....

14. It was deemed of the greatest importance that Negro students live and associate with people of their own race for psychological reasons.[12]

After many lengthy debates, the Lutheran Church decided to open a separate school for African Americans. On March 2, 1903, a temporary beginning of Lutheran participation in African American education was begun in Concord, North Carolina, with the construction of a small school house in a small Lutheran church. The school was named Immanuel Lutheran College. It opened with five African American students who expressed a desire to study for the Lutheran ministry. A short time later, the college moved to Greensboro, North Carolina.

African American Baptist Schools

Even during the antebellum period, African American Baptists became very much involved in the education of the race. Independent churches in the North as well as in slaveholding states were actively educating African Americans in small educational settings, sometimes in basements or Sunday school areas of the churches. Prior to the Civil War, African American Baptist cooperative ventures led to the establishment of educational boards within the denomination. The leadership of these boards saw the tremendous and urgent need of education for the race and initiated, with the help of white Christians and philanthropists, a strategy for the achievement of literacy on the part of the general population of African Americans. The education of the race was a tremendous undertaking.

At the close of the Civil War, the percentage of illiteracy among the African American population almost overwhelmed the churches. The experience of slavery had been devastating to the race. In 1850, the total free African American population twenty years of age or over was 219,520; of these, 90,522 were reported as unable to read or write. There were 113,629 free African Americans in the South; of these, approximately one-half were illiterate.[13] Further complicating the problem, the former slaves emerged from the Civil War almost completely illiterate. Hence, the need for an aggressive program of education became both critical and urgent for the survival of the race in America.

Fortunately, the end of the Civil War also ushered in a new era of opportunities for African Americans to receive an education. The federal government as well as church groups became involved. Initially, the Freedmen's Bureau under the leadership of General Oliver Howard, who was appointed by President Abraham Lincoln to the new position, took on much of the early leadership in African American education, especially in the South. He urged the U.S. Congress to pass legislation designed to broaden the role of the bureau to include education. Congress acquiesced and passed a bill over the veto of President Andrew Johnson, and the bill became law on July 16, 1866. Subsequently, the Freedmen's Bureau spent significant sums of money toward the organization and development of schools for the race. Not only did the bureau organize schools itself but participated financially with benevolent agencies already engaged in such work, especially the American Missionary Association.

The tendency toward cooperation on the part of the Freedmen's Bureau gave new momentum to benevolent agencies, northern philanthropists, and denominational missionary boards to expand their involvement in the education of African Americans. An example of a major contributor to the education of the race was George Peabody, who established the Peabody Fund which granted $3,500,000 toward the training of teachers for the educational needs of the freedmen. But a major problem faced by these strides was the menace of violence from radical rebels in the South. Teachers of both races were often victims of intimidation and mob violence, especially from the Ku Klux Klan and other ex-confederate hate groups. Some schools were completely burned down.

It was in such a social milieu that African American Baptists became one of the pioneers of education for the race. Leaders from various parts of the nation realized that the church faced the urgent challenge to reduce illiteracy among the disadvantaged in order to realize racial progress. Hence, they committed themselves, in cooperation with other groups, to the development of an aggressive educational enterprise. This became one of the greatest contributions of the African American Baptist Church to the advancement of human dignity and productivity. Educational progress was the only sure means for the race to gradually overcome the dehumanization and severe psychological scars of American slavery. This urgency motivated preachers and other educators to rise above the restraints of the existing social milieu.

Two types of educational institutions developed among African American Baptists: 1. Cooperative schools for the raced established primarily with the financial and human resources of white organizations; and, 2. Independent African American Baptist schools which utilized almost exclusively teachers and administrators from the African American community. Cooperative schools for the race were developed primarily by the American Baptist Home Mission Society. It played a major role in the intellectual and cultural development of African Americans, focusing primarily on higher education institutions. The work of the American Baptist Home Mission Society consisted of sending missionaries to work among the race, establishing and supporting schools, and support for teachers. Most of the earliest colleges for the race were financed, administered, and staffed by white American Baptists. They were the leaders of cooperative ministries in the establishment of such schools as: Richmond Theological Seminary in Richmond, Virginia, founded 1867 and incorporated 1876; Shaw University in Raleigh, North Carolina, founded 1865 and incorporated 1875; Atlanta Seminary in Atlanta, Georgia, founded originally in Augusta in 1867 and transferred to Atlanta in 1879; Roger Williams University in Nashville, Tennessee, in 1864; Leland University in New Orleans, Louisiana, in 1870; Benedict College in Columbia, South Carolina, in 1887; Bishop College in Marshall, Texas, in 1881; Selma University in Selma, Alabama, in 1878; State University in Louisville, Kentucky, in 1873; Florida Institute in Live Oak, Florida, in 1873; Spellman Seminary in Atlanta, Georgia, in 1881; Arkansas Baptist College in Little Rock, Arkansas, in 1887; Home Institute in New Iberia, Louisiana, in 1888; Mather School in Beaufort, South Carolina; and, the Bible and Normal Institute in Memphis, Tennessee. White Baptists made tremendous investments in the organization and operation of these schools.

The first independent African American Baptist School was Guadalupe College. Subsequently, others were founded in rapid succession: Houston College in Houston, Texas, 1885; Virginia Theological Seminary and College in Lynchburg, Virginia, 1888; Walker Baptist Institute in Augusta, Georgia, 1888; Western College in Independence, Missouri, 1890; Friendship Baptist College in Rock Hill, South Carolina, 1891; Meridian Baptist Seminary in Meridian, Mississippi, 1897; Central City College in Macon, Georgia, 1899; Central Texas College in Waco, Texas, 1903; East Texas Normal and Industrial Academy in Tyler, Texas;

and Morris College in Sumter, South Carolina, 1905. Significantly enough, most of these schools were founded by African American Baptists in the South where the overwhelming majority of the race resided. However, a small number were established in the North and West. In 1901, the Colored Baptist Convention of Maryland organized the Clayton-Williams Academy and Biblical Institute in Baltimore, Maryland; the Maryland Baptist Missionary Convention organized the Lee and Hayes University in Baltimore, Maryland, in 1914; the Independent Colored Baptist Convention organized in 1928 the Williams and Jones University also in Baltimore; and the United Baptist Missionary Convention of Maryland organized in 1942 the Maryland Baptist Center and School of Religion in Baltimore. These Baltimore schools were basically the result of rivalry among Maryland's African American Baptists. Two other independent schools were organized especially for the education of ministers: Central Baptist Theological Seminary in Topeka, Kansas, and Northern Baptist University in Rahway, New Jersey.

Not only were African American Baptists involved in higher education pursuits, but they also participated extensively in elementary and secondary education with the organization of independent Baptist associational schools. The state of North Carolina was foremost in the strides of Baptists to organize private secondary schools. Some of the teachers and preachers who graduated from Shaw University played major roles in establishing these schools, such as Alexander Hicks of Plymouth, North Carolina, and E.H. Lipscombe of Dallas, North Carolina. The school at Plymouth developed into a state normal school while the one at Dallas existed for several years and became extinct. These two pioneer movements inspired local African American Baptist associations to get involved. Other high schools were organized by church associations throughout the state of North Carolina. Unfortunately, the majority of such schools closed with the rise of state support for secondary schools.

Similarly, the rise of state support for higher education institutions tended to adversely affect the growth and development of African American Baptist colleges. Some were forced to merge with other institutions to maximize resources. The colleges, seminaries, and Bible schools that did survive had to struggle with limited physical buildings, poor faculty salaries, limited library facilities, and educational supplies. Nevertheless, some of the schools were able to meet state and national standards for certified education. A brief survey of these institutional stories will reflect the remarkable strides of the Baptist educational enterprise.

WAYLAND SEMINARY

The Wayland Seminary was a pioneer educational institution for the intellectual and moral development of African Americans. It was opened in the Nineteenth Street Baptist Church of Washington, D.C., under the auspices of the American Baptist Home Mission Society of New York City. The school was named in honor of Dr. Francis Wayland who was quite instrumental in the organization and maintenance of the seminary. Its focus was on the education of African American religious leaders to meet the challenges of racial development during the early post-Civil War era.

Actually, Wayland Seminary resulted from a merger with another school which was organized in Washington, D.C., in 1864, namely, the National Theological Institute. For a brief period of time, the two schools existed concomitantly, but in 1869, they merged with Wayland Seminary. Many African American leaders were educated in Wayland Seminary. The course of instruction at Wayland Seminary was adapted to the special needs of the freedmen. The curriculum combined academic, normal, and theological courses designed to prepare the race for American citizenship. In 1889, Wayland Seminary was merged with Richmond Theological Seminary under the new name of Virginia Union University at Richmond, Virginia.

VIRGINIA UNION UNIVERSITY

The Virginia Union University was founded in 1865 by the American Baptist Home Mission Society. It was the society's first bold attempt to organize work among African Americans in the South; Richmond was once the capital of the Confederate States of America. Its early evolution was inextricably related to several other educational movements. Near the end of 1865, Rev. J. B. Binney, former president of Columbia College in Washington, D.C., came to Richmond and started a night school, the Richmond Theological Institute for Freedmen. The school idea failed because he could not find a location to establish an institution for the freedmen.

Fortunately, the work was continued by Rev. Nathaniel Colver, an abolitionist and biblical professor at the University of Chicago. In 1867, he was asked to continue the work and secure a permanent site. Rev. Colver succeeded in this endeavor by leasing the Lumpkin's Slave Jail property from its owner. The new site was named the Colver Institute. Subsequently, the trustees and other officials of the American Baptist Home Mission Society decided to make it a school for ministers only; hence, the name was changed to the Richmond Theological Seminary. The Society elected Rev. Charles Corey to serve as the president, and he remained in this capacity until 1899.

Because of its strategic location in a densely populated area, the school grew rapidly. In 1870, it moved to a new location at the Union Hotel in Richmond. It remained in this location until 1898 when the Home Mission Society decided to move Wayland Seminary to Richmond and merge it with Richmond Theological Seminary. The merger was then named Virginia Union University. With the sale of the Wayland Seminary property in Washington, the society was able to use the funds to purchase a new location for the university at Sheep Hill, the old site of Nathaniel Bacon's plantation. The school soon assumed its university structure with Wayland Seminary becoming the college department and Richmond Theological Seminary the graduate school of religion.

In 1932 Hartshorn Memorial College, a women's Christian school, also merged with the growing and viable institution of higher learning. The last school to join the "union" was Storer College in 1964. It was the oldest institution dedicated to the education of African Americans in West Virginia. Initially, Storer College had been closed in 1955 and officially merged into Virginia Union University in 1964. Each of these schools had been led by white Baptists. The American Baptist Home Mission Society delegated the management of Virginia Union University to its various trustees and administrators. However, the African American Baptists of the General Baptist Convention of Virginia gradually assumed greater responsibility for the operation of the University. They made increasing financial contributions and desired greater input into faculty and staff issues. In 1936, Dr. John M. Ellison, born in Virginia in 1889, became the first African American president of Virginia Union University. This began a trend toward greater African American Baptist control of educational issues at the university.

Very significantly, Virginia Union University has developed into one of the leading universities for higher education; and, among the earliest to be accredited by the Southern Association of Colleges and Secondary Schools. Its School of Religion shares with Howard University School of Religion and the Interdenominational Theological Center of Atlanta University the distinction of accreditation by the American Association of Theological Schools.

Moreover, Virginia Union University represents a symbol of cooperation between American Baptists (formerly Northern Baptists), Southern Baptists, and African American Baptists to facilitate quality education for the African American race. Higher education is not limited to African Americans at the university but is open to all races and nationalities. But the student body still remains predominately African American.

Shaw University

In 1865, Shaw University was established by Rev. H. W. Tupper of Massachusetts under the auspices of the American Baptist Home Mission Society. Initially, Rev. Tupper began a theological class of freedmen in the old Guion Hotel in Raleigh, North Carolina, on December 1, 1865. Out of this theological class, he received the idea of establishing a university. The actual university was started in a "negro cabin" on the outskirts of the city. The work of this small school developed slowly, but, Rev. Tupper was determined to develop a significant institution for the higher education of African Americans in the state of North Carolina.

Accordingly, Tupper made appeals to other white men in the state who sympathized with the plight of African Americans. Hence, the construction of a building to house the university was made possible by liberal contributions from Elijah Shaw of Wales, Massachusetts; J. Estey and Company; Gen. Andrew Porter; George M. Moore; and other men from New England. Several African American men of the city also contributed to the construction of the first building, which was erected at the corner of Blount and Cabarrus Streets in Raleigh. The school remained in this location for several years under the name of Raleigh Institute.

Needless to say, the establishment of the Raleigh Institute was not without severe difficulties in Raleigh, where the local white residents were opposed to such education for African Americans. Rev. Tupper, a northern sympathizer with the race, was not received with kindness or cooperation. In fact, he was threatened with violence for persistence in such an endeavor. Rev. J. A. Whitted, a pioneer African American historian, observed:

> President Tupper and wife spent a night in a corn field in the rear of their humble cabin, having been threatened by the Ku Klux. Every moment of these hours of anxious suspense they expected to see the flames consume their home and all their earthly effects, but a kind, all-wise Providence guarded them through the long night watches, and when the welcome dawn tardily appeared the humble cabin was still standing and in devout thanksgiving they returned to the kindly shelter.[14]

In 1870, a new day dawned for Raleigh Institute. The Barringer property, comprising about ten acres with a mansion, was bought for $15,000 to house the expanding school. In 1872, nearly half of the Shaw building was completed at a cost of $15,000. Two year later, the Estey building, a school for girls, was finished at a cost of $25,000. In 1875, the school was incorporated as Shaw University. It became the first college for African Americans in North Carolina to receive the "A" rating by the state Department of Education and the first such institution south of Washington to limit itself strictly to college and theological work.

After its incorporation, Shaw University was expanded to reflect true university status. President Tupper first envisioned the establishment of a medical department. By 1908, the university had developed the Leonard Medical School in addition to normal, theological, and industrial departments, and the school of law, theology, and pharmacy. The medical school was led by prominent white physicians in the city of Raleigh. This expansion did not develop with some growth pains. By 1914, financial considerations necessitated the termination of the Leonard Medical School along with the new Leonard Hospital and the Law School. The closure of these professional schools was a serious blow to the institutional development of the university. All that remained of the medical school was the continuation for a brief period of time of a two-year course in pharmacy. However, during its brief lifetime, the Leonard Medical School graduated 396 medical students. [15]

Another serious situation that developed in the life of Shaw University centered around racial issues prominent on campus. Early in the twentieth century, African American students became increasingly aware of the prominence of white leaders in the administration of the institution. Several of the student leaders began to organized efforts to obtain greater African American control of the university. In 1914, a student protest movement erupted on campus, designed to remove President Meserve and obtain the service of an African American president. Some students even left Shaw to enroll in other schools because of the tension at Shaw University.

On January 21, 1914, T.L. McCoy of the *Norfolk Journal and Guide* surveyed the impact of the student protest movement, and he sided with the administration, suggesting that it had a negative effect on the overall program of the university. This support from a major African American newspaper proved to be encouraging news for the administration. However, gradually African American Baptists gained greater control over the university, leading to administrative changes and more African American faculty.

Meanwhile, the university shifted its emphasis from the professional schools to liberal arts education and the Shaw Divinity School. It specialized, more or less, in the general field of education. For many years, it provided most of the African American teachers for the state. Many notable professionals are among Shaw's alumni; among them are such distinguished persons as Ms. Angie Brooks, a world leader of the United Nations from Liberia; Dr. James E. Shepard, founder of North Carolina State University at Durham; and James Y. Eaton, member of the North Carolina Legislature in 1899.

In the 1960s, Shaw University experience perhaps its most important period of growth and development under the leadership of President James E. Cheek, a young African American scholar who led the university to redevelop its total curriculum and to expand the physical facilities. He was able of acquire significant sums of federal government money to construct several new buildings and to upgrade the academic programs. The faculty increased from 36 to 71 and the student enrollment from 667 to 1,052. He made further plans for increasing faculty salaries by approximates thirty percent and to increase capital outlay for new constructions to approximately $5 million.

President Cheek also addressed the issue of what he felt was too much control of the university by the General Baptist State Convention of North Carolina. On the one hand, he tried to encourage greater financial support from the Baptists of the state, but at the same time limit their direct involvement in the internal affairs of the university. This was a dilemma faced by most other administrators in church-related colleges and universities. Guarded care had to be taken to assure the freedom of professional educators to develop and administer the curriculum of the schools.

ROGER WILLIAMS UNIVERSITY

The beginning of the work of the American Baptist Mission Society in Nashville, Tennessee, was in 1864 when Rev. H.L. Wayland was appointed as a missionary-teacher for the city of Nashville. After eight months he resigned and was succeeded by Rev. D.W. Phillips. In 1864, Rev. Phillips organized a class of African American youths in his house, then moved it to the basement of the First Colored Baptist Church of Nashville. In 1866, the Roger Williams University was organized and housed in an abandoned government building. The school opened with accommodations for about forty-five young men and twelve young women. For about ten years, the university remained in this old government building.

In 1882, the board of the Home Mission Society decided to incorporate the institution, but incorporation was not effected until January 1883. Initially it was named Nashville Institute, and the name was changed to Roger Williams University after its incorporation. To be sure, the Home Mission Society contributed the principal financial support for the development of the university. After 1905, the African American Baptists of Tennessee began their support of the school and slowly gained some control of its administration. By 1908, the responsibility for the operation of the school shifted from the society to the Negro Baptist Missionary and Educational Convention of the state of Tennessee.

Fortunately, the Roger Williams University from the very beginning maintained a high reputation for thorough academic training. In addition to the training of African Americans, it was one of the pioneer institutions in the state for the education of Native Americans. Unfortunately, in 1929 the university experienced budget deficits, low student enrollment, and administrative problems which greatly concerned the African American Baptist leadership in the state. Many felt that the school could no longer survive under these conditions, and the fate of it was soon sealed.

LELAND UNIVERSITY

In 1870, Leland University was founded in New Orleans, Louisiana, for the education of African Americans to prepare them for Christian citizenship, either as ministers, teachers, or tradesmen. The school was open to all qualified persons without distinction of race, color, or religious opinions. It initially developed out of the labors of two American Baptist missionaries, Rev. J.W. Horton and Rev. Jeremiah Chapman. These men were appointed by the American Baptist Home Mission Society to "engage in the work of instructing colored ministers and students for the ministry."[16] In 1869, Holbrook Chamberlain and his wife, of the Baptist Free Mission Society, arrived on the scene and assisted the missionaries in the establishment of the school. The new school was named Leland University after the maiden name of Mrs. Chamberlain, who was a direct descendant of Rev. John Leland.

The curriculum of Leland University consisted of courses necessary for quality in normal and industrial education. However, the school also maintained a strong program of religious studies since the great aim of its founding was for the education of African American preachers. Equally important, the school served as a center for Protestant polemics against the strong Roman Catholic influence in the city of New Orleans.

Benedict College

During the early days of reconstruction in South Carolina, the Baptist denomination did very little in efforts to begin a strong institution for higher learning for the freedmen of the state. It was not until 1870 that a substantial effort evolved with the founding of Benedict College in Columbia, South Carolina. The site seemed ideal since Columbia was the capital of the state. Funds were made available for the purchase of the site through the generosity of Mrs. B.A. Benedict of Providence, Rhode Island. It consisted of approximately eighty acres of land.

The American Baptist Home Mission Board led the way in the establishment of this school. This was quite usual in the founding of African American colleges. Due to the large contribution from Mrs. Benedict, the board decided to name the school in honor of the deceased husband of the donor, Deacon Stephen Benedict. In 1871, the school was opened under the presidency of Rev. Timothy D. Dodge. The school was later incorporated under the name of Benedict College.

The founding of Benedict College signaled a new era in educational opportunities for African Americans in South Carolina, a state that had previously led the way in establishing "Black Codes" against the education of slaves in the antebellum South. According to the census of 1880, there were 604,332 African American people living in the state. Many of these people were still illiterate. Benedict College played a major role in decreasing the illiteracy in the state. The student body more than doubled in the early 1880s. African Americans, young and old, took advantage of the quality of education at the school.

Initially, the focal point of concern at Benedict College was the education of teachers and preachers for the large African American population of the state. A strong program in Christian morals permeated the entire curriculum of the institution. This was true of most of the early church-related schools. Other schools like Benedict College did not succumb to the wave of secularism in education.

By the turn of the century, the curriculum of the institution was greatly expanded in the liberal arts. Gradually, the general program of the school developed into a very strong institution of higher learning. On November 2, 1924, the school was legally incorporated and became a chartered institution, possessing full college powers under the laws of the state. The institution was organized into two schools—the College of Liberal Arts and the School of Theology. Each school was designed to meet the unique educational needs of African Americans.

BISHOP COLLEGE

The need for an institution of higher learning for African Americans of the Southwest beyond the Mississippi River was recognized during the early period of the Reconstruction Era. Dr. Nathan Bishop, a former secretary of the Home Mission Board Society of the American (Northern) Baptist Convention, was first to articulate this concern concretely: "I have $10,000 to put into a school in Texas, when the time has come."[17] This was the inspiration to establish Bishop College in Texas. In 1881, the college was founded through a cooperative effort of white Baptists (North and South) and African American Baptists in the state. Initially, the college was located in Marshall, Texas. This was a pioneer movement of cooperation between separate Baptist denominations in the United States. It signaled the willingness of these denominations to cooperate on important issues affecting African Americans.

Bishop College was established as a liberal arts school, but it provided educational opportunities for children and adults from kindergarten through undergraduate years. During the administration of its first president, S.W. Culver, the institution was chartered in 1886 under the laws of Texas. Incorporators were members of the American Baptist Home Mission Board, representatives of the Southern Baptist Convention, and several African American Baptist associations in Texas.

The academic program of the school was geared to prepare preachers and teachers and to provide professional training for lawyers, physicians, and dentists. In 1886, Bishop College established a cooperative relationship with the Richmond Theological Seminary in Richmond, Virginia, making it possible for advance students to enter seminary; and, with Shaw University in Raleigh, North Carolina, to accept the professional students from Bishop College for admission to the schools of law and medicine at Shaw. Hence, African American Baptists beyond the Mississippi River were linked with those of the East in cooperative educational programs.

Bishop College, like most private African American colleges, was initially administered by white presidents. It was not until 1929 that the school elected its first African American president, Dr. Joseph J. Rhoads, a native of the local community and a graduate of the college. Under his leadership the high school department was eliminated, and the school was given unconditional rank as a senior college by the Texas State Board of Education. At that time, it became one of the two schools west of the Mississippi River to be rated by the Southern Association of Colleges and Schools. Significantly enough, this academic distinction was accomplished under the leadership of an African American president.

Several other achievements of the Rhodes administration include: a junior college extension opened in Dallas in 1947; a graduate program leading to the Master of Education degree initiated in1947; and the organization of the Lucy Kirk Williams Ministers' Institute. The latter shared with the Hampton Institute Ministers Conference as one of the two greatest short-term training centers for in-service ministers and lay church leaders, especially musicians, in the United States. Also, Bishop College joined the United Negro College Fund in 1944.

In May 1951, Dr. Earl L. Harrison, pastor of Shiloh Baptist Church in Washington, D.C., became interim president during the illness of Dr. Joseph J. Rhoads. Following the retirement of President Rhoads in August 1951, Dr. Harrison assumed full duties of the presidency but declined a permanent appointment. During this brief administration, Dr. Harrison succeeded in realigning the Baptist Missionary and Educational Convention of Texas with Bishop College, thereby opening the doors for greater financial support. Earlier concerns had resulted in the withdrawal of some support from the convention.

In December 1951, the board of trustees elected Dr. M.K. Curry Jr. to the presidency of Bishop College. His long tenure was crowned with many accomplishments, including the elimination of the graduate program in teacher education; raising the minimum endowment of $300,000 in 1952-1955; upgrading faculty appointments; and the renovation of the campus with funds from the United Negro College Fund Capital Campaign. He also led in the relocation of the college to Dallas, Texas, in 1961.

Bishop College has made many outstanding contributions to the intellectual, religious, and social life of Dallas and the nation. Early in January 1964, Bishop College participated in the organization of the Dallas-Fort Worth Metropolitan Inter-University Council composed of administrators from nine of the colleges and universities in the area and the Southwest Center for Advance Studies to promote inter-institutional cooperation. It also participated in the organization of the Texas Association of Developing Colleges, a consortium of six traditionally African American colleges committed to improving the quality of undergraduate instruction, reducing unnecessary duplication of course offerings, and promoting cooperation among the participating institutions. Even with such a legacy, unfortunately the college was forced to close due to financial reasons.

State University of Louisville

State University of Louisville, Kentucky, founded in 1879 as the Kentucky Normal and Theological Institute (later named Simmons University), was one of the pioneer independent African American Baptist institutions of higher education in the United States. It grew out of a general discussion among African American Baptists at the close of the Civil War relative to the best means of elevating the race and teaching true citizenship. These Baptists organized themselves into a "General Assembly" for the purpose of "establishing a college for the education of ministers and teachers".[18] In 1886, they purchased a site at Frankfort but were too poor to start the school. In 1869, they changed their name to the General Association of Colored Baptists of Kentucky and, by a bare majority, decide to change the location for the school project from Frankfort to Louisville. The actual founding of the Kentucky Normal and Theological Institute was the culmination of almost a decade of planning. In the annual session of the General Association of Colored Baptists of Kentucky, the leadership of the association drew up an application and petitioned the state legislature for a charter. This was granted, and the leadership of the association soon raised sufficient funds to purchase grounds and buildings for the school. It was finally opened in February 1879.

Rev. E.P. Marrs and his brother H.C. Marrs were especially instrumental in the development of the new school. They were the first administrators of the institution. Specifically, Rev. E.P. Marrs served as manager and his brother the assistant manager. The first teacher was Rev. W.R. Davis. William H. Steward, who was employed in the Louisville post office, was elected chairman of the board of trustees. His large financial contributions were responsible for the economic growth and development of the school.

In 1884, the school's name was changed to the Baptist State University. It operated under the new name until 1918 when Simmons University was the name given to the college. By 1929, the school developed into a university with the organization of a liberal arts college, a theological department, and a preparatory school. It was also recognized as a standard college by the Kentucky State Department of Education.

Simmons University enjoyed significant growth for several decades. Under the leadership of President C. H. Parrish, the university enjoyed unprecedented growth with an enrollment of 467 students, 33 theological students, and property valued at $750,000 in 1922. The National Baptist Year Book, compiled by Dr. C.H. Parrish, reported also that year the university's endowment of $54,000. Unfortunately, the following decades witnessed a gradual decline in the vitality of Simmons University. In 1943, the *National Baptist Bulletin*, edited by Roland Smith, reported the school only as a theological institution with only 73 students.

However, the school still struggled to operate as one of the pioneer African American Baptist independent schools in the United States.

Selma University

In 1873, the Colored Baptist Convention at Alabama decided, while in session at Tuscaloosa, to establish a school for preachers and other church leaders. The leadership of the convention was anxious to develop an educated pastoral ministry for their churches. In this endeavor they asked the assistance of the white Baptists, but the white brethren said that the idea was not practical. Nevertheless, the local African American Baptists went to work among themselves and succeeded in opening a school at Selma, Alabama, in 1878.

Subsequently, the convention purchased property comprising about thirty-six acres with a building at the cost of $3,000 located in the suburbs of Selma. The school was initially named the Alabama Baptist Normal and Theological School, later called Selma University. In 1880, the school was adopted by the American Baptist Home Mission Society to receive support. This support played a major role in the growth and development of the institution.

In the year 1881, Rev. W.H. McAlpine, a formal slave, was elected to the presidency of Selma University. Under his leadership, the school became one of the prominent institutions for the education of African American leaders. In 1895, the school changed its name to the Alabama Baptist Colored University, and in 1908, to Selma University again. It struggled for several years to improve its academic standing, and in 1919 the Alabama State Department of Education accredited the teacher's professional course in the junior college for the granting of teachers' certificates. By 1970, Selma University was organized into a coeducational four-year institution. Like other church-related schools, Christian principles permeated the basic curriculum of the college.

Arkansas Baptist College

Arkansas Baptist College in Little Rock, Arkansas, was originated by the African American Baptists of the state in their annual convention at Hot Springs, Arkansas, in August 1884. In November of the same year the school then known as The Baptist Institute was opened at Mount Zion Baptist Church. It was operated until April 1885 under the direction of Rev. J.P. Lawson, a white Baptist minister of Joplin, Missouri, but was forced to close at that time because of insufficient funds. Later during the year of 1885 the Mount Pleasant Baptist Church was secured as a location, and Rev. Harry Woodsmall, a general missionary of the

Baptist denomination for the states of Arkansas, Louisiana, and Mississippi, helped with the reorganization of the plans for the continuation of the school. Articles of association were drawn up, and the institute was legally organized and incorporated under the laws of the state. The new corporation was named Arkansas Baptist College.

Subsequently, the African American Baptists of Arkansas purchased a city block from Attorney Blake Turner for the sum of $5,000. They were able to pool their resources to construct a modern facility for the school upon this site. Like other early schools, the theological department was the most prominent feature of the college, designed for the education of ministers to serve the Baptist churches. However, the college specialized in the education of teachers as well. Through the years, the college did not waver from its basic mission.

BUTLER COLLEGE

In 1903, Butler College was established under the name of East Texas Baptist Industrial Academy and operated under that name for about twenty-three years. It was founded by the East Texas Baptist Association for the primary purpose of developing an educated African American ministry and providing Christian education for other youth. The association developed the structure of a college with the desire to exercise continual influence or control of its fundamental operation, specifying that the moderator would serve as the president. Hence Rev. C.M. Butler, who had been moderator of the association for twenty-nine years, became the first president of Butler College. He served in this position for nineteen years until his death in 1924.

The leadership of the East Texas Baptist Association soon realized that the general African American population of the area needed additional educational opportunities, which could be met by the school. Hence, they upgraded the academy to a junior college. In 1924, following the death of Rev. C.M. Butler, the grammar school was dropped, and the curriculum concentrated on a high school program, a liberal arts junior college, and a school of theology.

In 1931, the East Texas Baptist Association found it necessary to seek the cooperation of other Baptists to operate the college successfully. Driven by necessity, the association extended an invitation to the Texas Baptist Convention to participate in a joint ownership of the property. The proposal was accepted by the Texas Baptist Convention, and the school was subsequently owned and operated jointly by the two Baptist bodies. By September 1947, the college had advanced its program to that of a senior college and was approved in 1949 by the state of Texas as an accredited four-year liberal arts college.

Initially, the Butler College served as a feeder for Bishop College. It operated as a cooperative institution rather than a competitor to Bishop College. This cooperative relationship between the two colleges enabled Butler College to gain financial support from African American Baptists throughout to state of Texas.

AMERICAN BAPTIST THEOLOGICAL SEMINARY

In 1913, African American Baptist and Southern Baptists launched a new era of cooperation in the cause of theological education with the founding of the American Baptist Theological Seminary. Initially, the Southern Baptist Convention appointed a committee of nine to "advise and confer with the colored brethren" regarding the establishment of a theological seminary for African American Baptists. This action was the real beginning of Southern Baptist activity for the establishment of the new school project.

Actually, the appointment of the committee for commission by the Southern Baptists was the culmination of much discussion within the convention. As early as 1872, the Southern Baptist Convention expressed real interest in the religious education of African American Baptists. Its Committee on the Colored Population recommended several activities in this direction: 1. white Baptist ministers were encouraged "to preach for them as frequently and regularly as they may have opportunity"; 2. local Southern Baptist churches were urged "to encourage the formation of Sunday schools among them, and aid in the instruction of teachers for such schools," and 3. the Home Mission Board was to seek ways for "the establishment of an institution for the education of the colored preachers."[19] This action set in motion a series of events. The year 1876 witnessed the beginning of ministerial institutes for African American Baptist preachers. In 1899, the Home Mission Board encouraged white ministers to assist in the development of good libraries for African American preachers. Many such activities led to the appointment of the commission for the establishment of the American Baptist Theological Seminary.

The National Baptist Convention, U.S.A., expressed a deep interest in the proposed project for a new theological school for training African American Baptist preachers. Prior to 1913, Dr. L.K. Williams, Dr. O.L. Bailey, and Dr. C.B. Bailey talked about such a project. Out of their dialogue, the decision was made to bring the matter before the National Baptist Convention, U.S.A., and the Southern Baptist Convention for deliberate action. Hence, both conventions decided to move forward with the establishment of the American Baptist Theological Seminary. In 1926, Dr. L.K. Williams, president of the National Baptist Convention, U.S.A., reported to the convention that the Southern Baptist Convention would build and equip the building necessary to the operation of the school if the National Baptist Convention would purchase and pay for the land. The board of directors would be appointed by the two conventions. However, the National Baptist Convention was to hold the majority representation of two-thirds of the total membership, giving the Southern Baptist Convention one-third of such board membership. Also, the leadership of the National Baptist Convention desired further controlling interest by specifying that the president of the school must be a member of their convention. On September 14, 1924, the American Baptist Theological Seminary was finally organized in Nashville, Tennessee. In 1934, the convention acquired the property formally occupied by the Roger Williams University for the new seminary.

Virginia Baptist Theological Seminary (later named Virginia University of Lynchburg)

The Virginia Baptist Theological Seminary and was founded by the Virginia Baptist State Convention during its annual session in May 1887, at Alexandria, Virginia. On February 24, 1888, the school was incorporated by an act of the General Assembly of Virginia. Under the provision of the charter a committee was appointed to purchase a suitable site in Lynchburg, Virginia. A building was erected with a cornerstone in July 1888. On January 13, 1890, the school was opened to give a thorough and practical education to African American youth. By 1896, the enrollment numbered 200.

Rev. P. F. Morris was elected the first president of the school, but on account of failing health resigned before the school building was completed. Hence, the real pioneer leader of the Virginia Theological Seminary and College was Gregory Willis Hayes, a graduate of Oberlin College, who succeeded Rev. P. F. Morris. He started his administration under tremendous disadvantages—a depleted treasury on the part of the Virginia Baptist State Convention and with no apparent source for financial aid. However, he proceeded with great determination to secure resources for the erection of a substantial building on a beautiful hill in Lynchburg. Under his dedicated and determined leadership, the "school on the hill" made tremendous progress in the education of African Americans. The free-spirited philosophy of Gregory Will Hayes' "Self-help and Spiritual Independence" invigorated and inspired many of the great leaders of the race who passed through this unique institution. It placed major emphasis on the values of teaching African American culture and achievement in the various fields of human endeavor.

The mission of the school was to provide unique educational experiences in liberal arts and theology permeated with the idea of "self-help" and "self-direction." Among the noted presidents who articulated this unique style of education were Reverends R.C. Wood, W.H.R. Powell, Vernon Johns, and M.C. Allen. Specifically, Rev. M.C. Allen was foremost in his emphasis on the philosophy of "Self-help and Spiritual Independence." His major emphasis was on exceptional African American preaching. In 1952, he published a standard textbook for the school entitled the *Virginia Seminary Formula for Effective Preaching*. This little book was used by all theological students on both the college and seminary levels.

Equally important was the school's emphasis on "black power." To be sure, Rev. M.C. Allen was one of the earliest men in the United States to place major emphasis on the empowerment of African Americans. He preached and lectured on the subject a decade before the beginning of the modern black power movement of Stokely Carmichael and other civil rights leaders. President Allen made sure that all of the students of the college and seminary would be exposed to the historic glory and heroes of Africa and the United States. Hence, many students from Virginia Seminary and College became leaders in the civil rights revolution in the United States as well as proponents of African nationalism.

African Methodist Episcopal Church Schools

The African Methodist Episcopal Church was the pioneer denomination in the organization of independent schools utilizing its own human and financial resources. Unlike African American Baptists who depended so heavily on cooperation from white denominations, African American Episcopal Church leaders moved forward in the education of the race with their own administrators, teachers, and financial resources. Leaders of the denomination firmly believed in offering the type of education to African Americans that would prepare them for productive citizenship in American society. This education was to express the intrinsic worth of African American people.

During the antebellum period, local pastors of the denomination were encouraged upon their appointment to establish schools in the churches to which they were appointed. In 1834 the Philadelphia Conference adopted a resolution presented by the Committee on Temperance as follows: "It shall be the duty of every minister who has charge of a circuit or station, to use every effort to establish schools wherever convenient and to insist upon parents of children sending them to school."[20] Hence, basements or other Sunday school rooms in various churches became schools for the education of African Americans.

On October 30, a convention composed of delegates from Baltimore, Philadelphia, and New York Annual Conferences met in Bethel Church in Philadelphia, Pennsylvania, to devise plans to educate the ministry in order that they might become equipped to assume the grave responsibilities and duties assigned to them.[21] In 1847, the denomination pioneered its first school for the education of African Americans in the United States—Union Seminary and Farm, established near Columbus, Ohio, on December 1, 1847, following the purchase of a tract by the Ohio Conference. The school was later merged with Wilberforce University after the purchase of the school by the church in 1863.

Sherman L. Green Jr., in his article entitled "The Rationale Underlying the Support of Colleges Maintained by the African Methodist Episcopal Church," summarized the establishment of this school:

> According to Dr. Samuel T. Mitchell, M.A., alumnus and third president of Wilberforce, "When the property of Wilberforce was offered for sale, Bishop Daniel A. Payne at once saw the adaptabilities of the school to the needs of the church and those of the race. At the meeting of those having it for sale, Bishop Payne, with no money or time to consult his church or brethren, with uplifted hands cried out, "Gentlemen, in the name of God, I purchase this property for the African Methodist Episcopal Church to be consecrated forever to the sacred cause of Christian education…." Inspired by the leadership of Bishop Payne, this "noble apostle of education," other leaders of the church organized schools throughout the South to educate the clergy and train the newly emancipated Negro slaves to assume the duties and responsibilities of citizenship and to enable them to make contributions to church and society to the full measure of their capacities.[22]

WILBERFORCE UNIVERSITY

Wilberforce University was organized by the Methodist Episcopal Church in 1856 in Wilberforce, Ohio, for the higher education of African American youth. Among its first board of twenty-four trustees were the Hon. Salmon P. Chase, then governor of Ohio, and a powerful advocate for fugitive slaves; and Reverends Daniel A. Payne and Richard S. Rust. Dr. R.S. Rust was elected as its first active president. As previously mentioned, Bishop Daniel A. Payne later purchased the college property for $10,000 for the African Methodist Episcopal Church.

Soon after Bishop Payne purchased the college, the building was burned to the ground on April 14, 1865. Subsequently, he led the way for the reconstruction of another building to house the college. Serving as the president of Wilberforce, Bishop Payne was able to construct a four-story brick building on the original site. Senators John Sherman and Charles Sumner were able to inspire the U.S. Congress to appropriate $28,000 for the building project and the work of the college. Similarly, the will of Chief Justice Salmon P. Chase contained as its first bequest, $10,000 for Wilberforce University, and the executors of the Avery estate in Allegheny City added $10,000 to its endowment.[23]

Allen University

On December 24, 1880, Allen University was established in Columbia, South Carolina, as an outgrowth of Payne Institute. It was located on four acres of land, with four cottages and one main building which had forty-two rooms. Rev. David Henry Johnson was the first president of Allen University. The university developed the following departments: Theological, Law, Classical, Normal, Musical, Intermediate, Graded, and Domestic Economy.

Edward Waters College

In 1885, the African Methodist Episcopal Church in Florida organized the Edward Waters College in Jacksonville, Florida. The primary responsibility for the operation of the college fell to the African Methodists of the state. The purpose of the college was to give African American youth of the area a thorough training both intellectually and industrially. The curriculum was designed to afford youth opportunities for study from grammar school to college. The school offered additional courses in sewing, printing, and tailoring. It sought to reach the masses through adult education program opportunities.

Morris Brown College

In 1881, the Morris Brown College was founded in Atlanta, Georgia, under the strong strides of John Wesley Gaines, later bishop in 1888, of Wilkes County, Georgia. He purchased four acres of land for $3,500 for the location of the college, contributing the first $1,000 out of his pocket. The money for the erection of the first buildings was raised by North Georgia Conference of the A.M.E. Church. Bishop Gaines personally raised a substantial amount of this money by subscriptions. He raised $2,500 by advertising with the James Armstrong Soap Company of Baltimore, Maryland.[24] In 1896, Rev. James M. Henderson, a graduate of Oberlin College in Ohio became the president of Morris Brown College. In 1894, Turner Theological Seminary was organized at Morris Brown College. Initially, the school operated both as a high school and college, but the high school was discontinued in 1932. Subsequently, the college was renamed the Morris Brown University.

The Morris Brown College was named in honor of Bishop Morris Brown, the second bishop of the A.M.E. Church, who succeeded Bishop Richard Allen. He was born in Charleston, South Carolina, on January 8, 1770. When Rev. Brown became intricately involved in religious and social issues in Charleston by organizing the first A.M.E. church in the Deep South, he was implicated and jailed because of the Denmark Vesey Insurrection of 1822. Subsequently, he moved to Philadelphia but later returned to Charleston. Because of his strong influence in planting the A.M.E. Church in the South, founders of Morris Brown College decided to name the school in his honor.

Paul Quinn College

The impetus for the founding of Paul Quinn College extended back to the establishment of the proposed "Conference High School" in Austin, Texas, in 1874. In 1881, Paul Quinn College was organized and located in Waco, Texas. Initially, the college was named Waco College, but later named after Bishop Paul Quinn. Among the founders of the college was Richard H. Cain, later elected a bishop in the A.M.E. Church in 1880. The founders of the college maintained a firm belief in self-reliance and administered the college under African American leadership.

In 1900, the property of the college consisted of twenty acres of land worth $65,000; two brick buildings and one brick addition; ten wood frame buildings; eight teachers, and 225 students. Rev. I. M. Burgan, a graduate of Wilberforce, was elected the president of the college to succeed H. T. Kealing. George F. Richings observed: "The growth of the school has been steady and solid. Bishop Atticus G. Haygood, while agent for the Slater fund, visited it and said it was the best managed and conducted school he had seen."[25]

Western University

The Western University was organized out an earlier school named Freedman's University at Quindaro, Kansas by Rev. Eben Blatchley, a white Presbyterian minister, in 1862 for the purpose of training African American youth. After his death in 1877, the school was donated to the A.M.E. Church. After this time, the denomination organized the educational movement into the Western University with the following departments: Theological, Preparatory Normal, Normal Industrial, and Collegiate. During the administration of Bishop Henry M. Turner, Western University experienced its greatest growth.[26] Financial pressure from the Great Depression led to its closing in 1943.

Campbell-Stringer College

The Campbell-Stringer College was organized out of two schools in 1887 in Vicksburg and Friars, Mississippi. George F. Richings noted:

> Owing to their unfavorable location, and in order that the endowment of the church would not be divided between several educational institutions, through the wisdom of Rt. Rev. W.B. Derrick, D.D., Bishop of the A.M.E. Church, presiding over the Eighth Episcopal District, and the trustees of said colleges, it was agreed upon to unite these two institutions of learning, and locate them in the city of Jackson.[27]

The ministers and laymen of the A.M.E. Church in Mississippi constructed a two-and-a-half story frame building to house the chapel, library, literary society, College of Law, Medicine, Music, Theology, Industries, and the recitation-rooms of the College of Letters. The aim of the college was to give African American students the benefit of a diversified curriculum.

Kittrell College

Kittrell College was founded in 1886 and incorporated in 1887 in Kittrell, North Carolina. John R. Hawkins was the founder of Kittrell Institute, later named Kittrell College. In 1900, the college property consisted of sixty acres and four buildings, which was valued at $15,000. The college owned a variety of livestock which provided opportunities for students to work out a part of their college expenses. The college consisted of the Scientific and Normal or Intermediate Departments, with Joseph S. Williams as principal.

In 1896, the General Conference of the A.M.E. Church convened in Wilmington, North Carolina, and elected John R. Hawkins, founder of Kittrell Institute, the first layman as the secretary of the Department of Education of the A.M.E. Church. He became very instrumental in increasing denominational funding for Kittrell College and other educational institutions of the denomination.[28]

A.M.E. Church Theological Schools

The African Methodist Episcopal Church maintained its early emphasis on the importance of a trained pastoral leadership. All of its colleges made Christian education a vital part of their curriculum. However, the denomination saw the benefit of organizing distinct theological seminaries. Hence, Payne Theological Seminary was organized in Wilberforce, Ohio, in 1894; Turner Theological Seminary in Atlanta, Georgia, in 1884; and the Dickerson Theological Seminary in Columbus, South Carolina. These seminaries developed comprehensive programs in Theology. Payne Theological Seminary was able to attain associate membership in the American Association of Theological Schools, and Turner Theological Seminary became affiliated with the Interdenominational Theological Center in Atlanta, Georgia.

African Methodist Episcopal Zion Church Schools

Almost from its beginning in the antebellum period, the African Methodist Episcopal Zion Church has sponsored educational opportunities for African Americans. The first A.M.E. Zion Church in New York had accommodations for a school. During this early period, most of the schools in New York operated from various churches. Some state funds were available to assist in the operation of these schools for African Americans. Among some of the early teachers of these schools were A.M.E.Z. Church leaders such as James Varick, George Collins, and William Miller.[29] In 1820, the John Street A.M.E.Z. Church erected a larger building with an additional building for the church school.

Christopher Russ, the second bishop of the A.M.E. Zion Church, was founder and first president of The Phoenix Society in 1833 in New York City, which spread to other urban areas of the North which made proposals and worked for the moral and spiritual upward mobility of African Americans and instructed them in literature and mechanical arts.

In 1844, the A.M.E. Zion denomination made its first attempt to establish a connectional institute of learning through an action taken by the General Conference. A constitution was drafted for the establishment of a connectional manual labor school under the supervision of the General Conference. By 1848, plans for the school were completed and was to be located in Essex County, New York, and be known as Rush Academy. Rush Academy was incorporated by the State of New York in 1864.

Livingston College

As previously mentioned, the African Methodist Episcopal Zion Church experienced tremendous church growth after the Civil War. The leadership of the denomination readily recognized the extensive need for educational opportunities of African American church leaders in particular, and in general the vast numbers of illiterate laity. Frederick Douglass and Booker T. Washington were uttering strong criticism about the poor educational state of African American pastors. Hence, the North Carolina Conference of the A.M.E.Z. Church started discussions to create an educational institution. In 1879, the Zion Wesley Institute was started in Concord, North Carolina. Unfortunately, the school was too dependent on the inadequate funds from the local churches in North Carolina and was forced to close in 1881.[30]

Bishop J.W. Hood, president of the Board of Trustees of Zion Wesley Institute; and Rev. J.C. Price were not willing to give up on the failed A.M.E.Z. institute. In 1881, they attended the Ecumenical Conference of the Methodist Episcopal Church in England with the expectation of securing some funds for restoration of Zion Wesley Institute. Rev. J.C. Price was able to inspire the delegates and visitors to the Conference to donate $9,100 for the Zion Wesley Institute which inspired the Zion A.M.E. Church of Concord to offer seven acres of land for a site to erect buildings and locate the school permanently. However, the trustees decided that Salisbury was a better location for the Institute. In 1882, the Board of Bishops adopted Zion Wesley Institute as a connectional school, electing a faculty with Rev. J.C. Price as president at the meeting in Chester, South Carolina. On October 1882, the institute was opened at the new location in Salisbury, North Carolina, and the name was changed to Zion Wesley College. Subsequently, the college name was again changed to Livingston College in honor of David Livingston, the famous missionary explorer of Africa. It opened with five day students but soon grew to have a large student body.

The mission of Livingston College was to give a thorough literary training to young African American men and women, without regard to denomination, to assume positions of leadership in the United States. Livingston College maintained a strong emphasis on moral and spiritual education as well as the liberal arts and industrial education. For a brief period of time, Livingston College received some financial support for its industrial program from the Slater Fund. The students of the carpentry shop of the industrial department responded by making and repairing all the furniture used in the college, such as bedsteads, chairs, tables, desks, washstands, and dressers.[31]

Fortunately, Livingston College grew rapidly and became one of the leading colleges in the South for the education of African Americans. During its formative period under the leadership of Rev. J.C. Price, Dr. W.E.B. Dubois noted, "The star of achievement which Joseph C. Price, a black boy of those days, hitched his wagon to the founding of a school for colored youth, a sort of black Harvard…."[32] Its students were sufficiently prepared academically to gain admission into graduate and professional institutions. Many of the prominent leaders of the African Methodist Episcopal Zion Church received their undergraduate education at Livingston College. By 1901, 130 students graduated from Livingston College; some were law students and others were pastors of some of the largest churches in the connection.

Hood Theological Seminary

In 1900, the General Conference of the African Methodist Episcopal Zion Church made plans for the establishment of a theological department at Livingston College. At the Board of Bishops meeting in Rock Hill, South Carolina, on March 13, 1901, a committee was appointed to devise a plan for the establishment of the theological department. Dr. George Lincoln Blackwell, a graduate of Livingston College and Boston University School of Theology, became the first dean of the Theological Department of Livingston College. Subsequently, the Board of Trustees decided to name the department Hood Theological Seminary, in honor of Senior Bishop J.W. Hood. The leadership of the new seminary sought to make it the equal to any such institution in the South.

Clinton Junior College

The leadership of African Methodist Episcopal Church entered the field of African American education with the intention of establishing schools in major areas where their churches were located, desiring first to have a school in each presiding elders' district and later one in each bishops' district. In 1879, Rev. Charles Calvin Pettey of Wilkesboro, North Carolina, opened the Pettey High School with 50 students, which was accepted by the General Conference of the A.M.E.Z. Church as a connectional school in 1880. Later the school was incorporated as Lancaster Normal and Industrial Institute. However, the school was later taken over by the State of South Carolina.

Afterwards, the General Conference shifted its attention to Clinton Institute, which was founded in 1894 in Rock Hill, South Carolina. The school was named in honor of the presiding Bishop I.C. Clinton, who established the school officially within the connection. The first president of Clinton Institute was Robert J.

Crockett, who served until 1908 when he became principal of Lancaster Normal and Industrial School. Later, the school improved its academic standard to the extent of being recognized by the South Carolina State Department of Education and the American Association of Junior Colleges. Subsequently, the school was in the position of granting State Teachers' Certificates.[33]

LOMAX-HANNON JUNIOR COLLEGE

The Lomax-Hannon Junior College was organized in 1893 as Greenville High School by Bishop Thomas H. Lomax of the East Alabama Conference at Butler Chapel in Greenville, Alabama. The first principal of the high school was Rosebud Simpson, who was succeeded by Rev. S.B. Boyd in 1900. In 1900, the oldest A.M.E.Z. Church's school in the state was merged with the Lomax High School which later became Lomax-Hannon Junior College.

Other schools organized by the A.M.E. Zion Church included Zion Institute in Mobile, Alabama, with Rev. R.A. Morisey serving as its principal; Greenville High School, later Greenville College, 1887; Atkinson College, established at Madisonville, Kentucky in 1889 as Atkinson High School; Eastern North Carolina Academy, founded in 1904 by Rev. William H. Sutton, as the Industrial Academy at New Bern, North Carolina; Walter-Southland Institute, founded by Bishop C.R. Harris in 1892 as Ashley County High School at Wilmot, Arkansas; Dinwiddie Institute, at Dinwiddie, Virginia, later becoming the Dinwiddie Agricultural and Industrial School of the A.M.E.Z. Church, opened in 1910; and Johnson Memorial Institute, founded as Johnson Rural High School at Batesville, Alabama.

The joint ventures of white denominations and African American denominations in the founding of various schools for African Americans throughout the South resulted in a progressive movement of reducing illiteracy among African Americans. African Americans entered these schools in large numbers following the Civil War. By the turn of the century, the numbers of African Americans attending schools increased tremendously, resulting in a constant decline of illiteracy.

To be sure, the African American church and schools played key roles in the elevation of the race during the first decades after emancipation. Not only did they help decrease illiteracy, but they also motivated the establishment of Christian family life, general economic progress through the development of a work ethics, moral and self-esteem growth, self-help venues, and growth in the number of independent businesses. Each area was addressed by African American preachers and teachers with a sense of urgency for racial progress. Each of the African American denominational schools responded to the educational needs of the race in changing environments.

Toward the end of the 1890s, philosophical debates emerged among African American educators. Divergent positions were taken regarding the goal of higher education. Questions were raised concerning whether the emphasis should be on the agricultural, mechanical and industrial, or should African Americans be exposed to the traditional western academic training in arts and humanities, and professional education. At issue was the educational philosophy of Booker T. Washington in opposition to that of Dr. W.E.B. Dubois. Characteristically, many of the denominational schools adopted a combination of the two educational positions.

During the twentieth century, the denominational schools faced tremendous competition from other better established African American schools and the white colleges after the historic 1954 Supreme Court decision ending segregation in educational institutions. Denominational schools found themselves having to compete with economically secure institutions for students and highly qualified faculty. The early part of the twenty-first century became characterized as a "turbulent period." Many of the race's highly qualified students elected to attend white colleges. Declining financial stability and administrative instability challenged some of the schools' ability to maintain accreditation. Student financial aid and scholarship programs became inadequate to meet the needs of many African American students. Some school administrators found themselves struggling to develop relevant curriculum to equip students with skills appropriate for the rapidly changing century. Hence, some of the schools were forced to close during this competitive period. Those that did survive had to advance aggressive plans for financial stability, faculty development, and student recruitment.

(Endnotes)

[1] John Hope Franklin, *From Slavery to Freedom* (New York: Vintage Books, A Division of Random House, 1967) 81.

[2] Hugh Victor Brown, *A History of the Education of Negroes in North Carolina* (Raleigh, N.C.: Irvin-Swain Press, 1961) 11.

[3] Franklin, 98.

[4] *The Journal of Negro Education*, Summer, 1960, 223.

[5] Ibid., 289.

6. William T. Alexander, *History of the Colored Race in America* (Kansas City, Missouri: Palmetto Publishing, 1887), 487.

7. *The Journal of Negro Education*, 252.

8. Ibid., 253.

9. Ibid., 254.

10. Ibid., 264.

11. Ibid., 300.

12. Ibid, 300-304.

13. *Negro Population 1790-1915*: (in the U.S.) (Washington, DC: Government Printing Office, 1918), 405.

14. J.A. Whitted, *A History of the Negro Baptists of North Carolina*. (Raleigh, N.C.: Presses of Edward and Broughton Printing Co, 1908), 15.

15. *Journal and Guide*, Norfolk, Virginia, April 25, 1914.

16. *Baptist Home Missions in North America*: Including a Full Report of the Proceedings and Addresses of the Jubilee Meeting, and a Historical Sketch of the American Baptist Home Mission Society, Historical Tables, Etc. 1832-1882 (New York: Baptist Home Mission Rooms, 1883), 456.

17. Ibid., 460.

18. Ibid., 458.

19. *Proceedings of the Southern Baptist Convention*, 1872, 24.

20. *Journal of Negro Education*, 319.

21. Ibid., 319.

22. Ibid., 320.

23. G. F. Richings, *Evidence of Progress among Colored People* (Philadelphia: G.F. Ferguson, 1901), 120-121.

24. Ibid., 135-36.

25. Ibid., 137.

26. Ibid., 138.

27. Ibid., 139.

28. Ibid., 131-132.

29. Walls, 301.

30. Richings, 143-144.

[31] Ibid., 150.
[32] Walls, 310-311.
[33] Ibid., 319-320.

Chapter 8

THE SOCIO-POLITICAL TRADITION OF AFRICAN AMERICAN CHURCHES

African American independent churches evolved as veritable schools of political science in the context of changes in America culture. Early pastors had to develop special skills in relating to the politics of church life. This was especially true in churches where the vote of lay members was crucial in the democratic decision-making process. Moreover, pastors had to manage clusters of block voting based on growing class consciousness and differences in local churches. Similarly, members of local churches and independent denominations were given unique experiences in democratic procedures during congregational meetings and deliberations in denominational assemblies and conventions. Even after emancipation, these skills were utilized by African Americans who entered the political life of the United States.

During the antebellum period, African American church leaders were challenged to meet the needs of the race in local and emerging national political struggles. They served as middlemen between the powerful white political machinery, advocates of better treatment of slaves, the abolition of slavery, and the general crimes against humanity persistent in the South. They were also challenged to develop a new theology which would relate a relevant appraisal of God in Christ for slaves who had been overly exposed to white racist theology. The new theology or anti-racist theology had to be interpreted to slaves with little or no understanding of the providence of God in the dynamics of history with rays of hope for freedom, salvation and human dignity. It was not totally eschatological in nature, as generally supposed, but largely committed to improve the quality of life for oppressed people in the social milieu of the period.

Henry Highland Garnett

Bishop H. M. Turner

The African American church grew up in response to two strong motivational sources: the social isolation of racism and discrimination in white churches, and the emerging social preaching of slave preachers and free African Americans. In their own meager way, those preachers reflected on the desperate plight of slaves and even the limited social and economic opportunities of free African Americans, necessitating a new form of Christian messages designed to meet the practical needs of the race. Hence, the African American church was practical in all aspects of life and thought. The voice of protest, wherever possible, became a strong element in church life, relating to anti-Christian thought of many white Christians in the South and the racism throughout the North. With an unswerving commitment to justice and righteousness, those preachers responded to the challenge of "preaching in the Spirit" reflective of the providence of God. They had a strong sense of being called by God to elevate the minds and spirits of oppressed people. The genius of slave and free African American preachers was manifested in the way they took the theological tradition of white America, which was designed to make slaves in the South and better second-class citizens in the North, and turn their new theology into a mighty power for the ultimate liberation of oppressed people.

How did slave and free African American preachers come to such creative intellectual awareness? To be sure, their methodology of "doing theology" during the slavery period must be examined. Perhaps a little archaic, but they found in the Old Testament stories something radically different from the interpretations of the white pulpit. In order to counter the tradition which held that subordination to the superior white race is the African's natural and moral condition, the pulpit of the African American church sought and found a new orientation for the liberation of the race. From this storehouse of divinely revealed material, liberation minded preachers created symbols and enigmatic phrases which were congruent to an emancipating theology emphasizing the fatherhood of God and the brotherhood of all people. If humanity has one Father, then brothers do not have the right to oppress a so-called weaker or inferior brother. Moreover, the brotherhood of humanity implied the fundamental equality of all people.

Commencing with the old slave preachers progressively to the educated ministry of the contemporary African American church, the centrality of social and political thought has permeated, fundamentally, traditions of the church movement. The church has addressed most aspects of social reforms, such as the abolition of slavery, prison reforms, racist legislations, temperance, segregation, discrimination, women's rights, human rights, civil rights, sexism, gay rights, and affirmative action. However, there were some conservative denominational leaders of churches which felt that some of these issues were beyond the ministry of the Christian church. They felt that there must be a separation between the concerns of church and state. For them, secular issues must remain the exclusive concerns of agencies of the state. Nevertheless, a sufficient number of preachers, often called "race men" and civil rights leaders, so influenced the African American church that it could be styled a major socio-political force in American culture, serving as the conscience of the nation.

African American Churches and the Abolitionist Movement

Roots of the Abolitionist Movement penetrated the young and fertile soil of the colonial period of American history. There were some early voices from colonial pulpits that spoke against the peculiar institution of slavery. Notably, some Quakers and Puritan clergymen spoke from their pulpits against the harsh natured of American slavery, but when the expansion of the slave trade developed these voices were primarily limited to the North. In 1776, the Quaker Anthony Benezet led the Society of Friends to expel its slaveholding members. In a more institutional manner, a group of Philadelphia Quakers organized an anti-slavery society. During the next two decades similar organizations were formed in many states, including Maryland (1790), Virginia (1791), and Delaware (1794).[1] However, the evolution of the National Period witnessed a more concerted effort to counter the rising tide of the slave trade in American life. The abolitionist movement passed into a more aggressive stage during the labors of William Lloyd Garrison, Henry Clay, John Brown, and other friends of oppressed people.

Not only white churchmen, but also church women took an active interest in the improvement of the plight of slaves and the abolitionist movement. Conspicuous among them were two sisters, Sarah and Angelina Grimke born in Charleston, South Carolina, into a slaveholding family. Angelina was very sympathetic toward the plight of slaves, and as a child she collected and concealed oil and other simple remedies so that she might steal out by night and alleviate the suffering of slaves who had been whipped. At age fifteen, she refused to be confirmed in the Episcopal Church because some words in the ceremony tended to support slavery. Two years later, she refused to accept a gift of a slave girl from her mother. She later joined the Presbyterian Church and labored with the officers of the denomination to participate in the antislavery cause. Her sister Sarah moved to the North and joined the Society of Friends in Philadelphia. In 1830, Angelina joined her sister in Philadelphia and published an essay entitled an "Appeal to the Christian Women of the South" to be circulated in the South and handed it to the Anti-Slavery Society in the city. When copies of the appeal reached Charleston, they were seized by a mob and publicly burned.[2] Many other women were prominent in the antislavery cause.

The first formally organized society against slavery was founded in Philadelphia in 1775, and it was incorporated fourteen years later under the name of "The Pennsylvania Society for Promoting the Abolition of Slavery, the Relief of Free Negroes Unlawfully held in Bondage, and for Improving the Condition of the African Race," which became a federation of other state societies. Subsequently, it became known as the American Convention for Promoting the Abolition of Slavery.

Elijah Embree, a slaveholder of Tennessee, was one of the earliest white abolitionists from the South who joined the Quakers in 1812, and soon thereafter made provisions for his slaves to be emancipated. His influence was felt through the Manumission Society of Tennessee. In order to spread the idea of manumission, Elijah Embree published a weekly newspaper called the *Manumission Intelligencer* in 1819 which later became a monthly paper in 1820 called *The Emancipator*. These were among the first periodicals in the United States to advocate the abolition of slavery. After his death, the legacy of white abolitionism passed on to another Quaker named Benjamin Lundy, who published a paper called *The Genius of Universal Emancipation*, which was an antislavery journal published in Baltimore. Benjamin Lundy's writings influenced the mission of William Lloyd Garrison, the most notable northern white abolitionist, who published a widely read periodical named *The Liberator*. On January 1, 1831, Garrison issued in Boston the first number of this periodical. The South reacted strongly against the antislavery articles in *The Liberator* and almost every day brought him letters from pro-slavery men containing threats of violence and even assassination.

Next to William Lloyd Garrison, Wendell Phillips (1811-1884) became the most prominent New England abolitionist. He was drawn into the movement in 1835 when he witnessed a mob leading William Lloyd Garrison through the streets of Boston in response to his objectionable abolitionist activities. For the next thirty years, Wendell Phillips rendered public support to the mission of his new friend Garrison. However, he did not completely follow the path of Garrison but attempted to steer a middle course between Garrison's Christian anarchism and the political abolitionist philosophy of men like Charles Sumner and Thaddeus Stevens. Nevertheless, the two notable white abolitionists remained dynamic forces in the abolitionist cause.

The earliest known African American voices against the institution of slavery came in the form of slave songs. They were uttered in symbolic language to maintain secrecy among the protest-minded slaves fearful of the certain violent response of slave masters. This indigenous American music prepared the spirit of protest which became prevalent in the abolitionist movement. Prior to the actual organization stages of the movement, certain African Americans captured the spirit of protest against the institution of slavery. To be sure, slave preachers in the "invisible institution" uttered protest messages against slavery in the most dangerous social context of the expanding southern institution. Unfortunately, those protest sermons were not recorded for examination by historians. Even most of the protest sermons of slave preacher in the separate church movement were not presented in manuscript form. Hence, only a few sermonic voices can be studied from the early antebellum period. These voices came largely from the North where there was a sizable number of free African Americans and the evolution of the separate church movement.

As early as March 8, 1777, the following petition was addressed by slaves in Boston to state officials:

> The petition of a great number of negroes, who are detained in a state of slavery in the very bowels of a free and Christian country, humbly showing—
>
> That your petitioners apprehend that they have, in common with all other men, a natural and inalienable right to that freedom, which the great Parent of the universe hath bestowed equally on all mankind, and which they have never forfeited by any compact or agreement whatever. But they were unjustly dragged by the cruel hand of power from their dearest friends, and some of them even torn from the embraces of their tender parents—from a populous, pleasant and plentiful country, and in violation of the laws of nature and of nations, and in defiance of all the tender feelings of humanity, brought hither to be sold like beasts of bruden, and, like them, condemned to slavery for life—among a people possessing the mild religion of Jesus—a people not insensible of the sweets of national freedom, nor without a spirit to resent the unjust endeavors of others to reduce them to a state of bondage and subjection.
>
> Your Honors need not to be informed that a life of slavery like that of your petitioners, deprived of every social privilege, of everything requisite to render life even tolerable, is far worse than non-existence.
>
> In imitation of the laudable example of the good people of these States, your petitioners have long and patiently waited the event of petition af-

ter petition, by them presented to the legislative body of this State, and cannot but with grief reflect that their success has been but too similar.

They cannot but express their astonishment that it has never been considered, that every principle from which America has acted, in the course of her unhappy difficulties with Great Britain, bears stronger than a thousand arguments in favor of your humble petitioners. They therefore humbly beseech Your Honors to give their petition its due weight and consideration, and cause an act of the legislature to be passed, whereby they may be restored to the enjoyment of that freedom, which is the natural right of all men, and their children (who were born in this land of liberty) may not be held as slaves after they have arrived at the age of twenty-one years. So may the inhabitants of this State (no longer chargeable with the inconsistency of acting themselves the part which they condemned and opposed in others) be prospered in their glorious struggles for liberty, and have those blessings secured to them by Heaven, of which benevolent minds cannot wish to deprive their fellow–men....[3]

One of the seven signers of this petition was Prince Hall, a member of the Boston Free African Society which established contacts with the Philadelphia Free African Society, and founder of the first African American Masonic order in the United States, which would play a decisive role in the freedom movement of African Americans. In his correspondence to the Philadelphia Free African Society, Prince Hall proposed to organize a lodge in Philadelphia, and Absalom Jones, James Forten, and Richard Allen played major roles in the advancement of the masonic movement.

When Prince Hall first came to America in 1765 from Barbados, he joined the Methodist Church and observed the working of freemasonry during the Revolutionary War, and he applied for his full masonic rights, which were granted September 12, 1784. Subsequently, the joint venture with the members of the Philadelphia Free African Society became successful when the African Lodge of Boston granted the request for a lodge in Philadelphia. The lodge elected Absalom Jones as the Worshipful Master and Richard Allen as the Treasurer.[4] This action placed these masonic leaders in unique positions to cultivate freedom thought for the liberation of African American people.

Similarly, in 1779 a group of slaves petitioned the New Hampshire legislature for the abolition of slavery in the state. Nineteen slaves addressed the following petition to the legislature:

To the Honorable, the Council and House of Representatives of said state, now setting at Exeter in and for said state: The petition of these subscribers, natives of Africa, now forcibly detained in slavery in said state most humbly sheweth, That the God of nature gave them life and freedom, upon the terms of the most perfect equality with other men; That freedom is an inherent right of the human species, not to be surrendered, but by consent, for the sake of social life; That private or public tyranny and slavery are alike detestable to minds conscious of the equal dignity of human nature; That in power and authority of individuals, derived solely from a principle of coercion, against the will of individuals, and to dispose of their persons and properties, consists the completest idea of private and political slavery; That all men being amenable to the Deity for the ill improvement of the blessings of His Providence, they hold themselves in duty bound, strenuously to exert every faculty of their minds to obtain that blessing of freedom, which they are justly entitled to from that donation of the beneficent Creator; That through ignorance and brutish violence of their native countrymen, and by the sinister designs of others (who ought to have taught them better), and by the avarice of both, they, while but children, and incapable of self-defense, whose infancy might have prompted protection, were seized, imprisoned, and transported from their native country, where (though ignorance and un-Christianity prevailed) they were born free, to a country, where (though Christianity and freedom are their boast) they are compelled and their posterity to drag on their lives in miserable servitude; Thus, often is the parent's cheek wet for the loss of a child, torn by the cruel hand of violence from her aching bosom; Thus, often and in vain is the infants' sigh for the nurturing care of its bereaved parent, and thus do the ties of nature and blood become victims to cherish the vanity and luxury of a fellow mortal. Can this be right? Forbid it gracious Heaven!

Permit again your humble slaves to lay before this honorable assembly some of those grievances which they daily experience and feel. Though fortune hath dealt out our portion with rugged hand, yet hath she smiled in the disposal of our persons to those who claim us as their property; of them we do not complain, but from what authority they assume the power to dispose of our lives, freedom and property, we would wish to know. Is it from the sacred volume of Christianity? There we believe it is not to be found; but here hath the cruel hand of slavery made us incompetent judges, hence knowledge is hid from our minds.... Is this authority assumed from custom? If so let that custom be abolished, which is not founded in nature, reason nor religion. Should the humanity and benevolence of this honorable assembly restore us that state of liberty of which we have been so long deprived, we conceive that those who are our present masters will not be sufferers by our liberation, as we have most of us spent our whole strength and the prime of our lives in their service; and as freedom inspires a noble confidence and gives the mind an emulation to vie in the noblest efforts of enterprise, and as justice and humanity are the result of your deliberations, we fondly hope that the eye of pity and the heart of justice may commiserate our situation, and put us upon the equality of freemen, and give us an opportunity of evincing to the world our love of freedom by exercising ourselves in her cause, in opposing the efforts of tyranny and oppression over the country in which we ourselves have been so long injuriously enslaved.

Therefore, Your humble slaves most devoutly pray for the sake of injury liberty, for the sake of justice, humanity and the rights of mankind, for the honor of religion and by all that is dear, that Your Honors would graciously interpose in our behalf, and enact such laws and regulations, as you in your wisdom think proper, whereby we may regain our liberty and be ranked in the class of free agents, and that the name of slaves may not more be heard in a land gloriously contending for the sweets of freedom. And your humble slaves as in duty bound will ever pray.

Portsmouth November 12th, 1779 [5]

Although there were only about 150 slaves in the state of New Hampshire when the petition was presented, the legislature rejected the petition. However, the new state constitution of 1784 declared that "all men are born equally free and independent."

In 1797, four illegally manumitted slaves from North Carolina, who had fled to the North to escape re-enslavement, petitioned Congress to consider "our relief as a people." Shortly thereafter, a group of free African Americans of Philadelphia appealed directly to Congress to revise the federal laws concerning the African trade and fugitive slaves and adopt "such measures as shall in due course emancipate the whole of their brethren from their present situation."[6]

A seminal document of the early antebellum movement for the abolition of slavery was the Walker's Appeal. David Walker (1785-1830), a militant abolitionist, was a free African American because his mother was free and his father was a slave in Wilmington, North Carolina. The law established that a child's status followed that of his mother. Although Walker was free, the circumstances of his childhood in the South were harsh. He traveled extensively in areas in North Carolina observing the brutal treatment of slaves and decided to move to the North. When he left Wilmington, he moved to Boston where he engaged in selling second-hand clothes. Walker rendered tremendous services to fugitive slaves, making his house a refuge for them. His bitter attitude toward slavery did not diminish when he moved to the North. This was evident with the September 1829 publication of his essay entitled, "Walker's Appeal in Four Articles Together with a Preamble to the Colored Citizens of the World but in Particular and very Expressly to Those of the United States of America." It was one of the most bitter denunciations of slavery ever printed in the nation. In radical language, Walker cited several factors contribution to the oppressed situation of African Americans, namely slavery, ignorance, "the preachers of Jesus Christ," and the African colonization movement. He urged upon the race to utilize violent means if necessary to ameliorate the conditions.

The southern white leadership was quick to react to Walker's "Appeal." The governor of North Carolina denounced the essay as "an open appeal to their slaves' natural love of liberty…and throughout expressing sentiments totally subversive of all subordination in our slaves; the mayor of Savannah requested the mayor of Boston to arrest and punish David Walker. In response to Walker and other abolitionists, South Carolina Congressman J. H. Hammond declared in 1836, "I warn the abolitionists, ignorant and infatuated barbarians as they are, that if chance shall throw any of them into our hands, they may expect a felon' death."[7]

About the same time of the publication of Walker's "Appeal," Robert Alexander Young, a free African American and a militant abolitionist, published a pamphlet on slavery entitled, "The Ethiopian Manifesto, Issued in Defence [sic] of the Blackman's Rights, in the Scale of Universal Freedom." In this pamphlet, Young issued a severe warning to slaveholders who violated the natural right of men to be free. Also, he inspired slaves to take serious their right and to use militant means, if necessary, to gain freedom.

In 1831, African Americans decided to participate in more institutionalized structures for the abolition of slavery. Initially, they organized a specific convention to deal with the issue of slavery called th Annual Convention of the People of

Colour. On January 6, 1832, in the midst of stormy conditions, the New England Anti-Slavery Society was organized in the basement of the African Baptist meeting house on Belknap Street in Boston, Massachusetts. This was the first association organized on the principle of immediate emancipation. Accordingly, African American Baptists were prominent in the genesis of the Abolitionist Movement. They were not totally dependent on white abolitionists to carry the full responsibility of the great movement for the immediate emancipation of slaves. In fact, some of the white abolitionists were not completely in accord with the idea of immediate emancipation, but suggested a gradual approach to the issue. Though the twelve signatures affixed to the previously drafted declaration of principles of the society were those of white abolitionists, about one quarter of the seventy-two first signers of the constitution were African Americans.

From its beginning, the New England Anti-Slavery Society entered upon an aggressive stride of agitation to destroy the institution of slavery in the United States. This society was probably responsible for more antislavery addresses and petitions throughout New England than had taken place during the previous decades. So successful was the aggressiveness of the society that it became the prototype of similar societies which from that time forth sprang up in increasing numbers all over the North.

In 1840, another biracial antislavery society was organized with more of a national scope named the American and Foreign Anti-Slavery Society, with a sizable number of African American clergy as co-founders. This clergy membership consisted of J.C. Beman; his son Amos G. Beman, who was the pastor of the Temple Street African Church in New Haven; Christopher Rush, second bishop of the A.M.E. Zion Church; and five Presbyterians—Samuel E. Cornish, Theodore S. Wright, Stephen H. Gloucester, Henry Highland Garnet, and Andrew Harris, pastor of St. Mary's Street Church in Philadelphia. All of these clergymen became powerful leaders in the Abolitionist Movement. Also in 1840, there were other strong African American clergymen who were prominent in the abolitionist movement. Among the clergy group were Charles B. Ray of New York; James W.C. Pennington of Hartford; Samuel Ringgold Ward—all Congregationalists; Nathaniel Paul, a Baptist who was active in the Albany Anti-Slavery Society; Episcopalian Alexander Crummell, who served as secretary of the New York State Anti-Slavery Society; and Daniel A. Payne, Bishop of the A.M.E. Church.

The African American abolitionists adopted multiple strategies in their struggles against slavery. Among them were the publication of a newspaper, several antislavery tracts, and the organization of annual national conventions. The national convention movement afforded them a national forum to address the issues through addresses and other venues to alert the race regarding the movement in the North and South. Prominent preachers, newspaper editors, and other talented speakers addressed the wide variety of issues about the slavery power establishment.

Among the prominent African American abolitionist clergymen was James W.C. Pennington, who was himself born a slave on a plantation in Maryland. In 1828 he fled through the woods, reaching freedom in Pennsylvania. Pennington was aided by two white Quakers who hid him until it was safe to continue his escape to New York. After a brief period, he was called into the Gospel ministry and became the pastor of a Presbyterian church and a dynamic leader of the antislavery convention movement in the years preceding the Civil War. In order to escape the possible return to slavery, he purchased his freedom to prevent prosecution under the Federal Fugitive Slave Laws.

Perhaps the most radical of all, Henry Highland Garnet became very active in the convention movement. Like Pennington, Garnet was born into slavery in Maryland. He was born on the Eastern Shore in Kent County, on December 23, 1815. His father was a slave on the plantation belonging to Colonel William Spencer. The parents of Henry Highland Garnet made their successful escape to freedom, leaving him alone. He later gained permission from his slave master to attend a funeral, enabling him to escape to freedom in a covered wagon. He made his escape through Wilmington, Delaware, ultimately arriving in New York. In New York, Garnet met and established a close friendship with Alexander Crummell, and together the two boys attended the "old African Free School" on Mulberry Street. Very early in life, Garnet became a Sunday school student in the First Presbyterian Church under the pastorate of Rev. Theodore S. Wright. Later, he was licensed and ordained into the Presbyterian ministry and later became pastor of a white Presbyterian Church in Troy, New York. Subsequently, he published a newspaper called the *Clarion* and entered the antislavery campaign.[8]

Garnet became a strong proponent of self-help for African Americans to take on greater responsibilities for the abolition of slavery. While not rejecting the role of white abolitionists, he believed that there were some issues that African Americans should deal with among themselves. This philosophy led him to become one of the most militant of the abolitionists, a militancy so serious that he often would wear a pistol. When he delivered a militant address to the convention in Buffalo, New York, in 1843 calling for a violent overthrow of the slave masters by slaves themselves, the abolitionist movement reached a decided turning point. Although the assembled delegates rejected a resolution supporting his militancy by one vote, subsequent conventions treated the question of violence with much more sympathy, and by 1854 violence was being openly advocated.

In 1843, the African American Baptists of Ohio organized the first exclusively racial antislavery society in the United States, namely, the Union Anti-Slavery Baptist Association. About the same time, the Providence Anti-Slavery Baptist Association and the Middlerun Anti-Slavery Baptist Association were organized in the state of Ohio. In 1837, African American Baptist women in New York organized the Roger Williams Baptist Anti-Slavery Society as an auxiliary to the American Anti-Slavery Society. To be sure, these church-related associations were extremely significant in advancing the abolitionist strides of the era.

African American abolitionists throughout America faced many hardships and dangers in their quest for the immediate abolition of slavery. Sometimes there were tremendous deferential opinions within the organizational structures, but providentially, consensus was reached. As one might expect, the few southern abolitionists faced the greater danger. Most of the preachers especially were targets of suspicion relative to abolitionist tendencies. Southern whites were scrupulous in their scrutiny of African American preachers during the late antebellum and early stages of the Civil War eras. Nevertheless, African American leaders from both the North and South kept the pressure on for the abolition of slavery. Several prominent African American leaders attracted the scrutiny of the slavery power establishment.

As early as 1818 James Forten, a prominent abolitionist who influenced William Lloyd Garrison to embrace the idea of human equality, was invited to address the American Convention for Promoting the Abolition of Slavery, a white organization, to relate African American opinions regarding the work of the American Colonization Society. The society had enjoyed widespread support of slaveholders in the South who desired an alternative to the radical ideas about the immediate end of slavery. Many prominent political leaders had given their support to the society including John Marshall, James Monroe, and Henry Clay. Even some of the white antislavery leaders supported the mission of the society, including Benjamin Lundy, who formed the Union Humane Society in 1815; Lewis Tappan, Gerrit Smith, James G. Birney, Theodore Weld, and Elizur Wright.[9] They favored a scheme to relocate manumitted slaves to West Africa. James Forten made a strong speech on the subject relating African American opposition to the American Colonization Society. Most African Americans claimed America as their new home and had no desire to return to Africa. Rather, they preferred the challenge of assimilation into American society. After considering the speech made by James Forten, the convention decided to issue a report opposing colonization on the grounds that African Americans were generally opposed to the scheme.

In 1817, Bishop Richard Allen of the A.M.E. Church joined James Forten and other prominent leaders in Philadelphia in developing strong opposition to the American Colonization Society. They opposed the Society and all African Americans who supported emigration, urging the "Humane and Benevolent Inhabitants of Philadelphia" to reject any attempt to colonize African Americans in Africa. They described such attempts as an "outrage, having no other object in view than the benefit of the slave-holding interests of the country." Several years later, opposition on the part of African American people had risen to a fever pitch. Meetings were held in Baltimore, Boston, New York, Hartford and New Haven to express opposition to "men of mistaken views" who were supporting colonization, while those of Lyme, Connecticut, described colonization as "one of the wildest projects ever patronized by enlightened men."[10]

Moreover, the First Annual Convention of the People of Colour was held in Philadelphia in June 1831. A committee reported:

> And lastly, your Committee view with unfeigned regret, and respectfully submit to the wisdom of this convention, the operations and misrepresentations of the American Colonization Society in these United States. We feel sorrowful to see such an immense and wanton waste of lives and property, not doubting the benevolence of some individuals engaged in that cause. But we cannot for a moment doubt, but that the cause of many of our un-constitutional, unchristian, and unheard-of sufferings emanates from that unhallowed source, and we would call on Christians of every denomination firmly to resist it.[11]

During the same convention session, a conventional address suggested:

> The Convention has not been unmindful of the operations of the American Colonization Society, and it would respectfully suggest to that august body of learning, talent, and worth, that, in our humble opinion, strengthened, too, by the opinions of eminent men in this country, as well as in Europe, that they are pursuing the direct road to perpetuate slavery, with all its unchristian like concomitants, in this boasted land of freedom; and, as citizens and men whose best blood is sapped to gain

popularity for that institution, we would, in the most feeling manner, beg of them to desist; or, if we must be sacrificed to their philanthropy, we would rather die at home. [12]

Lott Carey, a Baptist preacher, reacted sharply to the criticism of the free African Americans of Philadelphia. He responded in a letter written from Liberia, West Africa, which he addressed to a gentleman in Richmond on September 24, 1827: "Before I left America, and ever since then, the colored people in about Philadelphia, have been making efforts in opposition to the scheme of colonizing the free people in Africa; and as some of their very recent publications have reached this place, I felt that injustice to the cause, and my own feelings, I ought to undertake to point out to them their situation."[13] Carey proceeded to answer their objections by pointing out several things about the nature of the African mission. First, he suggested that the African was separate in spirit from the American Colonization Society. Carey made a clear distinction between a search for "missionary grounds" and "colonizing grounds." He explained, "Africa suffers for gospel truth, and she will suffer, until missionaries can be sent, and settled in different parts of her continent."[14] Secondly, Carey affirmed that the providence of God was the primary motivating factor in the Christian missions in Africa. He believed that the success of the African mission was the results of divine providence.

Another prominent African American minister was an emigrant to Sierra Leone, West Africa, under the auspices of the American Colonization Society named Rev. Daniel Coker, one of the founders of the African Methodist Episcopal Church. He departed the United States in 1820 with a small group of other mission-minded individuals. Like Lott Carey, Coker utilized the American Colonization Society as a means to the end of African missionary activity.

Bishop Richard Allen struggled with mixed emotions relative to the mission of the American Colonization Society regarding the slavery question. He addressed a lengthy letter to the editor of the *Freedom's Journal* expressing his thoughts and emotions:

To the Editor of the Freedom's Journal:

Dear Sir:

I have for several years been striving to reconcile my mind to the colonization of Africans in Liberia; but there have always been and there still remain great and insurmountable objections against the scheme. We are an unlettered people brought up in ignorance, not one in a thousand has a liberal education.… It is said by the southern slave-holders that the more ignorant they can bring up the Africans, the better slaves they make.… Is there any fitness for such people to be colonized in a far country, to be their own rulers?… Is it not for the interest of the slave-holder, to select the free people of color out of the different states, and send them to Liberia? Will it not make their slaves uneasy to see free men of color enjoying liberty?

It is against the law in some southern states, that a person of color should receive an education under a severe penalty.… We were stolen from our mother country and brought here. We have tilled the ground and made fortunes for thousands and still they are not weary of our services. But they who stay to till the ground must be slaves.…

I have no doubt that there are many good men who do not see as I do; and who are for sending us to Liberia, but they have not duly considered the subject—they are not men of colour. This land, which we have watered with our tears and our blood, is now our mother country; and we are well satisfied to stay where wisdom abounds and the Gospel is free.[15]

Apparently, Bishop Allen opted to remain in general opposition to the American Colonization Society as a viable vehicle to address the freedom of slaves.

Dr. Martin R. Delany, like Bishop Richard Allen, held mixed views regarding the emigration of African Americans. He was born in 1812, the son of free African Americans in Charleston, West Virginia, but later settled in Chambersburg, Pennsylvania, where he was educated. He moved to Pittsburg to study medicine and commenced publication of *The Mystery,* which became a journal for the African Methodist Episcopal Church. From 1847 to 1849, Dr. Delany worked with Frederick Douglass in publishing the *North Star* while studying medicine at the Harvard Medical School. He opposed the emigration policy of the American Colonization Society, but not necessarily the emigration of African Americans. In 1852, he wrote an essay entitled "The Condition, Elevation, Emigration, and Destiny of the Colored People of the United States." His was the voice of an African American intellectual who entered the cause of abolition.

Not only did African American leaders of the abolitionist movement oppose the American Colonization Society, but they were more adamant in their opposition to passage of the Fugitive Slave Laws. These laws were passed by the U.S. Congress first in 1793 and later in 1850 to deter slaves from fleeing to non-slave states for freedom. The 1793 act denied runaway slaves the right to testify at their trials and the benefit of a jury trial. However, some states in the North passed personal liberty laws providing the right to trial for fugitives. Moreover, the 1793 law which became part of the United States Constitution explicitly provided that "no person held to service or labor in one State, under the laws thereof, escaping into another, shall, in consequence of any law or regulation therein, be discharged from such service or labor; but shall be delivered up on claim of the party, to whom such service or labor may be due."[16] The Compromise of 1850 was a more definitive law to help slaveowners and an attempt to preserve the Union, which was threatened by tension between the North and the South over the spread of slavery to the western territories, and imposed severe fines and imprisonment on U.S. marshals and citizens who helped or failed to apprehend runaway slaves. There were several provisions of the law which established certain specific rights of the slaveholders to reclaim fugitives. An owner whose slave had run away could go to any court of record in his own state and make an affidavit to that effect. Included in the affidavit were three points: (1) that the fugitive had escaped; (2) that he owed service or labor to the claimant; and (3) a general description of the fugitive.[17] However, the law only hardened opposition and was defied by the abolitionists, further fueling the South's desire for secession.

African Americans throughout the North held anti-fugitive slave law meetings. At one meeting, Martin R. Delany stated that African Americans were obligated to defy the law, urging that he hoped the ground would refuse his body if a slaveholder crossed his threshold and he did not lay him a corpse at his feet. Similarly, the Underground Railroad intensified its operations to assist slaves in their quest for freedom. On October 7, 1850, some 1500 African Americans of New York assembled in Zion Chapel for a protest meeting against the fugitive slave laws. A few weeks later, some from Elmira vowed that they would defy the fugitive slave laws at the sacrifice of their lives. Ten days after the laws went into effect, a group of African Americans in Pittsburg held a meeting at the public square, and they condemned the Pennsylvania congressmen who had supported the "slave bill," which they declared to be a deadly blow at liberty. Defiance of the laws became something of a new commandment to abolitionists throughout the North.

Between 1851 and 1860, even some northern state legislatures sought measures to minimize the effects of the fugitive slave laws. They enacted what was called Personal Liberty Laws which were generally designed to safeguard state officers for not enforcing the Fugitive Slave Laws of 1850. They provided that the slave could secure counsel; he was to have the benefit of habeas corpus; of trial by jury; prohibited the use of jails for holding runaway African Americans; and a heavy fine or penalty was imposed for the seizure of any free person. The South countered by having these laws declared unconstitutional, insisting that the Fugitive Slave Law be strictly enforced.

The threat posed by the Fugitive Slave Law awakened a new urgency for fugitive slaves to move to Canada for the security of their freedom. Even some free African Americans migrated to Canada. Most cites in the North experienced at least a small exodus of African Americans. About 40 fugitive slaves left Boston within sixty hours after the law went into effect, which affected the African American churches. The A.M.E. Church lost 85 members to the exodus while the smaller Zion Methodist Church lost 10 members. The congregation of the Twelfth Street Baptist Church decreased from a membership of 141 to 81 members, and two of its deacons were retained only because the members had raised $1300 to buy their freedom.

Similarly, African American churches in New York were adversely affected by the Fugitive Slave Law. The Colored Baptist Church of Buffalo lost 130 members after the pastor told the congregation that he found biblical precedence for running away but none that warranted fighting. At the Colored Baptist Church of Rochester, the pastor who came from Kentucky was one of the earliest to leave the city and was soon followed by 112 members of his congregation, leaving only two members. At Pittsburg, a small group of about 200 left for Canada even before the law was signed. They carried firearms, having vowed that they would die before being taken back into slavery.

Shortly after the Fugitive Slave Law was passed, Henry Wilson reported a case in Maryland when an agent of a slaveholder appeared in New York, armed with the power of attorney from Mary Brown, and a certified copy of the act itself, cut from a common newspaper, in search of James Hamlet, a husband and father, a member of the Methodist church, and a resident in the city for about three years. He was seized while at work, hurried into a retired room, tried in haste, and delivered to the agent. He was then taken by the son of the marshal to Baltimore and lodged in the prison of the notorious Hope H. Slater until he could be returned to Mary Brown.[18]

The most notable of all African American abolitionists was Frederick Douglass, a former slave from the Eastern Shore of Maryland who opposed slavery, clauses of the United States Constitution supportive of slavery, colonization, and the complicity of white churches of the South in the continuation of slavery. He utilized two powerful tools in the abolitionist cause: the publication of his autobiography entitled *Narrative of the Life of Frederick Douglass*, in 1854; and his newspaper, *The North Star*. In his address to the national convention of the Free Soil party on August 11, 1852, meeting in the Masonic Hall in Pittsburg, Frederick Douglass severely criticized the Fugitive Slave Law. Because an alleged runaway might be carried away without trial by jury, "the colored man's rights are less than those of a jackass," since the latter could not be seized and taken away without submitting the matter to twelve men. He went on to offer a solution, suggesting "The only way to make the Fugitive Slave Law a dead letter is to make half a dozen or more dead kidnappers. The man who takes the office of a bloodhound ought to be treated as a bloodhound."[19]

Frederick Douglass proved to be a sharp critic of slavery in the United States even while he visited England. In an address entitled "American Slavery Is America's Disgrace" delivered on March 25, 1847, in Sheffield, England, he sharply criticized American churches for their complicity in the continuation of slavery. He argued that the "auctioneer's block stood in the same neighborhood as the pulpit" and that "revivals of the slave trade and revivals of the Bible societies went together." Even more critical, he observed that in the United States:

> Slavery had there no defender equal in ability and perseverance to those sent from the bosom of the Church. It came clothed in all the sacredness of the pulpit, and professing to have the sanction of the Bible and of God. Thus, when slavery was opposed in the street, it fled to the church, to prayer-meetings, to the conferenced, to the Bible society, to the tract society, and there it bows down, and goes to pray.[20]

When Douglass returned to the United States, he intensified his attacks on all supporters of slavery, individual and collective.

Slave Revolts and African American Churches

Abolitionist Frederick Douglass, a Methodist exhorter, was a strong advocate of resistance to slavery, supporting slave rebellions and other radical means of African American freedom. He noted the underlying mentality toward resistance to slavery throughout the long period of the system in the United States. Prior to the organized efforts of the abolitionist movement, slaves in various parts of the South, even during the earlier colonial period, had expressed their contempt for the system by violent episodes against their masters. In some cases, white indentured servants made common cause with African American slaves in rebellions against their masters. The spirit of resistance apparently was nurtured in experiences of African

American slave preaching, expressing freedom motifs from the Old Testament. Increasingly, many notable African American preachers, who had themselves been slaves, developed in their sermons some radical ideas on how freedom should be attained. Frederick Douglass once observed: "I know there is a spirit among the slaves which would not much longer brook their degradation and their bondage. There are many Madison Washingtons and Nathaniel Turners in the South, who would assert their right to liberty, if you would take your feet from their neck, and your sympathy and aid from their oppressors."[21]

In Virginia, where there was a large population of slaves, slave unrest and revolts were more frequent than in most of the states in the Lower South. Such conspiracies like Gabriel Prosser in 1800 and Nat Turner in 1831 attained national notoriety. The conspiracy of Gabriel Prosser was planned in great secrecy on the plantation of Thomas Prosser, a harsh slave master, located near Richmond. Apparently utilizing the Bible account of Israel's liberation from slavery, he was able to inspire a large number of slaves who took an oath to fight for their freedom. The plan was to seize an arsenal and several other strategic buildings of Richmond and then proceed to a general slaughter of all hostile whites. He hoped that with such a brave venture some fifty thousand African American slaves would join the militant stride for freedom. However, the plot was exposed by a faithful slave and Governor James Monroe secured the federal cavalry to destroy the undisciplined "army" of Gabriel Prosser.[22] When Gabriel Prosser was captured, he refused to implicate any of his fellow conspirators. However, the fact that such a large number of slaves were involved caused Governor Monroe to enter secret correspondence with Thomas Jefferson with the view of securing a grant of land to which troublesome slaves could be banished. However, the proposal was never acted upon.[23]

Between 1800 and 1820, the slave holders of Virginia were greatly alarmed by slave conspiracies and revolts. Soon after the Gabriel Prosser conspiracy, Governor Monroe was notified in 1802 of a plot in Nottaway County, resulting in the execution of several African Americans suspected in the scheme. Other plots were subsequently exposed in 1808 and 1809, necessitating almost continuous patrol service. During the summer of 1814, Lynchburg and Caroline County requested arms and troops for protection against the plots of slaves in the areas. To be sure, Virginia with its large concentration of slaves had to exercise vigilance to maintain its security.

The next major slave uprising to excite fear on the part of the white establishment was planned by Denmark Vesey in Charleston, South Carolina, in 1822. He was a native of St. Thomas in the West Indies and migrated to Charleston as a free African American. He had purchased his freedom in 1800 from the proceeds of a lottery prize in Charleston and found employment in the city as a carpenter. Soon after his arrival, Vesey acted on his inspiration from the successful freedom movement in Haiti and the principles of the French Revolution in an effort to liberate African American slaves in South Carolina. He preached against the brutalities of slavery and urged war against slave holders. His plan included the recruitment of a white man to purchase guns and powder for his proposed army; Charleston was to be captured and burned; the shipping of the city seized; and all the slaves would sail away for the West Indies. Similar to other rebellions, a faithful house slave exposed the plot and severe reprisals were instituted.[24] A few members of the A.M.E. Church in Charleston were involved, but the leaders in the church had kept clear of the conspiracy. Authorities of the city gradually discovered the leaders in the plot, thirty-five of whom were hanged, and thirty-seven were transported beyond the limits of the United States. Vesey accepted his fate courageously and was hanged without revealing the names of his fellow conspirators.

The Nat Turner rebellion in Southampton, Virginia, in 1831 was the most crucial in awakening severe socio-political repercussions for African Americans throughout the South. Nathaniel Turner was born October 2, 1800, in Southampton, Virginia, the son of a slave named Nancy. His family lived on the plantation of Benjamin Turner. He was an unusually intelligent child, learning to read and write with such skill and rapidity that impressed other individuals in the local slave community. Tradition maintained that his mother predicted he would be a future prophet, and her prediction remained with Nathaniel throughout his formative years. Turner devoted himself to the study of the Bible with its implications for the struggles of the slave community. Having experienced visions of white and black spirits fighting in battles, Nathaniel concluded that God was revealing to him that he was challenged to liberate slaves. In his later confession, Nat Turner explained:

> On the 12th of May, 1828, I heard a loud noise in the heavens, and the Spirit instantly appeared to me and said, "The serpent was loosened, and Christ had laid down the yoke he had borne for the sins of men," and that I should take it on and fight against the serpent, for the time was approaching when the first should be last and last should be first, and by signs in the heavens that it would make known to me when I should commence the great work, and until the first sign should appear I should conceal it from the knowledge of men.[25]

On the appearance of the sign, which was to be the eclipse of the sun in February 1831, he was to arise and slay the enemies of his people. Immediately after the sign, the seal on his lips would be removed and the rebellion must commence.

During February 1831, Nat Turner devised, together with four friends Sam Edwards, Henry Porter, Nelson Williams, and Hark Travis, which he called the war council, specific plans for launching the war against slave owners. On August 21, the insurrection commenced by night with the massacre of John Travis and his family sparing neither age nor sex. They proceeded from house to house killing as many white people as possible with the expectation that other slaves would join in the war. Some fifty other slaves actually joined in the rebellion, utilizing axes and knives to kill indiscriminately. The white power system responded by calling several artillery companies from Richmond, Petersburg, Norfolk, and Portsmouth, along with one cavalry company to conquer Nat Turner's army. During the hand-to-hand combat, most of Turner's army fell while he escaped to the swamps, eluding the whites for nearly three months. The military operations resulted in the death of sixty-one white persons and more than one hundred slaves. During November, Nat Turner was captured, tried, convicted, and executed.

To be sure, the Nat Turner insurrection sent shock waves throughout the South, resulting in severe repercussions for all African Americans. The Richmond Whig declared that should another insurrection occur whites would follow by putting the whole black race to the sword. Soon, most states in the South passed strict "Black Codes" designed to control the total life experiences of slaves and some free African American sympathizers. Henry Wilson reported:

> There were in 1847 in the State of Virginia several thousand free negroes. Though they were denied many of the essential rights of citizenship, they were a quiet and law-abiding people. Still they were objects of slaveholding distrust; their presence was regarded as inimical to the interest of slavery; and, during that year laws were enacted against their remaining in the state. In the revised constitution of 1851 it was provided that slaves thereafter emancipated, if they remained in the State more than twelve months, should forfeit their freedom, and be reduced to slavery under such regulations as might be prescribed by law.[26]

Earlier, the state of Virginia had prohibited meetings or schools of slaves and free African Americans for educational purposes, and in 1848 it had forbidden free African Americans from leaving the state for such purposes on the penalty of forfeiture of right to return. In 1847, Virginia reenacted a law that white persons should be punished for instructing slaves and that postmasters must give notice to justices of the peace of the presence of antislavery publications. Two years later, a law was passed by the same legislature denying citizenship to free African men.[27]

Similar restrictive policies were adopted by the state of Maryland in response to the Nat Turner insurrection and other slave revolts. In 1830, there were 52,938 free African American and 102,994 slaves in Maryland; 62,078 free and 89,737 slaves in 1840; 74,723 free and 90,368 slaves in 1850; and 83,942 free and 87,189 slaves in 1860 throughout the state. Hence, the passage of restrictive laws and local policies greatly affected a significant population of African Americans in the state. Henry Wilson reported:

> In 1842, there was a slaveholders' convention in Annapolis, Maryland, at which, as if the laws of that State were not inhuman and unchristian enough, it was proposed, even at that late date, to make them still more oppressive and wicked. Among other propositions, hardly less degrading and cruel, they proposed to the legislature to prevent the emancipation of slaves by will or deed; to prevent free negroes from coming into the State; to sell free persons of color, convicted of crime, into slavery out of the State; to repeal the act allowing manumitted negroes to remain in the State without a certificate; to require free negroes to give security for their good behavior; to forbid free negroes from holding real estate; and also to prohibit them from holding meetings after sundown.[28]

Another action taken after the Nat Turner insurrection was a law passed in 1846 which denied to African Americans the right to testify in cases in which any white person was concerned, although as far back as 1809 it had admitted the testimony of slaves against free African Americans. By the new constitution of 1851, the legislature was forbidden to pass any law abolishing the relation of master and slave; but, ample powers were given for the government, regulation, and disposition of the free African American population of the state.[29]

These regulations impacted the African American churches throughout the state. Beginning in the late 1700's, African Americans had organized separate churches among various denominations. Some of the pastors had participated in the education of slaves as well as free men in Sunday schools and other settings. They also advocated for the legal rights of slaves in Maryland courts. However, slaves remained at the mercy of their masters and court officials in seeking some form of justice. Certainly, there were instances of Christian slaves being denied human rights and justice in the court system.

However, the most radical Black Codes were formulated in the lower South, responding to the Nat Turner rebellion. There were cases of violence against African American Christians in various parts of the South. An example of this was the case of Avery Watkins, an African American preacher of Rockingham, North Carolina, and grandfather of Rev. R.H.W. Leak, a prominent minister in the A.M.E. Conference of North Carolina. He was charged with having endorsed the Nat Turner insurrection because of certain remarks he made in a private conversation with his family. It was reported that Rev. Watkins had related to them some of Nat Turner's plans and actions in Southampton County where he had recently visited his grandmother. This was sufficient cause for a mob to interrupt a camp meeting to lynch him in 1831.[30] Similar violence erupted throughout the South as more and more legal restrictions were enacted and social pressures applied to ensure security from slave revolts.

The various insurrections of African American slaves had dire consequences on their plight in the South. Upon discovery that Nat Turner was a preacher, rumors spread throughout the South that such preachers were guilty of using preaching as a means to incite their race to servile insurrection. Hence, legislations were passed to prevent African American preachers from instilling freedom ideas in the minds of slaves. According to Carter G. Woodson, in 1832 Virginia passed a law to silence African American preachers, making it impossible for them to function except in compliance with very rigid regulations and in the presence of certain discreet white men. In 1833, Alabama made it unlawful for slaves or free Negroes to preach unless before five respectful slaveholders and when authorized by some neighboring religious society. Georgia enacted a law in 1834 providing that neither free Negroes nor slaves might preach or exhort an assembly of more than seven unless licensed by justices on the certification of three ordained ministers.[31]

The Civil War and Reconstruction

The prelude to the Civil War witnessed many powerful political and social movements in America which both directly and indirectly affected African American churches. White American churches of the South, adjusting to the economic necessity of slavery for new economic developments with the invention of the cotton gin, intensified their support of selective biblical ideas supporting the institution of slavery. Cotton was king in the economy of the South from 1815 to 1861, and the principal bulwark of his throne was slavery. Samuel Elliot Morison and Henry Steele Commager reported: "Almost sixty per cent of the slaves in the United States, in 1850, were employed in growing cotton. Like rice, sugar, and tobacco, it was a plantation crop, requiring continuous attention of a sort that the most ignorant Negroes were well able to perform."[32] By 1860, the production of cotton had so increased that it valued two-thirds of the total exports of the United States. Faced with such a lucrative marker, the pulpit of the South could not withstand the pressure of not supporting the socio-political and economic necessity of slavery. They were even supportive of the dissolution of the Union in order to counter the abolitionist movement; the increasing number of free states admitted to the Union with the drawing of the Mason-Dixon Line; the election of President Abraham Lincoln; and to maintain their institution of slavery. White Christian pastors and politicians throughout the South forged a union of theoretical considerations for secession from the United States and the establishment of the Confederate States of America.

South Carolina, where extensive talks in churches and political forums had been advanced for succession should Abraham Lincoln be elected president, was the first state to secede from the Union. As soon as the election was certain, the South Carolina legislature summoned a state convention, and on December 20, 1860, the convention met at Charleston and unanimously declared "that the Union now subsisting between South Carolina and other states under the name of 'The United States of America' is hereby dissolved. The state's position clearly stated "Declaration of…Secession" was broadcast throughout the southern states, followed by tracts—such as "The South Alone, Should Govern the South"—appealing to the sister states to form a southern confederacy. Other southern states soon followed rapidly the example of South Carolina and decided to organize a new federal government on February 8, 1861, with constitutional support for the continuation of slavery and the southern way of life.

The delegates from the southern states met in Montgomery, Alabama, to consolidate the formation of the Confederate States of America and the drafting of a new constitution. These delegates were experienced men in the formation and interpretation of constitutional laws, for they had been focusing their attention for several years on how to find support for the southern agenda in the United States Constitution. Aside from making explicit the protection of slavery and states' rights to take slave property into the territories, the authors of the Confederate Constitution made no changes to indicate that they wanted a different kind of country from what they had left. They wanted to correct what they perceived as evils in the former U.S. Constitution and to protect the southern way of life.[33] Several clauses in the new constitution specifically related to the perpetual dehumanization of African Americans and the slave system, as expressed in the following excerpts:

> We, the people of the Confederate States, each State acting in its sovereign and independent character, in order to form a permanent federal government, establish justice, insure domestic tranquility, and secure the blessings of liberty to ourselves and our posterity—invoking the favor and guidance of Almighty God—do ordain and establish this Constitution for the Confederate States of America.
>
> Article I, Sec. I.—All legislative powers herein delegated shall be vested in a Congress of the Confederate States, which shall consist of a Senate and House of Representatives….
>
> 3. Representatives and direct taxes shall be apportioned among the several States which may be included within this Confederacy, according to their respective numbers, which shall be determined by adding to the whole number of free persons, including those bound to service for a term of years, and including Indians not taxed, three-fifths of all slaves….
>
> Sec.9.—The importation of Negroes of the African race, from any foreign country, other than the slaveholding States and Territories of the United States of America, is hereby forbidden; and Congress is required to pass such laws shall effectively prevent the same….
>
> 2. Congress shall also have power to prohibit the introduction of slaves from any State not a member of, or Territory not belonging to, this Confederacy….
>
> 4. No bill of attainder, or ex post facto law denying or impairing the right of property in Negro slaves, shall be passed….
>
> Article IV…Sec.2.—The citizens of each State shall be entitled to all the privileges and immunities of citizens of the several States, and shall have the right to transit and sojourn in any State of this Confederacy, with their slaves and other property; and the right of property in said slaves shall not be thereby impaired….

3. No slave or other person held in service or labor in any State or Territory of the Confederate States, under the laws thereof, escaping or unlawfully carried into another, shall, in consequence of any law or regulation therein, be discharged from such service or labor; but shall be delivered upon claim of the party to whom such slave belongs, or to whom such service or labor may be due....

—*The Constitution of the Confederate States of America.*

After the completion of the Constitution of the Provisional Government of the Confederate States of America, the delegates proceeded to formerly organize their new governmental leadership. They selected Jefferson Davis, a former Mississippi senator in President Buchanan's administration (1857-61) and forceful spokesman for southern rights, as the new president of the Confederate States of America. After delivering his inaugural speech on February 18, 1861, seeking to assure everybody that the intentions of the new government were peaceful and that "no reason or justice" existed for the United States to violate that peace, Jefferson Davis proceeded with the formation of his administration, resulting in the birth of a new nation in opposition to the United States of America.

The formation of the Confederate States of America posed new challenges to churches in both the North and the South. Most churches in the North, biracial as well as separate African American, remained strong in their support of the Union. In 1862, the Ohio Baptist Convention passed patriotic resolutions which became typical of many other resolutions from church denominations in support of the Union. These church leaders avowed it to be their right and duty as Christian citizens to tender sympathy and support to those trusted with the government, and they promised to uphold the armies "in their endeavors to crush the wicked rebellion" and to "offer up their prayers and supplications daily" in this behalf. They warmly approved the proclamation of Abraham Lincoln declaring liberty to slaves and promised support in carrying out that proclamation "till our beloved country shall be purged of the accursed blot" which they declared to be "both the cause of the war and the chief means in our enemy's hands of carrying it on."[34]

In the South in general, with the exception of independent African American churches, churches celebrated the establishment of the Confederacy. As early as the initial inception of the Confederacy, white Christians in Montgomery celebrated the election of Jefferson Davis with joyous acts. Even some African American slaves who had not been influenced by the African American freedom oriented pulpits celebrated with their masters the formation of the new government. This was followed by a series of church resolutions in strong support for the new government. In 1861, the Southern Baptist Convention adopted a series of resolutions on the state of the country, prepared by Dr. Richard Fuller, of South Carolina. "After recounting the steps taken by the South in separating from the Union, he stated that the South desired a fair and amicable adjustment which was repelled by the government at Washington, and since the United States government insists upon letting loose hordes of armed soldiers to pillage and desolate the entire South," and since the northern churches and pastors, whom he had hoped would interpose and protest against the appeal to the sword, are "breathing out slaughter and clamoring for sanguinary hostilities, therefore be it resolved that the formation of the Confederate States of America be approved; that the Divine direction be invoked upon those who rule them and that the Confederate States and also the King of Jesus Christ may prosper; that the Presidency of the Confederacy and the Confederate Congress be assured of their sympathy and confidence; that every principal of religion and patriotism calls then to resist invasion; and that prayers be offered for those from their families who are in the armies "to cover their heads in the day of battle, and give victory to their arms."[35] This spirit of religion and patriotism within the Confederacy was sufficient to inspire significant numbers of African Americans to serve in non-military positions as well as soldiers in the new nation. Many slaves expressed their patriotism through prayers for their masters in the army and dedicated labor on the plantations. Separate African American churches remained rather passive on socio-political issues in the Confederacy. Patriotism was expected of all individuals in the South.

During the Civil War, religion was very strong in the Confederate armies. Both Generals Lee and Jackson were men of strong religious conviction and gave great encouragement to the work of chaplains with their soldiers. During the nights, hymns and spiritual songs were often heard in Confederate military camps. William Warren Sweet reported:

> In the years 1863-1864 a great revival swept through the army of northern Virginia and thousands of Episcopalians were all active in their cooperation in religious work in the Confederate army. The Episcopalians furnished nearly a hundred chaplains, the Southern Methodists more than two hundred while Baptists, Catholics and Presbyterians sent their full quotas.[36]

With this overwhelming support from these white Christian churches, it became very difficult for African American church leaders in the South to resist the persistent flow of patriotism toward the Confederate States of America. They had to decide whether to become patriotic to the homeland in the South or to support the liberation of slaves. Giving the precariousness of their situation, most African American church leaders opted to become silent relative to their circumstances in the Confederate States of America. They avoided mentions of socio-political conditions in the South but emphasized the necessity of preaching Bible-based messages without social implications. This factor was further intensified due to the limited, and in most cases absence, of any theological education on the part of most church leaders. Due to the restrictive laws of the post-Nat Turner insurrection, most were partially illiterate, especially the slave preachers in rural areas. However, they were still able to instill a sense of personal worth and hope for the oppressed people of the Confederacy.

African American churches of the North were still very much involved in the movement for the end of slavery. Their leaders were strong supporters of President Lincoln and the Union cause during the Civil War. Frederick Douglass related a lengthy story of his impression of both President Lincoln and Vice President Johnson. He observed:

> No stronger contrast could well be presented between two men than between President Lincoln and Vice-President Johnson on this day. Mr. Lincoln was like one who was treading the hard and thorny path of duty and self-denial; Mr. Johnson was like one from a drunken debauch. The face of one was full of manly humility, although at the topmost height of power and pride, the other was full of pomp and swaggering vanity.[37]

Douglass observed in President Lincoln a strong commitment for the betterment of African Americans, but Vice President Johnson did not seem to have a similar commitment. To be sure, there were some divided opinions circulating even in the North relative to the end of slavery in the Confederate States. Douglass went on to relate his experience in trying to meet with President Lincoln. He related:

> On this inaugural day, while waiting for the opening of the ceremony, I made a discovery in regard to the Vice-President Andrew Johnson. There are moments in the lives of most men, when the doors of their soul are open, and unconsciously to themselves, their true characters may be read by the observant eye. It was at such an instant I caught a glimpse of

the real nature of this man, which all subsequent developments proved true. I was standing in the crowd by the side of Mrs. Thomas J. Dorsey, when Mr. Lincoln touched Mr. Johnson, and pointed me out to him. The first expression which came to his face, and which I think was the true index of his heart, was one of bitter contempt and aversion…. I turned to Mrs. Dorsey and said, "Whatever Andrew Johnson may be, he certainly is no friend of our race"….

In the evening of the day of the inauguration, another new experience awaited me. The usual reception was given at the executive mansion, and though no colored persons had ever ventured to present themselves on such occasions, it seemed now that freedom had become the law of the republic, now that colored men were on the battle-field mingling their blood with that of white men in one common effort to save the country, it was not too great an assumption for a colored man to offer his congratulations to the President with those of other citizens. I decided to go, and sought in vain for some one of my own color to accompany me…. It was finally arranged that Mrs. Dorsey should bear me company, so together we joined in the grand procession of citizens from all parts of the country, and moved slowly towards the executive mansion…. Recognizing me, even before I reached him, "Here comes my friend Douglass." Taking me by the hand, he said, "I am glad to see you. I saw you in the crowd to-day, listening to my inaugural address; how did you like it?"… I replied, "Mr. Lincoln, that was a sacred effort."[38]

The friendship between Frederick Douglass and President Lincoln remained steadfast throughout the Civil War period.

Another important African American clergyman was Rev. Hiram R. Revells, who became one of the two African Americans who served in the United States Senate after the Civil War. He was born a free man at Fayetteville, North Carolina, in 1822. He later migrated to Darke County, Ohio, and then to Galesburg, Illinois, to graduate from Knox College. He united with the African Methodist Episcopal Church and became a preacher at the age of twenty-five. When the Civil War began, Revells assisted in raising the first regiment in Maryland and the first one in Missouri. He became a strong spokesman for the Union cause and the freedom of slaves.

Bishop Daniel A. Payne was another strong advocate for the freedom of slaves and the support of Abraham Lincoln. He was especially concerned about the passage of a bill for the emancipation of slaves in the District of Columbia. He remarked:

> It was my fortune to be there when it occurred, and to participate in the joys of the occasion. The sermon I preached on this event was put in pamphlet form for the use of posterity. At that time I was the presiding bishop of the Second Episcopal District of the A.M.E. Church, of which Washington and Georgetown, D. C. were my head-quarters. On Friday afternoon, April 11, 1862, Congress passed the bill abolishing slavery in the District of Columbia. The following Monday night I called President Lincoln to know if he intended to sign the bill of emancipation, and thereby exterminate slavery in the District of Columbia? Having been previously informed of my intention to interview him, and having on my arrival at the White House sent in my card, he met me at the door of the room in which he and Senator Washburn were conversing. Taking me by the hand, he said: "Bishop Payne, of the African M.E. Church? I answered in the affirmative; so with my hand in his he led me to the fire-place, introduced me to Senator Washburn, and seated me in an arm-chair between himself and the Senator.[39]

Bishop Payne strongly urged the president to sign the bill which was approved on April 16, 1862.

During the Civil War, African American Christians played significant roles in the Union cause. To be sure, the enlistment of African American troops in the Union Army in late 1862 was a defining moment for the expression of their patriotism. Even before that date, they had been performing a variety of important contributions to the Union War effort serving in non-military and semi-military activities. Nearly 200,000 freedmen served as laborers, teamsters, cooks, carpenters, nurses, and scouts for the Union forces. Frederick Douglass was the foremost clergyman who argued for the right of African American men to serve in active duty for the Union. Initially, President Lincoln was reluctant to recruit African American soldiers, fearing that the slave states which supported the Union would retaliate. However, with the increase in Union casualties, the Bureau of Colored Troops was established in 1863. Shortly, the first African American regiment was formed, namely the 54th Massachusetts Volunteer Infantry, which set the precedent for other African American soldiers by providing skills and valor. These initial soldiers were inspired by the churches in Massachusetts in general and those of Boston in particular. Mark Anthony Bradley, who was born in Sussex County, Delaware, in 1847 and later became a minister of the A.M.E. Zion Church, entered the United States service September 9, 1864 when he was assigned to the Thirtieth United States Colored Troops. More than 175,000 African Americans responded to serve in the army, and over 70,000 of them became casualties during the course of the bloody war.

Among several clergymen who directly served the military were Rev. J.H. Anderson of Frederick, Maryland, and Rev. Elias P. Marrs, who served as a soldier in the Union Army of Kentucky. During 1863, when Baltimore was threatened by an invasion of the Confederate Army, Rev. A. W. Wayman, pastor of Bethel A.M.E. Church, along with many other African Americans, were arrested by the police and carried to the outskirts of the city to assist the U.S. government in constructing some barracks for the defense of the city. To be sure, many of these men, some specialized craftsmen, were members of local African American churches in Baltimore.

African American church leaders clearly saw the Civil War as a divine providential means for the liberation of oppressed people. This spirit was reflected in Julia Ward Howe's "Battle Hymn of the Republic," which inspired many soldiers to give their lives for the cause of freedom. It was the Civil War that paved the way for the Emancipation Proclamation, new amendments to the Federal Constitution which granted citizenship and voting rights for all citizens, the Freedmen's Bureau, and other provisions for the progress of the race. Church leaders throughout the North envisioned the ultimate triumph of the abolitionist movement would be decided on the battlefields. The triumph of the Union was signaled on April 1865 with the surrender of General Robert E. Lee to General Ulysses Grant at Appomattox Courthouse in Virginia; subsequently, President Abraham Lincoln, along with some former slaves, occupied the Confederate Manson in Richmond, Virginia.

Reconstruction and African American Christians

The end of the Civil War and the national challenges of reconstruction was a period of rapid church growth among African Americans. At the close of the War, large numbers of former slaves were attracted to separate African American churches, especially Baptists and Methodists. Significant numbers of churches left biracial denominations to join these Baptists and Methodists. The movement gained impetus even during the latter part of the Civil War. They found in these denominations a greater freedom of expression than in other Christian movements. Worship experiences were more conducive to the excited spirit of the freedmen. Their limited educational background, many still illiterate, posed no limitation on opportunities for upward mobility in congregational life.

African American Baptist churches gained the majority for membership largely because the freedmen found in the polity of Baptist churches the absence of control which characterized more structured denominations. Baptist churches were destined to play a preponderant role in the religious, social, and political future of the race. These rapidly growing churches soon became the training forum for black leaders to emerge and actively participate in the Reconstruction of the Union. More specifically, they were schools in political activity. The challenge of Reconstruction drew heavily on the energy and physical or human resources of the denomination. Some of the best qualified preachers were lured from exclusive pulpit ministries to enter Reconstruction politics.

However, the leadership role of these African American preachers, called "race men," who entered politics as well as Methodists and other denominations, was a tremendous challenge to their energy, perseverance, and resourcefulness. They were often objects of criticism from both southern whites and some African Americans. Attitudes of stress and desperation on the part of the two races in the defeated South were causes of tremendous difficulties for African American church leaders. Poverty, fear, anger, and dislocation became the shared experiences of many from both races.

Neither whites nor African Americans were exempted from the tremendous upheavals of the Civil War. The Reconstruction Period was characterized by the vast destruction caused by the war; deep sectional strife between the North and South; racial hatred; widespread desolation in southern family life with the destruction of many plantation houses; and mounting diseases. Confederate soldiers, upon returning home from the battlefields, often found their houses destroyed; blackened chimneys stood sentinel over cold ash heaps that once were houses. Throughout the South, fences were down, weeds had overrun the fields, windows were broken, and livestock had disappeared. The assessed valuation of property drastically decreased in the decade after 1861. The banking industry was crippled with the loss of Confederate currency.

More fundamental, from the white perspective, than the destruction of property and the paralysis of business was the disappearance of the South's basic economic institution. Slavery, so fundamental to the southern way of life with a growing aristocracy, had ended as the advancing Union armies carried news of the Emancipation Proclamation and the confiscation acts into the deep South. The emancipation of slaves meant to whites not only the loss of property, but loss of cheap labor too. These economic and social problems enraged southerners against all the northern whites entering their beloved South and the emancipated and elevated African Americans, particularly the religious and political leaders.

A brief survey of the tremendous rage of many southern whites against African Americans, in particular, will give some indication of the tremendous challenge of African Americans in their quest for freedom and human dignity as defined by the American ethos expressed in Federal Law. One will readily recognize from the following attitudinal survey of whites and the general plight of African Americans at the close of the Civil War the reality that Reconstruction was a formidable challenge to the African American church. It took the best and strongest minds and untiring labor of the race to advance new anthropological definitions of the race sufficient to lift a dehumanized people to advancing heights of dignity and freedom.

What was the socio-political situation of African Americans in which their churches found them at the emancipation? More than the poverty of some whites before the Civil War and the new widespread poverty, was a situation of poverty, illiteracy, and dehumanization with an element of despair on the part of the freedmen. In 1902, Rev. J.W.E. Bowen, pastor of Ashbury Methodist Episcopal Church in Washington, D.C., and field secretary of the Missionary Society of the Methodist Episcopal Church, reflected on the situation of the freedmen:

> The story of the burdens and disadvantages of the Negro at the beginning of his days of freedom has not yet been committed to paper. ... No other people ever had more disadvantages to contend with on their issue into freedom. They were seduced, deceived, misled. Their habits of industry was destroyed, and they were fooled into believing that they could be legislated into immediate equality with a race that, without mentioning superiority of ability and education, had a thousand years' start on them. They were made to believe that their only salvation lay in aligning themselves against the other race, and following blindly the adventurers who came to lead them to the promised-land. It is no wonder that they committed great blunders and great excesses.[40]

Still more revealing was a reflection of the same year by Rev. M.C.B. Mason, senior corresponding secretary of the Freedmen's Aid and Southern Educational Society of the Methodist Episcopal Church, observed:

A generation ago, he had practically nothing. He started out with scarcely a name—poor, ignorant, degraded, demoralized, as slavery left him. Without a home, without a foot of land, without the true sense of real manhood, ragged, destitute, so freedom found him. He stood at one end of the cotton row with his master at the other as he stepped into the new and inexperienced life before him his master still claimed him and the very clothes upon his back. Under these peculiar circumstances and amid these peculiar difficulties he began life for himself.[41]

Hence, the freedmen had deep emotional scars mixed with a degree of animosity toward southern whites. In such a moral and socio-political situation, African American church leaders were challenged to provide radical ministries, in terms of intensity, sufficient to elevate the race.

Southern whites had the psychological challenge of adjusting to defeat and poverty, on the one hand, and, on the other, the reconstruction of their immediate social and political institutions at the close of the Civil War. The question of Reconstruction—that is, of readmitting the seceded states to their former position in the Union—was one which deeply agitated the country during 1866-1867. Major differences of opinion relative to the basic issue of federalism and freedmen' rights had divided the Nation. Chief among them was the problem of racism. It was racism that prompted most of the debates and divided opinion during the Reconstruction Period. A major difference of opinion existed between President Andrew Johnson and the U.S. Congress over the political technicalities of Reconstruction. Congress advocated a policy of "radical reconstruction" while Johnson desired the continuation of Abraham Lincoln's conciliatory policy of reconstruction. Each had specific plans of readmitting the seceded states to the Union. President Johnson recognized loyal governments as existing in Virginia, Tennessee, Arkansas, and Louisiana. In cases of the other states, he appointed provisional governors with the authority to call conventions to establish permanent governments and restore the states to their former rights, as soon as they should repeal their ordinances of secession, repudiate their Confederate debit, and ratify the amendment which Congress proposed for the abolition of slavery.

With these conditions most of the states in question complied, but Congress would not recognize them as reconstructed without further guarantees. Accordingly, it proposed a fourteenth amendment to the Constitution providing, among other things, that when the right of voting is denied by a state to any citizen, the basis of representation in such state shall be reduced in the proportion which the number thus excluded shall bear to the whole number of citizens in the state. This was especially objectionable to southern politicians. When the amendment became a part of the Constitution in 1868, a major challenge was advanced to those political leaders in the South who would limit the voting rights of African Americans. They wanted to maintain the white-controlled Democratic Party in the South. One strategy of the Party was to cooperate with President Johnson in challenging the passage of Congress's radical Civil Rights Bill. Senator Lyman Trumbull had successfully led Congress to pass a bill to protect the voting rights of African Americans. But Southern Democrats succeeded in encouraging the President to veto the bill. Frederick Douglass, George Downing, and several other African Americans had led a delegation to meet with President Johnson to encourage his support of the bill. But the Southern Democrats were more successful with the president, who spurned the overtures of the African American delegation. Nevertheless, Congress passed Trumbull's Civil Rights bill over the veto of President Johnson. Abolitionists throughout the Nation were overjoyed with passage of the bill.

The liberal stance of President Johnson toward the South was especially attacked in Congress by Senator Charles Sumner of Massachusetts. Referring to the President's address to the Congress, Senator Sumner said: "It is a direct appeal to the worst passions and worst prejudices of those rebels who, being subdued on the battlefield, still resist through the aid of the President of the United States."[42] Behind this charge was the idea that President Johnson, being a southerner, shared the racist tendencies of the old Confederate States of America. Surely, the president would reestablish the old political leaders in the South without any requirement of a change in attitude over racial matters to be reflected in the legal codes of the states. Congress rightly recognized that this would lead to the political victory of the South.

The Radical Congress did not challenge the president's policy of Reconstruction on mere opinions of a general nature. Rather, it made a comprehensive investigation of the socio-political situation in the South to determine racial attitudes reflected in public opinion relative to Reconstruction. On December 13, 1865, a joint committee of the two chambers of Congress was appointed with direction "to inquire into the condition of the States which formed the so-called Confederate States of America, and report whether they or any of them are entitled to be represented in either house of Congress, with leave to report by bill or otherwise."[43] In 1866, the committee received testimonies from leaders throughout the South. Among individuals interviewed were some African Americans. Such testimonies proved to be a good sampling of the attitudes of southern whites toward the Union and a tremendous rage against African Americans.

On February 17, 1866, Robert E. Lee, the greatest military leader of the old Confederacy, testified to Congress relative to the issue of suffrage for African Americans in the South. He affirmed: "I think it would recite unfriendly feelings between the two races. I cannot pretend to say to what extent it would go, but that would be the results."[44] He assured the committee that southern political opinion was opposed to granting suffrage to African Americans. There was a general feeling that to give them suffrage was tantamount to the possibility of African American rule over whites in certain parts of the South. This was especially repugnant to white racists.

A more detailed account of the attitudes of the southern whites toward the politics of Reconstruction was expressed by other men from various walks of life in the southern states. On February 1, 1866, J.J. Henshaw, a practicing physician in Lovettsville, Virginia, when asked if southerners had the power would they reduce African Americans again to slavery, testified: "I do not think they would hesitate for a moment in doing so."[45] Similarly, Josiah Millard of Alexandria, Virginia, testified regarding the attitude of white Virginians toward African American emancipation: "They did not like it at all. They protested against it to the very last, and some of them in the country now are trying their very best to make the colored man believe that they are still theirs; that they are not free…. They say they have raised the Negroes, and have fed them all their lives, and it is the Negro's duty to work for them."[46]

Yet more racist, George S. Smith, a farmer in Culpepper, County Virginia, testified on January 31, 1866, regarding the attitude of white Virginians toward African Americans: "They would entirely extirpate him from the face of the earth. They would first commence with the Union men, and then they would take the Negro."[47] In this testimony, Congress could readily recognize that the South had been beaten on the battlefields but still persisted in its negative attitude toward the Union and African Americans. They still desired the forced removal of Union soldiers from southern soil and the oppression of African Americans.

In the deeper South, the attitude of whites was even more radical in nature and practice. D.E. Haynes, from Rapides Parish, Louisiana, stated what he felt to be the majority opinions of whites in this region: "If there was not interference from a superior power they would be in a worse condition than they were when in a state of slavery."[48] He believed that the presence of federal soldiers made possible a degree of security for African Americans in the state. Certainly, throughout the South a military presence was needed for the race to strive in the long road to security, citizenship, and upward mobility.

Fortunately, some African Americans were able to testify to the Joint Committee on Reconstruction regarding these crucial needs. They talked about the tremendous fears and apprehensions of the freedmen in the South. For example, Alexander Dunlop, a trustee of the First Baptist Church of Williamsburg, Virginia, testified on February 3, 1866, relative to the lack of security for the race:

> My purpose was to let the government know our situation, and what we desire for us if it can do it. We feel down there without any protection… we feel in danger of our lives, of our property, and of everything else…. I have suffered in the war; I was driven away from my place by Wise's raid; and so far as I, myself, am concerned, I do not feel safe; and if the military were removed from there I would not stay in Williamsburg one hour, although what little property I possess is there…. In case of the removal of the military, "nothing shorter than death" has been promised me by the rebels.[49]

Due to the intensity of the situation in Virginia, he saw the crucial need for greater protection by federal troops and an increase in the operation of the Freedmen's Bureau because many rebels had no respect for property rights and security for African Americans. The testimony of several other African Americans regarding conditions in the South reflected the precarious nature of the freedmen's condition. Their hope was for longer term protection from the federal government.

It was in this sort of precarious situation that African American church leaders tried to assume the dangerous and uncomfortable role of reconcilers between the races. They saw this as an absolute necessity for the security and progress of the race. To a certain degree, they realized some success stories, for a minority of white Christians did assist African Americans in religious and educational areas. There had always been a minority presence of white sympathizers toward African Americans in the South. Not all white Christians held slaves; and, even some slave owners manumitted their slaves before the Civil War. Hence, there were some small cracks in the slave power of the South before the war. African American church leaders were able to utilize this minority presence and expand the development of positive attitudes of southern white Christians and northern missionaries in the South for the edification of the race beyond the overthrow of Reconstruction. More specifically, African American churches provided opportunities for freedom, self-expression, economic cooperation, and release from the social barriers faced by the race in the emerging segregated society.

African American Churches and Moral Reform Movements

The experience of slavery was a tremendous challenge to the moral development of African Americans. The family as the basic unit of society had been seriously disrupted, especially on plantations, and the morals of the race had been accordingly lowered. Unfortunately, white men who had been initiators of negative morality among slaves were among the chief critics of the morals among the freedmen after the Civil War. African American church leaders were keenly aware of the need to restore Christian moral values within the race and felt the need to convince whites of the elevated morals of the race after liberation. There was always a strong need to be accepted or affirmed by the white race. Church leaders were anxious to avail themselves of different resources for the moral elevation of the race along the lines of Christian ethics. They were especially concerned over the issues of marriage, family life, sobriety, industry, and mutual respect for all humankind. Josephine Yates, a Christian woman, observed: "Emancipation and certain constitutional amendments brought freedom to the material body of the erstwhile slave, but the soul, the higher self, could not be so easily freed from the evils of that slavery had fastened upon it through centuries of debasement; and because of this soul degradation the Negro, no less than the South, needed to be physically, mentally, and morally reconstructed."[50] Again, Rev. J.W.E. Bowen marveled at the rapid progress of the race since emancipation:

> The marvel is, that the Negro has sufficient moral vitality left to cut his way through the whirlpool of licentiousness to the solid rock of Christian character. From the harem life of promiscuous and unnamable sins of slavery, some of which were natural and fatal growth of pagan vices, others the fruit of prostitution, to the making of one clean, beautiful, noble and divine family and home, covers a period of intense, moral, spiritual, and intellectual development, more significant than the geologic transformation of ages.[51]

His hope was that the future would be guided by the Hands of Providence to "chase away the curse of slavery." Rev. M.C.B. Mason observed that "any careful observer will see at once that in the field of ethics and morals a veritable revolution has taken place among Negroes during the present generation."[52] However, this progress was the result of many strides of church leaders during the early years after the Civil War.

A basic moral issue of considerable concern to the African American church was the matter of overindulgence in alcoholic beverages. Prior to the Civil War, alcoholism had been rather rare among the race except some overindulgence during Saturday nights on the plantations. Overindulgence was primarily a weekend affair. However, the problems and uncertainties of the new freedom and the stress of segregated life led to an increased number of African Americans indulging excessively in alcoholic beverages. This problem even manifested itself among some Christians of the race.

After the first decade of the post-Civil War era, some church leaders decided to align themselves with the National Prohibition Movement at least in spirit. In 1869, the National Prohibition Party was organized in Chicago. The effects of the movement were rapid. Thirty-two of the forty-eight states had after the 1870's, the majority of the states had adopted statewide prohibition legislation. In other states great sections were made "dry" by what was known as "local options," that is, towns and counties by popular vote decided whether or not the ban alcohol sales. As early as 1869, the Consolidated American Baptist Convention adopted a standing resolution: "That the use of intoxicating drinks is injurious and most destructive to morals, and we recommend all, over whom we have influence, to immediately abandon their use."[53] This resolution was published annually in the convention's publications. Shortly, a large number of African American Baptist churches included a statement in their church covenants to "abstain from the sale and use of alcoholic beverages." Nevertheless, the problem of alcoholism continued to be a real issue perplexing the churches.

In 1872, the convention took even stronger measures to encourage temperance among its members. J.H. Magee, Chairman of the Temperance Committee, offered a report which led the convention in a discussion of far-reaching significance:

> We, your Committee on Temperance, beg leave to submit the following as our report:
>
> Whereas, The sale and use of intoxicating liquors as a beverage, including wine, beer, and everything that produces intoxication, is of itself a gross immorality and sin against God and humanity.

1. Resolved, That it is the duty of every friend of God who is for the advancement of the Redeemer's Kingdom, to abstain from the use of such articles as will intoxicate, and also to discourage the distribution of the same by sale or otherwise, and do all in their power for the suppression of this worst of oppressors of mankind.
2. Resolve, That the members of this Convention, the pastors and deacons of our Churches, the superintendents of Sabbath Schools, teachers, and parents, are requested to totally abstain from the use of those articles, and use their influence against this great curse among our people.[54]

The use of alcohol as a beverage was deemed a moral wrong, and total abstinence was requested of all African American Baptists. They were the only major church denomination to recommend total abstinence, at least in principle, of its membership; still, this did not significantly curb alcoholism among Baptists and other Christian denominations.

By the turn of the century, alcoholism had continued to be a major concern of African American churches. Drinking among members of the churches was noted, and the ill effects of the habit on the social and moral development of the race were noted by many church leaders. Rev. Richard Spiller of Hampton, Virginia, offered an insightful comment to The Negro Young People's Christian and Educational Congress, held in Atlanta, Georgia, from August 6-11, 1902:

Whenever a movement is started in any county or State having for its object the destruction of the saloon, how hard it is to solicit the interest of the Negro in these movements. Not only is it true of the laity of the church, but it is also true of the preachers; not because they are intemperate, but because in childhood many of them were taught that strong drink was an excellent medicine. Where did the idea originate? It is one of the old relics of slavery, handed down by our fore parents. During the harvest seasons whisky was used just the same as water among the slaves; so much so that many of our old people felt that they were not prepared to worship without its aid. Hence there are churches to-day that will allow its members to deal in strong drink and hold membership in the church.[55]

He went on to suggest that temperance societies should be formed in Sunday schools and Christians should utilize the ballot to promote temperance legislation.

Similarly, Rev. D.W. Cannon of Albany, Georgia, recognized the political implications of alcoholism to voting and civil rights for African Americans, noting that some southern white politicians utilized moral issues against the race. He observed: "They contend that the drunken and vicious Negro has no right to so sacred a weapon of moral and social defense as the ballot. They say it is the free man's only defense against misrule and political usurpation, and since the Negro, through the agency of whiskey handlers, is the one most likely to vote indiscriminately, therefore the ballot or right to vote ought to be taken from him."[56] Whites often used moral issues regarding African Americans as justifications for disfranchisement, segregation, and limitations on other civil rights. They held that the race was morally depraved and lacked civilizing potentials.

Church leaders were quick to recognize the need to counter the public opinions of southern whites regarding the moral state of the race. Several different approaches were offered during the congress by African American ministers. Rev. W.D. Johnson suggested "total abstinence" and greater moral education for youth in the family setting as means of dealing with the problems of alcoholism and negative public opinions regarding the race. Rev. E.M. Jones of Montgomery, Alabama, urged ministers and laity to teach young people against the use of alcohol, noting that the extensive use of alcohol penetrated the membership of churches. He remarked: "If all the churches would exclude all the members who are guilty of drinking, you would be surprised to see how many vacant seats there would be in all these churches. And if all our conferences, associations, conventions, and synods could find out and fire all members who indulge, it would create a great ripple in the ministerial world."[57] He was greatly alarmed at the extensive use of alcohol and its crucial effects on upward mobility and racial progress. Generally, African American pulpits responded increasingly to the need of moral reform, especially through various agencies of the temperance movement.

Another strong supporter of temperance was Bishop M.H. Davis of the African Methodist Episcopal Church. In his Episcopal Address presented to the Thirty-Second Quadrennial Session of the General Conference held in Philadelphia in May 1944, Bishop Davis remarked:

> The ruin that writes the record of destruction to decent society may be found in alcoholic beverage. It combines against sober living, happy homes, honor in men, and purity in women, hope in humanity, and progress in achievement. Its last sentence is despair and death. The African Methodist Episcopal Church has in the

past and must in the future declare its opposition to this enemy of society. The bars, night clubs, and stores have united in spreading this deadly evil among our people, and especially our youth. The African Methodist Episcopal Church did oppose the traffic and use of alcoholic liquors. It is clearly seen that the accumulation of any group is unsafe in the hands of those who use alcoholic beverages.[58]

Between 1898 and 1921, Rev. Francis James Grimke devoted five sermons dealing exclusively with the need for wider church promotion of the cause of temperance. He cited poverty, degradation, high mortality rates, and demise of aspirations and dreams as causative factors in the use of alcohol. He advised:

Let us remember and with pride, that we started out as a church strongly committed to temperance; and, God helping us, let us be ever loyal to that pledge. The old Fifteenth Street Presbyterian Church began as a temperance organization, and, by the help of God, let one and all, husbands and wives, fathers and mothers, old and young, male and female, pledge ourselves that it shall ever be.... Unitedly, let us stand behind this movement that seeks to redeem this land from the blight of this terrible curse.[59]

The expansion of the Holiness and Pentecostal movements resulted in the development of doctrines specifically related to social ethics based on the general emphasis on personal sanctification and holiness. Hence, most of these churches prohibited the use of alcohol because such usage did not reflect the new birth in Christ. Specifically, the Apostolic Faith Mission Church of God and the Church of God (Which He Purchased with His Own Blood) generally required the abstention from the use of tobacco and alcohol. While not necessarily members of the temperance movement, these churches demonstrated a radical opposition to the drinking of alcohol and other narcotic drugs. Perhaps, it may be said that their success in promoting sobriety exceeded that of the mainline African American denominations.

Another socio-political issue with strong moral implications was the necessity of prison reform. African Americans were unjustly treated in the criminal justice system throughout the South. Many innocent individuals were convicted of crimes on insufficient evidence, and they were incarcerated in a vicious prison system. The treatment of convicts was cruel and extreme. Herbert Aptheker observed:

> ...most of the convicts are scattered over the State on farms, having no one to administer to their physical, moral, or spiritual needs but a host of inhuman, brutal convict guards. When a fresh convict is carried to the farms, he is taken down by the other convicts and beaten, at the command of the guard, and that, too, with a large piece of cowhide. The guard takes this method of taming the new comer.[60]

Many southern whites advocated a strong belief in the innate criminal minds of African American freedmen, suggesting a general moral depravity due to their race. Hence, they saw no significant moral issues in exposing the race to radically cruel and unjust treatment in the criminal justice system.

A classic example of this was the institution of the convict lease system. It was a system providing that a lessee could buy from the State the discipline of prisoners solely for gain. At the Prison Reform Convention, held in Atlanta in 1888, Dr. P.D. Sims of Chattanooga, Tennessee, declared that "the impoverished condition of the South succeeding the War of Rebellion, caused it to drift into the convict lease system, for which there were many excuses, but no justification."[61] In 1902, Attorney R.S. Smith, an African American, observed the cruel nature of the system when he said: "One of the greatest wrongs of the South is its convict lease system; and its lynch law, and its disfranchising statues are like unto it. Although the emancipation, written and promulgated by the immortal Lincoln, has been operative for more than thirty-six years, yet a species of slavery still exists there, fostered and nurtured by the statutes authorizing the convict lease system."[62] Culp went on to observe that one of the specific charges against the convict lease system was that "these unfortunate beings, without regard to sex, were huddled together in prison quarters like so many cattle."[63] Young boys and girls were especially victims of the system, who were "convicted of trivial charges and sent to the convict camp for the express purpose of securing to the lessees of convicts the benefit of their unrequited toil until they reached the age of majority."[64]

In his observations on convict labor, Booker T. Washington remarked:

> In Alabama eighty-five per cent of the convicts are Negroes. The official records show that last year Alabama had turned into its treasury $1,085,854 from the labor of its convicts. At least $900,000 of this came from Negro convicts, who were for the most part rented to the coal-mining companies in the northern part of the State. The result of this policy has been to get as many able-bodied convicts as possible into the mines, so that contractors might increase their profits.[65]

Profiting in convict labor was a general practice throughout the South.

Segregation and Discrimination Politics in the South

There were many forces at work to militate the social, political, and moral advancement of African Americans, devolving back to the southern white democrats' varied attempts to impede progress from post-Reconstruction civil rights gains. The Fourteenth Amendment to the Constitution which had given manhood suffrage to African Americans was soon to be challenged by local state laws. Some of the southern states had been forced to ratify the amendment in order to get back into the Union. Once these states regained their original status, they gradually and methodically worked against suffrage and civil rights for African Americans. One major strategy was to blame African American politicians, church leaders, and "carpetbaggers" for some of the so-called failures of the Reconstruction in the light of the southern ethos. This ethos was expressed in the writings of Charles H. Otken, a southern white historian, where he claimed that African Americans were "destitute of the rudiments of political knowledge" and therefore lacked the necessary skills for political leadership in the South.

Despite the Fourteenth Amendment to the Constitution, white political leaders of the South did everything they could to keep African Americans away from the pools and limit the political ascendancy of racial leaders. The federal government responded by the passage of the Fifteenth Amendment in which it was expressly declared that the states and the United States should never take the vote away from any citizen on the account of "race, color, or previous condition of servitude." However, the Supreme Court declared the Civil Rights Act of 1875 unconstitutional in 1883, ushering in a serious blow to the Reconstruction progress of African Americans. But a number of legislatures enacted legislation prohibiting discrimination in places of public accommodation.

The negative action of the U. S. Supreme Court set the stage for the triumph of white supremacy in the South. One of the most serious blows to African American citizenship was the rapid progression of disenfranchisement. In Mississippi, the first signal of disenfranchisement developed with a move in the state constitutional convention when the legislators undertook to write into their fundamental law a guarantee of white supremacy. In 1890, a convention met with the primary purpose of disenfranchisement of African Americans. A suffrage amendment was written which imposed a poll tax of two dollars, excluding voters convicted of bribery, burglary, theft, arson, perjury, murder, and bigamy, and also barred all who could not read any section of the state constitution, or understand it when read, or give a reasonable interpretation of it. Of course, this was to be enforced for African American voters only.

South Carolina followed Mississippi in the disenfranchisement of African Americans in 1895. By 1898, the pattern for the disenfranchisement had been securely established, with other southern states following the examples of Mississippi and South Carolina. By 1910, constitutional provisions for disenfranchisement were adopted in North Carolina, Alabama, Virginia, Georgia, and Oklahoma. These negative political developments ignited riots in several cities of the South.

Adamant in their strides to preserve the southern way of life, many segregationists responded with violence to any African American who dared to avail himself of the suffrage rights. The major agency of violence was the Ku Klux Klan, originally formed in Pulaski, Tennessee, by a group of young men for their own amusement. Dressed in ghostly costumes, they frightened the superstitious voters by appearing as the spirits of dead Confederate soldiers. The Ku Klux Klan movement soon developed violent strategies to curtail the voting rights throughout the South and to destroy the social, political, and economic progress of African Americans. Soon the KKK was joined by other white extremist and violent organizations, including the Knights of the White Camelia, White League, White Line, and other terrorist organizations. The small gains of African Americans from the Reconstruction were partially destroyed as many barns and houses burned, and many were whipped and lynched for attempting to vote for the Republican party, which most African American voters supported, calling it the "party of Lincoln."

African American church leaders reacted strongly against these violent attempts to impede the racial, political, and social progress of the race. The response of church leaders to the rise of violence and white racist control of politics and economic growth was varied. Some believed in the inevitable triumph of justice and righteousness in American democracy. Others were pessimistic in outlook. One example of the pessimistic group was Rev. Harvey Johnson, pastor of Union Baptist Church of Baltimore, who believed it was hopeless to suppose that white attitudes would improve regarding African Americans. He became widely known for his socio-political views regarding racial progress. Reverend Johnson was a strong advocate of self-help programs and freedom for the race which he made vocal in the National Baptist Convention, U.S.A., Inc., as well as in local Maryland state politics.

In the early 1890's, Rev. Harvey Johnson proposed a radical plan of separation between the races. Accordingly, he organized the "Texas Movement" which advocated setting aside the entire state of Texas for a sort of reservation or separate nation for African Americans. This movement did not take strong roots among the race. His plan was not as noteworthy as the earlier advocates of migration to Africa or other foreign lands. The failure of the Texas Movement did not stop him from attempting other viable approaches to the issue of segregation in American society. He became one of the foremost social thinkers and proponents of a social gospel among the race. His views were welcomed and highly respected, especially among African American Baptists. He preached and delivered many addresses that were saturated with socio-political thoughts. Locally, he led the fight that changed the Constitution of Maryland so that African American doctors and lawyers could practice their profession in the state. The law also provided that African American teachers could teach in public schools of the State.

Equally important, Rev. Harvey Johnson advocated the end of African American churches' dependence on white church organizations. He led the movement among the churches to declare their autonomy from white Baptists, resulting in the organization of the first African American Baptist convention in the state, the "Colored Baptist Convention of Maryland." Subsequently, the Clayton Williams Academy in Baltimore was organized for the training of ministers who would further the idea of separation from white Americans.

As early as 1897, Reverend Johnson delivered an address before the Seventeenth Annual Meeting of the National Baptist Convention, held in Boston, Massachusetts, entitled "A Plea for Our Work as Colored Baptists, Apart from the Whites." He advocated many seemingly radical ideas to the delegation:

> Yes, the white man is in a crisis and a panic in nearly every management confined to time, and still he is considered by us, and he considers himself, a manager and leader most sagacious, and yet so reckless, so unfaithful and unsuccessful has been his leadership in every capacity that confidence is destroyed everywhere.... We have leaders of our own, and the sooner we lay out plans and learn to follow them the better it will be for the Colored Baptist denomination.[66]

Subsequently, he continued to deliver sermons and addresses with strong separatist implications. He had little hope for the end of racism and segregation on the part of white America. Hence, African Americans must accept this fact and move on to develop their own institutions both religious and economic without the spirit of dependence on the other race. He came very close to advocating a "Black Power" ideology among the race.

Strangely enough, Rev. Harvey Johnson was accused by many African Americans as well as whites of being too extreme in his racial views. To be sure, his views were "radical" enough to challenge the white supremacy ideologies of the nineteenth and early twentieth centuries. Even more significant, he contributed a tremendous body of literary thought designed to correct the white man's negative views on the human potential of African American life, exposing the fallacies of white racism.

The turn of the century witnessed the emergence of a large group of African American Baptists and Methodists with the determination to participate in the evolution of the movement to counter racism and discrimination in the United States of America. In 1902 Nannie Helen Burroughs, a distinguished lay leader in the National Baptist Convention, U.S.A., Inc., issued "An Appeal to the Christian White Women of the Southland," to move their conscience on behalf of the African American man's struggle for equal treatment on the public transportation facilities of the nation. This pioneer African woman stated:

> We wish to appeal to you in behalf of the thousands of mothers in this land who have suffered in silence the unchristian humiliation to which they have been subjected in the Southland since the introduction of the separate-coach law....
>
> The separate-coach law in the Southland is not only a reflection upon our advancement, but a stigma upon us, and the better class of whites throughout the country consider it a stigma upon American civilization, and would join heartily in its removal.[67]

She appealed directly to the heartbeat of white Christian women to join African Americans in their struggle for fair treatment in the South. Nannie Helen Burroughs believed that all Americans should have equal access to public transportation. This could only be accomplished through active and cooperative efforts of southern Christians. Moreover, she recognized the powerful influence of white Christian women in southern politics. They were able, if only willing, to exert tremendous pressures to change public opinion in the segregated South. Generally, they held the keys to open public transportation facilities to all citizens of the nation.

Unfortunately, the appeal to white Christian women in the South was not generally effective because most of those women shared the same favorable opinions about segregated facilities in the South. A small minority responded, but the vast majority supported the status quo in the socio-political life of the South. The majority were not inclined to utilize the power of white churches to influence change in segregation politics. In fact, most white churches practiced and supported segregation. Fixed lined of segregation cut across all of southern society, including churches, schools, libraries, stores, medical facilities, public transportation stations, bathrooms, water facilities, housing, and communities. Specific laws in various southern states specified the segregation in those areas of public life.

Nevertheless, Miss Burroughs remained for many years a strong fighter for the civil rights of African Americans, as it was dear to her heart. She labored untiringly through the Women's Auxiliary of the National Baptist Convention, U.S.A., Inc., to aggressively use its influences and resources to aid the civil rights cause. Several women's groups subsequently led movements to petition the legislatures of Tennessee and Louisiana to repeal the obnoxious Jim Crow car laws. These brave women, like Miss Burroughs and many others, played a major role in the early civil rights struggles of the twentieth century.

In 1904, Rev. W. Bishop Johnson, pastor of the Second Baptist Church of Washington, D.C., delivered an address entitled "Citizenship, Suffrage, and the Negro" before the Baptist Ministers' Conference of Philadelphia, which surveyed the progress, challenges, and setbacks experienced by African Americans after the Reconstruction Period. He declared:

> The disfranchisement of the Negro is rank injustice, born of prejudice and race hatred. Everybody knows that the ballot placed in the Negro's hands is the badge of his citizenship, and has no more abuse by him than by the army of foreigners who are by political trickery and methods of perjury "made ready for voting" in State and National elections. The attempt to qualify electors by education or property qualifications or to keep back the growing numbers who desire to exercise the first and highest right of citizenship is a thing that the framers of the Constitution had never dreamed of….

> The citizen, in the hope of securing his rights, looks to the dominant political party. Where else should he look? The Republican Party is a synonym for freedom. It was born in the high and holy realms of human liberty. Its obligations to secure civil and political liberty to all citizens alike is as binding today as ever…. It has been the recipient of his votes since the right of suffrage was conferred upon him; it has narrowed down his political vision to where he has not been able to see salvation in any

other name.... Democrats don't want him; Lilly Whites won't have him; Populists never had any use for him, and his only hope is to manfully contend for what belongs to him in the house where he was born. He should speak out in the next campaign as never before. If Republicanism is powerless to stop lynching and all their horrible and hellish attendants, it should be made to put such legislation on the statute books as will forever crush it, since this barbarism is now confined to no section nor race and has become purely an American pastime, finding enthusiastic advocates in the United States Senate, among eminent lawyers, politicians, literary scholars, clergymen, and other public men, holding high positions that should stand for law and order....

The rapid growth of prejudice among the races is an alarming menace to citizenship. The...legislation that establishes the Jim Crow car is born of race prejudice and hatred.... It is a disgrace upon any State that citizens who stand for educational attainment, social purity, and material wealth, and everything that is helpful to the community should be made to suffer the insult to their manhood and respectability that is afforded by the Jim Crow car.[68]

In the case of *Plessy v. Ferguson*, the "Jim Crow" law segregating African Americans and whites on railcars was upheld "where there has been provision for substantially equivalent accommodations for each race, on the grounds of promoting the public comfort and preserving peace." Homer Plessy, a biracial African American, had been arrested in Louisiana where he had violated the state law requiring separate accommodations for the races in interstate travel. Plessy's contention that the Louisiana statute was unconstitutional was rejected by the Louisiana State Court and appealed to the United States Supreme Court. The Supreme Court also rejected his case.

Prominent church leaders across the nation were negatively impacted by the Jim Crow laws in the South. All major transportation facilities were required to accept the law by requiring separate seating for African American passengers once they entered southern states. Even passengers who had purchased first class tickets in northern states were not accorded the privileges once they entered the South. Church leaders and delegates to national conventions were often insulted by transportation officials when they demonstrated any form of resistance to the Jim Crow laws.

Nevertheless, several African American church leaders continued to sound their voices against such discrimination against American citizens. Significantly enough, certain foreign visitors from countries with peoples of color were exempted from those segregation laws. They were examined, sometimes being insulted, to determine their foreign status. This factor often created tensions between foreign visitors, especially from Africa, and African American citizens.

Another significant voice against the Jim Crow laws was that of Rev. William B. Reed, pastor of the First Baptist Church in Madison, New Jersey. In 1908, he issued strong socio-political statements in his *Echoes of the Emancipation Proclamation Relative to the Jim Crow Laws*:

> The [silence] of the President (Taft) to the savage wrongs of the South has done the colored race inestimable injury. His failure to ask for legislation, on the investigation of disenfranchisement laws, or reduction of Southern representation, has embroidered negro-haters and made them excessive in their mistreatment of the colored man. His announcement that there was no law against Jim Crow cars was a hard blow to a people whose hearts went out to him.
>
> The colored race will no more submit to Jim Crow law than disenfranchisement, its elder brother. And the operations of this inhumane rule will be an imposition, and not an accepted law with the entire race.
>
> It is not the principles of the Republican Party to impose on the colored man. If the President knew how respectable people of our race were treated, on trains and steamboats, etc., I believe he would have remained silent rather than fostered this unholy cause.... In the South we are not privileged to dining cars, railroad restaurants, sleeping cars, decent coaches or waiting rooms....[69]

To be sure, there were many tremendous socio-political developments taking place in American which overshadowed the appeals of African American leaders for justice and civil rights. The agrarian movement in the South and Southwest; the industrial revolution; and the conflicts between major industries and labor unions held the attention of leaders in national politics. The North was too engrossed in its major industrial concerns to be responsive to the so-called "Negro problem." The South acted toward African Americans as if the Fourteenth and Fifteenth Amendments did not exist.

What civil rights-minded church leaders had to deal with at the dawn of the twentieth century was the battle with other public issues to gain a significant hearing on the part of the economic and political systems of the expanding and developing republic. The first decade of the century was so dominated with other political and economic issues that basic human rights for African Americans were forced from the focus of national politics in America. The rise of "big business," industrialization, migration, immigration, and expansionism overshadowed the "Negro problem."

Accordingly, President William H. Taft was not really concerned about the issues raised by Rev. William B. Reed's *Echoes of the Emancipation Proclamation Relative to the Jim Crow Laws*. Truly the president, though essentially judicial and liberal in his political and social outlook, was not significantly sympathetic with the "Negro problem" in America. He was so preoccupied with the issue of how to relate to the tremendous influence of Theodore Roosevelt that many of the important national issues escaped him. The administration of President William B. Taft passed down in history as one of the worst failures in office in the whole past presidential list.

During the administration of President Woodrow Wilson, African Americans experienced some signs of relief. His administration was far more stable than the former president, William H. Taft. Under this new administration, Rev. W. B. Reed was able to note some progress of the race in the civil rights struggle:

> On the 21st of last June when the Supreme Court overthrew the Oklahoma Grandfather Clause and the Maryland election vote, there was handed down another decision of far-reaching significance. This decision overruled a sleeping car law passed by the legislature of Wisconsin. This law provided that the occupant of a lower berth could have the upper berth closed so long as it was not sold....

> This decision is in accord with our contention in our 1913 Report that when a man buys one ticket he has one space, one privilege—and has nothing to do with other space sold or unsold. We believe the time will soon come when these foolish train passengers will be sufficiently educated in matters of public decorum to know that they have nothing to do with the sold or unsold upper berth or the other seat occupied or unoccupied, which they did not pay for....

> The freedom of unrestricted travel is a right in this country of every law abiding citizen. We recognize no legality in the sign "white" and "colored," nailed in trains; and when political tyranny of those thirteen Democratic States is overthrown these signs will be done away with.[70]

Rev. W. B. Reed looked with tremendous disdain to the political significance of the Southern Democratic machine that was "[seemingly] getting the power they had before the Rebellion."[71] He realized that any political or legal gains made by African Americans would be null and void in the "Solid South" without the intervention of the federal government. The South had insisted on a "let us alone" policy in relation to the federal government, especially in matters dealing with the "Negro problem." They believed that local state governments knew better how to relate to the problem. For the South, the problem was a local states' rights issue. Rev. Reed was quite clear on the strategy of the Southern Democrats who were in the position to dominate the great committees of the House and Senate which originate tariff bills, internal revenue, corporation taxes, individual income tax, all the sources of government revenue, and all the appropriations carrying the great supply bills, both civil and military. Hence, the only way to break up that undue political power of the southern states and assure African Americans of their civil rights was to promote federal supervision of the elections in the South. Rev. W. B. Reed believed that it was absolutely necessary for African Americans to share some of the tremendous political power of the "Solid South" through the electoral process. Only under such conditions would the proper balance of power in American politics be assured. Doors must be opened for the race to participate in southern politics. Otherwise, the South would reestablish slavery under new names.

His observations were prophetic, for the South did in fact create a social and political situation of segregation, discrimination, and dehumanization which effectively placed the race in second-class citizenship. The proliferation of segregation laws in every corner of the race's life, literally from the cradle to the grave, took place in the South. The race was barred from both white hospitals and cemeteries; segregated public school systems were established; limited employment opportunities except in menial labor existed; many African American voters were purged from the voting rolls; and hazards of terror and mass injustice prevailed with larger numbers of African Americans being lynched annually. It became very clear to any detached observer that segregation was part of a deliberate pattern to degrade Africans Americans and deprived them of the rights that had been given after the Civil War. Hence, leading church leaders sounded the alarm regarding the eroding situation in the area of civil rights.

The Anti-lynching Movement

"Lynching is the black spot on America's soil," remarked Rev. L. B. Brooks, in his 1922 State of the Country address before the New England Baptist Convention.[72] He went on to say, "So long as America holds the record for its illegal taking of life, so long as the headlines of foreign papers carry in large letters, 'America burns another Negro,' just so long will her shame be world-wide."[73] Booker T. Washington remarked about lynching:

> In most parts of the United States the colored people feel that they suffer more than others as the result of the lynching habit. When he was Governor of Alabama, I heard Governor Jelks say in a public speech that he knew of five cases during his administration of innocent colored people having been lynched. If that many innocent people were known to the governor to have been lynched, it is safe to say that there were other innocent persons lynched whom the governor did not know about. What is true of Alabama in this respect is true of other States. In short, it is safe to say that a large proportion of the colored people lynched were innocent.[74]

Similarly, Rev. Francis J. Grimke expressed the basis of African American concern with the problem of lynching. He remarked:

> In the subject of lynching, the Negro has a general interest, and he has a special interest. A general interest in that he is an American citizen, interested in all that affects the present and future of welfare of this country. He hasn't had very much to encourage his patriotism. He has been oppressed, down-trodden, brutally treated; he has been told again and again, This is a white man's government, and everything has been done to make him feel like an alien. He is still patriotic, however.[75]

Lynching was one of the most inhumane practices in the history of the American republic. Hundreds of African Americans were lynched to "protect white womanhood from what they called 'Negro Male Coon or Brute,'" while southern whites, at the same time, used as common-law wives the daughters, sisters, and cousins of the same so-called Negro Brutes. Certainly, lynching was a widespread practice throughout the South. Rev. L. B. Brooks pointed out the following statistics on lynching:

> If you read the *Crisis Magazine*, the April number, the following facts are found on the question of lynching, that our proud Government had

allowed to go on without remedy:

> From the year 1889 there have been 3,443 known mob murders, 54 of them the victims being women. American mobs murdered 54 persons in 1921, four of whom were publicly burned at the stake. In only a few instances has prosecution of lynchers been attempted.[76]

He was a very strong participant in the ant-lynching movement, utilizing the pulpit of the Mt. Ararat Baptist Church of Rutherford, New Jersey, where he served as pastor, to advance the cause for freedom and protection for African Americans. His was also a very strong pen in the socio-political climate for the advancement of civil rights in the New England Baptist Convention. He was perhaps the first African American Baptist to lay the blame on the southern white clergy for the lynching. He protested:

> The white preachers of America can break up lynching, clean up the debauching evils of destructive prejudice, injustice, and civil robbery in all parts of our land; if the true dispensation of the Gospel is preached and practiced! ... But we find thousands of white preachers who hold the pulpit of the churches where lynchers are members, there men and women sit in the pew each Lord's Day who are members of State Legislatures, where corrupt laws have been enacted, lawyers, judges of the courts, and jurors who are vile and unjust to men because of their color or race; and are too cowardly to raise their voices against these criminals in high places. God cannot use these preachers because they are slaves of wicked man.[77]

The National Association for the Advancement of Colored People, a biracial organization with strong African American church ties, was organized in January 1909 as a result of a race riot in Springfield, Illinois. It played a major role in addressing the problem of lynching in America. Dr. W.E.B. Du Bois, its initial director of publicity, utilized *The Crisis* to advocate for justice and civil rights for African Americans. It addressed civil rights issues through the court systems and publications. The problem of lynching was addressed in a series of legal battles beginning in 1910. Many petitions and protests were sent to the House and Senate seeking support for anti-lynching legislation. In 1921, one congressman named Lemidas Dyer, a Republican from Missouri, decided to introduce a bill (H.R. 13) "to assure persons within the jurisdiction of every state the equal protection of the laws and to punish the crime of lynching." The bill would inflict a heavy fine upon any county in which a lynching occurred, requiring part of the money to be given to the victim's relatives. The measure was referred to the Judiciary Committee and reported out favorable on October 20, 1921.[78]

The Dyer Anti-Lynching Bill created a considerable amount of interest in African American communities. Many hopeful discussions centered on the absolute necessity of the bill's passage. It was hailed throughout the nation by racial leaders and liberal whites as a major step forward in the civil rights struggles of the early century.

Unfortunately, the initial excitement was premature because the "Solid South" political machine was able to block the passage of the Dyer Anti-Lynching Bill in the Senate through extensive filibuster. Consequently, the Republican leaders agreed to withdraw the bill on December 2, 1921. The fight over the bill in Congress did result in some improvement in race relations in the nation.

African American church leaders were not willing to accept the bill's failure in the Congress. Rev. W. J. Winston, a distinguished Baptist pastor and educator from Baltimore, offered a resolution on the Dyer Anti-Lynching Bill to the National Baptist Convention, U.S.A., Incorporated, urging:

> Whereas, the Dyer Anti-lynching Bill is fresh in the minds of our people, and by all indications will be re-offered in the coming Congress, a bill which should engage the mind and attract the attention of every colored patriotic American who believes in a square and fair deal to all, and especially should this bill be supported, since it has for its objective the destruction of the unholy and nefarious system of lynching which is a disgrace to American civilization, and enacting an adequate legislation for the amelioration of our condition and the respect for evenhanded justice and sympathy for the oppressed and persecuted.
>
> Resolved, That we urge our people to rally to the support of the candidates for election or re-election for Congress and the United States Senate who will solemnly pledge to vote for the passage of the Dyer Anti-lynching Bill and that each delegate be and is hereby requested to either write or interview his representative in Congress and the United States Senate, asking his assistance in the passage of the bill, thereby helping to correct the many wrongs having been perpetrated upon our people, and to protect a people who have never been traitors to the flag....[79]

The convention readily offered its support to the resolution, and African American Baptists across America worked for the passage of the bill. The struggle was destined to be long and lacking in hope. As late as 1936, The New England Missionary Baptist Convention was still lamenting over the failure of the bill in Congress, noting "No Party seems willing to pass a lynch law to stop Mob violence in the South. The Republicans refused to do so in the Senate, and the Democrats with the largest majority of America's history, have left the question for their successors to settle."[80]

In 1945 Father Divine, a Harlem cult leader, entered the fight for the anti-lynching legislation introduced in Congress. He announced his intention of blanketing Capitol Hill with hundreds of thousands of letters, telegrams, and a petition "with ten million signatures." He pledged the support of "all his angels and the resources of his far-flung kingdom into the anti-lynching movement."[81] The push for anti-lynching legislation continued well into the middle of the twentieth century when Rev. Adam Clayton Power Jr., a New York congressman, took up the cause. He helped to set the stage for the Civil Rights Revolution.

The Movement for the Enforcement of Voting Rights

The early twentieth century witnessed a surge in the law enforcement movement in the nation. Many of the nation's most distinguished and influential civil workers lined up behind the movement and constantly encouraged the national government to get more involved. The movement urged the enforcement of every law in the Constitution of the United States. The Women's Auxiliary of the National Baptist Convention, U.S.A., Inc., went on record to encourage the movement: "The Negroes of this country want to see the law obeyed—including the Fourteenth and Fifteenth Amendments. We have been asked to call your attention to the Law Enforcement Movement and distribute printed matter."[82] The Baptist women also suggested that the movement would be strengthened through greater participation in politics on the part of African American women:

> Negro women are in politics to make a new name for themselves and a new place for their race.... With Mrs. George S. Williams of Georgia, and Mrs. Mary Booze of Mississippi, as our spokesmen in the National Council of the Republican Party, we have the "understanding"—a foundation on which to stand—something to stand on and somebody who will stand on it.... We did not "get in" until last June when for the first

time in American politics, two Negro women were put on the National Committee of the most powerful political party.[83]

One of the strongest stands on the whole of law enforcement and political liberation of African Americans was delivered by Rev. W.J. Winston, who was the former president of Northern University in Long Branch, New Jersey, and pastor of the New Metropolitan Baptist Church of Baltimore, Maryland. His address was entitled, "Disfranchisement Makes Subject Citizens Targets of the Mob and Disarms Them in Courts." The central points of this address of protest include: (1) The disfranchisement of African Americans deprived them of their rights of citizenship "and chartered immunities"; (2) It made them victims of mob violence and exposed them to the "sham court trials" in the South; (3) African Americans economic development was hindered by disfranchisement; (4) They were denied active participation in the judicial process; and, (5) the rise of racism would go unchecked without the African American vote.[84] Rev. Winston readily recognized the grave danger disfranchisement posed to the actual survival of African Americans living in the South. Historically, the vast majority of the race resided in the South.

Giving the southern population demographic, the rise of organized crime, the resurgence of the KKK, and the failure of white America to enforce the federal laws weighed especially heavy upon African Americans. They were caught in the vicious wave of crime without the basic protection of law enforcement officers guaranteed to all citizens of the nation. Further compounding the problem, the courts of the nation were generally unfavorable to justice for the race. Many political and religious addresses on the local, state, and national levels were uniquely concerned with these basic issues in American democracy.

The Impact of Migration on Churches

The migration of African Americans, beginning in the 1890's, has been a phenomenon of far-reaching significance to the growth and development of the separate African American church movement. The changing economic and political situations in rural areas, especially in the South, were primarily responsible for the mass migration of the race to urban areas. Many were attracted by the expanding opportunities of urban life. Job opportunities, educational advancements, and access to the upward mobility of urban centers were seen as major motivations for migration. The rural South and Southwest were deficient in these opportunities.

Initially, African American Baptist and Methodist churches were principally concentrated in the rural South with all of its negative experiences. The members were often poor, illiterate, and dependent upon the soil of the South for subsistence. Unfortunately, the southern rural economy worked adversely to the subsistence of African Americans in general. Many who had been strong supporters of rural churches migrated to urban areas. With the general decrease in membership and support, the experienced and more qualified ministers left the traditional pastorate of several rural churches concurrently to a more lucrative full-time pastorate in urban areas. Baptists sought recommendations from friends or convention leaders for support in seeking new pastorates in small towns or larger cities. Methodist bishops assigned prominent rural pastors to larger urban churches. Similar policies were followed by other African Americans denominations, which resulted in many leadership crises in rural churches. Some were forced to consolidate in order to survive. Others were forced to close their doors.

There were several specific developments during and after the Reconstruction Period that forced a dilemma on rural churches. First, there was the development of the credit system in the rural south aimed at improving the general plight of the farming communities. The credit system encouraged the development of two types of farmers—the merchant farmers and the resident farmers. The merchant farmers were the wealthier class who usually resided in towns and upon whom the resident farmers depended for money and supplies to operate their farms. Invariably, African Americans were of the latter class and subject to tremendous exploitation. They were known as tenant farmers usually required to live in poor housing owned by the merchant farmers and were basically dependent upon the merchant farmers. Even the few that owned their little houses and farms were still dependent upon the merchant class. Both groups of tenant farmers were exploited by the merchant class. Usually, they were not granted bills for their credit nor receipts for payment of debt. Hence, they were at the mercy of merchant farmers' honesty or sense of fair-play. For the most part, the merchant farmers were not honest in their dealings with tenant farmers. The system was often a blueprint for bankruptcy for most African Americans, forcing such poverty upon the tenant farmers that they lost the little property which had been accumulated after the Civil War. Those tenants who were forced of necessity to live in the houses of the merchant class continued in a state of economic dependence.

Second, African Americans were often caught in the middle of the struggles between the white merchant farmers and resident farmers. Both classes became dependent largely on African American labor. They became competitors for such labor, and often bitter rivalry developed. Generally, African Americans were more inclined to work for merchant farmers as sharecroppers for two specific reasons. First, the share plan was a favorite one with most African Americans because it allowed them to be their own managers. The employer furnished the land, the mule, and necessary tools. African Americans were primarily responsible for providing a labor force, usually their wives and children. The merchant farmer generally received half the cotton and corn produced by the system. Secondly, the share plan with the merchant farmer allowed certain workers to enjoy a favorable social status in comparison to those who worked for the resident farmers. They had the social distinction of being identified with the wealthy class of farmers who lived away in the towns and small cities. Even at its best, however, the workers were often exploited.

African Americans who were identified primarily with the resident farmers were poor and more inclined to migrate to urban areas in search for a better life. They were often humiliated by the white farmers because of their complete slave-like dependence. The resident farmers could come to the house of an African American man and demand the labor of the family on any given day. Not only was this demoralizing, but the system kept many of the youth from school and other social experiences. Many men became victims of low self-esteem resulting from their diminishing credibility in family leadership. These major disadvantages forced many African Americans, especially young adults, to look to the urban areas of the North and Northwest for a better way of life.

By the turn of the century, a significant number of African Americans had migrated from the South, adversely affecting African American churches, especially in the rural South. This left the churches with small youth and young adult participation and fewer experienced and qualified pastors. Rural churches were faced with the problem of educating a group of people who would not return to the local church to demonstrate their skills and talents. Surely, these developments caused some weariness on the part of rural clergy. They saw their once-thriving and progressive churches diminish to centers of the very young and older adults.

The migration of rural African Americans to the urban centers of the North and Northwest impacted the churches in those areas. While there was a growth in membership, there were still some problems that had to be addressed. One major social problem was the cultural shock experienced by most of the migrants from the rural South in their encounter with city life. The fact that they were transplanted culturally had tremendous significance to the mental, emotional, and spiritual development of this class. Hence, the crucial task of urban churches was to help these migrants get over the cultural shock of their new environment and assimilate in the culture of these churches. Class differences soon developed within the growing urban churches. In a report to the Women's Convention, Auxiliary to the National Baptist Convention, U.S.A., Inc., the following observations were made relative to the African American migration to urban areas:

> Northern Negroes, as a group, look down with scorn on southern migrants. They are afraid that Jim Crow is coming North to live and move and have his being; that southern Negroes will southernize the North, instead of the North northernizing them....
>
> Only great souls can work side by side with and for their ignorant brothers—undaunted and unafraid. The task in the North is for big Negroes—spirited Hercules—who will put their whole souls to the task. Negroes who are not afraid of losing their northern prestige by lift in their southern brothers.[85]

In order to address these problems, the many northern churches developed unique cultural programs. One part of the programs was the transplantation of southern church music to urban churches. This was not without some difficulties because northern churches had identified with the music culture of their white church counterpart. Hymns and anthems were very much parts of the worship experience of these northern mainstream African American churches. Their members were proud of their cultural tradition.

Another part of the church cultural tradition was the introduction of rural or southern African American preachers to the leadership of urban churches. These preachers brought to the worship experience of the northern churches their unique style of preaching, which attracted more and more migrants into the churches. Summer camps, retreats, and prayer bands were developed to help alleviate the cultural shock experience caused by the migrants. Hence, they sought a balance in church culture between the northern and southern styles. Those migrants who were not able to assimilate into the church culture joined small storefront churches and sometimes cults.

Rev. L. K. Williams, president of the National Baptist Convention, U.S.A., Inc., remarked: "The migration of Negroes from the South to the North is a striking phenomenon of race friction and no movement since the Emancipation of the Negro has had so many potential eventualities as this one, yet concerning which some otherwise loquacious leaders have been tempted to maintain an unbroken silence."[86] He had an early fear that the Baptist churches of the North were not completely ready for African American migration from the South. Urban churches were able to meet many of the needs of the migrants as long as they were residing in well defined "black neighborhoods." However, the changing racial situation in urban areas seriously hindered the effectiveness of these urban churches in meeting the needs of the migrants. With the process of decentralizing "black neighborhoods," the traditional urban churches slowly lost a great deal of influence over migrants, and consequently the population grew much faster than church membership. Actually, a significant number of southern-born African Americans became secularized in their attempt to adjust to the urban cultural shock and opted not to affiliate with the churches. Their value system, largely nurtured by southern mores and folkways, was radically altered by the emerging secular culture of northern cities. Others, however, joined the non-traditional churches. Holiness and Pentecostal churches experienced the largest church growth from the migrants. Storefront churches and cults move in to fill the cultural gap between the migrants and the traditional African American churches. This tendency prevailed throughout the twentieth century.

However, towards the end of the twentieth century a new trend commenced with the reverse migration of African Americans from the North back to the South. This trend developed with the emerging group of retired workers seeking a familiar way of life back in their original social environment. Wearied and fatigued with the challenges of city life, these African Americans opted to escape to the familiar settings of their hometowns and communities. Some had accumulated sufficient wealth to build modern houses in rural and small towns of the South. It was these returnees who began the revitalization of rural African American churches. They brought with them the habits of tithing learned in the urban churches. With the infusion of their financial resources, emerging numbers of rural churches began the process of becoming full-time ministries and building educational facilities. Also, larger numbers of trained and experienced ministers opted to remain in the South, especially in sizable towns.

(Endnotes)

1. Sydney E. Ahlstrom, *A Religious History of the American People* (New Haven, CT: Yale University Press, 1972), 650.
2. Jesse Macy and Allen Johnson, *The Anti-slavery Crusade: A Chronicle of the Gathering Storm* (New Haven: Yale University Press, 1919), 40-42.

3 George Washington Williams, *History of the Negro Race in America 1619-1880* (New York: Arno Press, 1968), 404-405.

4 Charles Harris Wesley, *Richard Allen, Apostle of Freedom* (Washington, DC: Associated Publishers, 1935), 219.

5 Stanley I. Kutler, *Looking for America: The Peoples History, Second Edition, Volume I* (New York: W.W. Norton & Company, 1979), 125-127.

6 Melvin Drimmer, ed., *Black History: A Reappraisal* (New York: Anchor Books, Doubleday & Company, 1968), 207.

7 Martin Duberman, ed., *The Antislavery Vanguard: New Essays on the Abolitionists* (Princeton, NJ: Princeton University Press, 1965), 57.

8 George F. Bragg, *Men of Maryland* (Baltimore: Church Advocate Press, 1914), 54-55.

9 Ahlstom, 650-651.

10 John Hope Franklin, *From Slavery to Freedom* (New York: Alfred A. Knopf, Inc., 1965), 237.

11 Williams, 61-63.

12 Ibid., 68.

13 Miles Mark Fisher, *A Short History of the Baptist Denomination* (Nashville: Sunday School Publishing Board, 1933), 412.

14 James Barnet Taylor, *Lives of Virginia Baptist Ministers* (Richmond, VA.: Yale and Wyatt, 1837), 407.

15 Wesley, 219-220.

16 Stanley W. Campbell, *The Slave Catchers: Enforcement of the Fugitive Slave Law, 1850-1860* (New York: W.W. Norton & Son, 1968), 50.

17 Ibid., 39.

18 Henry Wilson and Samuel Hunt, *History of the Rise and Fall of the Slave Power in America* (Boston: J.R. Osgood and Company, 1875), 304-305.

19 Duberman, 124.

20 John W. Blassingame, *The Frederick Douglas Papers, Series One: Speeches, Debates, and Interviews, Volume II 1847-54* (New Haven: Yale University Press, 1982), 12-16.

21 Ibid., 130-131.

22 Joanne Grant, ed., *Black Protest: History, Documents, and Analyses, 1619 to the Present* (Greenwich, Conn.: Fawcett Publications, Inc., 1968), 38-39.

[23] E. Franklin Frazier, *The Negro in the United States* (New York: The Macmillan Company, 1957), 87.

[24] Grant, 42

[25] Wilson, 190.

[26] Ibid., 181-182.

[27] Ibid., 182.

[28] Ibid., 75.

[29] Ibid., 182.

[30] Edward A. Johnson, *A School History of the Negro Race* (Raleigh, N.C.: Edwards & Broughton, Printers and Binders, 1890), 90.

[31] Carter G. Woodson, *The History of the Negro Church* (Washington, D.C.: The Associated Publishers, 1921), 132.

[32] Samuel Elliot Morison and Commager, Henry Steele, Eds., *The Growth of the American Republic* (New York: Oxford University Press, 1915), 533.

[33] Charles Dowdey, *The History of the Confederacy* (New York: Barnes & Noble Books, 1955), 77.

[34] William Warren Sweet, *The Story of Religion in America* (New York: Harper & Brothers Publishers, 1950), 314.

[35] Ibid., 315-316.

[36] Ibid., 318.

[37] Frederick Douglass, *Life and times of Frederick Douglas* (Chicago, IL: J. S. Goodman and Company, 1882), 405

[38] Ibid., 406-407.

[39] Daniel Alexander Payne, *Recollections of Seventy Years* (New York: Arno Press, 1969), 146.

[40] D. W. Culp, *Twentieth Century Negro Literature* (Naperville, IL: J. L. Nichols & Company, 1902), 81.

[41] Ibid., 34.

[42] *The Annual Cyclopedia and Register of Important Events of the Year 1868, Volume VIII* (New York: D. Appleton and Company, 1869), 125.

[43] *Report of the Joint Committee on Reconstruction at the First Session Thirty-Ninth Congress* (Washington, DC: Government Printing Office, 1866), vii.

[44] Ibid., 134.

⁴⁵ Ibid., 138.

⁴⁶ Ibid., 28-29.

⁴⁷ Ibid., 16.

⁴⁸ Ibid., 62.

⁴⁹ Ibid., 56.

⁵⁰ Culp, 23.

⁵¹ Ibid., 33.

⁵² Ibid., 37.

⁵³ *Report of the Twenty-Ninth Annual Meeting of the Consolidated American Baptist Convention*, September 1869, 3.

⁵⁴ *Report of the Thirty-Second Annual Meeting of the Consolidated American Baptist Convention*, 1872, 27-28.

⁵⁵ J. W. E. Bowen and I. Garland Penn, *The United Negro: His Problems and His Progress; Containing the Addresses and Proceedings the Negro Young Peoples Christian and Educational Congress, August 6-11, 1902* (Atlanta, GA: D. E. Luther Publishing, 1902), 310.

⁵⁶ Ibid., 166.

⁵⁷ Ibid., 257.

⁵⁸ *The Episcopal Address Presented by Bishop M. H. Davis to the Thirty-Second Quadrennial Session of the General Conference of the African Methodist Episcopal Church at Philadelphia, Pennsylvania*, May 1944, Published by order of the General Conference of the African Methodist Episcopal Church, 40.

⁵⁹ Bowen and Penn, 310.

⁶⁰ Herbert Aptheker, ed., *A Documentary History of the Negro People in the United States* (New York: Citadel Press, 1951), 689.

⁶¹ Culp, 97.

⁶² Ibid., 92.

⁶³ Ibid., 92-93.

⁶⁴ Ibid., 93.

⁶⁵ Howard Brotz, *Negro Social and Political Thought: 1850-1920: Representative Texts* (New York: Basic Books, 1966), 459.

⁶⁶ Harvey Johnson, *A Plea for Our Work as Colored Baptists, Apart from the Whites* (Baltimore: Afro-American Company, Printers, 1897), 11-12.

67 Bowen and Penn, 522-533.

68 W. Bishop Johnson, *The Scourging of a Race: And Other Sermons and Addresses* (Washington, DC: Beresford Printers., 1904), 59-71.

69 William B. Reed, *Echoes of the Emancipation Proclamation* (Madison, NJ: W.B. Reed, 1908), 21-23.

70 William B. Reed, *"State of the Country Address," Delivered before the New England Baptist Convention, Forty-Second at Second Baptist Church*, Philadelphia, Pennsylvania, 1916, 22-24.

71 Ibid., 12.

72 L.B. Brooks, *"State of the Country," New England Baptist Convention, 1922*, 16.

73 Ibid., 16.

74 Brotz, 459.

75 Woodson, 292.

76 Brooks, 11.

77 Ibid., 21.

78 Robert H. Brisbane, *The Black Vanguard: Origins of the Negro Social Revolution, 1900-1960* (Valley Forge, PA: Judson Press, 1970), 61.

79 *Minutes of the National Baptist Convention, U.S.A., Inc., 1924*, 97-98.

80 *Minutes of the New England Baptist Missionary Convention*, 1936, 7.

81 *The Afro-American*, Baltimore, MD, July 6, 1940, 17.

82 *Minutes of the National Baptist Convention*, U.S.A., Inc., 1924, 301.

83 Ibid., 301.

84 J. W. Winston, *Disenfranchisement Makes Subject Citizens Targets for the Mob and Disarms Them in the Court of Justice* (Baltimore, MD: Varsity Press, undated manuscript), 4-10.

85 *Minutes of the National Baptist Convention, U.S.A., Inc., 1924*, 293.

86 L.K. Williams, *Annual Address to the National Baptist Convention, U.S.A., Inc.,* 1923, 17.

Chapter 9

THE NEW SOCIO-POLITICAL TRADITION OF AFRICAN AMERICAN CHURCHES

The Impact of a New Cosmopolitan Outlook

The political and intellectual movement for equal rights and freedom for African Americans assumed a new stance when World War I erupted, and later World War II. Historians have readily seen these wars as turning points in modern history. This was the beginning of the visible end of an era of stability in national politics and economics followed by social upheavals, economic changes, and international tensions on a global scale. The result was a significant and distinctive transition in the western mind. African Americans were introduced to divergent world cultures with aspirations for freedom and self-determination. Divergent philosophies of government—democratic capitalism, socialism, and communism—impacted the emerging intelligentsia of African Americans, especially influenced by Dr. W.E.B. Du Bois and politically minded clergy like Reverends Adam Clayton Power Jr., Leon Sullivan, M.C. Allen, and Vernon Johns. With their evolving interpretations of African American military involvement in the wars, there was a rather rapid widening of the emotional and intellectual outlook of the race. They felt that African Americans desperately needed a "New Deal" in civil rights.

To be sure, African Americans were not unaffected by the general transition in the western mind. Gone were the days of non-intervention in world military affairs. The socio-political thoughts of African American church leaders were now characterized by the assimilation of new worldviews of the United States and certain European nations. In other words, they began to think internationally. The wars' justifications forced them to see the racial problems of American culture in the light of world movements. The parochialism of post-Reconstruction thought gave way to a new intellectual approach to the racial problem with an expanding horizon. They were brought into closer contact with various socio-political problems around the world and their apparent interrelationships. African American leaders came to realize that the mob violence of the Ku Klux Klan and disfranchisement politics could now be viewed in the cosmopolitan milieu of dehumanizing political systems around the globe designed to quench the human spirit of freedom, equality, and justice. Deprived racial and ethnic groups around the globe were viewed by some church leaders as part of their united struggle for human dignity and freedom.

Initially, one crucial development precipitated by World War I was the attempt of white American proponents of racial supremacy to transplant their theories internationally. Rev. E.C. Morris, long-time president of the National Baptist Convention, U.S.A., Inc., was well apprised of the new international offensive of American proponents of white supremacy and alluded to it in such an argument in his last presidential address:

> What country would welcome the Turks in wholesale numbers among them? If the many false statements sent abroad about the morals of the Negro are allowed to go unchallenged, it will not be long before the doors of all great countries of the world will be shut in our faces…. The Negro does not desire to leave the United States, not even the South. But the South must change or the Negroes will seek homes in a more congenial clime.[1]

These words were designed to have a twofold effect. On the one hand, Rev. Morris wanted to counter the charges of the American proponents of white supremacy on the international front. Certain white American soldiers were reporting to Europeans that African Americans were deprived in morals and deficient in intellect. He believed in the moral and intellectual equality of the races. Also, on the other hand, Rev. E.C. Morris sought to advise African Americans to keep their options open. If the attitudes of white Americans, particularly in the South, did not radically change, then African Americans might determine that their interest might necessitate a migration to another part of the world away from the land of the "lynchers."

Rev. W. G. Park, who succeeded Rev. E. C. Morris in the presidency of the National Baptist Convention, U.S.A. Inc., remarked the same year:

> As a race we have made rapid progress, notwithstanding the many oppositions which have confronted us. The door of opportunity has been shut against us, the industrial mills have denied us, the factories have rejected us, prejudice and race hatred have met us in all the avenues of life. We, so to speak, have been forced to make brick without straw, but we are not discouraged. We have been loyal and patient in tribulations. We have fought and will fight to protect the flag under whose folds many of the members of our race unjustly bled and died…. As a race, we have

answered every call to arms from the Revolutionary War to the World War and have not insulted the flag. Search the record of 1812, the Civil War, the war with Spain, and the war with Mexico and you will find that the Negro soldier has done his bit in each and that his record for bravery and heroism cannot be questioned. In times of war, he has been a hero, and in times of peace, he has never been charged with harming a single chief magistrate, nor throwing a single bomb.[2]

Similarly, the African American Baptist church leadership of the New England Baptist Missionary Convention joined the ranks of other church leaders in the call for "A Square Deal" in American life. That leadership also recognized the tremendous importance of the recent world war to the so-called "Negro Problem." As early as 1919, Rev. W.B. Reed told the convention:

> The guns of the mighty have ceased their roaring, their forts are silenced, their navies gone, armies disorganized, and the people waiting for orders.... The armies of our allies with untold hardships, backed up with a willing sacrifice of the people got the victory, and from pools of mingled blood triumph has been written in history. We, in this, the forty-fifth annual session of our convention, rejoice with the rest of mankind over the victory of our armies and the triumph of a sacred cause. Any cause charged with complete liberties and rights of the weak is sacred....
>
> Victory has been won on the battlefields; the defeated enemy had made a most humiliating surrender; the last of our soldiers will soon tread upon home soil with the nation's acknowledgement of well done. But world or home democracy is not yet.[3]

When the war ended, African Americans were still waiting for the benefits of American democracy to advance freedom, economic progress, and civil rights for the loyal and patriotic race.

However, World War I did not make the world safe for democracy. Nations were still busy building up their military complexes at the expense of progressive social programs. Worldwide poverty had set in with the failure of the world's economies. The Great Depression seriously altered the socio-political mindset of world leaders. Out of the stress of economic insecurities in Europe, a very dangerous political ideology emerged which seriously challenged the peace won by the World War. The rise to power of Adolph Hitler and his political theories were perhaps the most radical international challenge to the progress of African Americans in particular, and generally democratic minded peoples of the world. The racial myth was given a potent international thrust with the development of Nazism as an ideology in Germany. While the European Jews were the primary objects of this myth, African Americans realized that the world with an ideology of Nazism was not safe for their progress. They saw clearly the fantastic potency of sheer mythology was part of the racist attitudes of many white Americans. Nazism and American racism were similar in social objectives. Perhaps, this affinity was part of the motivation for America's late involvement in World War II.

As early as 1938 Rev. J.H. Jackson, Corresponding Secretary of the Foreign Mission Board of the National Baptist Convention, U.S.A., Inc., recognized the growing threat of Adolph Hitler. He realized that the progress of the foreign mission programs of Christian organizations was directly related to world socio-political movements. Accordingly, Rev. Jackson remarked:

> As we look across the world today, we behold many discouraging signs and must admit the presence of many stalwart enemies of the Cross of Jesus Christ. These may be found in the form of materialistic philosophies, the secular mind and political states....
>
> Fascism and Nazism are demanding the loyalty and, in many instances, the sacrifice of the human personality to the orders and dictates of the State. In such political organizations man is not evaluated as an end in himself but the means to an end.... The totalitarian idea of man runs counter to the Christian concept of human personality and negates the sacred truths uttered by Jesus of Nazareth. Along with the development of the cult of the State there has risen the doctrine of the supremacy of race. To follow such a theory or view of life to its logical conclusion will naturally divide the world into many hostile camps where each race will be pitted against the other.[4]

Similarly, Rev. J.C. Jackson, president of the New England Missionary Baptist Convention, offered some insightful socio-political remarks in his address to that convention on June 18, 1942: "To begin with, I want it thoroughly understood that I want and hope the allies will win the War and destroy forever the spirit of dictatorship, but to do this the monster prejudice must be obliterated from the face of the whole earth. Prejudice is the most costly thing in the world today, and person or nation that possesses it, nurtures, and seeks to keep alive this monster, is to be pitied."[5] Rev. Jackson clearly understood the affinity between American racism and the ideologies of Fascism and Nazism. He was anxious to warn African Americans to keep a critical eye on world developments.

Among the major concerns of African American church leaders relative to the world wars was the issue of the abuse of African American soldiers. It was ironic that the military and civil leaders of America were not willing to deal justly with such soldiers on the battlefields to defend the American flag. The physical and psychological abuse of these soldiers was so severe that the National Baptist Convention deemed it necessary to issue a "Resolution on Abuse of Colored Soldiers":

> WHEREAS, There is much concrete evidence that native born colored American soldiers now in training in Army camps in the South have been in hundreds of instances subject of humiliations, discrimination, brutalities, and, in at least one case, a trainee was murdered, even when clothed in the uniform of the United States Army. And,
>
> WHEREAS, We are not only segregated but have been deprived of a fair proportion of officers and men, although there are thousands of patriotic and loyal men well qualified, and those taken in have been restricted to a few of the many regular services.
>
> WHEREAS, We seek not to take Negro soldiers from the South, for geography does not count in a democracy. We do ask that the War Department armed with power and authority use drastic measures to protect them from un-American practices of individuals and brutal mobs, just as would be done if Nazis, Communists, Ku Klux Clan or Night Riders attempted to humiliate, abuse, or intimidate white soldiers in the U.S. Army. Colored Americans are super patriots, 100 per cent American by birth and love of country, who are being trained to fight, and if need be to die for their native land and for democracy, although they do not fully share equally in its beneficences. Democracy is needed in the army.[6]

It was further observed that African American soldiers were "barred from enlisting in the U.S. Navy, except as messmen, flunkies and valets with no hope of promotion to the higher ranks."[7]

African American church women were also vocal regarding developments during World War II. They readily saw the relationship between world events and the racial problem in America. In 1944 Nannie H. Burroughs, a national leader in the Baptist denomination, gave a broad survey of the plight of the race in the national and international arena. She observed:

> The first stark reality the Negro will face in the post-war world will be that while he helped to beat Hitler into complete surrender that Hitler's kind of race prejudice is still unlicked, at home and abroad in the world.
>
> It is against this background that the Negro will have to fight his economic battle. He will have to compete with the very people whom he fought to help liberate. America will give aliens jobs and give the Negroes their walking papers.
>
> Let nobody fool you—we are in for a long, hard uphill battle on the American front. The pressure of the European war emergency will be gone. The army will be on world fronts. The home front battle will have to be fought by civilians—Negro and white—who want to free America from her home-made Hitler's.[8]

The astute observations of N.H. Burroughs were prophetic because successive decades were to witness many "home front battles." African Americans were later called upon to fight in the Korean and Vietnam wars while at home the battles remained unsettled. It was to these war issues, especially the Vietnam War, that the voice of Dr. Martin Luther King Jr. came to be heard internationally.

The Civil Rights Revolution

The Civil Rights Movement of the 1950's and 1960's has been described as the most remarkable revolution in the history of the United States. Slowly, events in the long struggle for civil and human rights took on the appearance of a movement designed to bring about the greatest change in the social fabric of American life since the Civil War. From half-hidden depths of impatience and mental aggression, African Americans pressed forward their revolution to a crescendo of protest in the middle of the twentieth century. Curiously enough, the revolution started long before it was recognized as such by white America. Certainly, the Civil Rights Movement of the middle of the century, revolutionary in intent and momentum, was a continuation of the earlier civil rights struggles of the past century. There was no period of the century wherein African Americans did not protest the injustices and inconsistencies of American democracy. Significantly, Baptists were foremost leaders in the new revolution.

The greatest link between the Civil Rights Movement of the turn of the century and the revolutionary Civil Rights Movement of the 1950's and 1960's may be linked to the person of Rev. Adam Clayton Powell Jr. He grew up in Harlem and was nurtured in the best socio-political tradition of the race and the Baptist denomination. In the early 1920's Harlem became a center for the social and political development of African Americans. It was the home of a dense population of many prominent members of the race, and other communities of the nation gained inspiration and guidance from the Harlem leaders of racial progress. The apex of Harlem's development in African American culture has been described as the Harlem Renaissance. Harlem was a cultural center for artists, writers, poets, and dramatists with such noted writers and poets as James Weldon Johnson, Langston Hughes, Countee Cullen, Sterling Brown, and Claude McKay. They influenced this young son of a Baptist pastor.

It was during this period of revitalization of cultural life among African Americans that Adam Clayton Powell Jr. received his nurture at the Abyssinian Baptist Church of New York under the pastorate of his father Rev. Adam Clayton Powell Sr. He was generally exposed to the most favorable traditions of the race. During his period of nurture, Adam Clayton Powell Jr. studied Marcus Garvey and became intrigued with the racial consciousness and pan-Africanism of Garvey's movement. Subsequently, he helped pioneer the tactics of mass action against racial discrimination. In 1931, he led six thousand marchers to New York's City Hall to protest the barring of five African American physicians from the staff of Harlem Hospital. Subsequently, young Powell led innumerable demonstrations that focused public attention and racial energy on campaigns to open job opportunities for the race in the city. As director of relief efforts in Harlem during the Great Depression, Rev. Adam Clayton Powell Jr. helped to feed a thousand persons a week and later led rent strikes to protest evictions and slum conditions.[9]

After he inherited the pastorate of the Abyssinian Baptist Church, Rev. Adam Clayton Powell Jr. became a typical embodiment of the social gospel tradition of the African American church. In concomitance with his regular pastoral duties, he operated a day nursery for working mothers, a grocery store, and other services with a staff of twenty workers. Also, he was successful in promoting job opportunities and selective buying campaigns. All these accomplishments took place in the early 1930's.

The paramount contributions of Rev. Adam Clayton Powell Jr. to the Civil Rights Movement were rendered after his election to the Congress of the United States as Harlem's first congressman, giving him the position of one of the most celebrated politicians in American history. The congressional position paved the way for him to succeed Booker T. Washington and Dr. W.E.B. Du Bois as the single most powerful African American. From the outset of his political career, Powell set out on a persistent fight for civil rights with an international outlook. During the 88th Congress, he reminisced:

> Mr. Speaker, much has been said in recent months regarding the necessity of passing an effective civil rights bill. The urgency has been recognized as essential for America's proof to the world that she believes in democracy.
>
> The question of civil rights is no longer the problem of Negro people—it is the problem of all the people of the United States of America. Many fear that the United States may be finished as a great power in the eyes of the world unless it solves this problem and solves it now.
>
> However, on November 7, 1944, when I was elected to the 79th Congress of the United States of America, I pledged myself to dedicate my efforts to the task of making democracy work.[10]

These remarks reflected the quality of Rev. Adam Clayton Powell's commitment to the strength of the American republic, while remaining faithful to the patriotic spirit of earlier African American church leaders. Generally, no one desired the destruction of the republic, but to aid and inspire it on its march to justice, equality, and quality of life for all citizens.

At the outset of Powell's congressional career, he expressed a specific interest in the way African Americans were treated in the armed forces of the United States. Practices of discrimination were longstanding throughout the nation. In 1944, he introduced H.R. 2708: "A bill to prohibit race segregation in the Armed Forces of the United States after the termination of hostilities in the present war and the beginning of demobilization."[11] The bill failed in the 79th Congress but was reintroduced in the 80th Congress. During his speech to Congress, Powell said: "… The Negro people will stand ready at all times to defend this Nation, but they are saying, 'We want some of the democracy here now at home that you are trying to sell abroad to other people that you ask us to go ahead and fight for. We have proven our loyalty. We are asking for democracy now."[12] However, it was not until 1948 that some progress was made in the area of racial equality in the armed forces. But none of his bills and amendments on the cessation of discrimination and segregation in the armed forces passed the Congress and Senate of the United States. Generally, some relief came in the form of programs initiated by the Executive Branch of the government when the interests of the race was linked with national security during the Korean conflict.

The next area of major concern on the part of Rev. Adam Clayton Powell Jr. was the violence experienced by African Americans. As previously noted, the race was constantly victims of mob violence and other acts of crime in American life. He was forceful in his claims that America had a special responsibility to protect its citizens from violence at home as well as abroad. A series of anti-lynching bills had failed to pass the Congress, but Powell continued the pressure for the passage of a federal anti-lynching bill. By 1963, he had become weary of the failure of the Congress to pass protective legislation for the protection of African Americans. He gave a detailed speech on the issues of lynching and mob violence. Powell's bill H.R. 546 was the most comprehensive piece of legislation ever introduced in Congress for the protection of African Americans from lynching and mob violence. It was so comprehensive that all minorities were protected by the special provisions of the bill. Much of the legal thought behind the famous Civil Rights Bill of the 1960's was developed by Rev. Adam Clayton Powell Jr.

Another area of concern for Rev. Adam Clayton Powell Jr. was the issue of voting rights. He was especially critical of all tactics used by southern whites to prevent the race from voting. In the 79th Congress, he introduced a bill relative to "Poll Tax and voting." He challenged the rationale for such a requirement for voting, noting that financial considerations prevented the poor from voting. This was especially true of the farm laborers in the South. The majority of poor farmers was intimidated and denied voting privileges because they were not able to pay the poll tax.

During the 85th Congress, Rev. Adam Clayton Powell Jr. modified his earlier bill against the poll tax to include a Voter Registration Commission: "H.R. 7957 (Mr. Powell): To provide for the establishment of a Federal Voter Registration Commission to provide, in certain instances, for the registration of citizens of the United States for the purpose of voting in Federal and State elections, and for other purposes."[13]

A brief survey of other civil rights bills proposed by Rev. Adam Clayton Powell Jr. will reflect the depth and breadth of the Harlem politician's socio-political thought in his strides in the Unites States Congress. During the 79th Congress, he introduced a House Joint Resolution "proposing an amendment to the Constitution of the United States empowering Congress to grant representation in the Congress and among the electors of President and Vice President to the people of the District of Columbia"[14]100; a public accommodations bill "to assure to all persons within the jurisdiction of the United States full and equal privileges with respect to public conveyances and places of public accommodations, resort, entertainment, amusement, assemblage, and institutions"[15]; and, the school lunch programs amendment to "see that minority races have the same opportunity in the free-lunch program as do those of the majority race."[16]

The following sessions of Congress were characterized by an avalanche of civil rights legislation proposals from the pen of Rev. Adam Clayton Powell Jr. Included among these were: Interstate transportation bill H.R. 22 "To amend the Interstate Commerce Act so as to prohibit the segregation of passengers on account of race or color"[17]; Anti-segregation Day H.R. 3016 "Making May 17 in each year a legal holiday to be known as Anti-segregation Day";[18] Federal assistance for school construction H.R. 7535 "An amendment that school facilities of the States are open to all children without regard to race, in conformity with the requirements of the U.S. Supreme Court decision…";[19] Housing H.R. 12538 "To provide that Federal funds shall not be used for loans, grants, or other financial assistance to provide housing with respect to which there is any discrimination against occupancy on account of race, religion, color, ancestry, or national origin";[20] Fair labor standards H.R. 6887 "Extends protection of Fair Labor Standards Act to employees of large hotels, motels, restaurants, and laundries with gross sales of $1 million annually"[21]; Immigration H.R. 543 "Grants natives of British Guiana, British Honduras, the Virgin Islands, and the West Indies Federation unlimited access to the immigration quota for Great Britain"[22]; Manpower resource H.R. 7396 "Provide for a program of occupational training of the Nation's labor force…Provide for on- and off-the-job training and vocational training for the unemployed"[23]; and, Equal pay for women H.R. 11677 "to prohibit discrimination on account of sex in the payment of wages by certain employers engaged in commerce or in the production of goods for commerce and to provide for the restitution of wages lost by employees by reason of any such discrimination."[24] In 1963, Rev. Adam Clayton Powell Jr. summarized the importance of this avalanche of civil rights bills in rather suggestive language: "Civil rights to me is what Israel is to the Jew or as sacred as Ireland is to an Irishman or Catholicism is to a Catholic."[25]

Unfortunately, the vitality of Rev. Adam Clayton Powell's civil rights career in the United States Congress was overshadowed by a political scandal. His personal standard of public morality left a lot to be desired. He sought to justify the congressional ethics violations allegations against him: "As a member of Congress, I have done nothing more than any other member and, by the grace of God, I intend to do not one bit less."²⁶ This philosophy of public morality was unacceptable to both his African American constituency and the members of the House of Representatives of the United States. He openly rebelled against many rules set down by whites, drove expensive foreign cars, dined at exclusive restaurants, and made regular trips abroad. The big blow to his political career came on March 1, 1967 when 307 legislators voted for his exclusion from the 90th Congress. He became the first congressman in those times to be excluded by a vote of the House.

Specifically, the grounds for Powell's exclusion from the 90th Congress were misuse of public funds and defying the courts (for months Powell had stayed away from New York to avoid arrest in a complicated libel suit begun after he called a Harlem widow a "bag woman" for corrupt police officials). Significantly, he was reelected twice during the scandal. In 1969, the Supreme Court reversed his expulsion from Congress, but by then Powell was suffering from cancer and spending most of the time in his Bahamian Eden of Bimini. In 1970, Rev. Adam Clayton Powell Jr. permitted himself to be either outvoted or outcounted in a Harlem primary. He lost by 150 votes.²⁷ He was defeated by State Assemblyman Charles B. Rangel. After his defeat, Powell retired permanently to his island home. The death of Rev. Adam Clayton Powell Jr. ended a great era of social activism wherein one man became an institution reflecting the basic thought of an emerging social revolution. Ron Daniels, executive director of the Center for Constitutional Rights, summarize the life and legacy of Adam Clayton Powell Jr., suggesting: "Despite his flaws and frailties, Adam Clayton Powell, Jr. left a legacy of extraordinary commitment, unfailing courage, exceptional skill and monumental accomplishments. We should always remember him as a great leader who put everything on the line so that his people might be liberated!"²⁸

Interdenominational Organizational Civil Rights Strides

To be sure, African American Baptists played a major role in the struggle for civil rights, but other denominations were not silent in the struggle. Much of the early struggle was characterized by individual voices from noted clergy and lay members of the churches and conventions. However, the tremendous difficulties related to segregation and discrimination necessitated a more organized effort to combat the challenge. As previously mentioned, the National Association for the Advancement of Colored People was the first major organization with strong interdenominational and interracial support to launch a major challenge to segregation and discrimination in the United States. African American clergymen from across the nation took active roles in the work of this organization. However, some of them came to the conclusion that African American churches should advance more inclusive programs of protest against the broader areas of the social condition of the race in the United States.

In 1934, several African American denominations organized the Negro Fraternal Council of Churches in Chicago, later known as the National Fraternal Council of Negro Churches, an ecumenical organization. It membership soon encompassed twelve major denominations, including the African Methodist Episcopal Church; the African Methodist Episcopal Zion Church; the African Orthodox Church; the Bible Way Church of Our Lord Jesus Christ Worldwide; the Christian Methodist Episcopal Church; the National Baptist Convention, U.S.A., Inc.; and the National Baptist Convention of America. The founding president was Bishop R. C. Ransom of the African Methodist Episcopal Church. The organization was concerned with interdenominational and social issues affecting the African American community.

In 1943, the executive committee of the Fraternal Council of Negro Churches, representing more than six million members, met in Chicago with Rev. William H. Jernagin, serving as its chairman. Bishop James A. Bray of Chicago served as president of the council, and Bishop R.R. Wright Jr. of Wilberforce, Ohio, served as executive secretary. The committee addressed such issues as African American representation at the peace table when World War II ends; the establishment of a national office in Washington, D.C. for closer contact with national legislators; discussions on the status of African American soldiers in the armed forces in America and abroad; agricultural involvement of the race; and civil rights issues.[29] Initially, the Washington bureau of the National Fraternal Council of Negro Churches, with Rev. William H. Jernagin serving as director, served as a lobby bureau to advance special national issues of the African American community including all hearings on bills introduced in Congress that affect the economic, social, and civil rights of the race. The office was officially set up following an interdenominational mass meeting at Shiloh Baptist Church of Washington, D.C. The special subcommittee for its organization consisted of Bishop W.H. Walls, Dr. W.H. Jernagin, and Reverends H.J. Callis, J.H. Marshall, C.T. Murray, and George A. Crawley.[30]

One of the initial issues of the Washington bureau was the matter of farmers. The council dispatched a telegram to President Roosevelt asking him to veto legislation introduced in Congress forbidding farmers to move from one county to another on the grounds that it would reduce southern farmworkers to peonage.

On May 15, 1943, the Fraternal Council of Negro Churches met in Nashville, Tennessee, and asked for full racial equality in the United States of America, specifying the issues of separate car laws and the poll tax. The council issued the following statement:

> We are told that World War II is a war of ideologies; Nazism and fascism and imperialism against democracy and Christianity; the super race vs. the human race.... If in ten years Hitler's hate propaganda could plunge the whole world into a war, why cannot our united American church build an effective counter propaganda of good will to all people? What is more necessary for the salvation of the modern world?... If hate be turned loose on colored citizens all minorities will suffer; Jews will not be safe, nor Catholics, nor Italian-Americans, nor German-Americans, nor Hungarian or Poles, nor Spanish, not Mexican, nor any others who differ from the majority.... We would suggest that the separate car laws and poll tax laws be repealed as no longer of service in the democracy; that equal pay to teachers and equal school facilities, with equal opportunities in home and farm loans, be given, and that a national security, including domestic and farm workers, health work be inaugurated; that educational programs be encouraged with national aid to those States economically unable to give full educational advantages to all children to the end that not only illiteracy shall be wiped out, but that every American shall have fair health and fair employment without reference to race, color or creed.[31]

By 1947, the council expressed its belief that the 79th Congress would enact more liberal legislation affecting the concerns of the race.

In 1949, Rev. W. H. Jernagin, leader of a delegation of seven members, spearheaded a successful effort to convince the Protestant National Study Conference:

> United States churchmen have to stand up and be counted in a freedom campaign at Home. As a result, the National Conference, attended by 470 representatives of 37 million American Protestants, went on record as urging Congress to enact promptly civil rights laws, including the "safeguarding of civil, political and economic rights of citizenship."[32]

Also, the National Conference further agreed that "the behavior of the country should be brought into harmony with the principles defined in the Human Rights declaration of the United Nations, and went on record as approving the end of colonialism in the world and aid for downtrodden peoples."[33]

In 1952, African American church denominations organized the National Fraternal Council of Churches, U.S.A., Inc., on the model of the National Council of Churches of Christ in the U.S.A. Its membership included Baptist conventions, the African Methodist Episcopal Church, the African Methodist Episcopal Zion Church, and the Christian Methodist Zion Church with headquarters in Atlanta, Georgia. The initial presiding officer of the organization was Bishop Stephen L. Greene of the Second Episcopal District of the A.M.E. Church. Initially, the organization was concerned with ecumenical concerns of the African American church and civil rights.

African American Social Revolution: 1956–1970

The Civil Rights Movement during the 1960's was a continuum of the socio-political struggles of previous decades. There were many forces at work which prepared the way for the African American Social Revolution. Momentum was gained through the political activity of Adam Clayton Powell Jr.' Presidents Roosevelt and Truman; and the United States Supreme Court. Each contributed to the approaching momentum of the revolution. Specifically, the United States Commission on Civil Rights provided a tremendous body of research data for a legal and political approach to the problem of race in the United States. It was created by the Civil Rights Act of 1957 as a bipartisan agency to study civil rights problems and report to the president and Congress. More specifically, the commission's function was to advise the president and Congress on conditions that may deprive American citizens of equal treatment under the law because of race, color, religion, or national origin.

African American leaders across the nation voiced their intimate knowledge of the data reflected in the commission's report. It was clear that the nation began with an obvious inconsistency between its precepts of liberty and justice and the actual social experiences of the race. The majority race saw the nation and its Constitution as a nation of the white man, by the white man, and for the white man. The social revolution which emerged was designed to bring a radical change in the very structure of life in the nation. It was about the destruction of the old southern way of life in order for the birth of the New South to be realized without racial discrimination and segregation. With the birth of the New South, it was believed possible for the restructuring of the entire nation.

On December 1, 1955, the match was struck to ignite the dynamo of the social revolution in the historical American experience. Nothing less than an unexpected and dynamic revolution began when Rosa Mae Parks boarded the Cleveland Avenue bus in Montgomery, Alabama, and sat down in the "Whites Only" section on the bus. She demonstrated great courage in her "no" response to the bus driver's demand for her to surrender the seat to a white man. She was arrested for defying the Jim Crow law of Alabama. News reports of Rosa Mae Parks' arrest swept through the African American community and proved to be the catalyst for a different style of protest.

Shortly after the bus incident, the African American clergy leadership of Montgomery, Alabama, met to consider the significance of the new development. They could not discount the brave move of Rosa Mae Parks. Her courage called for them to match it by exercising a new form of leadership in the "heart of Dixie." She was not new to the protest movement, but an early activist in the in the effort free the "Scottsboro Boys," young men at the center of a celebrated case in the 1930's. To free her, the clergy decided to call on the community to stage a bus boycott for the following Monday morning. They utilized their pulpits on Sunday to set the stage for the boycott. Rev. Martin Luther King Jr., a local Baptist pastor of the Dexter Avenue Baptist Church of the city, accepted the monumental task of mimeographing and distributing printed material within the community. The power of the pulpit in shaping public opinion and community solidarity over a crucial issue proved effective, for the bus boycott was almost a hundred percent successful.

However, Rosa Mae Parks' decision that provoked the Montgomery bus boycott was not without precedent. African Americans had exercised individual forms of protest against the Jim Crow laws of the southern states. Rev. J.C. Jackson, at the age of 76, sued the Southern Railroad because he had been beaten by a white passenger when he and Rev. S.A. Young were traveling to attend the National Baptist Convention, U.S.A. Rev. Jackson said that "he was attacked by J.T. Hudson of Decatur, Alabama, fully a half hour after the conductor had been told of threats allegedly made by the white man against colored passengers."[34] His suit for $50,000 was based on the "claim that a public carrier is responsible for the protection of its passengers against harm inflicted by fellow passengers if the proper authorities have been duly warned of the imminence of such danger."[35] Another example was the suit made by Rev. Ollie Flemings, pastor of the St. Stephen CME Church of Winchester, Virginia, against the Greyhound Bus Company because he was forced to leave a bus in Alexandria, Virginia, when he refused to take a rear seat during his travel from Baltimore. "When the bus stopped in Alexandria after leaving Washington," Rev. Flemings said, "…the driver sought to have him move from a seat, three rows from the back, to the extreme rear seat. He stated that the driver became so insistent when he refused that he thought it best to leave the bus rather than chance physical violence."[36] Similarly in 1942, Reverends J.C. Austin, pastor of the Pilgrim Baptist Church of Chicago; and William McDowell, pastor of Mount Vernon Baptist Church, obtained warrants against E.M. Holt, a general passenger manager agent of the Pennsylvania Railroad because "the alleged refusal of the railroad official to grant the complainants first class accommodations, for which they had paid, when they attempted to board the company's train bound for Nashville, Tenn., to attend the National Baptist Convention."[37] These cases were among many other protests made by African Americans regarding discrimination and segregation on public transportation vehicles.

A classic example of an earlier boycott was led by Rev. Theodore Judson Jemison, pastor of the Mt. Zion First Baptist Church in Baton Rouge, Louisiana. In 1953, he organized the nation's first bus boycott, achieving integration in only eight days. Apparently, the white power structure in Baton Rouge was not as adamant in the enforcement of Jim Crow as those encountered by Rosa Mae Parks in Birmingham, Alabama. They responded to protest pressure more readily.

Apparently, Rev. Martin Luther King Jr. and Rev. Ralph David Abernathy were knowledgeable of such precedents in boycotts and protests in other parts of the nation. In order to confront the white power structure, the two ministers led the community to form the Montgomery Improvement Association, boycotted the bus lines, and referred their case to the state court and then to the United States Supreme Court. The Montgomery Improvement Association demanded courteous treatment of African Americans on public transportation facilities and the hiring of bus drivers from the racial community. Both the district court and the Supreme Court ruled that segregated busing was unconstitutional.

Throughout the initial days of the movement, the community looked to Rev. Martin Luther King Jr. as their supreme spokesman. This was part of a strategy developed by Rev. Ralph David Abernathy with several other clergy leaders and other strong community leaders to maintain community solidarity behind Rev. Martin Luther King Jr., when confronted by deliberate attempts on the part of the white system to fragment the movement.

The initial victory of the Montgomery Improvement Association propelled Rev. Martin Luther King Jr. into a position of national and international prominence and led to the organization of the Southern Christian Leadership Conference. The new regional organization consisted of approximately one hundred southern clergymen with the belief that civil rights leadership must be revitalized by churches and church leaders. This new organization, with several affiliate groups—such as the Alabama Christian Movement for Human Rights organized in 1956—became active in the areas of voter registration, protest, and citizenship training. From the beginning of the Southern Christian Leadership Conference, Rev. Martin Luther King Jr. inspired the movement to be guided by the principles of nonviolent resistance.

Christian men, women, and youth were inspired by the nonviolent resistance philosophy of Rev. Martin Luther King Jr., causing the desegregation of numerous public facilities including fast food restaurants throughout the South. Lunch counter sit-ins to desegregate public eating facilities were held by students in Greensboro, North Carolina, beginning in February 1960. This protest triggered similar demonstrations in several other southern cities. In December 1961, Rev. King responded to a call from Dr. W.G. Anderson to come to Albany, Georgia, and to assist other civil rights leaders seeking to integrate that city's public facilities. Consequently, the white power structure had him jailed along with hundreds of other African Americans. This time, Rev. King became disappointed by their apparent lack of success in the Albany campaign. However, he remarked from the jail cell prophetically: "In the next few months, we will see one of the most vigorous assaults on segregation ever undertaken in the South."[38] Subsequently in 1963, sit-in protests were held in Birmingham, Alabama (described then as the most segregated city in America), to protest segregation of eating facilities, again resulting in Rev. King's arrest along with some two thousand others.

Following the mass arrest tactics of the segregationists, the Civil Rights Movement gained even more momentum, causing many shopping areas to encounter severe economic setbacks as more and more African Americans joined in the marching. Again, segregationists resorted to violence against the demonstrators, releasing trained police dogs and fire hoses on participants in the demonstration. This brought national attention from the news media which ultimately led to the success of the demonstrations and other civil rights movements in the South.

The general success of the Southern Christian Leadership Conference attracted the negative attention of some federal officials. The Federal Bureau of Investigation, under the direction of J. Edgar Hoover, started a program of surveillance of Rev. Martin Luther King Jr., and other civil rights leaders. They were considered political dissidents. Director Hoover especially targeted King and sought to discredit him and the SCLC as fronts for the Communist Party. King, like many others in the earlier twentieth century, had to dispel this charge in public opinion. Gradually, he was able to convince many public leaders of his innocence.

Rev. Martin Luther King Jr., the famous leader of the African American Revolution, was raised in the Baptist traditions of the South and later educated in liberal theology at Boston University where he received a doctorate in theology. During his academic career, King was highly influenced by the social ethics of Christianity and the philosophy of Mahatma Ghandhi of India. He was able to synthesize the thought of Ghandhi with the social gospel of Christianity. A third ingredient was later introduced into King's synthesis—the socio-political theories of Henry David Thoreau. From this synthesis emerged his commitment to passive resistance and nonviolent protest. With this academic background, Rev. King was able to meet the challenge of the African American Revolution, advocate for Americans of all races in support of equality, and focus on the Civil Rights Movement of the 1960's. To be sure, the new movement challenged his intellectual, moral, and psychological skills. At times, the pressures were almost overwhelming and caused King tremendous physical and emotional stress.

Several years after the Montgomery bus boycott, Rev. King left Montgomery and returned to Atlanta where he became associate pastor, along with his father, of Ebenezer Baptist Church. However, he realized that it was impossible for him to leave behind or drop out of the Civil Rights Movement. He had established a reputation of working for the elimination of segregation and discrimination in America. In Atlanta, King settled down as the executive head of the Southern Christian Leadership Conference. This position afforded him the opportunity to specialize in civil rights leadership.

One very potent characteristic of Rev. King's socio-political thought for the movement was an emphasis on the significance of history to the plight of African Americans. He once remarked:

> Whenever I am asked my opinion of the current state of the civil rights movement, I am forced to pause; it is not easy to describe a crisis so profound that it has caused the most powerful nation in the world to stagger in confusion and bewilderment. Today's problems are so acute because the tragic evasion and defaults of several centuries have accumulated to disaster proportions…. What might once have been a series of separate problems now merge into a social crisis of almost stupefying complexity.

> I am not sad that black Americans are rebelling; this was not only inevitable but eminently desirable. Without this magnificent ferment among Negroes, the old evasions and procrastination would have continued indefinitely. Black men have slammed the door shut on a past of deadening passivity. Except for the Reconstruction years, they have never in their long history on American soil, struggled with such creativity and courage for their freedom.[39]

Rev. Martin Luther King Jr. was able to identify the tremendous power of African Americans in the "magnificent ferment" and plan an appropriate strategy to unite that power for the Civil Rights Revolution. He realized that the race was now wide awake to the life-and-death struggles necessary for victory in the revolution. However, he was careful to manage the dynamics of the movement for the implementation of nonviolent resistance on their part. They were trained to meet the violence of the southern system with nonviolence. It was his synthesis of social ethics in Christianity with socio-political thoughts that provided the frame of reference for civil disobedience and nonviolent protest of an unjust system.

In 1963 Rev. Martin Luther King Jr. joined with other major African American leaders to launch a March on Washington for "Jobs and Freedom." This was the largest interracial assembly of American citizens ever executed in the history of the nation. Americans from all walks of life gathered in the capital city to ask President John F. Kennedy and the U.S. Congress for a fair employment practices commission and the power for the Justice Department to step into civil rights disputes on state and local levels. Already pending was a proposal by the president to enact a civil rights bill. On June 19, 1963, President John F. Kennedy asked Congress to enact the most comprehensive legislation on civil rights since Reconstruction. The March on Washington, with King's "I Have a Dream" speech, became the key motivating factor for the eventual passage of the Civil Rights Bill under the presidential leadership of President L. B. Johnson.

Participation in the March on Washington was the apex of Rev. Martin Luther King Jr.'s civil rights career. After the march, he transitioned much of his focus to the war in Vietnam. His interests extended far beyond the crisis in America to other global concerns with human right and justice. Rev. King was led to see the global need to merge civil rights with human rights. He relentlessly opposed the war in Vietnam and the right of the Vietnamese to self-rule without American interference. His view of peace extended beyond Vietnam to the liberation of third-world nations, criticizing the U.S. military for its deployment "to maintain social stability for our investments" not only in Vietnam but in "counter-revolutionary action" in Guatemala, Peru, and Columbia.[40] The global focus of Kings' thoughts and struggles inspired the world to take note, ultimately earning him the Nobel Peace Prize.

Towards the end of the century, the rise of white conservative political agendas slowly began to modify the Civil Rights Bill with special attacks on affirmative action programs. Most of the economic gains of African Americans were the direct results of affirmative action in the job market. African American church leaders throughout the country were alarmed at the rapid change in public opinion about affirmative action. Many opposed the appointment of Clarence Thomas to the Supreme Court because he seemed opposed to the economic policy regarding affirmative action. The Jewish community joined with African American leaders in their efforts to preserve the progress made under affirmative action. In 1990, several prominent African Americans and Jewish leaders met at the national office of the American Jewish Committee to announce their support of the Civil Rights Act of 1990, introduced by Senator Edward Kennedy, Representative Hawkins, and a group of bipartisan co-sponsors. The legislation was designed to overturn a series of restrictive decisions of the Supreme Court that would weaken job discrimination laws. Dr. Benjamin Hooks, executive director of the N.A.A.C.P., who chaired the meeting remarked: "It is sad and tragic in 1990 when freedom is breaking through all over the world—with Mandela freed in South Africa and the nations of Eastern Europe throwing off the yoke of communism—that we have a regressive, backward-looking, narrow majority of the Supreme Court that is trying to re-segregate and destroy freedom in this nation."[41] Dr. Hooks saw the need for the NA.A.C.P. to move in a new direction in the civil rights crisis. Likewise, the Unites States Catholic Conference voiced its support in remarks calling the Civil Rights Act of 1990 "vital legislation" which will "strengthen and enhance our nation's commitment to fight racism and other forms of unjust discrimination."[42] Unfortunately, President George Bush vetoed the Civil Rights Act. Again, African Americans attempted to reawaken liberal white support for civil rights in the United States. This became a lasting part of the new agenda of African American church leadership toward the turn of the century.

The Black Power Movement and a New Social Agenda

The death of Rev. Martin Luther King Jr. signaled the beginning of the end of the African American Social Revolution. A new style of leadership struggled to amass support to continue progress in civil rights in the nation. Some even lost faith in the socio-political philosophy of Rev. King. The rise of Black Power advocates completely overshadowed the nonviolent and passive resistance ideology. The Black Power Movement gained new momentum with the 1968 meeting of the National Committee of Negro Churchmen in St. Louis. One of its organizers, Rev. Benjamin F. Payton of Columbia, South Carolina, described the committee as "an effort to relate to the black power movement without adopting a philosophy of separation or black supremacy."[43] The committee consisted of representation from major African American denominations as well as the Black Catholic Caucus.

However, violence broke out in many major metropolitan areas in the North as well as the South. Young African Americans had built up hostilities over news reports of churches being bombed; vicious dogs let loose on women and children; and other vicious acts performed by hate groups and individuals. The riots resulted partly to avenge the assassination of Rev. Martin Luther King Jr., and more strongly to vent the internal emotions smothered by nonviolent demonstrations. Consequently, many African Americans looked with approbation on the riots, some crying "Burn, baby, burn."

The result of the race riots was the virtual breakdown of the cohesive community force that propelled the Civil Rights Revolution. A power struggle emerged between new aspirants for the leadership vacuum created by the death of Rev. Martin Luther King Jr. To make matters worse, some African Americans no longer saw the need for a new leader in the style of Rev. King in the civil rights struggle. They became apathetic because the "Great Society" had dawned upon the American experience. Furthermore, liberal whites gradually withdrew from the movement because they were reluctant to be linked with a violent movement in the nation. Hence, the close of the 1960's set the stage for a gradual decline in the Civil Rights Revolution.

A large number of the former leaders of the movement were later to be found in prominent positions within the system. They became convinced that the Great Society was finally ready to be inclusive of all Americans. A significant number of the race did experience upward mobility; however, it was reserved for a select group. The masses were still poor and estranged from the mainstream of American life. The following decades brought high unemployment among the race, street violence, drug addiction, and a gradual decline of the family and church. Ironically, young African Americans deserted the primary institution which had won their initial advancement in the economic and political life of the nation. Admittedly, some of these problems resulted from the general rise of secularism and the new morality in American culture. Hence, the race was caught up in the general spirit of the age.

Just before the close of the decade of the 1960"s, African American church leaders began to realize that a major threat to the gains of the Civil Rights Revolution had surfaced in the American experience. On the economic front Rev. Leon Sullivan, a native of Charleston, West Virginia, and pastor of the Zion Baptist Church of Philadelphia, began to urge the race more aggressively to involve itself in President Richard Nixon's "Black Capitalism" program. As early as 1969, Sullivan had addressed the annual meeting of the Allegheny Conference on Community Development utilizing for his subject, "People's Power." Even prior to the end of the Martin Luther King Jr. era, he had been active in utilizing boycotts from businesses and urging businesses to make more jobs available for the race. But after King's death, Rev. Sullivan pushed with new energy an economic plan for the race, largely reminiscent of the thoughts of Booker T. Washington. He had previously urged:

> Ultimately, I think, the black man will require a fair share of ownership in the American economy. And that will come in large part through his own efforts. Thus, he will gain self-respect through self-help.
>
> A man is not free until he owns something and has self-prided. This is not to say that riots and disruption may not be productive of gains in their own peculiar way. Many of my people are locked up in a box of deep prejudice and segregation and ignorance, and they can't get out. The only way they can let you know they are there is just to pound on the box and even knock down the sides.[44]

Rev. Sullivan continued to utilize his Opportunities Industrialization Centers, a global self-help training program, to advance economic potentials of black capitalism. He opened more than one hundred centers across the nation; trained many unskilled workers; and obtained employment for the newly trained workers in American industries. This emerged as one of the greatest economic movements in the United States and parts of Africa. He made a tremendous impact on America and Africa. Millions of dollars and other resources were utilized by this great leader's creative genius to improve the quality of life for a large number of people.

The tremendous success of Rev. Sullivan in the economic development realm gained for him the honor of becoming in March 1971 a member of the Board of Directors of General Motors (GM), thus becoming the first African American to serve on the board of a major corporation. In this prestigious position, he sought to apply economic pressure on the country. At that time, GM was the largest employer of native Africans in South Africa.

In 1990, Rev. Leon Sullivan took the bold step of trying to bring about closer relations between African Americans and Africans. He convened the first African-African American Summit in Abidjan, Cote d'Ivoire, in West Africa with the attendance of several African dignitaries and over twenty representatives of the African diplomatic corps. The following African American leaders attended the Summit: Dr. Benjamin Hooks, Rev. Joseph Lowery, Dr. Dorothy I. Height, the Honorable William Gray III, and Rev. Jesse Jackson. The summit was planned to focus on the creation of a pragmatic and positive strategy to help deal with "the development of Africa, to create closer cooperation between Africans and African Americans, and better American and African relationships for the support of Africa."[45]

In 1990, Rev. Sullivan had developed a comprehensive self-help plan for the socio-economic and political development for the continent of Africa, called the Sullivan Principles. Specifically, the Sullivan Principles effectively isolated South Africa by demanding all U.S. companies to stop doing business in the country and calling for the total embargo of South Africa. Like most African American church leaders, Rev. Sullivan was highly critical of apartheid and sought to fight the system with the same aggressive energy of the Civil Rights Revolution in the United States.

Beyond South Africa, he duplicated the Opportunities Industrializations Centers in several African countries, providing job skills training and educational opportunities for economically deprived Africans. This resulted from his organization International Foundation of Education and Self-Help, which was the driving force of the African program. The effective economic power of this organization was sealed in an agreement with the U.S. Agency for International Development in three African countries. In the signing ceremony, Rev. Sullivan announced that the new organization would coordinate the new AID grant in cooperation with the Africare agency, and with Nigeria, Niger, and Guinea. Hence, a form of African capitalism emerged in the poor regions of the continent. Rev. Sullivan remarked:

> This is the first agreement of this kind, with the Agency for International Development to allow the foundation to purchase debt owed to United States commercial banks in exchange for local currency which will be used to support human development programs in the three African countries.... With the multiple effect, the $2.1 million grant will more

than double the availability of funds for the purpose of supporting self-help programs in these countries.[46]

He estimated that the grant from AID would help the foundation reach over 40,000 grassroots people in the three participation countries.

Rev. Ralph David Abernathy, co-partner with Rev. Martin Luther King Jr., continued to be a major participant in the Civil Rights Movement after the death of Rev. King, becoming the new leader of the Southern Christian Leadership Conference. His voice was loudly heard during the 1970's, warning African Americans not to allow the gains of the revolution to be lost. He made many forceful attempts to remind the race to continue in the struggle because racism and discrimination still existed in the South, as well as in other parts of the nation. The first major task assumed by Rev. Abernathy was to complete King's dream for the racially mixed Poor People's Campaign in Washington, D.C., designed to be a major confrontation between the "haves" and the "have-nots." He decided to canvas federal officials for their support for certain demands of the Campaign, called an Economic Bill of Rights, to include guaranteed annual income, guaranteed jobs, and billions of dollars more for social and economic programs for the poor.

Initially, Rev. Abernathy encountered significant opposition from officials in Washington. Significantly, Rev. Walter Fauntroy, vice chairman of the D.C. City Council, opposed the Poor People's Campaign. His fear, along with other members of the council, was that such a tremendous move would cause violence in the city. African American newspapers criticized Rev. Fauntroy for his stand against the Poor People's Campaign, suggesting that he should endorse the drive and the United Front or resign the City Council and the SCLC. However, he received strong support from other members of the City Council and refused to resign. This represented early signs of disunion within the movement. Nevertheless, Rev. Abernathy and the SCLC were able to erect Resurrection City, a plywood and canvas encampment designed to accommodate about 3,000 marchers from different parts of the Nation intending to remain in Washington for an extended period of time. Resurrection City was located between the Lincoln Memorial and the Washington Monument. During the opening ceremony, Rev. Ralph David Abernathy assured: "This is a nonviolent movement…. We shall not destroy person or property," noting that violence "is impractical and immoral."[47]

Perhaps the strongest support for the campaign came from the Juneteenth rally which was a longtime traditional celebration among African Americans as June 19 is the anniversary of the freeing of slaves in Texas. The rally expected to bring about 50,000 people in support of the Poor People's Campaign. However, much of the support failed because Bayard Rustin, veteran civil rights leader who organized the 1963 March on Washington, resigned as coordinator of the Juneteenth rally after a dispute with Rev. Ralph David Abernathy over a statement of goals for the campaign.[48] This dispute impacted the attendance at the rally. But the march proceeded and impacted the socio-political climate in the United States.

In 1971, Rev. Abernathy's attention was directed toward the armed services of the United States. He criticized the draft as "the hand-maiden of militarism" and a new form of slavery for the poor and the black that must be abolished. He observed that "the very existence of an unlimited manpower pool has lured presidents into waging undeclared wars with draftees carrying most of the fight." In a statement read by an aide to the Senate Armed Services Commission, Rev. Abernathy called for an end of the Selective Service System and a shift to an all-volunteer army.[49]

In 1971, a serious struggle emerged in the Southern Christian Leadership Conference between Rev. Ralph David Abernathy and Rev. Jesse Jackson, who was director of SCLC's Operation Breadbasket with its headquarters in Chicago. After a day-long meeting, the SCLC's executive committee relieved Rev. Jackson of his position with Operation Breadbasket and placed him on leave status with pay, hoping to prevent a split in the Civil Rights Movement. However, Rev. Jesse Jackson decided to resign the position and organize a new movement, Operation PUSH. Clearly, this reflected the existence of significant power struggles within SCLC.

Notwithstanding internal differences within the Civil Rights Movement, Rev. Ralph David Abernathy and other African American church leaders made possible the election of President Jimmy Carter. They were highly impressed with Carter's stand on civil and human rights issues. Perhaps the linkage of the politics of human rights with civil rights was the most significant achievement of the post-Revolution decade.

As previously mentioned, the tensions between the SCLC and Rev. Jesse Jackson represented the beginning of a decline in the influence of the organization. Jackson's new Operation PUSH organization soon overshadowed the SCLC. Rev. Jackson, a young friend of Martin Luther King Jr., rivaled the leadership of the old regime of civil rights leaders in the popular sentiment of African Americans. The American press tended to focus more on Rev. Jesse Jackson than on Rev. Ralph David Abernathy. He appeared as a dynamic and energetic leader in the eyes of the public. Operation PUSH (People United to Save Humanity) became a powerful springboard for his jump into the position of almost undisputed leadership in the African American community. The new organization was designed to specialize in mass voter registration and education. It developed a twelve-point platform:

1. PUSH for a comprehensive economic plan for the development of black and poor people. This plan will include status as underdeveloped enclaves entitled to consideration by the World Bank and the International Monetary FUND;
2. PUSH for the revival of the labor movement to protect the organized workers and to organize unorganized workers;
3. PUSH for humane alternatives to the welfare system;
4. PUSH for a Survival Bill of Rights for all children up to the age of 18, guaranteeing their food, shelter, medical care and education;
5. PUSH for a Survival Bill of Rights for the aging, guaranteeing adequate food, clothing, shelter, medical care and meaningful programs;
6. PUSH for full political participation including automatic voter registration as a right for citizenship;
7. PUSH to elect to local, state and federal offices persons committed to humane economic and social programs;
8. PUSH for humane conditions in prisons and sound rehabilitation programs;
9. PUSH for a Bill of Rights for veterans whose needs are ignored;
10. PUSH for adequate health care for all people based upon need;
11. PUSH for quality education regardless of race, religion, or creed, and,
12. PUSH for economic and social relationship with nations of Africa in order to build African Afro-centric unity.[50]

These challenges of the platform of Operation PUSH soon caught the attention of the American socio-political power system. Rev. Jesse Jackson was well on the way to sustained national attention.

Initially, Rev. Jesse Jackson's PUSH facilitated agreements with major American companies to hire and do business with minorities. Also, PUSH's Project Excel inspired many young African Americans to stay in school and achieve academically. Subsequently, Rev. Jackson emerged as a symbol of upward mobility to a large number of the nation's African American youth.

In 1980, Rev. Jesse Jackson came to Baltimore to meet with the Ministerial Alliance to encourage the membership to participate in the Pilgrimage March for Jobs, on May 17, 1980. He was very critical of national politics, suggesting that neither African Americans nor the poor in general could be satisfied with the balanced budget controversy. The impact of a balanced budget meant for Rev. Jackson a drastic loss of jobs for minority Americans. Accordingly, he traveled throughout the nation to encourage African American church leaders to challenge the political agenda of national politics.

By the end of 1982, Rev. Jackson had experienced some significant success in his attempt to improve the economic life of minority Americans. Five of the six major companies targeted by PUSH since 1981 actually signed trade agreements totaling approximately $1.5 billion. These companies included the Southland Corporation, Coca-Cola Company, Kentucky Fried Chicken Corporation, Seven-Up Company, and Burger King Corporation. Only Anheuser-Busch refused to negotiate with PUSH. Consequently, Rev. Jackson launched a national movement designed to pressure the companies of Anheuser-Busch to back economic development programs of African Americans and other minorities.

On November 3, 1983, Rev. Jesse Jackson decided to expand his leadership for the civil rights struggles of African Americans. He wanted to position himself with more political power. He shocked the nation when he announced his candidacy for the presidency of the United States. Initially, the old civil rights regime did not take Rev. Jackson's candidacy under serious consideration. But slowly, he gained momentum when he organized the Rainbow Coalition behind the theme, "Run, Jesse, run." This theme was chanted even in some parts of Africa.

The presidential campaign caused Rev. Jackson to enter some new areas in the struggle for human rights and freedom. One of the high points of his quest for the presidency was his attempt, without the approval of President Ronald Reagan, to secure the release of captured U.S. Navy air-man Robert Goodman Jr. This event gave Rev. Jesse Jackson nationwide media attention. He planned a "moral appeal" to President Hafez Assad of Syria to release Lt. Goodman as "a humanitarian gesture." News of the success of this mission was heard around the world. African Americans and so-called third-world peoples were especially excited over his success. Hence, he was able to endear himself in the popular sentiment of the worldwide black community and consequently a few from the old civil rights regime began to side with him. By and large, Rev. Jackson's primary support came from the African American and Hispanic communities rather than the leadership of churches.

Slowly, Rev. Jesse Jackson broadened his focus to some very sensitive issues in American politics. He challenged the presence of U.S. Marines in Beirut, suggesting that the multinational force withdraw and be replaced by United Nations troops or other neutral forces. Like the experience of Rev. Martin Luther King Jr., Rev. Jackson's shift in focus to very sensitive political issues resulted in diminishing popularity and increased hostility toward him from other national leaders. The mass media also gave him some negative editorials.

As an ordained Baptist minister and associate pastor of the Fellowship Missionary Baptist Church in Chicago, Rev. Jesse Jackson viewed his quest for the presidency as a special mission. This sense of mission colored all of his political stances. He remarked: "I want to inspire hope in our young people and let them know that America can offer them more than unemployment, dope, jails, and the military."[51] Hence, he took strong and unrelenting positions against nuclear proliferation; criticized the United States' role in El Salvador and Nicaragua; and called for the recognition of Fidel Castro' administration in Cuba. Again, all of these issues were especially sensitive to the political leadership of the United States. His presidential candidacy reached its' highest point at the 1984 Democratic National Convention when he made a major address, the first of its kind by an African American, to the nation and the world community. During the address, Rev. Jackson was especially critical of the presidency of Ronald Regan. In terms of President Regan's domestic policies, he stated:

> "While Reaganism is largely subjective, supply side economics is more objective. Reaganism was used to impose Reaganomics. Reaganism is the perception. Reaganomics is the reality. We are fatter now, but less secure. Many who were once basking in the sun of Reaganism have now been burned to a crisp with Reaganomics. In 1980, many thought they saw a light at the end of the tunnel in Reaganism. But in 1984, we now know it was not sunshine, but a train coming this way."

Proclaiming the inclusiveness of the Rainbow Coalition and President Reagan's foreign policies, Rev. Jesse Jackson remarked in the address:

> The Rainbow Coalition includes Asian Americans, now being killed in our streets—scapegoats for the failures of corporate, industrial and economic policies. The Rainbow is making room for young Americans.

Twenty years ago, our young people were dying in a war for which they could not even vote....

Twenty years later, young America has the power to stop a war in Central America and the responsibility to vote in great numbers. Young America must be politically active in 1984. The choice is war or peace. We must make room for them....

The Regan administration's...plans and preparations to launch and win a limited nuclear war, and its commitment to "Star Wars" has left the world a much more unstable and dangerous place in which to live.

We are at a nuclear stand-off in Europe. We are mining the harbors of Nicaragua and attempting to covertly overthrow a legitimate government there.

Under this administration, we have been at war and lost the lives of American boys in Lebanon, Honduras and Grenada. Under this administration, one-third of America's children have come to believe that they will die in a nuclear war. The danger index for everyone is increasing—and it is frightening.[52]

Some political strategists thought that the new national exposure of Rev. Jackson and his success in increasing the numbers of African American voters would greatly affect the campaign of Walter Mondale. However, the social protest mode of his campaign did not gain many votes, and even most African American elected officials opposed him and supported Walter Mondale for president. In an interview with Lerone Bennett Jr., Rev. Jackson blamed his defeat on white media and "a crisis of confidence of black leaders" that cost him, he said, two key states at a critical stage of the campaign. The charismatic leader also discussed his post-convention plans and called for a new crusade "to expand and heal" every American institution.[53]

Rev. Jesse Jackson did not give up on his quest for the presidency of the United States, but ran again in 1988. This time his Rainbow Coalition adopted a more moderate policy. He supported the election of both David Dinkins as mayor of New York City, and Douglas Wilder as governor of Virginia. However, both politicians paid very little attention to Rev. Jesse Jackson's candidacy. Their support and that of most African Americans went to Governor Michael Dukakis of Massachusetts as the Democratic candidate for president. Realizing the probability of his defeat, Rev. Jackson hoped to win sufficient support for Dukakis to choose him for the vice presidency, but this too failed. With the Democratic party being divided between Dukakis, Jackson, and Gore, and the Republican party being united, Republican Vice President George Bush won the presidency of the United States of America. Consequently, Jackson moderated his political aspirations.

In the 1990's, Rev. Jesse Jackson joined other civil rights and human rights leaders in their opposition of apartheid in South Africa. He made his first trip to South Africa since 1979, calling apartheid a sin and warned the South African government that it faced "chaos" if it backtracked on reforms. At the Johannesburg airport, Rev. Jackson said the world waited with "bated breath" for the white minority government to free imprisoned black leader Nelson Mandela, also saying "We must encourage the president of this country to seize this moment to rise above political circumstances in the name of history and conscience and the value of a new South Africa," in response to reforms announced by President Frederick de Klerk.[54] He urged de Klerk to proceed with reform policies, and he continued a long and hot battle with the South African government until the release of Nelson Mandela was achieved.

Returning to the domestic front of the civil rights movement, Rev. Jesse Jackson stepped up his campaign for statehood for the District of Columbia. He urged President Bush to end his opposition to such statehood. Jackson, elected as "shadow senator" to lobby on behalf of statehood, said in a letter to President Bush that creating a state of "New Columbia" from non-federal property in Washington was "Morally right, rationally sound, economically feasible, and constitutionally permitted."[55] He was joined in this campaign by D.C. Mayor Sharon Pratt Dixon and other distinguished leaders, declaring May "Statehood Month."

In his eight-page letter written as president of the National Rainbow Coalition, Rev. Jackson focused on the costs to the District for supporting the federal government and the inequities he said were forced upon residents by current arrangements. He said that District residents pay more than $1 billion in federal taxes, well above the national average; and the taxes exceeded the payments of all but one state. The movement "Taxation without Representation" continued into the twenty-first century.

In May 1999, Rev. Jackson resumed his international political campaign by leading a delegation of religious leaders to Yugoslavia, hoping to secure the release of three captive American soldiers and provide President Slobodan Milosevic with "an honorable way" to resume peace negotiations. The delegation included rabbis, Muslim clerics, Serbian-American leaders, Rev. Joan Brown Campbell of the National Council of Churches, and other leaders. Without the approval of President Clinton, Rev. Jackson and the delegation negotiated the successful release of the three prisoners of war. Also in 1999, he brokered a cease-fire agreement between Sierra Leone's government and rebel forces who then resumed peace talks.

The beginning of the twenty-first century witnessed several areas of involvement on the part of Rev. Jesse Jackson on both domestic and international fronts. On the international front, he became critical of Condoleezza Rice's advice to President Bush on the wars on terrorism in Iraq and al-Qaeda operatives in Afghanistan; civil conflicts in various parts of Africa; and the violation of human rights internationally. He led Operation PUSH to form a relief fund for victims of a tsunami disaster. His vision for international human rights and freedom has continued to expand in this century. On the domestic front, he cautioned African Americans to be careful about their donations to various relief organizations for the Hurricane Katrina disasters in New Orleans and other Gulf States, fearing that some of the funds might not reach many of the desperate African Americans in the areas. He urged African Americans to form through their churches a new organization specifically for the relief of members of the race in affected areas. Moreover, he continued his struggles against the new trend to attack affirmative action programs in the United States, urging the passage of more secure civil rights legislation; called a summit of African American leaders to support health care programs for large numbers with such benefits; and, contacted Tavis Smiley, former PBS late-night talk show host, for the leaders to develop a list of priorities to be submitted to politicians seeking support from African American voters. To be sure, the struggles on the part of African American church leaders for a new priority agenda for the new century became central in the socio-political movement.

Another prominent African American church leader both before and during the twenty-first century was Rev. Alfred Sharpton. A Pentecostal minister of the Church of God in Christ and born in New York City, He became a social activist similar to Rev. Jesse Jackson. As a young man, he developed an organization known as the National Youth Movement. He tied the new movement to the Civil Rights Movement of the sixties by appropriating the language and tactics of the sixties. He, like Jackson, linked his name with the legacy of Rev. Martin Luther King Jr.; used protest demonstrations to gain media attention; and drew parallels between Brooklyn and the old South. He became critical of conservative African American leaders who seemed resistant to strategies of the Black Power Movement and identified the existing power structure of New York as acting contrary to the vital interests of the African American community. Rev. Al Sharpton developed close ties with officials of the *New York Amsterdam News* and other newspapers to advance his movement in the city. He joined Jesse Jackson's campaign for African American economic development linked with black capitalism. He was appointed by Rev. Jesse Jackson as New York City's director of Operation Breadbasket.

In 1990, Rev. Sharpton served as president of the National Black Farmers Harvest and Business Corporation and national director for the United We Stand Food Program of the SCLC. He related that the program was not aimed at African Americans only, suggesting: "We want to produce a marriage between Black and Hispanic farmers in the South to Black consumers in the North."[56] Also in 1990, he and Attorney Alton Maddox founded the United Front Movement to fight racism in the southern and eastern regions of the nation. He stood at the forefront of marches to protest the racial violence at Howard Beach, Queens, New York, which led to the death of Michael Griffith on December 20, 1986. He was arrested and remarked: "The only reason that I am freely submitting this morning is to make it clear that New York City is a town where people who protest nonviolently go to jail."[57] In the rape case of Tawana Brawley, Rev. Sharpton fully supported the claim of the victim, being outraged at the publication of a book by *New York Times* reporters entitled, *Outrage: The Story behind the Tawana Brawley Hoax*. He said that the book was a phony publication. He provided moral support to Don King who went to jail for manslaughter; but, King was convicted and went to jail on the charge. The notoriety of his socio-political involvements led him to a position of national attention.

In order to establish himself nationally, Rev. Al Sharpton decided to enter the American political arena. Initially, he ran for the United States Senate by entering the New York Democratic primary in 1992; and, later ran for President. His political ambition drew the negative attention of the F.B.I. which sought to discredit his leadership. However, he continued to be a major figure in the socio-political struggles of African Americans in the twenty-first century. Among some twentieth-century political issues confronted by Rev. Sharpton were the American response to the bombing of the World Trade Center; the race baiting attacks on Fernando Ferrer by Mark Green during the Democratic primary; the Persian Gulf War; the conflict in Lebanon; and the treatment of Muslims in Palestine by the Israeli government.

Other major African American church leaders of the twenty-first century include: Rev. Andrew Young, mayor of Atlanta and U.S. Ambassador to the United Nations; Joseph Lowery of the NAACP; Rev. Walter Fauntroy, member of the

D.C. City Council; Rev. Wyatt T. Walker, noteworthy civil rights advocate; Rev. Benjamin Chavis, former executive director of the Commission for Racial Justice of the United Church of Christ and later executive director of the NAACP; Rev. Floyd H. Flake, member of Congress; and many others who stand in the forefront of socio-political causes for African Americans and international human rights and freedom.

During the closing days of the first decade of the twenty-first century, Barack Obama became the first African American U.S. senator from Illinois. Subsequently, the African American church, Hispanic Americans, and young white Americans played key roles in supporting his bid for the presidency of the United States of America. His actual election to the presidency invigorated and electrified the vast majority of American citizens. It was the most radical change in the history of American politics. African Americans were given their greatest moment of pride in being American citizens. Internationally, President Obama was cheered as the leader of the free world. He advanced a foreign policy of negotiation rather than military confrontation, thus gaining tremendous respect from other world leaders. He made the bold decision to negotiate with the Cuban leadership and reestablish a diplomatic relationship with Cuba, opening doors that had been closed for more than fifty years. On the home front, President Obama was able to overcome the opposition of conservative Republicans in the passage of a comprehensive health care program, often called ObamaCare. Through it all, the African American church has remained strong in supporting the programs of America's first African American president.

(Endnotes)

[1] *Minutes of the National Baptist Convention*, U.S.A., Inc., 1922, 52.

[2] Ibid., 63-64.

[3] W.B. Reed, "The State of the Country," *New England Baptist Convention, Newport, RI* (Newport, RI., Mercury Publishing Company, 1919), 5-7.

[4] *Minutes of the National Baptist Convention*, U.S.A., Inc., 1938, 100.

[5] *Minutes of New England Baptist Convention*, 1942, 31.

[6] *Minutes of the National Baptist Convention*, U.S.A., Inc., 1941, 52.

[7] Ibid., 52.

8. *Minutes of the National Baptist Convention*, U.S.A., Inc., 1944, 267-68.
9. David M. Alpern, "The Black Revolution's Adam" *Newsweek*, Vol. 79, April 1972, 17.
10. *Congressional Record*, Vol. 109, Part 2, 88th Session, 1963, 20519.
11. Ibid., 20519.
12. Ibid.
13. Ibid., 20524.
14. Ibid., 20519.
15. Ibid., 20520.
16. Ibid., 20522.
17. Ibid., 20532.
18. Ibid., 20524.
19. Ibid., 20525.
20. Ibid., 20526.
21. Ibid.
22. Ibid., 205293
23. Ibid.
24. Richard Harwood, "Harlem's Rep. Adam Clayton Powell: There Is Nothing Ordinary about Him." *Washington Post*, April 6, 1972, 1.
25. *New Pittsburgh Courier*, December 8, 2004, A-6.
26. *The Baltimore Afro-American*, January 2, 1943, 19.
27. *The Baltimore Afro-American*, March 23, 1943, 6.
28. *The Baltimore Afro-American*, May 15, 1943, 21.
29. *The Afro-American*, Baltimore, Maryland, March 22, 1949, 8.
30. *The Baltimore Afro-American*, March 9, 1949, 115.
31. *The Baltimore Afro-American*, January 23, 1843, 1.
32. Ibid., 1.
33. *The Afro-American*, September 24, 1946, 14.
34. *The Journal and Guide*, January 2, 1943, 1.
35. *Chicago Defender*, January 13, 1990, 30.

36 Edward Guinan, *Peace and Nonviolence Basic Writings* (New York, NY: Paulist Press, 1973), 122-123.

37 *Chicago Defender*, January 13, 1990, 48.

38 *Chicago Defender*, March 10, 1990, 42.

39 *The Afro-American*, September 22, 1990, Section D.

40 *The Richmond Afro-American*, November 2, 1968, 21.

41 Martin Luther King, Jr., *Stride Toward Freedom: The Montgomery Bus Boycott* (New York, NY: Harper and Row, 1958), 95.

42 *The Grand Rapids Times*, February 1-7, 1991, 1.

43 *The Black Chronicle*, March 22, 1990, 7.

44 *Journal and Guide*, Norfolk, Virginia, May 18, 1968, 1.

45 *Richmond Afro-American*, June 22, 1968, 1-2.

46 *The Richmond Afro-American*, February 20, 1971, 12.

47 *National Edition Pittsburg Courier*, January 1, 1972, 1.

48 *Chocolate Singles*, Vol. 3, No. 5, March 1984, 12.

49 *Baltimore Afro-American*, July 21, 1984, 5.

50 *Ebony*, Special Issue, August 1984, A Johnson Publication, 166.

51 *Afro-Times*, February 10, 1990, 2.

52 *The Capital Spotlight*, May 23, 1991, 3.

53 *The Dallas Weekly*, May 10-16, 1990. 3.

54 *Afro Times*, July 21, 1990, 3.

Chapter 10

EMERGING TRENDS IN AFRICAN AMERICAN CHURCH LIFE

The late twentieth century and early twenty-first century ushered in some social, moral, and denominational innovations in the life of African American churches. Many of the challenges existed earlier, but they confronted the new leadership in ways forcing them to reexamine and reconsider many of the beliefs systems, practices, and structures of modern church life. Secularism, the post-Civil Rights Revolution, the new morality, ecumenism, family planning, gender consciousness, and the emergence of new structures for ministry relevant for church growth caused church leaders to respond in new ways to changes in public opinion regarding the nature and purpose of the Christian church. Increasingly, African American churches were compelled to respond to new thoughts and currents among the laity and liberal-minded pastors of churches. They were impacted by the currents of change in society and, accordingly, advocated change in church structure and life.

Currently, the most characteristic description of contemporary African American church life is transition. Everywhere in the life of churches, transition is the order of the day. All denominations are caught in the tidal wave of unprecedented changes. In order to understand these mighty forces, a critical analysis of the causative factors precipitating the transition in church life is necessary.

One very significant stimulus of transition in African American church life is the impact of the Civil Rights Revolution of the 1960's which precipitated a change in the old Southern ethos where the majority of the race still resides. The racist ethos that once permeated the region as well as the nation is rapidly changing under the pressure of new civil rights legislation, educational philosophy, and new styles of social intercourse between whites and African Americans, exposing the black race to the wave of thoughts and practices of the majority population. New opportunities for the race to participate in the evolution of the new ethos of southern life and the broader American experience are apparent throughout the region. Previously, segregation had shielded the race from many of currents of secular life experienced by southern whites in suburban areas. But the barriers are rapidly disappearing as more and more members of the race are experiencing upward mobility and relocation to the suburbs of many southern cities.

On the political scene, African Americans occupy some strategic positions in both local and national political life. Many small towns as well as large cities are now led by African Americans as mayors and city council members. Most of these politicians came to power through the adoption of liberal platform ideas of the Democratic party. The election of President Barack Obama and his liberalism, combined with the emerging previous liberalism of the Democratic party, has had a tremendous impact on the African American church community. Positively, liberalism has made possible the upward mobility of Christians and other members of the race; but negatively, this liberalism has eroded some of the fundamental Christian beliefs and practices of larger denominations such as Baptists and Methodists, and slowly impacts Holiness and Pentecostal groups. However, the Holiness and Pentecostal groups offer the greatest resistance to the new wave of change. For the most part, they still seek to preserve traditional biblical foundations for church life. But the wind of change still blows on all Americans.

The Ecumenical Movement and African American Churches

Traditionally, African American denominations operated within rather closed confines in their unique belief practices. They saw these practices or styles of church life as defining evidence of their biblical rights of existence and witness to the world. For them, their denomination defined the lifestyle closest to the New Testament church and informed moral and spiritual decisions as expressions of the Protestant Reformation and subsequent revivalism in America. But gradually, they came to the realization that other Christian denominations shared many similar beliefs and practices. Universal church union ideas precipitated partly by the World Council of Churches and the Second Vatican Council inspired the emergence of dialogue among many Christian denominations. They became less reluctant to accommodate the possibility or even the probability of the authenticity of other Christian belief systems. Protestant Reformation theology did not prevent Christian Americans from welcoming Pope John Paul II to the United States in 1987. The National Council of Churches called on "all Christians to seize this moment as an opportunity for renewed common witness before a divided and hurting world."[1] Affirming the Roman Catholic Church's point of view, Pope John Paul II told African American Catholics that their race must be given equal opportunity to share in American wealth and that the Church "can never remain silent in the face of injustice."[2] In his speech at the New Orleans Superdome, the Pope deplored that African Americans suffered a "disproportionate share of economic deprivation" and that he stood united with their efforts to "achieve full dignity."[3] Some twenty-seven church leaders were slated to meet with the Pope, including the Rt. Rev. Philip R.

Cousin, AME presiding prelate and president of the National Council of Churches; the Rt. Rev. J. Clinton Hoggard, presiding prelate of the AMEZ Church and in 1956 elected executive secretary of the World Methodist Council; and the Rt. Rev. Richard O. Bass Sr., presiding prelate of the CME Church. This spirit of openness on the part of African American church leaders was rather unprecedented toward the Roman Catholic Church. As previously mentioned, African American Christians were not as dogmatic about their denominationalism as other racial groups. Hence, the ecumenical spirit was more attractive to them even at an early period of denominational development.

African American Methodists have had a long history of strides toward union within Methodism. As early as 1864, the initial effort for union between the AME Church and the AME Zion Church came soon after emancipation at the twelfth session of the AME Zion Church General Conference in that year. Talks were finally dismissed after some points of disagreement were never resolved.[4] Denominational leadership was the only factor separating the two bodies. Each had copied, for the most part, the doctrines and structure of the white Methodist Episcopal Church. Subsequently, the major three Methodist denominations such as the African Methodist Episcopal Church, the African Methodist Episcopal Zion Church, and the Christian Methodist Episcopal Church have held repeated conferences and dialogues for the unity of Methodism. To be sure, the World Methodist Conference played a significant role in the more recent strides for union among African Methodists. The World Methodist Council, a federation of Methodist bodies that promotes ecumenical, evangelistic, educational, and historical emphasis among autonomous Methodist bodies in various different countries, was organized to facilitate fraternal cooperation. Named the World Methodist Council in 1951, it is the successor to the Ecumenical Methodist Conference, which was convened at ten-year intervals from 1881. The expansion of its influence into the African Methodist movements led to the revitalization of union strides among the denominations.

Serious dialogue for the union of African American Methodism extents back to the 1890's when the AME Church and the AME Zion Church entered dialogues at the episcopal level. In 1893, Bishop Alexander Waters made the following remark in his episcopal address:

> One of the most important questions which have ever been presented to Colored Methodism is the organic union of the A.M.E. Zion and A.M.E. Churches. This matter was submitted to the general conferences of the

two churches at their last sessions. By an almost unanimous vote they agreed to submit to the Annual-Quarterly Conferences and churches the following name as the title of the United Church: "African-Zion Methodist Episcopal Church." A Joint session of the Boards of Bishops of the two churches met in Washington, D.C., on July 1892, and prepared terms of union, etc., which will be submitted to this conference ere it adjourns. When an affirmative vote has been taken by a majority of all the annual and quarterly conferences, and two-thirds of all the churches, these two churches shall be declared one. A joint meeting of the Bishops will then be called to issue a call for a United General Conference, which shall consummate the Union. I am glad to inform you that every annual conference of both churches that has met since the joint meeting of the Boards has voted in favor of such a union. God grant that the good work may go on. I believe the Lord is in the movement, hence, I believe in its final consummation.[5]

The majority of both denominations voted in favor of the union. However, some strongly divisive opinions among certain AME bishops inhibited the plans for union. Following the failure for union, both denominations sought to blame the other for such an unfortunate failure.

With the failure of union between the AME Church and the AME Zion Church, the AME Zion Church soon looked toward the CME Church for a possible union within Methodism. In 1900, the AME Zion Church appointed its commission for union dialogue, followed by the C.M.E. Church's appointment of its commission in 1902. The joint commissions of the two denominations met in Israel CME Church, Washington, D.C., October 7, 1902, and drew up Articles of Agreement to the General Conference of 1904.[6] Subsequently, the idea of a Tri-Federation Council of Bishops emerged among the African Methodist denominations in 1908. This Tri-Federation Council of Bishops met in the Big Zion AME Zion Church, Mobile, Alabama, and issued a strong declaration favoring organic union. After a series of negotiations, the Tri-Federation met with another failure for organic union among the Methodist denominations.

Interest within African American Methodism for organic union did not vanish with the early failures. By the early 1980's, the AME Zion and the CME Church revisited the idea of union and participated in serious dialogue for the union of the two denominations. They set a target date of 1985 for effectuating the union. The

Steering Committee of the Joint Commission on Union met in Atlanta, Georgia, at the West Side Community CME Church, with Bishop Clinton R. Coleman of the AME Zion Church serving as chairman. The commission reviewed earlier reports and prepared recommendations for a later Joint Commission of the denominations in Charlotte, North Carolina, in 1985. The bishops issued the following statement in a letter:

> Dear Members of the Joint Commission:
>
> You have been given the task of working on a document for the Union of the AMEZ Church and the CME Church for approval and transmission to the members for study and comment.
>
> We are convinced that the depth and characteristics of the new denomination to be formed out of the existing ones may be fully seen and understood as each one works for the church to become visibly one.
>
> A united church is God's gift to our broken humanity and marks his actions among us.
>
> We expect your attendance in our important Charlotte meeting and your best efforts in doing the work for our progress towards church union.
>
> Sincerely,
> Your Chairpersons,
> Bishop William M. Smith
> Bishop Chester A. Kirkendoll[7]

A timetable for union was established by the steering committee which met in Memphis, Tennessee, which outlined the process for union involving three phases designated as the "Principles of Union." The denominations appointed a standing subcommittee to address the Principles of Union including: Basic Affirmations; Reasons for Union; The Faith of the United Church; The Structure of the United Church; The Ministry of the United Church; Judicial Administration; General Church Administration; and Educational Institutions.[8]

The Charlotte, North Carolina meeting set the stage for continual dialogue between the two denominations. Concomitantly, the major African Methodists bodies organized a pan-Methodist commission in 1985. The commission, authorized by the general conferences of all four denominations, discussed other areas of possible cooperation toward union including curriculum production, marketing, leadership training, college recruitment, mission outreach, evangelism, social witness, and educational events focusing on the origins of Methodism.[9] Beyond specifically denominational issues, the commission issued a political statement on apartheid in South Africa, affirming:

> We join with Christians and with people of good will everywhere. People in all of the religions of the world condemn the diabolical system of apartheid which is rooted in hatred and violence, and which if left unchallenged, can lead to international violence involving the major nations of the world....
>
> We further appeal to the South African government to free all of the political prisoners, including Black leaders such as Nelson Mandela and Allen Boesak. Such leaders must be involved in the development of a new inclusive government if that government is to be representative of the total population.
>
> In recent weeks, many of the nations of the world have expressed indignation over the outrage of apartheid in South Africa through economic sanctions. We appeal to all nations to join those which have already acted to deplore this blight on humanity and to heal this malignant disease of blatant racism in South Africa.
>
> Finally, we appeal to the administration of our own government to take more seriously the role of this nation as the leader of the free world. Black people, and all other freedom-loving people in this nation, were disappointed over the anemic gestures made by the president to frustrate, sabotage, and pre-empt the actions of the United States Senate in its effort to press strong sanctions against South Africa. We the African Methodist Episcopal Zion Church and the Christian Methodist Episcopal Church, both separately and corporately, express our indignation with both apartheid in South Africa and President Reagan's efforts through the undermining of constructive engagement to support it.
>
> We further call on President Reagan as the leader of the free world to use his moral and political influence to end apartheid in South Africa and help to create a more just political system.[10]

In 1991, an even bolder step toward union within Methodism took place with dialogue between the African American Methodist denominations and the United Methodist Church during a meeting at St. Simons Island, Georgia. The denominations took steps to tighten their common ties of heritage by authorizing a joint commission to study possible union. The denominational leaders approved a resolution requesting each body of bishops to "petition their respective General Conferences to authorize a study commission for the purpose of exploring possible merger. Again, the commissions failed to receive popular support from the denominations. Nevertheless, the African Methodist Episcopal Church General Conference did approve a proposal forming a covenant with the Consultation on Church Union. By an overwhelming majority, delegates to the Louisville, Kentucky, conference approved a resolution which recognized the long history of the African Methodist Episcopal Church's participation in the COCU and embraced the covenanting proposal.[11]

The twenty-four-member Commission on Pan-Methodist Cooperation comprised of representatives from the African Methodist Episcopal denominations and the United Methodist Church met in Atlanta at the Interdenominational Theological Center to deal with organizational issues for the next four years. The initial conference was established to "discern collegiality and collectiveness" on issues that make a difference in the lives of the members of the four Methodist denominations, as stated by the outgoing president of United Methodist Bishop Felton E. May of Washington, D.C. Sharing the pan-Methodist vision for union, retired United Methodist Bishop F. Herbert of Riverdale, New York, said, "Union may not be possible in our lifetime, but the longest journey must begin with one step."[12] Nevertheless, the ecumenical offer of the United Methodist Church was viewed by both optimism and skepticism in 1998 by the bishops of the African Methodist Episcopal denominations. The main issue that emerged was the historic racism of the United Methodist Church. Realizing the divisive nature of this issue, the United Methodist Commission on Christian Unity and Interreligious Concerns authorized a task force to work on an "act of repentance and reconciliation" for the denomination "to remember or learn the story about how the historic Black churches were founded."[13]

The black caucus of the United Methodist Church had been working since 1968 to address the issue of racism in the church. It was organized as a forum for African American Methodists who remained in the denomination to define issues and develop strategies for change within the United Methodist Church. Furthermore, the caucus sought to empower African American Methodists for effective witness and service; involve then in the struggle for economic justice; and to expose racism at all levels of the denomination, its agencies, and related institutions. The caucus has done a tremendous job in countering racism and promoting the upward mobility of the race within the denomination. Nevertheless, the Commission on Unity agreed that the denominations were not ready for organic union.

Unlike the African Methodist denominations, the congregational polity of African American Baptist local churches made strides toward church union more difficult. However, there has been a long history of dialogue between the National Baptist Convention, U.S.A, Inc., the National Baptist Convention of America, and the Lott Carey Baptist Foreign Missions Convention. Dialogue has centered on the issues of cooperative programs for missions, evangelism, education, and racial progress. The emerging prominence of the denominations in civil rights issues resulted in an openness to others religious bodies for participation in socio-political struggles worldwide. This factor resulted in the gradual rise of liberalism among many of the leaders of the denominations and their wiliness to cooperate with people of divergent religious ideologies.

The membership and leaders of the African American Baptist denominations in the Baptist World Alliance did encourage some dialogue for union or at least cooperation between the denominations, and the subsequent organization of the Progressive National Baptist Convention. For many years, Rev. J.H. Jackson represented the politically conservative wing within the African American Baptist movement. However, he did express early moderate interest in the ecumenical movement. While serving as secretary of the Foreign Mission Board of the National Baptist Convention, U.S.A., Inc., Rev. Jackson recognized that the scope of the convention needed to be more universal; hence, in 1937 he attended as an observant the Life and Work Movement at Oxford University and the Faith and Order Movement at Edinburgh University, which later merged to form the World Council of Churches in 1948. Prior to 1937, the convention was represented only in the Baptist World Alliance. He reminisced: "Those meetings in England inspired me toward re-thinking the concept of 'the-many-but-the-one' concept of Christianity."[14] He noted that the convention had been represented at every assembly of the World Council of Churches since its inception.

To be sure, Rev. J.H. Jackson was highly influenced by the spirit of the ecumenical movement as other Christians from divided Christianity expressed their similar interest. In 1961, he went so far as to visit the Roman Catholic Pope, relating: "One of the most rewarding experiences in the realm of the ecumenical movement was, for me, my visit with Pope John XXIII in December of 1961. In a forty-five-minute audience with the pope in Vatican City, we shared our mutual concern for the peace of the world and for a hope of closer religious fellowship among all the people of God."[15] During the audience with the pope, Rev. Jackson inquired about the proposed Second Vatican Council regarding its significance for Christian unity. He desired to obtain the Pope's point of view regarding the prospect for greater cooperation between Protestants and Roman Catholics. Subsequently, Rev. Jackson attended as an observant the meeting of the Second Vatican Council as the representative of the National Baptist Convention, U.S.A. Inc.

More liberal views emerged through the leadership of the Southern Christian Leadership Conference and the Progressive National Baptist Convention. Moreover, cooperation with the American Baptist Churches, U.S.A., contributed to the emergence of liberalism among African American Baptists and the emergence of new trends such as women in ministry, openness to the Million Man March under the leadership of Louis Farrakhan, gay rights dialogue, and the general acceptance of the platform issues of the National Democratic Party. Many African American Baptist churches held dual membership in the American Baptist Churches, U.S.A., and the Progressive National Baptist Convention, Inc. In the South, some African American Baptist churches also held dual membership with the Southern Baptist Convention and one of the national African American Baptist conventions. Often, this dual membership with biracial groups was partly for economic reasons, like retirement programs which were lacking in their conventions. The practice of dual membership was not limited to liberal wings of Baptist churches, for conservatives too looked to the biracial denominations for better educational and economic benefits. Even some churches like the First Baptist Church of Baltimore held membership in the American Baptist Churches, U.S.A., the National Baptist Convention, U.S.A., Inc., and the Lott Carey Baptist Foreign Mission Convention. In reality, most of the churches in the Lott Carey Baptist Foreign Mission Convention held membership in the larger Baptist conventions. For the most part, African American church leaders did not view the Lott Carey Baptist Foreign Mission Convention as an independent denomination because it specialized in foreign missions. To be sure, there were no radical lines of separation between African American Baptist denominations except leadership considerations.

Signs of cooperation between the National Baptist Convention, U.S.A., Inc., and the National Baptist Convention of America were seen in 1998 when the two bodies came together for a joint worship program in Dallas, Texas. Rev. T.J. Jemison, president of the National Baptist Convention, U.S.A., Inc., remarked at the joint session: "President E. Edward Jones of the National Baptist Convention of America and I enjoy a good working relationship.... We have been able to lead our conventions to work together on a number of projects, and we have each preached sermons at each other's conventions."[16] However, President Jemison added that the joint session did not indicate a possible merger of the two bodies despite rumors and speculations about such a merger. Nevertheless, in 2005 four of the historic African American denominations met in a joint session in Nashville, Tennessee. This was the first time the National Baptist Convention, U.S.A., Inc., the National Baptist Convention of American, the Progressive National Baptist Convention, and the National Missionary Baptist Convention of America agreed to meet in a joint session to "forge a united voice to address social and political issues affecting all Blacks."[17] Rev. William J. Shaw, president of the National Baptist Convention, U.S.A., Inc., stated: "There has to be more focused effort to include minorities in the mainstream of this nation's life in terms of ownership of economic resources, inclusion in the political structure, educational commitment, and changing the practices that make for the incarceration of so many people of color."[18]

The ecumenical spirit was not limited to African American Methodist and Baptist denominations, but it has more effectively penetrated biracial denominations with minority memberships of African Americans. Large numbers of African Americans opted to remain within predominately white denominations. Although in many instances they had separate churches, they still held membership in the majority denominations in the American experience. Most of such denominations were ecumenically oriented. Through the international influence of ecumenical bodies various American Protestant denominations, the Roman Catholic Church, and even the Greek Orthodox Church have been responsive to the spirit of ecumenism. Vatican II and the worldwide growth of the Roman Catholic Church greatly accelerated the worldwide ecumenical movement. In 1964, Vatican II promulgated a document on the Eastern Catholics churches which solemnly declared that "the churches of the east like those of the west have the right and duty to govern themselves according to their own special disciplines," affirming the equality of the eastern and western traditions of Christianity.[19]

Prior to Vatican II, the Eastern Orthodox Church had demonstrated an interest in ecumenism. In 1919, the denomination under the leadership of Patriarch Germanos of Constantinople, called for all Christian churches to form a "league of churches." They "became the first church to call for a permanent organ of fellowship and cooperation between the churches."[20] The Roman Catholic Church responded under the leadership of Pope Benedict XV by creating the Congregation for the Oriental Churches in May 1917, and the Pontifical Oriental Institute in Rome. Hence, the ecumenical spirit between the two churches predated Vatican II.

During the Second Vatican Council, Pope John XXIII appointed Augustin Cardinal Bea, an ecumenical-minded cardinal and biblical scholar, to serve as president of the new Secretariat for Promoting Christian Unity. In his announcement of the council, the pope spoke of an "ecumenical council" and explained that it should be considered as an invitation to all Christians who were separated from the Apostolic See to seek even more eagerly than before that unity for which Christ prayed on the eve of his suffering. However, he insisted that the council would serve the purpose of Christian unity only indirectly, insofar as it would offer a precious picture of the truth, unity, and love which reigned in the Catholic Church, and thus spur on all Christians who are separated from the See of Peter to strive even more than heretofore for the unity which Christ intended his church to have.[21] The founding of the Secretariat for Promoting Christian Unity was warmly welcomed by non-Catholic opinion, which included the executive committee of the World Council of Churches.

Augustin Cardinal Bea, president of the Secretariat for Promoting Christian Unity, offered the following summary of the nature of the ecumenical work of the Second Vatican Council:

> The official document by which the Council was convoked appeared on Christmas 1961. It contained two points of interest for the ecumenical movement. Firstly, it explicitly stated that it was within the competence of the Council to review the complex of doctrinal and practical questions which had a bearing on Church unity. Among these were numbered the language of the litany, mixed marriages, religious freedom, the nature of the Church, and other similar questions.
>
> Secondly, the document entrusted to the Secretariat for Unity the task of establishing relations also with the non-Catholic churches of the East. As a consequence, our efforts to bring non-Catholic observers to the Council took on greater dimensions.[22]

The majority of the observers, including Rev. J. H. Jackson, publicly declared that the audience with the pope while attending the Council made a deep impression on them because of the pope's simplicity and kindness. Many of the observers were also able to establish cordial relationships with bishops in the council. This was facilitated by the secretariat in the weekly private sessions for observers at the council. Its new approach to non-Catholic churches, not as adversaries but as separated brethren seeking unity in Christ, has resulted in a broad range of active consultations, joint sponsorship of programs and conferences, joint publishing ventures, and collaboration in service programs. A Joint Working Group has been established with the World Council of Churches to consider subjects of mutual concern in the quest for unity, such as the Joint Theological Commission on Catholicity and Apostolicity, the Pontifical Council on the Laity, and the Pontifical Commission on Justice and Peace, have been set up to channel joint action in various areas.

The American Roman Catholic churches responded to the Second Vatican Council in varied ways. Religious liberalism had already become a trend within the American churches. Pope John Paul II found it necessary to place some restraints on American bishops by establishing some new rules requiring bishops' conferences to reach unanimous agreement issuing declarations on issues of doctrine. If the bishops could not reach such unified agreement, they must get approval from the Vatican, "which will not give it if the majority requesting it is not substantial."[23] These conferences in America evolved from the Second Vatican Council reforms.

Pope John Paul II was very much aware of moves for innovations stemming from large countries like the United States and Brazil where Roman Catholic leaders have been the most outspoken on some questions of church policy. Liberation Theology and secularism were progressively influencing social and political changes in the Americas. Liberation Theology invigorated liberation movements. The pope was especially concerned about the pressure from American bishops to address the issues of homosexuality, abortion rights, family planning, and the ordination of women in the ministry. He issued a document specifically affirming that there could be no debate about the church's opposition to ordaining women. He emphasized that actions by national bishops' conferences must be in line with the Vatican when dealing with "new questions posed by the accelerated social and cultural changes characteristic of present times."[24] In spite of the duplicity of the church in international homosexual scandals and the virtual acceptance of abortion and family planning issues, the pope affirmed the traditional positions or official policy of the Vatican. He was especially concerned about the liberal inclinations of the American church.

With the increase of African American migration to strong centers of Roman Catholicism, African Americans increasingly joined the Roman Catholic Church in the United States. In 2005, it was estimated that the African American population was four percent of the 61 million Catholics in the United States, or about 2.5 million African Americans. The National Black Catholic Website projects that Catholics of African descent make up more than 200 million, or about twenty percent of the Catholics worldwide.[25] Some who joined the church came from Protestant backgrounds and brought with them these tendencies to their new church. Specifically, they urged radical changes in worship, such as the introduction of gospel music, revived interest in Pentecostal experiences, and Afrocentric cultural expressions. In 1987, a delegation of African American Roman Catholics from the United States told the worldwide Synod of Bishops that the church should grant more decision-making positions to "often ignored" Black laypeople.[26] The rationale was that since the laity contributed to the finances of the church, they should have a greater voice. Also, the delegation called the Women for Faith and Family presented a document to Cardinal Eduard Gagnon, president of the Vatican's Pontifical Council for the Family, and asked that he turn it over to Pope John Paul II. The group said the document, called "Affirmation for Catholic Women," expresses backing for traditional church teaching on reproduction, marriage, the family, and the role of men and woman in church and society.[27] All in all, Cyprian Davis summarized the evolving significance of African American Roman Catholics:

> Black Catholics were part of the gradual transformation of both the American Catholic Church and African American society. They also emerged from mission status as recipients and dependents to a community that not only began to find its voice, as Thomas Wyatt Turner had hoped, but also began to make itself heard and heeded in the social and cultural revolution following the Second World War. Blacks also increased in numbers; they too made their presence recognized in the monolithic structures of American Catholicism, even when their demands generated cracks and fissures in the solid front of what some labeled as a "white, Euro-American church." In fact, the black Catholic community, more than any other ethnic group, brought about the Catholicization that made the American church "Catholic" in the full historical meaning of that word.[28]

Father George Stallings, a controversial African American priest, posed a tremendous challenge to the authority of the Vatican with the introduction of uncompromising Afrocentric tendencies in church life. He emerged as one of the most radical and liberal-minded priests in the United States. He had been raised as a Roman Catholic and decided to go into the priesthood while still a teenager. After completing his education in Rome, Stallings was ordained in 1974. His first appointment as a priest was St. Teresa of Avila Roman Catholic Church, an African American parish in the archdiocese of Washington, D.C. Concomitant to his parish ministries, he became a lecturer at St. Mary's Seminary in Emmitsburg, Maryland, and at the Washington Theological Union. For a short period, Father Stallings realized a successful career in the Roman Catholic Church as an educator and priest. He enjoyed a relationship with the National Black Catholic Clergy Caucus which was headquartered in Washington, D.C.

The first real challenge to Father Stallings' career came in the form of an alleged incident of sexual impropriety. This brought some tremendous criticism of his ministry. Soon differences developed between Father Stallings and his superior Archbishop James Hickey, and the Roman Catholic Church in general. He accused the archbishop and the Roman Catholic Church of racism. Consequently, he was removed from his parish to a new assignment as a special evangelist for the archdiocese for work within the African American community. This move simply caused more tension between Father Stallings and the Roman Catholic Church.

The mutual tension between Father Stallings and the Roman Catholic Church resulted in Stallings' decision to organize an independent church movement. He organized his own Imani Temple African American Catholic Congregation in June 1989 at Howard University. In May 1990, Father Stallings was installed as the first bishop of his African American Catholic congregation. The episcopal ordination of Father Stallings was performed by The Most Rev. Richard W. Bridges, archbishop of the Independent Old African Churches of California. Initially, the two bishops discussed the possibility of merging the two churches. After the ordination, Bishop Stallings indicated that his mission would be to establish new churches throughout the United States. By 1998, AACC had churches in Louisiana and even on the African continent, including Nigeria and Ghana. Also, he affirmed: "We have not split at all from the traditional Church. There is only one church; there are many approaches, many avenues to be a part of the one Church."[29] Bishop Stallings organized other churches, which served as examples of Afrocentricity in the United States.

In many ways unlike the Roman Catholic Church, the major Lutheran denominational churches—such as the Lutheran Church of America founded in 1962, the American Lutheran Church founded in 1960, and the Lutheran Church-Missouri Synod, each founded through mergers with smaller bodies—sought unity within Lutheranism and with the Episcopal Church. The Lutheran Church of America represents the most ecumenical of the Lutheran denomination, holding membership in the World Council of Churches, the National Council of Churches, and the Lutheran World Federation. Also, the American Lutheran Church holds membership in the World Council of Churches and the Lutheran World Federation. The three denominations organized the Lutheran Council in the United States to serve as a common agency for them to cooperate in various endeavors in social ministries that did not compromise their respective theological positions.

In 1991, the Evangelical Lutheran Church in America and leading officials of the Episcopal Church endorsed proposals aimed at establishing full communion between the two denominations. Under the Proposed Concordat of Agreement, ordained clergy of the denominations would be able to serve congregations of the other denomination, and church members would be able to receive communion in churches of either body. The concordat was released by Presiding Bishop Edmond Browning of the Episcopal Church and Presiding Bishop Herbert Chilstrom of the Evangelical Lutheran Church of America. Subsequently, the two denominations convened a Christian Unity workshop to study the proposal for the denominations to enter full communion, which would allow them to share the sacraments among their members and "make provisions for an orderly exchange of ordained ministers." Significantly, African Americans hold membership in the Episcopal Church and the Lutheran denominations.

The Protestant Episcopal Church, which derived its heritage from the Church of England, has sought cooperation with the twenty self-governing national or regional churches within the Anglican Communion, and more recently with the Evangelical Lutheran Church in America. As with all the churches of the Anglican Communion, the Protestant Episcopal Church has maintained the ancient Catholic sacraments, creeds, and order of the church. The unity among these diverse churches is rooted in their common ancestry; their full communion with the Archbishop of Canterbury and with one another; their prayer books, which establish the body of common faith; and their increasing common action in many relationships.[30] The concordat with the Evangelical Lutheran Church represents its ecumenical outreach beyond the churches of the Anglican Communion.

In the worldwide arena of ecumenism, the Protestant Episcopal Church, like several other American denominations, has adopted policies inconsistent with the Roman Catholic Church and the Orthodox Church. The role of women in the church has been a major block to cooperation with the two other worldwide denominations. The Episcopal Church, the United Methodist Church, Lutheran churches, some Presbyterian churches, and other American denominations have adopted policies regarding women in ministry which make church cooperation with the Roman Catholic Church and the Orthodox Church impractical. The decision of the Episcopal Diocese of Massachusetts to elevate the Rev. Barbara Harris to be a bishop of the Church greatly frustrated the ecumenical spirit of the two worldwide denominations. The Vatican responded by issuing a 119-page letter from Pope John II once again affirming the Roman Catholic Church's opposition to women in the priesthood. Both the Roman Catholic Church and the Orthodox Church have remained adamantly opposed to women's ordination and since 1976, when the Episcopal Church voted to permit the ordination of women to the priesthood, have warned the issue threatens the ecumenical quest for church unity.

The United Church of Christ was formed in 1957 through the union of the General Council of Congregational Christian Churches and the Evangelical and Reformed Churches. The United Church of Christ has significance in the ecumenical movement in that it combines two forms of polity: congregationalism and presbyterianism. Also, it has a large membership of African American churches. The denomination holds membership in the National Council of Churches, the World Council of Churches, the International Congregational Council, and the World Alliance of Reformed Churches.

One of the most prominent and controversial members was Rev. Benjamin Chavis, who was ordained in North Carolina in 1980, and later assumed a national position within the United Church of Christ to end domestic and international racism. In 1993, he was hired to lead the NAACP but later fired, disclosing that he allocated a large number of the organization's funds to quiet sexual harassment allegations. While in leadership of the NAACP, Rev. Chavis became a strong advocate of establishing a working relationship between African American churches and the Nation of Islam. In 1996, he organized the National African-American Leadership Summit, unveiling an agenda inclusive of a broad base "politically blind to party affiliation" for leadership in the civil rights cause. He said: "Our goal is to transform the political system by practicing the principle of self-determination and by affirming a God-centered, spirit-filled, mass movement for empowerment."[31]

This philosophy of broad-based leadership for the African American community made it easy for Rev. Benjamin Chavis to transition and to support movements beyond the Christian church. His ecumenical scope transcended any Christian denominational limitation to include any religious group involved in the cause of racial empowerment. Allying himself more closely with Louis Farrakhan, Rev. Chavis helped the Nation of Islam's leader to organize the Million Man March in

1995. This was not completely unique for Christian ministers, for men like Calvin Butts, George A. Stallings, Johnny Youngblood, Jessie Jackson, and Al Sharpton became supportive of the Million Man March, which became a stimulant for ecumenism. However, the real crisis in the Christian career of Rev. Chavis evolved when he decided to join the Nation of Islam and assume the name, Benjamin Chavis Muhammad. Subsequently, the North Carolina commission of the United Church of Christ voted to recommend his termination as a minister. He argued his case before the Church and Ministry Commission of the UCC's Eastern North Carolina Association, urging, "The God who called me to the Christian ministry is the same God who called me to the ministry of Islam. There is only one God."[32] Initially, the United Church of Christ temporarily suspended Chavis from peaching, administering the sacraments, or performing other pastoral duties for the 1.5 million-member denomination. In March 1997, Benjamin Chavis Muhammad promised to build a bridge between Christians and Muslims to confront African Americans' socio-political issues. To be sure, much of the ecumenical spirit of the African American church was related to cooperation in the causes of social justice, human rights, and economic progress.

The Affirmative Action Debate

The passage of the Civil Rights Acts was the most defining moment in the socio-political history of progress for African Americans in the twentieth century. It opened doors that had been tightly closed from the initial appearance of the race in America in 1619. Heretofore, jobs and political offices once reserved for white Americans were opened to African Americans who once experienced only second-class citizenship. Economic and political progress for large numbers of the race appeared in direct response to the affirmative action legislation. A desegregated "Great Society" was the long-range goal of the legislation. In his "Great Society" speech of 1964, President Lyndon B. Johnson declared: "The Great Society rests on abundance and liberty for all. It demands an end to poverty and racial injustice, to which we are totally committed in our time."[33] Sar A. Levitan and Robert Taggart evaluated the sociopolitical significance of the Great Society in an article entitled, "In Defense of the Great Society," suggesting:

> President Johnson's vision of a Great Society, contrasting so markedly with the phlegmatic ideology of the preceding decade, stirred the nation. Under the banner of the Great Society, there was a dramatic acceleration of governmental efforts to insure the well-being of all citizens, to equalize opportunities for minorities and the disadvantaged, to eliminate, or

at least mitigate, the social, economic, and legal foundation of inequality and deprivation. Congress moved ahead on a vast range of long-debated social welfare measures and pushed on into uncharted seas.... The essence of the Great Society was increased federal intervention to assist the disadvantaged and disenfranchised by providing needed goods, services, and income and by changing the socioeconomic system.[34]

Not only did the Great Society bring unprecedented changes to the plight of African Americans in general, but it also greatly enriched the dynamism and economic advancement of the African American church. New economic resources for church growth and development were created, and a new generation of highly skilled clergymen and laity was created. This resulted from the varied approaches to affirmative action. In terms of economic growth, the legislation required businesses to hire a racially mixed and balanced workforce of members of minority groups which led to the expansion of the African American middle class. This economic growth greatly increased the economic power of the churches. In terms of public and private school education, affirmative action resulted in the adoption of admission polices reflecting integration, diversity, and multiculturalism. This opened new doors for higher education for African American clergy and laity. Major theological schools adopted admission policies on racial inclusiveness. Hence, African American churches experienced an increase of professionally trained clergy leadership. Such policies in employment and education were labeled "quotas."

The affirmative action legislation was generally deemed of paramount importance by many African Americans for their progress in voting rights, employment, political advancement, and quality education. Racial progress was viewed as dependent upon the continuation of the policy throughout the nation. Hence, racial leadership carefully guarded against potential threat to affirmative action. They were carefully critical of conservative African American Republicans. The appointment of Justice Clarence Thomas to the U.S. Supreme Court was opposed by many clergy and lay African Americans. African American newspapers were also generally opposed to his nomination. They saw the potential threat to affirmative action stemming from an alignment of Justice Thomas with other conservative justices to establish a majority voting bloc within the Supreme Court. As predicted, Justice Thomas, along with Sandra Day O'Connor, William Rehnquist, Antonin Scalia, and Anthony Kennedy delivered a decisive blow to affirmative action when they ruled that it was unconstitutional to "set aside" contracts for minorities, or for that matter do anything else to redress past wrongs of a society, unless that minority can pinpoint and prove that anyone in that society or the society itself has wronged that minority individual, no matter the obvious result or the appearances.[35] The decision was especially damaging to the minority group's progress in education. Seemingly, the 5-to-4 ruling of the Supreme Court damaged the more than fifty years of school desegregation advances when it delivered a blow to public school districts in Louisville, Kentucky, and Seattle, Washington, declaring their racial integration programs unconstitutional. However, the Supreme Court did rule that race may sometimes be used as one component of schools' diversity plans.[36] This opened an avalanche of claims against the policy of "quotas" in education and employment policies.

Just before the Supreme Court decision, Rev. Jesse Jackson had seen the potential threat to affirmative action when he urged President Clinton to convene a White House conference on jobs and racial issues and criticized him for ignoring urban problems in his State of the Union address. Rev. Jackson requested that he and ministers affiliated with the Rainbow Coalition be invited to a White House meeting to discuss ideas relating to jobs, racial justice, and gender equality. Rev. Jackson and Rev. Wyatt Tee Walker, chairman of the minister's group, claimed that President Clinton spent a lot of time in the address discussing welfare reform and the work ethic but did not address job program initiatives, no economic stimulus package, and no urban policy. They suggested that there was increasing racial and gender polarization in the nation that demanded presidential attention.

In 2006, the Bush administration continued the road toward limiting the affirmative action program by filling the permanent ranks of the Justice Department's Civil Rights Division with lawyers who had strong conservative credentials but little experience in civil rights. The previous policy of hiring civil rights lawyers based on civil rights experience was terminated in 2002 by John Ashcroft, attorney general of the United States. Subsequently, the hiring became politically oriented with further challenges to the success of affirmative action. The gradual erosion of affirmative action continued to be a challenge throughout the administration of President Barack Obama.

The Reparations Movement

The Reparations Movement gained national attention when James Forman, executive director of the Student Nonviolent Coordinating Committee, with the assistance of the League of Black Revolutionary Workers prepared a document called the "Black Manifesto," which was adopted by the National Black Economic Development Conference in 1969. In May 1960, James Forman interrupted the Sunday service at the Riverside Church in New York, reading from the "Black

Manifesto" and calling for reparations from the whites to African Americans for historic and ongoing repression. In the first phase of this program, white churches and synagogues would pay $500 million to be distributed to African Americans and black community groups. Subsequently, the Reparation Movement gained some recognition on the part of African American church leaders. In May 1993, Rev. Jesse Jackson, at a summit of African and African American leaders held in Libreville, Gabon, raised the issue of reparations. In order to gain further support for reparations, the "Millions for Reparations Rally" was held on August 17, 2002, the 115th birthday of the Honorable Marcus Garvey, in Washington, D.C. Conrad W. Worrill, national chairman of the National Black United Front, suggested the rationale for reparations for what was called the "African Holocaust of Enslavement" including: the trans-Atlantic slave trade; destruction of the African family; raping of African women; fugitive slave laws; colonizing of our African culture; KKK night riders and lynching; denied our forty acres and a mule; Jim Crow laws; fighting and dying in imperialistic and white supremacist wars; the crack epidemic; and the jailing of freedom fighters. It was urged that as the result of the African Holocaust and the genocide against African people in the United States, the race must step up and demand reparations as advocated by the National Coalition of Blacks for Reparations in America. The movement cited the fact that since the U.S. government paid some $1.2 billion to Japanese living in the country for their internment during World War II, African Americans should be paid for all money collected by the Internal Revenue Service since 1913 and the continued inequality toward the race in denying its constitutional rights. Nevertheless, the reparations movement has not gained substantial support from within the African American church community nor from the liberal white community.

Upward Mobility in Denominational Life

The inclusion of women and minorities in the denominational structures of African American and biracial denominations has been a long and controversial struggle in Protestant denominational and Roman Catholic church life. Issues like the ordination of women in ministry, election of African American bishops in biracial denominations, and election of archbishops of the race in the Roman Catholic Church evolved as highly sensitive issues in ecumenism and western Christianity. African American Methodism, Pentecostalism, and certain biracial denominations were the pioneers in the ordination of women and the general upward mobility of African Americans in church life. Inspired by leaders and laity in these denominations, African Americans commenced struggles within others Protestant denominations and the Roman Catholic Church to increase the numbers of their participation in the upward structures of their particular church, especially as membership increases became more evident.

The Episcopal Church made some early strides for African American leadership. In 1962, the Rt. Rev. John Melville Burgess was elected the first African American bishop of the denomination and first African American canon of the Washington Cathedral. He was elected first as suffragan bishop of Boston where he served until 1967, when he became coadjutor bishop of Massachusetts until his retirement in 1975. In 1988, Rev. Canon Herbert Thompson Jr., became the first African American bishop of the Episcopal Church in Ohio. He became bishop of the Episcopal diocese of Ohio where there were less than 10 percent African American membership. Bishop Thompson served as coadjutor to the Rt. Rev. William G. Black, the prelate until 1992. After Bishop Black's retirement, Bishop Thompson became the prelate of the diocese. At that time, there were about 32,000 Episcopalians in 84 parishes and missions in the southern half of Ohio. In 1977, the Rt. Rev. John Thomas Walker became prelate of the Washington, D.C., diocese of the Episcopal Church. The Rt. Rev. Orris George Walker Jr., became the first African American bishop of the Episcopal diocese of Long Island, New York, in 1991. Significantly, the Long Island Episcopal Diocese was the third largest district in Episcopal Church in the United States with 155 congregations and over 90,000 members in Brooklyn, Queens, Nassau, and Suffolk. In 1988, Bishop Franklin Turner became the suffragan bishop of Pennsylvania. The Rt. Rev. Walter D. Dennis became suffragan bishop of New York in 1997. After these historic elevations, the Episcopal Church continued to make progress in the upward mobility of African Americans.

Similarly, African Americans experienced upward mobility within the United Methodist Church, the Evangelical Lutheran Church of America, and the Pentecostal Assemblies of the World. Rev. Sherman Hicks became the first African American bishop the Evangelical Lutheran Church of America; Rev. Joseph Bethea became the first African American United Methodist bishop in South Carolina in 1988, marking upward mobility of African Americans among United Methodists. Also in 1988, the Pentecostal Assemblies of the World elected Rev. Norman L. Wagner as the bishop of the 41st Episcopal District of the Pentecostal Assemblies of the World, encompassing the entire continent of Europe. Bishop Wagner was able to develop an international appeal for the denomination through his weekly television program, "Power of Pentecost," which was chosen by the Pentagon to be the first African American worship program to be televised on the Armed Forces Radio and Television Network, the largest and most expansive network in the world. The denomination has more than 2,000 churches worldwide.[37]

On July 19, 1993, the United Church of Christ adopted a new policy which opened the doors for the upward mobility of African Americans and other races in the life of the denomination. The General Synod set a pioneering goal for the UCC to "truly become a multiracial and multicultural church in all its settings." A pronouncement voted by delegates to the biennial synod affirms that the church should embody the diversity of all races, ethnicities, and cultures as gifts to the human family and rejoice in the variety of God's grace. Specifically, the synod advised that the church "consciously elect, now and evermore, significant numbers of persons of all races, ethnicities, and cultures to policy making positions throughout the church."[38] The synod announcement defined a multicultural and multiracial church as one that develops new churches in racial and ethnic communities, develops multilingual resources, shares financial resources to empower local racial and ethnic congregations, uses inclusive, equitable procedures for calling and placing ministers at all levels of the church, and affirms affirmative action goals. In response to the synod's action, Rev. Benjamin Chavis remarked: "This is a defining moment in the United Church of Christ. I am happy the church was courageous enough to take this important step forward. This will make broader our base and make us a better church."[39]

Within the Roman Catholic Church, African Americans have made significant strides toward upword mobility in the structure of the church. Much of the success of African American Roman Catholics may be attributed to the work of the Josephites, a religious community of Catholic priests belonging to the St. Joseph's Society of the Sacred Heart which trained and ordained African American priests. In fact, the first African American ordained in the U.S., Charles Randolph, was trained at the Josephites' seminary. They oversaw and staffed 14 high schools, 67 elementary schools; and, cared for more than 38,000 students. Many of these students assumed significant roles in the church. In 2001, there were more than 135 priests and brothers involved in Josephite society missions. Earlier in 1989, the National Conference of Bishops passed resolutions to seek ways to give African American Catholics a greater and more meaningful role in the church's activities. It noted the tremendous increase in the race's presence from 900,000 in 1969 to two million in 1989. However, the total Roman Catholic membership in the United States was 53 million with only 13 of the 300 bishops being African Americans.

There were about 1,100 predominantly African American parishes in the United States.

Following a plea by an African American nun, Sister Thea Bowman of Canton, Mississippi, the Bishops' Conference voted to refer a proposed document from the Bishop's Committee on Black Catholics to its administrative board. The document urged greater representation of African American Catholics throughout the church and integration of African American cultural symbols into local parishes and liturgies. In the document, the thirteen African American bishops affirmed that "the church and nation are still burdened with racism, and there has been a serious defection of blacks from the church to Protestant denominations where they feel more at home."[40] In 1988, Bishop Eugene A. Marino, a native of Biloxi, Mississippi, became the first African American Roman Catholic archbishop in the United States. He was appointed by Pope John Paul II as the third archbishop of Atlanta, Georgia. Initially, Bishop Marino served as spiritual director of Saint Joseph's Seminary in Washington, D.C.; later elected Vicar General of the Josephites; and auxiliary bishop of the Archdiocese of Washington. The archdiocese of Atlanta consisted of 156,000 Catholics in 65 parishes. After an alleged sexual scandal, Archbishop Marino resigned and was replaced by Bishop Wilton D. Gregory, appointed archbishop by Pope John Paul II. Archbishop Gregory, a native of Chicago, was the first African American Roman Catholic to serve as the president of the U.S. Conference of Catholic Bishops, which was at the height of the clergy sex abuse crisis when he was appointed archbishop. Noteworthy is the fact that the archbishop was able to lead the American Roman Catholic Church through the crisis while he served as the president of the U.S. Conference of Catholic Bishops.

Women in Ministry

Generally, the women's movement in America impacted church life among African American Christians in all denominations. As previously mentioned, African Methodism and Pentecostalism responded to the challenge of women in ministry throughout the twentieth century. Women were licensed, ordained, and served as pastors of local churches in some African American Methodist and many Pentecostal churches. In some cases, they were prominent organizers of Holiness and Pentecostal churches. Periodically, some women clergy were invited to be speakers in African American churches before their denominations gave specific approval of women in ministry. An early example of this was the rise of Rev. Era Ferrell of the Emmanuel Christian Church of Baltimore, Maryland. Rev. Wilbur Waters, who served the church until his death in 1956, was followed by Rev. Era Ferrell serving as interim pastor until the church called Rev. Sidney Daniels. During her pastorate, large crowds worshipped at Emmanuel Christian Church. There were other examples of women in ministry in several other denominations. However, the emergence of women in ministry in many traditional denominations was a major change of events. This was especially true of African American Baptists and other African American churches in traditional biracial denominations. However, the winds of change and transition pressed hard on the doors of these churches to respond positively to the women's movement. Women who were already active in other denominations influenced the laity in these traditional denominations to become receptive of women in ministry. Clergywomen were also rapidly gaining theological education which gave them further power to influence the Christian witness.

One of the most shocking signs of change in the role of women in African American Baptist church life came in 1979 when the tradition-oriented Baptist Ministers' Conference of Baltimore and Vicinity admitted, under the leadership of its President Rev. Vernon Dobson, women preachers for the first time to its membership. Admitted to the conference were Rev. Lydia Starks, pastor of the Fellowship Baptist Church of Baltimore; Rev. Minnie Robinson, associate minister of Mt. Lebanon Baptist Church of Baltimore; and Rev. Agnes M. Alston, associate minister of Gillis Memorial Christian Community Church of Baltimore. The fact that some women ministers were already accepted in a few local Baptist churches gave impetus to the acceptance of women in the conference. However, the decision of the conference to admit them to its membership sent shock waves through African American Baptist life. The vast majority of Baptist churches still did not open their doors to women in ministry. In fact, the Baptist Ministers' Conference of Washington, D.C., and Vicinity severed its longtime relationship with the Baltimore Conference in protest of the conference's action. They believed that the Baltimore Ministers' Conference had made a radical departure from the traditional faith and practice of Baptists, especially in the southern areas of the United States. Such changes had already begun in northern areas under the influence of the American Baptist Churches, U.S.A. The New England Missionary Baptist Convention was already experiencing the pressure of the women's movement. The decision of the Baltimore Baptist Ministers' Conference impacted the convention in its debates over the question of whether or not to ordain women.

Once the initial door was open, women clergy readily applied for membership in the Baltimore Conference and other Baptist ministers' conferences in various cities. They became active in the total life of ministers' conferences throughout various parts of the nation. The tremendous attendance of women clergy at the Hampton Ministers Conference, a major ecumenical event, greatly added to the momentum of acceptance of women clergy. With the beginning of the George A. Crawley "Women in Ministry Hour" at the Hampton University Ministers' Conference, major women pastors and educators across the nation addressed a large body of church leaders. Among the women who participated in the "Women in Ministry Hour" were Rev. Susan Johnson Cook, Evangelist Winifred Morris, Rev. Cynthia Hale, Rev. Debra Martin, Rev. Debra L. Haggins (who became university chaplain, and executive director & treasurer of the Hampton University Ministers' Conference), and other leading voices among African American women. Toward the end of the twentieth century women had gained substantial acceptance in church life across denominational lines. However, the Southern Baptist Convention, U.S.A., persisted in its traditional position against the acceptance of women in the clergy.

During the latter part of the twentieth century, the women's movement also pressured the leadership of biracial denominations for the acceptance of women in clergy positions. The United Methodist Church responded early to the acceptance of women in the clergy. In fact, the representatives of the Wesleyan tradition were predominant among advocates of the expansion of women's sphere. As early as the late nineteenth century two prominent Methodist women advocated the expansion of the role of women in ministry. Phoebe Palmer's works, *The Way of Holiness* first published in 1843, and *Promise of the Father*; and Frances Willard's *Woman in the Pulpit* were used to promote the right of women in the pulpit. Specifically, Palmer as a theologian, redefined John Wesley's doctrine of sanctification in such a way that would lend credence to women in ministry. In both *Promise of the Father* and *The Way of Holiness*, Palmer declares that Wesley himself licensed Sarah Mallet to preach at the Manchester Conference of 1787, by giving her a written note saying: "We give the right hand of fellowship to Sarah Mallet, and have no objection to her being a preacher in our connection, so long as she preaches the Methodist doctrine, and attends to our discipline.[41] Hence, early theological developments and traditions opened the way for the denomination to elect Bishop Marjorie Matthews as its first woman bishop in 1980. Subsequently, the church elected two women to the episcopacy. The two women bishops were Rev. Susan Morrison of Baltimore, Maryland, program coordinator of the church's Baltimore Conference; and, Rev.

Sharon B. Christopher. By 1997, the Black Clergywomen Support Group was formed among United Methodist women to promote, develop, and support and enhance opportunities for African American clergywomen in the United Methodist Church. At that time, there were approximately four hundred clergywomen in the denomination. The top priorities of the support group were: developing a system of networking; understanding the appointment process; and, mentoring young women in the ministry. By 1999, women had gained tremendous influence within the denomination. In 1999, Rev. Martha Orphe was appointed superintendent of the Pittsburgh District of the United Methodist Church. The influence of the movement progressed beyond denominational lines.

The Episcopal Church adopted an early policy toward the ordination of women. In November 1972 the House of Bishops, meeting in New Orleans, issued the following official statement: "It is the mind of this House that it endorses the principal of the Ordination of Women to the Priesthood and of the Ordination and Consecration of Women to the Episcopate." However, the General Convention of September 1973 refused to authorize the ordination of women as presbyters and bishops.[42]

By 1988, the women's movement had made sufficient strides for the ordination of women in the denomination to culminate in the ordination of Rev. Barbara Harris, an African American Episcopal priest and social activist, to be elected suffragan bishop of the Diocese of Massachusetts, the nation's largest Episcopal diocese. She had been a longtime participant and leader in the struggle for justice and freedom internationally. At her election in Boston, Bishop Harris stated that she will continue to work for the cause of freedom and justice. Her election was highly applauded by clergy of other denominations. Rev. Benjamin F. Chavis Jr., executive director of the United Church of Christ Commission for Racial Justice, remarked:

> The election of Bishop Harris is a victory for all women. In too many places throughout the world and in the United States, women are still victimized by the sin of sexism. We take note that the Episcopal Church, after centuries of struggle and debate, has taken an important step forward in history. It is our hope that all church denominations and religious bodies will become institutions where women will enjoy equal justice, respect, status, and support.[43]

In 2006, the Episcopal Church took the radical step of installing Bishop Katharine J. Schori as its first female presiding bishop. Her selection as the 26th presiding bishop of the Episcopal Church, the denomination's highest office, was hailed as a breakthrough for women and for inclusion of gays and lesbians, which she supports. It also made her a target in an international battle over opposing views on sexuality and interpretation of Scripture that have pushed the worldwide 77 million-member Anglican Communion toward schism. Even in the United States, several conservative dioceses have rejected her authority and asked Archbishop of Canterbury Rowan Williams, the Anglican spiritual leader, to place them under the jurisdiction of another leader.

The question of the ordination of women confronted the Lutheran Church in American, almost at the same time as among Episcopalians. In 1970, the ordination of women was approved by the Lutheran Church in America and by the American Lutheran Church. A proposal for ordination of women was presented at the 1971 Missouri Synod convention but was defeated by a 674 to 194 vote. But by 1985, the tide had turned among Lutherans. At that time, the number of ordained women in the Lutheran Church in America had increased by 20 percent since a favorable approval for such ordinations had been accepted. The Church's Division for Professional Leadership reported 367 of the church's approximately 7,000 active pastors were women. Moreover, the number of women enrolled in theological schools increased annually.

As early as 1956, Presbyterian churches had developed an open-door policy toward the ordination of women. With the merger of the United Presbyterian Church in the United States of America and the United Presbyterian Church of North America to form the United Presbyterian Church in the United States of America, the question of ordaining women continued to gain official acceptance. The United Presbyterian Church Form of Government stated that "every congregation shall elect men and women from among its active members, giving fair representation of all ages and of all ethnic minorities of that congregation, to the office of ruling elder and the office of deacon."[44] This policy led to the general acceptance of the ordination of women in all levels of church government.

Similar policies toward the ordination of women were advanced in several other biracial denominations. The Church of God in Christ has enjoyed a longtime policy of ordaining women. In 1951, the denomination organized the Women's International Convention to strengthen and reaffirm its commitment to the fellowship and spiritual growth of women in ministry. In 1998 Rev. Kay Ward, director of continuing education at Moravian Seminary, became the first woman elected as bishop in the Moravian Church of America. The only major churches that still resist the women's movement are the Roman Catholic Church and the Orthodox Church.

The African Methodist Episcopal Church was an early denomination within the African American church experience to ordain women in ministry. By 2000, the church elected Rev. Vashti McKenzie as the denomination's first female bishop. In 2004, the Rt. Rev. Vashti McKenzie was appointed president of the bishop's council. Her appointment to the high Episcopal office took place at the AME Church Quadrennial Conference in Cincinnati, Ohio, and marked a significant change in the church's attitudes and proceedings. Also, her election opened the doors for the denomination to elect two other women bishops in 2004. During the 47th Quadrennial Conference of the AME Church, Rev. Sarah Francis Davis and Rev. Carolyn Tyler Guidry were elected bishops.

By 2005, the number of women in ministry had rapidly increased to a point which led Rev. Caria Jo Howlett, a chaplain from Evanston, Illinois, to found the National Consortium of Black Women in Ministry as a forum and resource for African American women in ministry. The consortium was specifically designed to provide professional training and networking opportunities and a job resource center for ministers just out of seminaries. Rev. Howlett also indicated that the consortium will be a voice for African American women in communities throughout the nation facing poverty, disease, and racial and gender-based injustices. Moreover, she indicated her hope that the consortium will eradicate injustice for women in other denominations.

The Rise of Megachurches

Two significant trends in the contemporary African American church are the decrease in membership of traditional churches and the rise of megachurches. Megachurches are classified as those churches with attendance of more than 2000 congregants in attendance at worship services , usually consisting of middle class and highly educated African Americans. These churches evolved toward the end of the twentieth century. They pose a tremendous challenge to tradition-oriented churches in urban America. Often they are both admired and envied by the leadership of the tradition-oriented churches. The decrease in membership in traditional churches, especially in urban areas, constitutes a major challenge to many leaders in the African American church. Church growth among these churches, except among Holiness and Pentecostal churches, seemingly has reached its apex in major cities. On the other hand, megachurches modeled after the electronic church movement have continued to enjoy phenomenal growth. They have maximized the utilization of mass media—such as, newspapers, radio, and television, and modern electronic devices—to advance church growth. Also, they have adopted growth strategies from broader business models for growth and development. To be sure, they are organized, developed, and administered on the models of big business.

New Shiloh Baptist Church
Baltimore, Maryland
2015

The rapid proliferation of megachurches toward the end of the twentieth century into the twenty first century of American church life can be attributed in part to the rise of television evangelism. Radio ministries have long been a major evangelistic tool for church growth. But with the rise of television ministries and the utilization of computer technology, African American churches have advanced to new levels of growth unprecedented in the historic experience of the African American church. Nationally, there are more than 50 mega churches in urban and suburban communities with memberships ranging from 6,000 to 20,000 members. They are usually led by strong charismatic leaders with specialized supporting staff. Each paid and sometimes volunteer staff member coordinates a designated ministry as assigned by the charismatic pastor-bishop. They tend to avoid evoking perceptions of conventional church by utilizing new models for congregational life called "ministries." This allows thenm to transcend the traditional model of African American church life. These ministries tend to focus on the sociopolitical and economic needs of the African American community. They are diverse by design to reflect the full gamut of spiritual, social, and psychological needs of members who enjoy a unique sense of empowerment.

A classic example of a megachurch is The Potter's House, one of the largest churches in the United States with a membership exceeding 30,000, located in the booming Dallas-Fort Worth metropolis in Texas. This prominent urban church was organized and developed by Bishop T.D. Jakes. He developed The Potter's House from a small store-front church to an internationally known megachurch. Jakes was born June 9, 1957, in South Charleston, West Virginia. From his youth onward, he was devoted to the Gospel ministry, by founding and serving as pastor of Greater Emmanuel Temple of Faith, a small storefront church in Montgomery, West Virginia. He became known for ministering to drug addicts, the homeless, prostitutes, single mothers, and others of dire circumstances. Later, he moved to Dallas and organized the new church destined to be a megachurch. He is the author of thirty books, a Grammy-winning gospel singer with dynamic sermons broadcasted on the Trinity Broadcasting Network and Black Entertainment Television. His phenomenal success became the subject of a 2001 *Time* magazine cover story that queried "Is This Man the Next Billy Graham?" Among his many popular success stories includes Bishop Jakes' movie, *Woman, Thou Art Loosed*, a movie that tackles the subject of child molestation. The day the film opened Bishop Jakes promoted it in an appearance on *The Oprah Winfrey Show* on October 1, 2004. The film is a joint venture between Jakes' for-profit T.D. Jakes Enterprise and Reuben Cannon, a Hollywood producer. The fictional story intersperses graphic scenes of sexual abuse, drug use, and domestic violence with Jakes preaching at Los Angeles revivals and ministering to the condemned prisoner. The film is based on his first book by that title which Jakes wrote in 1993. Unable to find a publisher, Jakes decided to self-publish the book which has sold more than seven million copies. A subsequent book entitled *He-Motions: Even Strong Men Struggle*, was designed to reach out to men who are absent from the church. The film represents one of the most dynamic and creative ministries of the African American church experience.

His tremendous success led both Presidents George Walker Bush and William Jefferson Clinton to invited Jakes for White House conferences. During these conferences, Bishop Jakes advocated for the needs of African American communities nationally. Subsequently, Jakes remarked:

> African Americans are making grave mistakes in allowing themselves to be controlled or owned by a particular political party. I think that when it is presumed that we're going to vote a particular way, frankly, the Democratic Party takes us for granted because they feel like they own us.... And the Republican Party fails to provide the things that would draw us because they feel they can't get us. And I think we need to approach politics from a non-partisan posture and make the parties fight

for our allegiance by coming up with agendas that are of interest to people of color.[45]

In May 2005, Bishop Jakes continued to advance his tremendous pulpit ministry by addressing a 5,000-member audience at the Mount Airy Church of God in Christ in Philadelphia on the subject, "The Power of Words." The event was a partnership between Bishop Gilbert Coleman of the Freedom Christian Bible Fellowship, and Bishop Ernest Morris pastor of Mount Airy Church of God in Christ. The partnership between Bishop Coleman and Bishop Morris worked to bring other megachurch leader along with Bishop Jakes to evangelize the Philadelphia metropolitan area. They made plans to bring Bishop Noel Jones, a California pastor who often appeared on BET; and the late Bishop Eddie Long, then-pastor of the 25,000-member New Birth Missionary Baptist Church located in the suburbs of Atlanta, Georgia. However, the ministry of Bishop Jakes became the central focus of the partnership. He continues to be the principal speaker at major religious conferences and conventions.

In 2004, Bishop Jakes addressed the Kingdom Conference 2004 for the New Psalmist Baptist Church, Baltimore, Maryland, with some 8,000 persons in attendance at a convention center, including delegates from Sweden. Bishop Walter Scott Thomas coordinated the development of specific classes for men, women, youth, children, young adults, singles, pastors, and musicians. Bishop Jakes spoke to the congregation about "conflicted anointing." The response was like one of an extraordinary evangelistic crusade. Also, in the same year Bishop Jakes, along with Bishop Paul S. Morton of the Full Gospel Baptist Church Fellowship International, addressed the "Ministry of Excellence Empowerment Conference" in Woodbridge, Virginia. The organization of such conferences became models for other megachurches.

Bishop Walter Scott Thomas, a "son in the ministry" of Rev. Harold A. Carter of the New Shiloh Baptist Church of Baltimore, the first megachurch in the city, developed the New Psalmist Baptist Church from a small church structure in 1975 to a megachurch with several thousand members. By 1996, the church has grown from 200 to 7,000 members in a new location with expanded facilities. At the new location in Baltimore, Bishop Thomas developed programs of evangelism, missions, discipleship training, and education. Early in his church growth ministry, he teamed up with Bishop John Bryant in mass evangelistic crusades. In addition, the church has a national television broadcast, "Empowering Disciples." Between 1998 and 2002, Bishop Thomas served as president of the Millennium Association of Pastors, hosting conferences and establishing a framework for ministry in the new millennium. He also served as president of the Hampton Ministers' Conference, at Hampton University in Hampton, Virginia. Also, he led in the formation of the "Kingdom Association of Covenant Pastors." He was assisted by Rev. Leah White of Greater Faith Baptist Church, Bishop Oscar Brown, Rev. Carl Solomon, Rev. William Curtis of Philadelphia, and Rev. Arthur Jackson of Florida. On July 20, 2005, Rev. Walter Scott Thomas was elevated to the bishopric. Assisting in the induction into the bishopric were Bishop Larry Trotter, presiding prelate of the United Covenant Churches of Christ; Bishop Neil C. Ellis, third presiding bishop of the Full Gospel Baptist Fellowship International and pastor of Mount Tabor Full Gospel Baptist Church; and Rev. Harold A. Carter, pastor of New Shiloh Baptist Church of Baltimore. Currently, Bishop Thomas continues to be instrumental in the elevation of other African American clergy to the bishopric.

As previously mentioned, Rev. Harold A. Carter was among the earliest to develop a megachurch in Baltimore. He was a native of Selma, Alabama, and he was nurtured spiritually at the Tabernacle Baptist Church in Selma. He was called to the ministry and became pastor of Court Street Baptist Church in Lynchburg, Virginia. In 1965, Rev. Carter was called to the New Shiloh Baptist Church in Baltimore, where he increased the membership to such a capacity that the church had to move to a new location. On May 27, 1990, he led the church to occupy its new location on Monroe and Clifton Avenue in the city. The new massive structure expanded facilities for a variety of church growth ministries including a clothing center, music center, chapel for creative arts, Saturday church school (which became a model for growth), theological center, Outreach Center for Child Development, and Christian bookstore. The New Shiloh Baptist Church became a megachurch with more than 3,000 members, which set a precedent for church growth in Baltimore. Some of Rev. Carter's sons in the ministry, like Bishop Walter Thomas, became leading pastors in several areas of the nation. Other megachurches in Baltimore include Bethel AME with some 5,000 members under the leadership of Rev. Frank Reid; Living Word Christian Center, with more than 2,000 members under the leadership of Rev. David Brown; and Mount Pleasant Baptist Church and Ministries, under the Bishop Clifford Johnson. In other Maryland urban areas, megachurches are located in various urban areas including: Ebenezer AME Church in Ft. Washington, with more than 3,000 members under the leadership of Rev. Granger Browning; National Church of God, also of Ft. Washington, with a membership of more than 3,000 members under the leadership of Rev. Stephen

L. Lowery; the First Baptist Church of Glenarden in Landover, with a membership exceeding 3,000, under the leadership of Rev. John K. Jenkins; the Jericho City of Praise also in Landover, with 7,000 members under the leadership of Rev. Betty Peebles; and the Full Gospel AMEZ Church, Temple Hill under the leadership of Rev. John Cherry. To be sure, the rise and development of megachurches has been remarkable in the state of Maryland as well as in other major urban areas in the United States.

Exploding Moral Crisis Debates

The evolution of "new morality" ethical standards in the United States set the stage for exploding debates centering about the changing social and political policies in the church and state. Such issues as drug addiction, abortion rights, capital punishment, stem cell research, family planning, and the homosexual liberation movement have evolved into heated debates among liberals and conservatives both in church and state. Within the church, liberal clergy and professional theologians have developed new approaches to the interpretation of ethics in the Bible, prompted by new extra-biblical discoveries, the women's theological emphasis, and liberation theology. Conservatives continue to hold traditional interpretations of the Bible and insist that Christian politicians must be guided in their decisions by the traditional values of the Christian church. Fundamentally, the African American church held tenaciously to the traditional values of Christianity—at least in matters of faith, but not always in practice.

The drug addiction debate centers around causative factors, the war on drugs, poverty, and the appropriate response of the African American church to individuals caught in addiction. To be sure, drug and alcohol addiction are not a new phenomenon in church life. However, the proliferation of addiction in communities across the nation has raised urgent questions about the church's response to the issue. Rapid increases in the numbers of addicts both within and outside churches; increases in the imprisonment of African Americans involved in the drug culture; violence on urban American streets; rapid destruction of the already volatile African American family; and the radical challenges to evangelism have forced the church to take stands on these exploding issues. African American church leaders throughout the nation have provided facilities for Narcotics Anonymous and Alcoholics Anonymous meetings, drug addiction counseling, homeless shelters for addicts, and support groups for families experiencing the presence of addicts in the home environment. They have also been critical of the detrimental effects of the government's war on drugs policies, some proposing the decriminalization of some drugs in order to decrease incarceration of large numbers of African American men. Actually, many have blamed the federal government for targeting African American neighborhoods for the infiltration of addictive drugs.

Rev. Cecil Williams, pastor of the Glide Memorial United Methodist Church in San Francisco, California, held a conference of more than 1,500 anti-drug activists to develop strategies and methodologies to address the addiction crisis in African American communities throughout the United States. Noting that the church must return to the "trenches," he called for increased anti-drug activism, observing that "It's recovery time, and we're going to march to the projects and reclaim the lives of our children, our brothers, and sisters."[46] Nevertheless, drug addiction continues to be a leading problem for African American families in both rural and urban areas.

As indicated, the culture of narcotic drugs, their sale and use, constitute the leading causes of crime and violence in African American communities. The legal system tends to deal more harshly with African American and Hispanic addicts and distributors than with others in society. More African American and Hispanic addicts and distributors are arrested and receive longer sentences of incarceration. The Lawyers' Committee for Civil Rights, a nonpartisan, nonprofit organization, was formed in 1963 at the request of President John F. Kennedy to involve the private bar associations to address racial discrimination. When the U.S. Sentencing Commission recently voted to retroactively reduce drug trafficking sentences, the Lawyers' Committee sent a letter to U.S. Sentencing Commission in support of retroactive application of the 2014 amendment which surveyed the disparities in nearly all areas of the federal criminal justice system. It noted that racial disparities persist at nearly every stage of the federal criminal justice system, leading to a prison population which African Americans and Hispanics are grossly overrepresented. The following statistics was noted in the letter, reporting that in 2010, 37 percent of the federal prison population was Black, 32 percent Hispanic, and 28 percent white; and that the Bureau of Justice Statistics reported in 2013 that African Americans and Hispanics represent over 75 percent of defendants charged in federal district courts. Moreover, the statistics do not reflect the large population of African Americans and Hispanics incarcerated in state correctional institutions on drug-related charges. Disparities in both the federal and states criminal justice systems alarm many African American church leaders.

Black-on-black violence, often drug-related, has also caused increases in incarceration of young African American men; some have traveled the route of capital punishment. Some studies have revealed a national condition wherein a disproportionate number of African American men have been executed in states where capital punishment remains legal, and many more wait out death row sentences in overcrowded jails. Rev. Jesse Jackson represents one major leader among many others who decry the capital punishment laws in the States. In marking the first anniversary of the execution in Texas of Shaka Sankofa (Gary Graham), Rev. Jackson called on Americans who oppose capital punishment to continue to move forward and do everything "we can to outlaw legal lynching in the country. He remarked: "We must continue to stay strong all around the world, and people must come together to stop the systematic killing of poor and innocent black people.... We must stand together in unity and to demand a moratorium on all executions."[47] Nevertheless, liberals and conservatives in political offices, as well as in some local churches, still debate the capital punishment issue in the United States.

Another controversial issue is gay and lesbian rights in the United States. As early as the 1960s, the gay and lesbian rights movement gained momentum in public dialogue and the national press. The movement was linked with the Civil Rights struggles of African Americans for social justice. Members of the movement felt that they were victims of discrimination and violence equally critical as that suffered by African Americans. During this period, gays and lesbians organized two highly political and activist groups, the Gay Liberation Front and the Gay Activist Alliance, whose goal was to overthrow the sex/gender hierarchy created by the dominance of patriarchy in American life. African American participation in these movements was overshadowed by their more urgent Civil Rights struggles. Some were even resentful of the gay and lesbian rights movement, viewing it as a competitive minority movement. However, gays and lesbians were active in the Civil Rights movement itself, kept on a low key and remaining in their "closets."

Several sociopolitical pressures negatively impacted the gay and lesbian rights movement toward the end of the 1960s: the rise of hate crimes against gays and lesbians; the continuing controversy over gays and lesbians in the military; and the opposition against homosexuality and homosexuals by conservative Evangelical churches. A major political setback took place in 1998 when Maine became the first state to repeal its gay rights laws, which prohibited discrimination against gays and lesbians in employment, credit, housing, and public accommodations, even though public opinion polls showed a two-thirds statewide majority in favor of the law.[48] This political signal motivated gays and lesbians to become more aggressive in their struggles.

The gay and lesbian rights movement in the United States has vacillated between successes and setbacks. In June 2003, the U.S. Supreme Court gave a major boost to gay rights, overturning a seventeen-year legal precedent that had allowed states to criminalize private homosexual conduct. In reaching that decision, the majority justices overturned a key legal precedent that had held that states were justified in criminalizing homosexual conduct because it violated the shared moral values in society. Gay rights activists were hopeful that the *Lawrence v. Texas* decision would mark a turning point in the fight to end what they saw as the second-class status of homosexuals in America. But their hopes were disappointed when the decision only intensified debates in courtrooms and legislative assemblies across the country, reflecting fundamental disagreement with the Supreme Court itself over the proper role of sexual morality in the law.

Gay marriage rights became another heated political and religious debate in the United States, which has prompted crucial battles between liberals and conservatives in the twenty-first century. In 2004, a Massachusetts court ruled that gay marriage is a constitutional right, which caused tremendous religious and political debates across America. In efforts to prevent Massachusetts-style court intervention, several states sought to define marriage in their constitutions as a union of one man and one woman. At issue were the most basic concepts in American life—the definition of family and marriage. Nevertheless, several states passed legislation recognizing gay marriages, including Maryland, a strong seat of Roman Catholicism. This signaled the growing influence of the gay rights movement in the United States.

Attitudes among African American Christians varied regarding the gay and lesbian movement. Church leaders across denominational lines recognized the presence of gays and lesbians in their local churches. Their presence in the music departments of churches was seemingly indispensable. They were the best or more talented musicians and soloists in many church choirs. Moreover, their presence was felt in Sunday schools and in the leadership of churches, even within the clergy. Nevertheless, gays and lesbians were expected to keep their sexual orientation in carefully guarded "closets." But with increased social acceptance of homosexuality, gays and lesbians gradually began to come out about their sexual orientation and to demand that their rights be protected. This factor brought the movement into a stage of general controversy regarding causative factors of homosexuality and the appropriate moral response of Christian churches.

In February 1997, the United Methodist Church took its initial stand on homosexuality in a three-page document entitled: "The More Excellent Way: God's Plan RE-Affirmed." The document affirms: "The United Methodist Church's position on homosexuality stated in the 'Social Principles' and the Book of Discipline; The lifelong commitment between one man and one woman as the only appropriate form of marriage; 'The Disciplinary standards for ordination' excluding 'self-avowed practicing homosexuals' from the ranks of the ordained; and, Support for 'ministries of transformation' for homosexuals 'to wish to leave such lifestyles.'"[49] The document was signed by both clergy and laity. It concluded with an appeal: "As a people of God, let us leave behind this distraction and move forward, shining forth the light of the Gospel of Jesus Christ into the dawning of a new millennium."[50] However, in 2003 the campaign to have United Methodists and other mainline Protestant denominations to normalize homosexual activity was motivated by Dr. Theodore Jennings Jr., in his book entitled, *The Man Jesus Loved: Homoerotic Narratives from the New Testament*. The book makes the radical claim that Jesus Himself was a homosexual. This position was diametrically opposed to the historic position of the United Methodist Church, which was restated in 2004 affirming that homosexual practice is incompatible with Christian teaching. The Bishops Council of the church strongly opposed same-sex marriage.

By October 1995, significant dialogue within the Evangelical Lutheran Church inspired the denomination to prepare a statement on sexuality. The Division for Church and Society decided to draft a message for consideration at the Church Council in 1996 on issues regarding areas of apparent consensus within the church. The Church Council had asked the Division for Church and Society to begin work on a multi-authored volume on how Lutherans do ethics, with a companion document to be prepared for congregational use. The volume was to deal with the debate surrounding human sexuality in the Bible. The church decided to develop outreach strategies to gay and lesbian people, especially in communities where there are large populations of homosexual persons, either with new ministries or through existing congregations. With the encouragement of the denomination's 1995 Church-wide Assembly, the Conference of Bishops issued a letter to the church in March saying:

> The debates and controversy surrounding homosexuality sometimes have turned bitter.... We ask all our members to join us in repentance

for hurtful actions toward others, and in forgiving when we have been the objects of anger or hate. The way we face our differences on the issues surrounding homosexuality can be an important expression of grace for our particular church body and for the communities in which we live.... We invite gay and lesbian persons to join with other members of this church in mutual prayer and study of the issues that still divide us, so that we may seek the truth together.[51]

With reference to same-sex marriage, the Evangelical Lutheran Church policy expects ministers to refrain from all sexual relations outside marriage, which it defines as "a lifelong covenant of faithfulness between a man and a woman."

Rev. R. Albert Mohler Jr, a leading conservative voice in the Southern Baptist Convention and president of Southern Baptist Theological Seminary in Louisville, Kentucky, set the stage for future conservative postures regarding homosexuality, expressing in March 1995, that tolerance of homosexuality illustrates the depth of moral problems in the United States. He said: "Evangelicals are accused of being homophobic. But if we take the apostle Paul seriously, we cannot overemphasize the sin of homosexuality.... The first act of compassion is to tell the truth.... We must certainly strive to see the family is not legally redefined. We must seek to prevent any effort to have homosexuality classified as a civil right."[52]

In 1992, the Southern Baptist Convention terminated the membership of two of its churches for their liberal acceptance of homosexuality. The Olin T. Binkley Memorial Baptist Church in Chapel Hill, North Carolina, voted to rescind its oppositional statement toward homosexuality when it decided to license a gay divinity student to preach. The newly stated position of the church, the first of its kind among Southern Baptists, stated that a person's sexual orientation should not be considered in the ordination process. Similarly, the Pullen Memorial Church reaffirmed their decision to bless a homosexual union.

The Southern Baptist Convention, consisting of about 16 million members, voted overwhelmingly in June 1999 to rebuke President Clinton for proclaiming June as Gay and Lesbian Pride Month and passed resolutions ranging from human embryo research to Kosovo. Rev. Wiley Drake of Buena Park, California, remarked: "We're not going to allow the president, especially since he is a Southern Baptist, to say that homosexuality is good."[53] Moreover, the resolution called on President Clinton to rescind his appointment of openly gay James Hormel as ambassador to Luxembourg; it also voiced opposition to a study published by the American Psychological Association that concluded the long-term effects of child sexual abuse were not as serious as many believed. Of all the Protestant denominations, the Southern Baptist Convention remained consistent with its opposition to homosexuality into the twenty-first century.

African American Baptist churches have been rather reluctant to publish statements regarding homosexuality; however, they have been vocal in preaching against homosexuality, regarding it as a sin. The late Rev. E.V. Hill, pastor of Mount Zion Missionary Baptist Church and nationally-renowned preacher, took a stand against the gay rights movement in California with the proposed passage of a bill that would recognize minority rights protection for homosexual men and women. He was particularly critical of the California Legislative Black Causus' decision to support the measure. Rev. Hill remarked: "I do not know of one single church in Los Angeles where proponents of this bill can speak and not be booed."[54]

In May 2005, Rev. Voddie Baucham Jr., a popular African American evangelist, submitted a joint resolution with attorney Bruce Shortt, calling on Southern Baptist churches to investigate whether their school district has a "gay-straight alliance" or other homosexual clubs. Also, the Baucham-Shortt resolution called upon churches to encourage parents' removal of their children from schools that have curricula or programs that treat homosexuality as an acceptable lifestyle. It was noted that groups like the Gay, Lesbian, and Straight Education Network and Parents, Families, and Friends of Lesbians and Gays worked with pro-homosexual student groups to promote the false notion of inherent homosexual, bisexual, or transgender identity, resulting in sexually confused students' "coming out" at younger and younger ages.[55] Such conservative oppositions toward homosexuality were significant factors in the proliferation of private Baptist schools. Conservative Christians sought to establish their own schools where traditional beliefs would be emphasized.

Debates about homosexuality and same-sex couples emerged early in the late 1980s and early 1990s within the Presbyterian U.S.A. and the Episcopal Church in the United States. The governing body of the Episcopal Church opened its meeting in 1991 deeply divided over same-sex couples and the ordination of homosexuals. The House of Bishops began the debate in the context of tremendous divided opinions regarding a proposal that Episcopal bishops clearly empowered to ordain homosexuals without demanding that they remain celibate should begin developing an official blessing for homosexual couples to live together permanently. At the convention, church leaders discussed the proposal, but a counterproposal was offered affirming the traditional position of the church against such a radically new policy. Approximately three thousand Episcopal delegates and observers at the General Convention of the Episcopal Church flooded into an open committee hearing to debate homosexuality, the Bible, and the obligations of the socially and religiously influential church.

Bishop William C. Frey, one of two bishops who opened the session with contrasting presentations, introduced the counterproposal to include in the canon law of the church a requirement that all clergy be committed to abstain from sexual relations outside of marriage. Although this traditional teaching was affirmed in1979 by the General Convention in a resolution that declared that it was not appropriate to ordain a practicing homosexual, the resolution was deemed only advisory, and a number of bishops did not act upon the traditional resolution. Even in 1979, a minority of Episcopal bishops publicly stated that they did not consider the resolution binding on their consciences. In 1991, Bishop Ronald H. Haines of Washington, D.C., ordained a woman who had publicly indicated her lesbian orientation and her relationship with another woman. Similarly, Bishop John S. Spong of Newark, New Jersey, stirred protest by ordaining an avowed active homosexual man. Subsequently, the Church's Standard Commission Human Affairs recommended that the General Convention unambiguously state decisions about ordaining homosexuals should be left to local dioceses and bishops; and that the church should find ways to bless "covenants of homosexual persons" who are in "faithful, committed relationships."[56]

The acceptance of homosexual ordinations in the Episcopal Church, U.S.A. caused an international storm of debate in the Anglican Church community. Approximately three hundred Anglican bishops meeting in Nigeria for the first African bishops' convention said that homosexuality was an "un-African practice and warned that congregations would turn away from a church that condoned homosexuality. Their statements highlighted the growing divide between the Anglican Church in Africa, which represented more than half the world's fifty million-strong Anglican population and the West. They were particularly angered by their American colleagues' decision to ordain an openly gay bishop, Bishop Gene Robinson, in 2003. The Anglican Communion has about seventy-seven million members around the globe, while Episcopalians make up just over two million in that body, a relatively small number, though the American church is a wealthy one.

The storm within the Episcopal Church, U.S.A. continued to brew over the issue of ordaining homosexuals. Although the church accepted liberal views regarding the issue, some conservative clergy still resisted the movement. The Episcopal

Bishop of Connecticut indicated his intention to punish six priests who were at odds with his support for the Episcopal Church, U.S.A.'s current positions on homosexuality issues. He indicated that the conservative priests had "abandoned the Communion."[57] This development clearly indicated that the conservative priests had become a minority within the church.

Similar battles developed among conservative and liberal leaders of the Presbyterian Church, U.S.A., over the issue of homosexuality. However, the governing body of that church overwhelming rejected a report in 1991 urging the church to relax its strictures against sexual relations among homosexuals and unmarried heterosexuals. As early as 1970, the church had taken a stand against homosexuality, stating: "We, the 182nd General Assembly (1970), reaffirm our adherence to the moral law of God as revealed in the Old and New Testament, that adultery, prostitution, fornication and/or the practice of homosexuality is sin."[58] Hence, the Presbyterian Church refused to follow the path of the Episcopal Church.

In 1985, Cardinal Joseph Bernardin voiced the position of the Roman Catholic Church regarding gay rights in a letter responding to reports of violence against gays and lesbians presented to him by the Illinois Gay and Lesbian Task Force. He wrote:

> I receive your letter on behalf of the Illinois Gay and Lesbian Task force and carefully reviewed the additional materials you sent. Naturally, I had been aware of violence and harassment against gays and lesbians, but the National Gay and Task Force (NGTF) study provided preliminary statistics which give me further indication of its intensity and extensiveness.
>
> Basically, as I understood your letter, you are asking me to play a leadership role in attempting to stop chronic violence against gays and lesbians by endorsing civil rights legislation which would allegedly protect them. There are two separate issues involved: (1) defending civil rights and (2) endorsing specific legislation. I will address both issues in this letter.
>
> Let me state clearly at the outset that I am not afraid to take an unpopular position in defense of human rights. However, I know you understand that any leadership I might provide in regard to such issues would have to be exercised within the parameters of the Catholic Church's teaching. That is simply my responsibility as a bishop.

I would first like to clarify the Catholic Church's position about homosexuality and gay/lesbian rights. Basically, the Church's mission is to proclaim Jesus Christ and his Gospel. Our values and understanding of the basic dignity of every human person—including gays and lesbians—are based on this. More specifically, four principles shape our teaching about homosexuality and gay/lesbian rights.

1. Some people, through no fault of their own, find themselves to have a homosexual orientation. This orientation is not in itself immoral or sinful. That is why the Catholic Bishops' 1976 pastoral letter, "The Gift of Sexuality," states: "Homosexuals, like everyone else, should not suffer from prejudice against their basic human rights. They have a right to respect, friendship and justice. They should have an active role in the Christian community."

2. There is no place for arbitrary discrimination and prejudice against a person because of sexual attraction. We especially deplore violence and harassment directed against such persons. Moreover, all human persons, including those with homosexual orientation, have a right to decent employment and housing.

3. However, homosexual activity, as distinguished from homosexual orientation, is morally wrong. A corollary of this traditional teaching of the Church is that patterns of life, sometimes referred as "lifestyles," which encourage immoral behavior are also morally objectionable. I agree with your assertion that there is a wide spectrum of gay and lesbian lifestyles. As a Church, we do not approve of those patterns of life or lifestyles which encourage, promote, or advocate homosexual activity.

4. Parents have the right to keep their children free during their formative years of any person(s) or influence(s) which might draw them toward homosexual practice or condoning homosexual activity.

Let me expand on this last point. We do not assume that many homosexuals are child abusers or seducers of young people. We have not recommended the firing of any persons of homosexual orientation from Church-related positions where they may be simply disliked. Moreover, we do not ask questions about sexual orientation in our Archdiocesan hiring procedures. Of course, any employee of a Church-related institution, acting in a non-professional manner on the job or seeking to teach in a way contrary to Catholic morality, would be subject to disciplinary action. That would include anyone who promotes or advocates a heterosexual lifestyle which we would consider immoral, as, for example, people living together without the benefit of marriage.

My own position, then, is this: I firmly deplore acts of violence, degradation, discrimination, or diminishment of any human person—including anyone with a homosexual orientation. I am especially concerned that such attitudes or acts might be found at times in institutions of this Archdiocese. At the same time, as a bishop in the Catholic Church, I am equally bound to teach that homosexual activity and patterns of life which promote it are immoral.[59]

The letter clearly contrasted the Roman Catholic Church's attitude toward homosexual orientation and homosexual activity.

Nevertheless, social and political challenges surrounding homosexuality have become a very sensitive issue in the American Roman Catholic experience, as allegations and incidents involving sex abuse on the part of priests have come to light all over the country. The tormenting problem of molesters in the priesthood represents one of the most crucial issues confronting the Roman Catholic Church in America and worldwide, often described as "the worst crisis the American church had ever faced." In 2003, the Archdiocese of Louisville had to pay 243 people who accused priests and employees of child sexual abuse more than $25 million. Between 1998 and 2003, the church paid out the following settlements: 1998, Lafayette, Louisiana: $18 million; 1998, Dallas, Texas: $31 million; 1999, Stockton, California: $13 million; 2001, Los Angeles, California: $5.2 million; 2002, Tucson, Arizona: $15 million; 2002, Providence, Rhode Island: $13.5 Million; 2002, Boston Archdiocese: $10 million; 2003; Manchester, New Hampshire: $6.5 million; and, 2003, Louisville Archdiocese: $25 million. The problem has persisted into the twenty-first century.

The magnitude and administrative management of the sex abuse scandal of the Boston Archdiocese astonished legal and public opinions in the United States. The allegations of sex abuse were sordid, the details shocking, and the number of cases was much higher than the public expected. A series of cases included: a Roman

Catholic priest molested more than 130 children; another pulled boys out of religious classes and raped them in a confessional; and, another seduced girls studying to become nuns by telling them he was "the second coming of Christ."[60] Church documents of the files of 138 priests in the Boston Archdiocese were made public at the request of attorneys representing alleged victims which revealed to the public the fact of a host of accusations of molestation, rape, sexual misconduct involving boys, girls, and some adults. Observers and victims' advocates pointed out that Catholic Church officials over decades sought to cover up the scandalous behavior, no matter how disturbing, sparking a national crisis over clerical molestation. The fallout was felt from church pews to the highest levels of the Boston Archdiocese, culminating with the resignation of Cardinal Bernard Law and the removal of 27 priests.

During the sexual scandals of Roman Catholic priests, Bishop Wilton Gregory, president of the U.S. Conference of Bishops, had the responsibility of charting an affirmative action course for the church. He traveled to Rome to give Vatican officials the ambitious policy of American prelates' approval to bar sexually abusive priests from church work. He realized that Vatican approval of the plan was necessary before it could be binding on the American Catholic Church community. Under the plan, bishops were required to remove abusive priests from public ministry and from boards comprised mainly of lay people to monitor how the church handles these conduct allegations. In 2003, Pope John Paul II approved changes in Vatican policy that will expedite dismissal of some clergy accused of sex abuse and give lay people a greater role at the church trials of alleged molesters. Bishop Gregory's leadership role in the new policies of the church in dealing with sex abuse greatly helped the American Roman Catholic Church to be seen in a more positive light.

However, incidences of child sexual abuse did not disappear from the American Roman Catholic Church experience. One particular case was the sex abuse conviction of Farther Maurice Blackwell, an African American priest in Baltimore, Maryland. His victim was Dontee Stokes, who charged that Father Blackwell had sexually abused him between 1989 and 1992; and, out of outrage, Stokes shot the accused priest. The jury convicted Blackwell of three of four counts, finding he abused Stokes in 1990, 1991, and 1992 but acquitted him of a charge relating to an alleged incident in1989, when Stokes was only thirteen years old. To be sure, the court conviction of Father Blackwell greatly distressed the African American church community in Baltimore and throughout the United States.

When one surveys retrospectively the historic experience of African American Christians from the standpoint of these modern trends, it seems evident that the period of slavery has impacted the religious, social, psychological, and political developments of the total African American church in America. The evolutionary persistence of racism and discrimination have served as defining moments in the successes and failures of African American Christians as they have struggled against almost insurmountable odds to advance the progress of the race. Often through the documentation and evaluation of primary sources in their sociopolitical milieu, this study has demonstrated the nature of the many struggles of African Americans in their strides to assimilate within American culture. African American churches of all denominations have contributed to the institutions, schools, foreign missionary enterprises, social dialogue, and participation in the humanitarian struggles for civil and human rights of all African Americans and other minority groups, as well as international movements for freedom and human development.

(Endnotes)

[1] *Los Angeles Sentinel*, September 10, 1987, C9.

[2] Ibid., C9.

[3] Ibid., C9.

[4] *The Star of Zion*, January 12, 1984, 6.

[5] William Jacob Walls, *The African Methodist Episcopal Zion Church: Reality of the Black Church* (Charlotte, NC: A.M.E. Zion Publ. House, 1974), 470.

[6] Ibid., 471.

[7] *The Star of Zion*, August 29, 1985, 2.

[8] *The Star of Zion*, October 3, 1985, 4.

[9] *The Star of Zion*, June 13, 1985, 1.

[10] *The Star of Zion*, October 17, 1985, 4.

[11] *The Philadelphia Tribune*, July 30, 1996, D6.

[12] *New Pittsburgh Courier*, January 18, 1997, B3.

[13] *New Pittsburgh Courier*, August 29, 1998, B5.

[14] J. H. Jackson, *A Story of Christian Activism: The History of the National Baptist Convention, U.S.A., Inc.* (Nashville: Townsend Press, 1980), 163.

15. Ibid., 500.

16. *New York Amsterdam News*, September 17, 1988, 36.

17. *New Pittsburgh Courier*, January 19-23, 2005, B2.

18. Ibid.

19. Timothy G. McCarthy, *Catholic Tradition: The Church in the Twentieth Century* (Chicago, IL: Loyola Press, 1998), 168.

20. Ibid., 178.

21. Samuel H. Miller, ed., *Ecumenical Dialogue at Harvard the Roman Catholic-Protestant Colloquium* (Cambridge, MA: Belknap Pr. of Harvard Univ. Pr., 1964), 43-44.

22. Ibid., 48-49.

23. *Philadelphia Tribune*, July 28, 1998, 7C.

24. Ibid.

25. *New Pittsburgh Courier*, April 13-17, 2005, A3.

26. *Los Angeles Sentinel*, November 5, 1987, C8.

27. *Florida Star*, October 31, 1987, 4.

28. Cyprian Davis, *History of Black Catholics in the United States* (New York: Crossroad Publishing, 1990), 239.

29. *The Post*, May 20, 1990, 4.

30. Leo Rosten, ed., *Religions of America: Ferment and Faith in an Age of Crisis* (New York: Simon & Schuster, 1963) 97.

31. *New Pittsburgh Courier*, August 10, 1996, A5.

32. *New Pittsburgh Courier*, May 3, 1997, A8.

33. Richard D. Hefner, *A Documentary History of the United States* (New York: A Signet Book, 2002) 415.

34. Natasha Zaretsky et al., eds., *Major Problems in American History since 1945: Documents and Essays* (Lexington, MA: Heath and Company, 1992), 317-318.

35. *The New York Amsterdam News*, June 17, 1995, 14.

36. *The Crisis*, September-October 2007, 6.

37. *Buckeye Review*, August 19, 1988, 1.

38. *Indianapolis Recorder*, August 14, 1993, C4.

39. Ibid., C4.

40. *The Birmingham World*, June 24, 1989, 1.
41. Rosemary Skinner Keller and Hilah F. Thomas, eds., *Women in New Worlds: Historical Perspectives on the Wesleyan Tradition* (Nashville: Abingdon, 1982), 91.
42. Rosten, 97.
43. *Chicago Defender*, October 24, 1988, 12.
44. George L. Hunt, *A Brief History of the Presbyterians* (Philadelphia: The Westminster Press, 1978) 197.
45. *New Pittsburgh Courier*, January 9, 2005, A6.
46. *New Pittsburgh Courier*, June 16, 1990, B3.
47. *New York Amsterdam News*, July 5-11, 2001, 5.
48. Claire M. Renzetti, Daniel J. Curran, and Shana L. Maier, eds., *Women, Men, and Society: Pearson New International Edition* (Boston: Allyn & Bacon, 1990), 180.
49. *New Pittsburgh Courier*, February 15, 1997, B3.
50. Ibid., B3
51. *The Philadelphia Tribune*, June 21, 1996, D2.
52. *The Philadelphia Tribune*, March 3, 1995, D3.
53. *The Philadelphia Tribune*, June 22, 1999, D5.
54. *Los Angeles Sentinel*, June 13, 1991, 3A.
55. *New Pittsburgh Courier*, May18-22, 2005, B2.
56. *The Black Chronicle*, July 18, 1991, 11.
57. *New Pittsburgh Courier*, May 11, 2005, B3.
58. *Minutes,* 1970, Part I, Journal, 889.
59. *Chicago Defender*, April 27, 1985, 35.
60. *The Sunday Tribune*, March 23, 2003, E3.

Bibliography

Aaseng, Nathan, *African American Religious Leaders*. New York: Facts on File, 2003.

Adams, C.C., *Negro Baptists and Foreign Missions*. Philadelphia: The Foreign Mission Board of the National Baptist Convention, U.S.A., Inc., 1952.

The Afro-American, September 27, 1952; May 4, 1935; January 23, 1960; November 2, 1968.

The Afro-American Magazine Section, February 13, 1960; September 22, 1990.

Afro Times, February 10, 1990; July 21, 1990.

Ahlstrom, Sidney E., *A Religious History of the American People*, New Haven: Yale University Press, 1972.

Ajayi, J.F. and Michael Crowder, Eds., *History of West Africa*. Philadelphia: New York: Columbia University Press, 1973.

Alexander, Archibald, *A History of Colonization of the Western Coast of Africa*. Philadelphia: William S. Martien, 1849.

Alexander, William T., *History of the Colored Race in America*. Kansas City: 1887.

Alpen, David M., "The Black Revolution Adam." *Newsweek*, Vol. 79, April 17, 1972.

The American Baptist: The Official Newspaper of Colored Baptists in Kentucky, Friday, February 26, 1988-Volume CXXVIII, No. 9.

Anderson, Mathew, *Presbyterianism: Its Relation to the Negro, Illustrated by the Berean Presbyterian Church*. Philadelphia: John McGill White & Co., 1897.

The Annual American Cyclopedia and Register of Important Events of the Year 1868, Vol. VIII, New York: D. Appleton and Company, 1869.

The Annual American Cyclopedia and Register of Important Events of the Year 1861, New York: D. Appleton and Company, 1862.

Annual Edition, 1924-1925, First Colored Directory of Baltimore City. Afro-American Office, Baltimore, Maryland.

Annual Report of the Corresponding Secretary, "Lott Carey Baptist Foreign Mission Society of the U.S.A, 1925-1926; 1930-1931; 1964

Aptheker, Herbert, Ed., *A Documentary History of the Negro in the United States*. New York: The Citadel Press, 1951.

Atlanta Daily World, February 14, 1993.

The Baltimore Afro-American, December 9, 1947; October 8, 1988; October 22, 1988; March 32, 1943; September 24, 1946.

Baptist Home Missions in North America: Including a Full Report of the Proceedings and Addresses of the Jubilee Meeting, and a Historical Sketch of the American Baptist Home Mission Society 1832-1882. New York: The American Baptist Home Mission Society, 1883.

Baptist Progress, Progressive National Baptist Convention, 1972.

Bay State Banner, September 25, 1986

The Birmingham World, July 6, 1940; June 24, 1989.

The Black Chronicle, July 18, 1991.

Boone, Clinton, *Congo As I Saw It*. New York: J.J. Little and Ives Company, 1927.

Boone, Theodore S., *Negro Baptist Chief Executives in National Places*. Detroit: A.P. Publishing Company, 1948.

Booth, Charles Octavis, *The Cyclopedia of Colored Baptists of Alabama*. Birmingham: Alabama Publishing Company, 1895.

Boyd, Jesse Laney, *A Popular History of the Baptists of Mississippi*. Jackson: The Baptist Press, 1930.

Bracket, Jeffery R., *The Negro in Maryland: A Study of the Institution of Slavery*. Baltimore: Johns Hopkins University Press, 1889.

Bradley, David Henry, *A History of the A.M.E. Zion Church, Part II 1872-1968*.

Bragg, George, *Men of Maryland*. Baltimore: Church Advocate Press, 1914.

Brinks, William and Louis Harris. *The Negro Revolution in America*, New York: Simon and Schuster, 1963.

Brisbane, Robert H. *The Black Vanguard: Origins of the Negro Social Revolution 1900-1960*. Valley Forge: Judson Press, 1970.

Brockway, Maude J., *Manual for Women's Missionary Society*. Nashville: The Sunday School Publishing Board, 1947.

Brooks, Charles H. *Official History of the First African Baptist Church Philadelphia, Pa.* Philadelphia: Charles H. Brooks, 1923.

Brooks, L.B., *State of Country.* New England Baptist Convention, 1922.

Brotz, Howard, Ed., *Negro Social and Political Thought 1850-1920.* New York: Basic Books, Inc., 1966

Brown, Hugh Victor, *A History of the Education of Negroes in North Carolina.* Raleigh, N.C.: Irvin-Swain Press, 1961.

Birmingham World, October 15, 1988.

Buckeye Review, August 19, 1988.

Burkett, Randall, *Garveyism as a Religious Movement: The Institutionalization of a Black Civil Religion.* Metuchen, N.J.: The Scarecrow Press, Inc., 1978.

The Call, Kansas City, Mo., August 11-17, 1989; April 13, 1989; June 23-29, 1989; June 30-July 6, 1989.

The Call and Post, September 19, 1991.

Campbell, Stanley W., *The Slave Catchers' Enforcement of the Fugitive Slave Law 1850-1860.*

Cantril, Hadley, *The Psychology of Social Movements.* New York: John Wiley & Sons, Inc., 1963.

The Capital Spotlight, May 23, 1991.

The Charlotte Post, October 4, 1990.

Chapman, Abraham. *Steal Away: Stories of the Runaway Slaves.* New York: Praeger Publishers, 1971.

Chicago Defender, February 11, 1989: October 29, 1988; August 29, 1987; January 13, 1990; March 10, 1990; October 24, 1988; April 27, 1985.

Chocolate Singles, Vol. 3, No. 5, 1984.

The Colored American, Vol. 1, No. 41, New York, October 14, 1837.

The Combined Minutes of the Forty-first Session of the General Conference of the African Methodist Episcopal Church, June 18-28, 1980.

Cone, James H., *Black Theology and Black Power.* New York: The Seabury Press, 1969.

Congressional Record, 88th Session, 1963.

Congressional Record, Vol. 109, Part 2, 88th Session, 1963.

Cook, Arthur N., *Africa: Past and Present*. Totowa, N.J.: Littlefield, Adams & Company, 1969.

The Crisis, September-October 2007.

Culp, W.D., *Twentieth Century Negro Literature, or A Cyclopedia of Thought: Vital Topics Relating to the American Negro*. Naperville, Ill.: Nichols & Company, 1902.

Daily Challenge, July 22, 1991.

The Dallas Weekly, May 10-16, 1990.

Dawson, Joseph M., *Baptists and the American Republic*. Nashville: Broadman Press, 1956.

Davis, Cyprian, *The History of Black Catholics in the United States*. New York: The Crossroad Publishing Company, 1992.

Davis, Noah, *Narratives of the Life of Reverend Noah Davis, a Colored Man*. Baltimore: Printed Solely for the Author's Benefit, 1859.

Detweiler, Frederick G. *The Negro Press in the United States*. Chicago: The University of Chicago Press, 1922.

Douglass, Frederick, *The Life and Times of Frederick Douglass Written by Himself: His Early Life As a Slave, His Escape from Bondage, and His Complete History to the Present Time*. Chicago: Park Publishing Company, 1882.

Douglas, William, *Annals of the First African Church in the United States of America, Now Styled the African Episcopal Church of St. Thomas*, Philadelphia: 1862.

Dowdey, Charles, *The History of the Confederacy 1832-1865*. New York: Barnes & Noble Books, 1955.

Drimmer, Melvin, Ed., *Black History: A Reappraisal*. New York: Anchor Books Doubleday & Company, 1968.

Duberman, Martin, Ed., *The Anti-slavery Vanguard: New Essays on the Abolitionists*. Princeton, N.J.: Princeton University Press, 1965.

Du Bois, W.E.B., *The Philadelphia Negro*. New York: Schocken Books, 1967.

East, James E. *Report of the Foreign Mission Board of the National Baptist Convention, U.S.A., Inc.* 1925,1926.

East, J.E., *Files of the Lott Carey Baptist Foreign Mission Convention*, Washington, D.C.

EBONY, Special Issue, August 1984, A Johnson Publication.

Eppse, Merl R., *The Negro, Too, in American History*. Nashville: National Publication Company, 1943.

Filler, Louis, *The Crusade against Slavery: 1830-1860*. New York: Harper & Row Publishers, 1960.

First Baptist Church, Williamsburg, Virginia. "How Our Church Began."

Fisher, Miles Mark, *A Short History of the Baptist Denomination*. Nashville: Sunday School Publishing Board, 1933.

Florida Star, October 31, 1987.

Frazier, E. Franklin, *The Negro in the United States*. New York: The MacMillan Company, 1957.

Franklin, John Hope. *From Slavery to Freedom: A History of American Negroes*. New York: Alfred A. Knopf, 1965.

Franklin, John Hope, *Reconstruction after the Civil War*. Chicago: The University of Chicago Press, 1961.

Forty-fifth Annual Report of the Foreign Mission Board of the National Baptist Convention, U.S.A. Inc.., by James E. East, September 9-14, 1925.

Freeman, Edward A. *The Epoch of Negro Baptists and the Foreign Mission Board, National Baptist Convention, U.S.A., Inc.*, Kansas City: The Central University Press, 1953.

Fuller, T. O., *History of the Negro Baptists of Tennessee*. Memphis: Haskin Print, Roger Williams College, 1936.

Gillett, E.H., *History of the Presbyterian Church in the United States of America*. Philadelphia: Presbyterian Board of Publication and Sabbath-School Work, 1864.

Gillard, John T., *Colored Catholics in the United States*. Baltimore: The Josephite Press, 1941.

Grant, Joanne, *Black Protest: History, Documents, and Analyses 1619 to the Present.*

Greenwich, Conn.: Fawcett Publications, Inc., 1968.

Green, Nathaniel E., *The Silent Believers*. Louisville, Ky.: West End Catholic Council of Louisville, Kentucky, 1972.

Gregg, Howard D., *History of the A.M.E. Church*. Nashville: AMEC Sunday School Union, 1980.

Griffith, Robert, Ed., *Major Problems in American History since 1945: Documents and Essays*. Lexington, Massachusetts: D.C. Heath and Company, 1992.

Guinan, Edward, *Peace and Nonviolence*. New York: Paulist Press, 1973.

Gurley, Ralph R., *Life of Jehudi Ashmun, Late Colonial Agent in Liberia*. New York: Negro University Press, 1835.

Guzman, Jessie P., Ed., *Negro Year Book: A Review of Events Affecting Negro Life 1941-1946*, Tuskegee, Alabama: The Department of Records and Research, Tuskegee Institute, 1947; 1952.

Hamilton, Charles V., *The Black Preacher in America*. New York: William Marrow & Company, 1972.

Handy, Robert T., *A History of the Churches in the United States and Canada*. New York: Oxford University Press, 1976.

Harwood, Richard. "Harlem's Rep. Adam Clayton Powell: There Is Nothing Ordinary About

Him." *Washington Post*, April 1972.

Hasseltine, William B., *The South in American History*. New York: Prentice-Hall, Inc., 1943.

Hastings, Adrian, *Church and Mission in Modern Africa*. New York: Fordham University Press, 1967.

Hatcher, William, *John Jasper*. New York: Fleming H. Revell Company, 1908.

Heffner, Richard D., *A Documentary History of the United States*. New York: Signet Book, 2002.

Hennessy, James Pope, *Sins of the Fathers: The Atlantic Slave Traders 1441-1807*. Castle Books, 2004.

The Herald, Savannah, Georgia, February 14, 1990.

Hervey, George Winfred, *The Story of Baptist Missions in Foreign Lands*. St. Louis: C. Barnes Publishing Company, 1884.

Hood, J.W., *One Hundred Years of the African Methodist Episcopal Zion Church*. New York: A.M.E. Zion Book Concern, 1895.

Hunt, George L., *A Brief History of the Presbyterians*. Philadelphia: The Westminster Press, 1978.

The Impartial Citizen, February 14-28, 1990.

Indianapolis Recorder, August 14, 1993.

Inventory of the Church Archives of Virginia, "The Negro Baptist Church in Richmond." Richmond: The Historical Records Survey of Virginia, June 1940.

Jackson, J. H. *A Story of Christian Activism: The History of the National Baptist Convention*, U.S.A., Inc. Nashville: Townsend Press, 1980.

James, Isaac, *The Sun Do Move: The Story of the Life of John Jasper*. Richmond: Printed by Whittet & Shepperson, 1954.

Jay, William, *Inquiry into the Character and Tendency of the American Colonization Society, and American Anti-slavery Societies*. New York: Negro University Press, 1835.

Johnson, Edward A., *A Social History of the Negro Race in America*. Raleigh: Edwards & Broughton, Printers and Binders, 1890.

Johnson, Harvey, *A Plea for Our Work as Colored Baptists, Apart from Whites*. The Afro-American Printers, 1897.

Johnson, William Bishop, *The Scouring of a Race, and other Sermons and Addresses by W. Bishop Johnson*. Washington: Beresford Printers, 1904.

Jordan, L.G., *Negro Baptist History, U.S.A.* Nashville: The Sunday School Publishing Board, 1930.

Jordan, L.G., *Up the Ladder in Foreign Mission*. Nashville: National Baptist Publishing Board, 1901.

Jordan, L.G., *The Eighth Annual Report of the Historian, National Baptist Convention, U.S.A., Inc.*, 1933.

Jordan, L. G. *The Ninth Annual Report of the Historian, National Baptist Convention, U.S.A., Inc.,* 1934.

The Journal and Guide, January 2, 1943.

The Journal and Guide, May 18, 1968.

The Journal and Guide, September 25–October 2, 1985

The Journal of Negro Education, Summer 1960.

July, Robert W., *A History of the African People*. New York: Charles Scribner's Sons, 1974.

Kauffman, Christopher J., Ed., *U.S. Catholic Historian*. Baltimore, 1986.

King, Martin Luther Jr., *Strides toward Freedom: The Montgomery Story*. New York: Harper and Brothers, 1958.

Kutler, Stanley I., *Looking for America: The People's History, Volume 1 to 1865*. New York: W.W. Norton & Company, 1979.

Kyle, Richard, *The Religious Fringe: A History of Alternative Religions in America*. InterVarsity Press, 1993.

Kletzing, H. F. and W. H. Crogman, *Progress of a Race, or the Remarkable Advancement of the Afro-American Negro*. Atlanta: J.L. Nichols and Company, 1898.

Kletzing, H. F. and W. H. Crogman, *Progress of a Race, or the Remarkable Advancement of the Afro-American Negro*. Atlanta: J.L. Nichols and Company, 1900.

Lewis, James K. *Religious Life of Fugitive Slaves and Rise of Colored Baptist Churches, 1820-1865, in What Is Now Known as Ontario*. New York: Arno Press, 1980.

Los Angeles Sentinal, September 10, 1987; November 5, 1987; June 13, 1991.

The Lott Carey Herald, September 1925.

Macy, Jesse. *The Anti-slavery Crusade: a Chronicle of the Gathering Storm*. New Haven: Yale University Press, 1919.

Master, Frank M. *A History of Baptists in Kentucky*. Louisville: Kentucky Baptist Historical Society, 1953.

Mathews, Donald G. *Religion in the Old South*. Chicago: University of Chicago Press, 1977.

McCall, Emmanuel L., *The Black Christian Experience*. Nashville: Broadman Press, 1972.

McCarthy, Timothy G., *The Catholic Tradition: The Church in the Twentieth Century*. Chicago: Loyola Press, 1998.

Minutes of the Consolidated American Baptist Convention, September 1869, 1871, 1872, 1877.

Minutes of the National Baptist Convention, U.S.A., Inc., 1922, 1924, 1933, 1938, 1941, 1944, 1956.

Minutes of the New England Baptist Convention, 1924, 1936, 1942.

Minutes of the Progressive National Baptist Convention, 1975.

The Mission Herald, 1907, 1910, 1919, 1934, 1970.

Mitchell, Henry H., *Black Preaching*. New York: J.B. Lippincott Company, 1970.

Manross, William Wilson, *A History of the American Episcopal Church*. New York: Morehouse Publishing Co., 1935.

Marden, Charles F., and Gladys Meyer, Eds., *Minorities in American Society*. New York: D. Van Nostrand Company, 1962.

Mbiti, John, *African Religion and Philosophy*. London: Heinemann Educational Books, Ltd., 1969.

Miller, Richard Roscoe, *Slavery and Catholicism*. Durham, N.C.: North State Publishers, 1957.

Miller, Samuel H. and G. Ernest Wright, Eds., *Ecumenical Dialogue at Harvard: The Roman Catholic-Protestant Colloquium*. Cambridge, Massachusetts: The Belnap Press of Harvard University Press, 1964.

Miyakawa, T. Scott, *Protestants and Pioneers: Individualism and Conformity on the American Frontier*. Chicago: The University of Chicago Press, 1964.

Morison, Samuel Elliot, *The Oxford History of the American People*. New York: Oxford University Press, 1965.

Murray, Andrew E., *Presbyterians and the Negro, a History*. Philadelphia: Presbyterian Historical Society, 1966.

National Edition Pittsburgh Courier, January 1, 1972.

Negro Population 1790-1915. Department of Commerce Bureau of the Census. Washington: Government Printing Office, 1918.

New Pittsburgh Courier, Dec. 8, 2004; August 29, 1998; January 19-23, 2005; April 13-17, 2005; August 10, 1996; May 3, 1997; January 9, 2005; June 16, 1990; February 15, 1997; May 18-22, 2005; May 11-15, 2005.

The New York Amsterdam News, September 17, 1988.

The New York Amsterdam News, June 17, 1995; July 5-11, 2001

The New York Page of the Afro-American, January 11, 1936.

Nichols, J.L. and William Crogman, Eds. *Progress of a Race, or the Remarkable Advancement of the American Negro*, Naperville, Ill.: J. L. Nichols & Company, 1920.

Noble, Frederick Perry, *The Redemption of Africa: A Story of Civilization*. New York: Fleming H. Revell Company, 1899.

The Northwest Dispatch, August 9, 1989.

Nuesse, C.J., *The Social Thought of American Catholics 1634-1829*. Westminster, Maryland: The Newman Book Shop, 1945.

Oliver, Roland, *A Short History of Africa*. Baltimore: Penguin Books, 1966.

Osbourne, William, *The Segregated Covenant: Race Relations and American Catholics*. New York: Herder and Herder, Inc., 1967.

Payne, Daniel A., *Recollections of Seventy Years*. New York: Arno Press and *The New York Times*, 1969.

Payne, Wardell J., *Directory of African American Religious Bodies: A Compendium by the Howard University School of Divinity*. Washington: Howard University Press, 1995.

Penn, I. Garland, *The United Negro: His Problems and His Progress*. Atlanta: The Lutheran Publishing Company, 1902.

Penn, I. Garland, *The Afro-American Press and Its Editors*. Springfield, Mass.: Willey and Company, 1891.

The Philadelphia Tribune, July 30, 1996; June 21, 1996; March 3, 1995; June 22, 1999

The Philadelphia Tribune, July 28, 1998.

Pius, N.H., *An Outline of Baptist History*. Nashville: National Baptist Publishing Board, 1911.

The Post, December 31, 1989; May 20, 1990.

Poulet, Don Charles, *A History of the Catholic Church, Volume II*. London: B. Herder Book Co., 1935.

Priest, Josiah, *Bible Defence of Slavery, and Origin, Fortunes, and History of the Negro Race*. Glasgow, Ky.: Published by Rev. W.S. Brown, MD, 1852.

Proceedings of the Baptist General Convention, 1817.

Proceedings of the Southern Baptist Convention, 1872.

Putnam, Mary Burnham, *The Baptists and Slavery, 1840-1845*. Ann Arbor, Michigan: George Wahr Publishers, 1913.

Raboteau, Albert J., *Slave Religion: The Invisible Institution in the Antebellum South*. New York: Oxford University Press, 1978.

Reed, William B., *Echoes of the Emancipation Proclamation*. Madison, N.J.: W.B. Reed, 1908.

Reed, William B., "State of the Country Address." Philadelphia: New England Baptist Convention, 1916.

Reed, William B., "State of the Country Address, 1919.

Renzetti, Claire M. and Daniel J. Curran, Eds., *Women, Men, and Society, Third Edition*. Boston: Allyn & Bacon, 1995.

Report of the Joint Committee on Reconstruction at the First Session, Thirty-Ninth Congress, Washington: Government Printing Office, 1866.

Report of the Fifth Annual Meeting of the Consolidated American Baptist Convention, September 1871; 1877; September 22, 1869.

Report of the Thirty-Second Annual Meeting of the Consolidated American Baptist Missionary Convention, 1872.

Review and Expositor, Vol. LXX No, 3. Louisville: The Southern Baptist Theological Seminary, Summer 1973, Theme of this issue, "The Black Experience and the Church."

Richardson, Harry V., *Dark Salvation: The Story of Methodism as It Developed among Blacks in America.* Garden City, N.Y: Anchor-Press/ Doubleday, 1976.

Richings, G. F., *Evidences of Progress Among Colored People.* Philadelphia: Geo. S. Ferguson Co., 1896.

Richings, G. F., 1900.

The Richmond Afro-American, August 25, 1962; November 2, 1968; June 22, 1968; February 20, 1971.

Rosten, Leo, *Religions of America.* New York: Simon and Schuster, 1963.

Rosten, Leo, ed., *Religions of America: Ferment and Faith in an Age of Crisis.* New York: Simon & Schuster, 1963

Ruben, Leslie and Brian Weinstein, Eds., *Introduction to African Politics: A Continental Approach.* New York: Prager Publishers, 1874.

Rupp, I. Daniel, *An Original History of the Religious Denominations at Present Existing in the United Sates.* Philadelphia: Humphreys, 1844.

Scharf, Thomas, *History of Baltimore City and County from the Earliest Period to the Present.* Philadelphia: Louis H. Everts, 1881.

Scherer, Lester B., *Slavery and the American Churches, 1619-1819.* Grand Rapids, Michigan: Wm. B. Eerdmans Publishing Company, 1975.

Schlesinger, Arthur M., Ed., *The Almanac of American History*, Barnes & Noble Books, New York 1983.

Shepperson, George and Thomas Price, *Independent Africa: John Chilembwe and the Origins, Setting, and Significance of the Nyasaland Native Rising of 1915.* Edinburgh: The University Press, 1958.

Shipley, David O., Ed., *History of Black Baptists in Missouri.* Kansas City: Missionary Baptist Convention of Missouri, 1976.

Simmons, William J., *Men of Mark: Eminent, Progressive, and Rising.* New York: Arno Press, 1968.

Simms, James M., *The First Colored Baptist Church in North America.* Philadelphia: J.B. Lippincott Company, 1888.

Sithole, Ndbaningi, *African Nationalism.* Cape Town: Oxford University Press, 1959.

"Souvenir Program of the 50th or the Golden Anniversary Celebration of the First African Baptist Church, Richmond, Virginia," Sunday, April 29, 1928.

The Star of Zion, February 1, 1990; September 23, 1982; October 1, 1987; May 13, 1982; January 8, 1987; May 24, 1990; October 15, 1981; August 10, 1989; September 28, 1989; February 12, 1987; January 12, 1984; August 29, 1985; October 3, 1985; June 13, 1985; October 17, 1985.

Sweet, William Warren, *The Story of Religion in America*. New York: Harper & Brothers Publishers, 1939.

Tate, Thad W., *The Negro in Eighteenth Century Williamsburg*. Williamsburg: The Colonial Williamsburg Foundation, 1965.

Taylor, James Barnett, *Lives of Virginia Baptist Ministers*. Richmond: Yale and Wyatt, 1837.

Thomas, Hilah F., and Rosemary Skinner Keller, Eds., *Women in New Worlds: Historical Perspectives on the Wesleyan Tradition*. Nashville: Abingdon Press, 1981.

Thornburgh, Emma Lou, *The Negro in Indiana: A Study of a Minority*. Indiana Historical Bureau, 1957.

Tupper, Henry Allen. *The Foreign Missions of the Southern Baptist Convention*. Philadelphia: American Baptist Publishing Society, 1880.

Twin Citizen Courier, June 20, 1985.

U.S. News and World Report, 1969.

Walls, William J., *The African Methodist Episcopal Zion Church: Reality of the Black Church*. Charlotte, N.C.: A.M.E. Zion Publishing House, 1974.

Watson, Francis B., *The Native Liberian Missionary Field*. Washington: Courant Press, 1956.

Walker, Thomas H.B., *History of Liberia*. Boston: The Cornhill Publishing Company, 1921.

Weatherford, W.D., *American Churches and the Negro: An Historical Study from Early Slave Days to the Present*. Boston: The Christopher Publishing House, 1957.

Wallerstein, Emanuel, *Africa: The Politics of Independence*. New York: Vintage Books, 1961.

Washington Post, April 1972.

Weisbrot, Robert. *Father Divine: The Utopian Evangelist of the Depression Era Who Became an America Legend.* Boston: Beacon Press, 1983.

Weinstein, Allen and Frank Otto Gatell, Eds., *American Negro Slavery: A Modern Reader.* New York: Oxford University Press, 1973.

Weishampel, J.F., *A History of Baptist Churches in Maryland Connected with the Maryland Baptist Union Association.* Baltimore: Printed and Published by J.F. Weishampel Jr., 1885.

Welbourn, F.B., *East African Christian.* London: Oxford University Press, 1965.

Wesley, Charles H.A., *Richard Allen, Apostle of Freedom.* Washington: The Associated Publishers, Inc., 1935.

West, Arson, *A History of Methodism in Alabama.* Nashville: Publishing House of the Methodist Episcopal Church, South, 1893.

West, Richard, *Back to Africa.* New York: Holt, Rinehart, and Winston, Inc., 1970.

White, B.S., *First Baptist Church Richmond, 1780-1955.* Whittet and Shepperson, 1955.

Whitted, J.A., *A History of the Negro Baptists of North Carolina.* Raleigh: Presses of Edward and Broughton Printing Co., 1908.

Wilkins, Roy, "Adam Powell: A Black Appraisal." *New York Times*, April 28, 1972.

Williams, George W., *History of the Negro Race in America, 1691-1880.* New York: Arno Press and the *New York Times*, 1968.

Williams, L.K., "Annual Address to the National Baptist Convention, U.S.A, Inc.," 1923.

Wilmore, Gayraud, *Black Religion and Black Radicalism: An Interpretation of the Religious History of Afro-America People.* New York: Orbis Books, 1983.

Wilmore, Gayraud, Ed., *The Journal of the International Theological Center*, Vol. XVI, Fall 1988–Spring 1989. Atlanta: The Interdenominational Theological Center, 1987.

Wilson, Henry, *History of the Slave Power in America, Vol. 1.* Boston: James R. Osagood and Company, 1875.

Winks, Robin W., *The Blacks in Canada: A History.* New Haven: Yale University Press, 1971.

Winston, W.J., *Disfranchisement Makes Subject Citizens Targets for the Mob and Disarms Them in the Courts of Justice*. Baltimore: Varsity Press, undated manuscript.

Winston-Salem Chronicle, May 9, 1991; February 13, 1992.

Wish, Harvey, *The Negro Since Emancipation*. Englewood Cliffs, N.J.: Prentice-Hall, Inc., 1964.

Woodson, Carter G., *The History of the Negro Church*. Washington: The Associated Publishers, 1921.

Woodson, Carter G., *The Works of Francis J. Grimke*, Vol. 11. Washington: The Associated Publishers, Inc., 1942.

Worrell, William H., *A Short History of the Copts*. Ann Arbor: University of Michigan Press, 1945.

Index

Abernathy, Ralph David, 154, 353, 361-362

Abyssinian Baptist Church, 81-82, 142, 229, 344

African Methodist Episcopal Zion Church, New Bern, N.C., 68

African Methodist Society, 63

Alabama Christian Movement for Human Rights, 354

Allen, M.C., 261, 338

Allen, Richard, Bishop, 56-62, 64, 69, 82, 105, 113-115, 132, 160, 201, 233, 264, 278 -

Alexander, Sandy, 85

American Baptist Missionary Convention, 142-143, 193-194

American Colonization Society, 54, 71, 285

A.M.E. Zion Church, 64

A.M.E. Zion Church, Manteo, N. C., 68

Amherstburg Baptist Association, Canada, 230

Amoci Divisional Baptist Association, 219

Apostolic Faith Mission Church, 176, 314

Archer Memorial AMEZ Church, Windsor, Connecticut, 66

Asbury, Francis, Bishop, 44, 60, 69

Austin, J. C, 353

Azusa Street Apostolic Faith Mission, 158

Baptist African Missionary Convention of Western States and Territories, 194

Baptist Foreign Mission Convention, 144-145 Bassett, Miles, 94

Bassett, Richard, 94

Bassett, Zachariah, 94

Beale Street Baptist Church, Memphis, Tennessee, 88

Bethea, Joseph, 493

Bethel AME Church, Indianapolis, Indiana, 99

Bethel AME Church, Baltimore, Maryland, 61-62, 115

Bethel AME Church, New York, 62, 139

Bethel AME Church, Philadelphia 61, 113

Blackwell AME Church, Jamestown, New York, 66

Boone, C.C., 211, 220, 421

Booth, L.V., 153,

Bowen, J.W.E., 164, 189, 232, 305, 310, 336 Bowman, Thea, Sister, 395

Boyd, R. H., 147, 150, 168,

Bragg, George F, 73, 106, 115, 160

Brown, C. S., 149, 213-214 Brown, Tillman, 98

Broyles, Moses, 94

Buchanan, J.I., 218

Burroughs, Nannie Helen, 319-320

Bryan, Andrew, 50

Burgess, John Melville, Bishop, 393

Carey, Lott, 46-48, 149, 192-193

Carter, Harold A., 154, 404

Cartwright, Andrew, 68, 204-205

Chavis, Benjamin, 370, 388-389, 394

Chavis, John, 45

Cheruiyot, Hezron K., 224

Chilembwe, John, 224-226, 431

Christian, Washington, 229

Church of God (Holiness) U.S.A., 173-174

Church of the Living God, Pillar and Ground of the Truth, Inc., 173-174

Clinton, J.J., Bishop, 125, 127-128

Clinton Memorial AME Church, 67

Clayton, Moses C., 83-84

CME Church, 170-171

Coker, Daniel, 61-62, 115, 192, 200-201, 286

Colored Methodist Protestant Israel Church, Baltimore, Maryland, 72

Colored Peoples' First Baptist Church, Baltimore, Maryland, 98, 168

Consolidated American Baptist Convention, 143-144, 194-195, 232

Cook, John F., 76

Cornish, Samuel, 75

Crosby, Solomon, 195

Crowdy, William Sanders, 173-174

Culver, Peter, 62

Cunningham, Henry, 82

Davis, M. H., Bishop, 118, 140, 160, 313

Davis, Noah, 84, 423

Delany, Emma, 225

Delany, Martin R., 287

Divine, M. J. "Father Divine," 182, 381

Douglass, Frederick, 53, 55, 65, 70, 81, 201, 267, 287, 289-291

Dupree, George Washington, 95

Dyer Anti-Lynching Bill, 327

East, James Edward, 207, 209

Ebong, Charles, 223

Emanuel Methodist Episcopal Church, 63

First African Baptist Church, Richmond, Virginia, 48, 80, 82-83, 432

First African Baptist Church, Trenton, New Jersey, 83

First African Society of Philadelphia, 66

First Baptist Church, Savannah, Georgia, 50

First Baptist Church, St. Louis, Missouri, 96

First Baptist Church, Toronto, Canada, 229-230

First Baptist Church, Baltimore, Maryland, 149

First Presbyterian Church of Color, Princeton, New Jersey, 76

First Zion Cathedral, Los Angeles, California, 98

Ford, Louis H., Bishop, 158

Fraternal Council of Negro Churches, 349-350

Free African Society, 58, 61

Free Christian Zion Church of Christ, 174, 176

Free Will Baptist Church of America, Inc., 169

Garnet, Henry Highland, 282-283

Garvey, Marcus, 182-183, 344, 392

Gayles, George Washington, 48-49

General Assembly of the Church of God in Christ, 158

General Association of Colored Baptist of Kentucky, 95-96

General Association of Western States and Territories, 97

General Baptist State Convention, 142

George, David, 50

Gregory, Wilton, Bishop, 395, 416

Gilfield Baptist Church, Petersburg, Virginia, 79

Gloucester, John, 74-75

Grace, Charles Immanuel, "Bishop Daddy Grace," 185-186

Grimke, Francis James, 314, 325, 434

Hall, Prince, 278

Haldimand (Baptist) Association, Canada, 230

Hammon, Jupiter, 44

Hampton University Ministers Conference, 397, 404

Hannon, Allen, 67

Harrison, Earl L., 255

Hooks, Benjamin, 357, 360

Hoosier, Harry, 44

Hubbard, E. D., 206-207

Hunter Chapel AME Church, Tuscaloosa, Alabama, 67

Jackson, J.C., 197, 218, 341, 352

Jackson, J. H., 151-153, 341, 380-381, 383, 417

Jackson, Jesse, 360, 362-369, 391-392, 407

Jakes, T.D., Bishop, 402

Jasper, John, 45-46, 54

Jemison, T.J., 157, 353, 381-382

Jernagin, W. H., 349-350

Johnson, Harvey, 317-319, 336

Johnson, W. Bishop, 145, 147

Jones, Absalom, 57-59, 61, 72

Jordan, L. G., 196, 225

Joy Baptist Church, 81

Kassavubu, Joseph, 220

Kiambu, Sebastian, B., 221

King, Martin Luther, Jr., 343-359

Liele, George, 50

Lott Carey (Baptist) Home and Foreign Mission Convention, 149-151, 205-206, 210-211, 232, 381

Martens, M. W., 206

Mason, M. C. B., 164, 305, 310

Malekebu, Daniel S., 226

Meachum, John Berry, 96-97

Memorial AME Zion Church, Rochester, New York, 65

Miller, A. Carlyle, 227

Morris, Charles S. 225

Morris, E.C., 145, 339

Mitchell, William, 230

National Baptist B.Y. P.U. Board, 148

National Baptist Convention of America, 146, 150

National Baptist Convention, U.S.A, Inc., 146-152

National Baptist Educational Convention, 145

National Baptist Foreign Mission Board, 147-153, 196

National Missionary Baptist Convention of America, 154

National Baptist Publishing Board, 147-150

National Baptist Benefit Association Board, 148

Nelson, Joswant Harman, M.D., 221

Metropolitan AME Church, Washington, D.C., 63

New England Anti- Slavery Society, 282

New England Baptist Missionary Convention, 143, 340

New Prospect Baptist Church, Anniston, Alabama, 85-87

Oblate Sisters of Providence, 89-92

Old Ship AMEZ Church, Montgomery, Alabama, 67

Orchard Street Methodist Episcopal Church, Baltimore, Maryland, 71

Original Free Will Baptist Church of North Carolina, 169

Pan Methodist Commission, 337-338 (Commission on Pan-Methodist Cooperation, 379)

Park, W. G., 339

Parks, Rosa Mae, 352-353

Paul, Thomas, 81

Payne, Daniel A. Bishop, 71

Pennington, James W.C., 282, 283

Pentecostal Assemblies of World, Inc., 173, 177, 226, 393

Pilgrim Baptist Church, 97

Pius, N. H., 148, 430

Pleasant Green Baptist Church, Kansas City, 97

Powell, Adam Clayton, Jr., 343-348

Preston, Richard, 231

Progressive National Baptist Convention, 153-154, 380

Prosser, Gabriel, 291

Providence Baptist Association, 141

PUSH (People United to Save Humanity), 362-363

Quinn Chapel AME Church, Chicago, Illinois, 99

Quinn Paul, 99

Quinn, William P., 99

Reed, William B., 322-324

Richardson, C. H., 195

Richmond African Missionary Society, 48, 192-195, 201

Rockwell AME Church, Charlotte, North Carolina, 67

Roger Williams Baptist Anti-slavery Society, 284

Rush, Christopher, Bishop, 65-67, 123, 282

Rush Metropolitan AME Church, Raleigh, North Carolina, 68

Seymour, William J., 157, 176-177

Sharp Street Memorial Church, Baltimore, Maryland, 70

Sharpton, Alfred, 368-369

Simmons, William J., 144

Summerville, Wendell Clay, 151, 222

Southern Christian Leadership Conference, 354-355

Spencer, Peter, 78

Stallings, George A. Bishop, 385-386

St. Francis Xavier Roman Catholic Church, Baltimore, Maryland, 90-92

St. James AME Church, Ithaca, North Carolina, 65

St. James AME Church, Winston-Salem, North Carolina, 64

St. James AME Zion Church, Red Bank, New Jersey, 67

St. John AME Zion Church, Omaha, Nebraska, 101

St. Mathew's Episcopal Church, Savannah, Georgia, 73

St. Stevens Episcopal Church, Savannah, Georgia, 73

St. Thomas Protestant Episcopal Church, Philadelphia, Pennsylvania, 72

Stone Street Baptist Church, Mobile, Alabama, 85

Sullivan, Leon, 338, 359-360 Taylor, A.M., 101

Taylor, Gardner C., 153

Thomas, Walter Scott, 403-404

Turner, Nat, 63, 291-295, 300

Uncles, Charles, Father, 90

Union Anti-Slavery Baptist Association, 141-142, 284

Union Bethel AME Church, Great Falls, Montana, 101

United American Free Will Baptist Church, 169

Vesey, Denmark, 291

Varick, James, Bishop, 62 65, 120-123

Walker, David, 281

Walker, Wyatt Tee, 391

Waters AME Church, Baltimore, Maryland, 63

Wendell Baptist Convention of Africa, 223

Wilks, William, 229

Williams, Cecil, 406

Williams, L. K, 260, 332

Williams, Peter, 120

Winston, W. J., 327-329

Wood River Baptist Association of Illinois, 142

Wright, R.R., Bishop, 139, 349

Yahweh, Yahweh Ben, 187

Zoar ME Church, Philadelphia, Pennsylvania, 61, 70

www.ingramcontent.com/pod-product-compliance
Lightning Source LLC
Chambersburg PA
CBHW081716100526
44591CB00016B/2407